NATION AND IDENTITY
IN CONTEMPORARY EUROPE

The resilience of nationalism in contemporary Europe may seem para-doxical at a time when the nation-state is widely seen as being 'in decline'. The contributors to this volume see the resurgence of nationalism as symptomatic of the quest for identity and meaning in the complex modern world. Challenged from above by the supranational imperatives of global-ism and from below by the complex pluralism of modern societies, the nation-state, in the absence of alternatives to market consumerism, re-mains a powerful focus for social identity.

Nation and Identity in Contemporary Europe takes a fully interdisciplinary and comparative approach to the 'national question'. Individual chapters consider the specifics of national identity in France, Germany, Britain, Italy, Iberia, Russia, the former Yugoslavia and Poland, while looking also at the external forces shaping contemporary perceptions and reactions: economic globalisation, European supranationalism, and the end of the Cold War.

Setting current issues and conflicts in their broad historical context, the book reaffirms that 'nations' are not 'natural' phenomena but 'constructed' forms of social identity whose future will be determined in the political arena.

Brian Jenkins is Professor of French Area Studies at the University of Portsmouth, where **Spyros A. Sofos** is Research Associate in the School of Languages and Area Studies.

NATION AND IDENTITY IN CONTEMPORARY EUROPE

Edited by Brian Jenkins and Spyros A. Sofos

London and New York

First published 1996
by Routledge
11 New Fetter Lane, London EC4P 4EE

Simultaneously published in the USA and Canada
by Routledge
29 West 35th Street, New York, NY 10001

Routledge is an International Thomson Publishing company I(T)P

Typeset in Palatino by
Ponting–Green Publishing Services, Chesham, Bucks
Printed and bound in Great Britain by
TJ Press (Padstow) Ltd, Padstow, Cornwall

British Library Cataloguing in Publication Data
A catalogue record for this book is available from the
British Library

Library of Congress Cataloguing in Publication Data
Nation and identity in contemporary Europe / edited
by Brian Jenkins and Spyros A. Sofos.
p.   cm.
Produced by members of a research group established at
the University of Portsmouth in 1993.
Includes bibliographical references and index.
ISBN 0–415–12312–7. – ISBN 0–415–12313–5 (pbk.)
1. Europe–Politics and government–1989–
2. Nationalism–Europe–History–20th century.
3. Ethnicity.   I. Jenkins, Brian, 1944–
II. Sofos, Spyros A., 1964–
D2009.N367   1995
320.5'4'09409045–dc20   95–25786
CIP

ISBN 0–415–12312–7 (hbk)
ISBN 0–415–12313–5 (pbk)

CONTENTS

List of Contributors   vii
Preface   ix

INTRODUCTION   1

Part I Nation and identity: theory and context

1 NATION AND NATIONALISM IN CONTEMPORARY
EUROPE: A THEORETICAL PERSPECTIVE   9
Brian Jenkins and Spyros A. Sofos

2 LANGUAGES OF RACISM WITHIN CONTEMPORARY
EUROPE   33
Martin Evans

3 IMMIGRATION, CITIZENSHIP AND THE NATION-STATE
IN THE NEW EUROPE   54
Mark Mitchell and Dave Russell

Part II Nationhood and nationalism in Western Europe

4 RECONSIDERING 'BRITISHNESS': THE CONSTRUCTION
AND SIGNIFICANCE OF NATIONAL IDENTITY IN
TWENTIETH-CENTURY BRITAIN   83
Kenneth Lunn

5 NATION, NATIONALISM AND NATIONAL IDENTITY IN
FRANCE   101
Brian Jenkins and Nigel Copsey

6 POST-WAR NATIONAL IDENTITY IN GERMANY   125
Gerd Knischewski

CONTENTS

Part III State, nation and region in Southern Europe

7 MULTIPLE NATIONAL IDENTITIES, IMMIGRATION AND
RACISM IN SPAIN AND PORTUGAL   155
David Corkill

8 ITALIAN NATIONAL IDENTITY AND THE FAILURE OF
REGIONALISM   172
William Brierley and Luca Giacometti

Part IV The nation-state after communism

9 THE FAILURE OF NATIONALISM IN POST-COMMUNIST
POLAND 1989–95: AN HISTORICAL PERSPECTIVE   201
Frances Millard

10 FROM SOVIET TO RUSSIAN IDENTITY: THE ORIGINS OF
CONTEMPORARY RUSSIAN NATIONALISM AND
NATIONAL IDENTITY   223
Paul Flenley

11 CULTURE, POLITICS AND IDENTITY IN FORMER
YUGOSLAVIA   251
Spyros A. Sofos

Part V Conclusion

12 CONCLUSION   285
Brian Jenkins and Spyros A. Sofos

Index   287

LIST OF CONTRIBUTORS

William Brierley is Programme Area Director for Area Studies and Subject Leader for Italian in the School of Languages and Area Studies of the University of Portsmouth. He has previously published on the Italian trade union movement, and on business culture in Italy. He has also published on language teaching methodology.

Nigel Copsey is Lecturer in European Studies at University College Stockton, a new college of the University of Durham in academic partnership with the University of Teesside. He received his Ph.D. from the University of Portsmouth for a thesis on the extreme right in contemporary France and Britain.

David Corkill is a Senior Lecturer in the Department of Spanish and Portuguese at the University of Leeds. He has published widely on the politics and economic history of Iberia and Latin America. Among his recent publications is *The Portuguese Economy since 1974* (Edinburgh University Press, 1993).

Martin Evans is Lecturer in French and European Studies at the University of Portsmouth. He received his Ph.D. from the University of Sussex for a thesis on French resistance to the Algerian war. He has published extensively on the theme of Franco-Algerian relations. He is currently researching the impact of colonialism on French national identity during the nineteenth and twentieth centuries.

Paul Flenley is Principal Lecturer in Russian Studies at Portsmouth University. He received his Ph.D. from Birmingham University for a thesis on labour organisations in the 1917 Russian Revolution. He has published a number of articles on the Russian Revolution. As editor of the *Journal of Area Studies* he edited issues covering questions of nationalism and national identity in Eastern Europe.

Luca Giacometti is a graduate in Political Science from the University of Genoa and a research student in the School of Languages and Area Studies of the University of Portsmouth. His research area is Italian national identity and the Leagues phenomenon.

Brian Jenkins is Professor of French Area Studies at the University of Portsmouth. He is the author of *Nationalism in France: Class and Nation since 1789* (Routledge, 1990) and, with G. Minnerup, of *Citizens and Comrades: Socialism in a World of Nation States* (Pluto Press, 1984). He is also co-editor of the reviews *Modern and Contemporary France* and *Journal of Area Studies.*

Gerd Knischewski is Senior Lecturer in German Politics and Society at the School of Languages and Area Studies of the University of Portsmouth. He is currently working on a project on 'history and memory: the example of Berlin'. He has published on law and German unification; war, memory and national identity.

Kenneth Lunn is Reader in Social History at the University of Portsmouth. He has published extensively on aspects of 'race', immigration and labour history in modern Britain and is one of the editors of *Immigrants and Minorities.*

Frances Millard is Reader in East European Politics at the University of Portsmouth and a specialist in Polish affairs. She has written numerous articles on Polish political and social policy issues. Her latest book is *The Anatomy of the New Poland: Post-Communist Politics in Its First Phase* (Edward Elgar, 1994).

Mark Mitchell is Dean of the Faculty of Humanities and Social Sciences and, with Dave Russell, has for the past ten years undertaken research in the field of race and racism in the United Kingdom and, more recently, across Europe.

Dave Russell is Programme Area Director for Social Studies at the University of Portsmouth. In collaboration with Mark Mitchell he has published work on state and society in South Africa, as well as 'race' and racism in Britain. More recently his research has focused on the politics of 'race' and immigration in a broader European context.

Spyros A. Sofos is Research Associate at the Faculty of Humanities and Social Sciences of the University of Portsmouth. He has recently completed his Ph.D. on populism, popular culture and political identity at the University of Kent. He has written a number of articles on populism, nationalism, cultural politics and political identity in southeastern, east-central European and Mediterranean societies.

PREFACE

Nation and Identity in Contemporary Europe is the work of a Research Group with that same title, established at the University of Portsmouth in 1993. The study of the national question has a long pedigree at this University, which was formerly the base for the British Research Group on Socialism and Nationalism (1976–84).[1] The renewed salience over the last ten years of the related issues of nationalism and national identity, race and ethnicity, migration and citizenship, has provided a point of convergence for the interests of social scientists and contemporary historians working in the field of European studies at Portsmouth.

This multi-authored volume therefore aspires to be something more than an edited collection of essays. It is the fruit of genuine collaboration, facilitated by a programme of research seminars where conceptual issues were explored and draft chapters presented and discussed. This dialogue allowed all contributors to develop a concern for the overall coherence of the book, and to work towards common terms of reference. We would not pretend to have arrived at a collective theoretical perspective, but in our shared insistence on the importance of global economic and political change as an explanatory framework, we hope at least to have ensured consistency of approach.

The preparation of this book owed much to the support and encouragement of others. The University of Portsmouth made a substantial allocation to the Research Group from Higher Education Funding Council development money, and this facilitated some necessary fieldwork and research leave. The editors are also grateful to the referees commissioned by Routledge to read the draft copy, who made many constructive and useful suggestions for improving the text. Finally, we would like to thank Heather McCallum, Associate Editor at Routledge, for her patience and tact, and for her unswerving faith in the success of this project.

Brian Jenkins
Spyros A. Sofos

NOTE

1 E. Cahm and V.-C. Fisera, *Socialism and Nationalism in Europe, 1848–1945* (3 vols), Nottingham, Spokesman, 1978–80.

INTRODUCTION

Brian Jenkins and Spyros A. Sofos

This book was conceived at a time of intense speculation about the future of nation-states and nationalism. On the one hand a variety of interrelated global processes seemed to be undermining the nation-state, both in terms of its political sovereignty and legitimacy, and in terms of its primacy as a focus for social identity. The globalisation of the market economy, accelerated by the end of the Cold War and the collapse of the Soviet bloc, and exemplified in Europe by the rapid development of supranational institutions, has increasingly set limits on the capacity of national governments to act independently. At the same time, alongside the decay of traditional ideologies based on the ties of class or religion, which often acted as mediating agencies of national identity, the impact of mass migratory movements has created more pluri-cultural societies which are less amenable to the historic 'homogenising' myths of nation-statehood.

On the other hand, these global processes have not yet weakened the appeal of what is commonly called 'nationalism' (though the definition of the term is, of course, notoriously contentious). This has been most dramatically demonstrated in the territories of the former communist regimes, but western Europe has not remained immune. At both state and sub-state level, 'nationalist' movements and ideologies have proved their resilience, and cannot simply be dismissed as desperate rearguard actions against the onward march of world history.

As the birthplace of the nation-state idea, Europe has been the fulcrum of these contradictions and conflicts. Here the concept of nationhood has deep roots, extending back to the mid-nineteenth century and in some cases well beyond, and assiduously cultivated over many generations. At the same time, the global processes referred to above have had a more dramatic political impact on Europe than on any other continent. Divided by the Cold War and then 'reunited', challenged economically by more powerful blocs, open to both 'post-colonial' and 'post-communist' migratory movements, Europe provides a fascinating laboratory for the study of the nation-state, and the associated problems of legitimacy, sovereignty and identity in the modern world.

1

This, then, is the broad historical context to which all the ensuing chapters refer. In recognition of this 'shared' European experience, the opening section seeks to lay some essential 'common ground'. The first chapter examines the theoretical tensions implicit in the concept of 'nation', focusing in particular on the 'malleability' of nationalism as a political project. Martin Evans widens the perspective, suggesting that the formation of all social and cultural identities necessarily involves a process of differentiation and demarcation, and that group identity is often reinforced by the stigmatisation of the 'other'. Concepts like nationhood therefore have an inherent capacity to 'exclude' as much as to 'include'. Finally in this first section, Mark Mitchell and Dave Russell consider how policies on migration and citizenship across the European Union are shaped by different national experiences and concepts of nationality.

Thus, though nationalism has 'generic' features, by very definition it also has peculiarities shaped by the experience of individual 'national' communities. Similarly, the global processes described above have not had a uniform impact across the continent. The remaining chapters are therefore 'country-specific', and in order to facilitate meaningful comparisons, these studies have been grouped into three parts. The division follows a broadly regional pattern (western, southern and eastern Europe), but the logic has been pragmatic rather than schematic. The objective has been to identify some comparable features (whether in terms of economic and political development, location within the international system, experience of global change) in order to reduce the number of significant variables. Those variables that remain will therefore often relate to the distinctive processes of nation-state formation in the countries that have been juxtaposed in this way.

Britain, France and Germany are deemed 'comparable' for a number of reasons. All three were relatively early 'industrialisers' and today have broadly similar economic systems and socio-occupational structures. All three are regarded as relatively stable liberal democracies. Each enjoyed 'great power' status in the recent past, and had to come to terms with a reduced influence in the post-war world of the 'super-powers'. Each was deeply implicated in the politics of the Cold War, and is now forced to reappraise its strategic interests. All three have experienced the full effects of market globalism, and of growing supra-nationalism in the European Union, and must reconcile these with traditions of national self-assertiveness. All are countries of immigration, and face the challenge of adapting national identity to the needs of a multicultural society.

The differences of emphasis which emerge in these three chapters are none the less instructive. In the case of the United Kingdom, 'Britishness' remains an elusive and fuzzy concept, whose symbolism is largely depoliticised and centres on the myth of a time-honoured, pragmatic 'British way'. Using the 1930s as an exemplar of how British identity has been constructed, and weaving this into a contemporary narrative, Ken Lunn reveals the distinctly political agenda behind the consensual imagery of British identity, which conceals social conflict and ethnic diversity behind a narrow and sentimental vision of 'Home-Counties' Englishness. In France on the other hand, the concept of 'nation' has always been highly politicised, closely related to the issue of state legitimacy, and therefore often deeply divisive. Reflecting on how nationalism in France has been harnessed to competing political projects of Left and Right, only to lose its potency and centrality in more recent years, Brian Jenkins and Nigel Copsey seek to explain its virulent resurgence on the periphery of French politics in the shape of the Front national. Finally, in the case of Germany, the concept of a culturally and linguistically defined German 'nation' has never found political expression in terms of a single 'state', except in the grim shape of the Third Reich. Gerd Knischewski reflects on the difficulties of forging a new sense of national identity in the wake of reunification, which has highlighted the tensions between the 'civic' and 'ethnic' models of nationhood.

Part III turns to the southern European states of Spain, Portugal and Italy, whose democratic systems were all born in the wake of long periods of authoritarian rule. In comparison to their northern neighbours they also share a more recent and uneven pattern of economic development, which has created strong regional disparities and a more diversified social structure incorporating both distinctly 'modern' and highly 'traditional' occupational groups. In the case of Italy and Spain in particular, relatively weak central state institutions mean that 'national identity' is based more on a layering of social and regional identities, and the accommodation of these subcultures is therefore necessary to the maintenance of social cohesion and political stability. While the absence of any ambition to play a 'world role' means that these states are less jealous of their 'sovereignty', and have adapted more comfortably to the implications of European integration, 'nationalism' has manifested itself at regional level as a challenge to the unitary state. Indeed, 'ethnic' tensions have been produced more by these inter-provincial rivalries than by the presence of 'immigrants' as such, who until recently have been relatively few in number.

If local and regional particularism appears to present a common problem in these three cases, the task of subsuming these allegiances within overall 'state identity' has met with varying success. Spain and Portugal are longstanding territorial states and, as David Corkill indicates, in the latter case a strong sense of national pride coexists quite comfortably with strong local loyalties and a sense of 'European' identity. In Spain, regional autonomy has partially defused the historic nationalisms of Basques, Catalans and Galicians, and may yet create a composite sense of identity as the basis for state legitimacy. In the case of Italy, on the other hand, as Bill Brierley and Luca Giacometti show, the cohesion of the state was largely based on traditional party allegiances, themselves rooted in class and religious loyalties, and the collapse of this system has revealed the historic weakness of Italian civic identity. Into this political vacuum have moved regionally based political movements like the Northern Leagues, and in the south the neo-fascist MSI, more concerned with the populist mobilisation of sectional interests than with genuine autonomist aspirations, while the 'flash movement' success of Berlusconi's Forza Italia reveals the status of the media as one of the few remaining institutions with 'nationwide' appeal.

Part IV brings together Poland, Yugoslavia and the Russian Federation, which all experienced long periods of state-socialism and therefore followed a distinct socio-economic and political path to modernity. In addition, all three societies experienced – in admittedly different ways – the recent collapse of the state-socialist regimes, and had to undergo a painful transition process to a market economy adapted to the realities of an increasingly global economic system. The formidable task of building new economic and political structures in an unstable climate of pent-up popular aspirations has provided fertile terrain for populism across Eastern Europe and the former Soviet Union. In many cases, this has taken the form of 'ethnic nationalism', which has already transformed the state map of the former communist world beyond recognition.

However, these three chapters are a salutary reminder of the profound singularity of each of the societies concerned. Thus in Poland, the transition to post-communism was eased by a strong tradition of religious, intellectual and trade union dissent culminating in Solidarity's ten-year struggle against the state-socialist regime. The emergence of an embryonic replacement leadership in 'civil society' helped to forestall populism. As Frances Millard indicates, given the country's ethnic homogeneity Polish nationalism focused consensually on anti-Soviet sentiments, and in the new context it has little to feed on. In the case of the Russian Federation, curiously enough, this most powerful of the former republics of the USSR initiated the formal dissolution of the Union, partly in the name of reassertion of Russian identity, and yet continued in some way to claim aspects of the Soviet heritage. It is this ambiguous relationship between Soviet and Russian identity, combined with the problems posed by the 'incongruence' between the territory and ethnic composition of the successor states of the Soviet Union, that Paul Flenley examines in his chapter. Finally, Spyros Sofos reveals how the 'internal dynamics' of communist Yugoslavia's federal structure favoured the 'ethnicisation' of its constituent Republics at the expense of state-wide identity, and how ethnicity was thus easily promoted as a primary social reference point once the communist regime disintegrated. Historically conditioned fears, suspicion and animosity thus provided an explosive mix, which led to the most destructive military confrontations of the post-war period in Europe.

This book does not pretend to provide comprehensive coverage of these issues in contemporary Europe. It could be argued that in the interests of geographical balance Scandinavia should have been included, and we are also aware of the claims of Belgium, Austria, the former Czechoslovakia, the Baltic states or the Ukraine, which like many other examples could have provided fascinating contrastive case-studies. The selection we have made has been dictated by the need to cover those countries which tend to attract the greatest academic and media interest. The choice has therefore been pragmatic, but subsequent volumes in this series, both collaborative works and monographs, will seek to redress the balance.

In each of the chapters that follow, the history of nation-state formation in the country concerned has been a necessary reference point in the elucidation of contemporary issues. Inevitably, the amount of historical background deemed relevant has varied considerably from case to case, as indeed has the mode of presentation, some authors preferring a thematic and others a more chronological approach. As editors, we have not endeavoured to impose a rigid template on contributors, preferring to allow them as specialists in their fields to find the most appropriate conceptual framework to develop their line of argument.

However, the primary focus is on the developments of the last ten to fifteen years, when the pace of global change has thrown into sharp relief the issues of state legitimacy and national identity in a variety of different contexts. Notwithstanding the effect of these deeper structural processes, it remains important to recognise that 'nation' is a social construct, and 'nationalism' a distinctly political project. Its analysis belongs not only to the realm of economic, social and cultural change, but also to the unstable and unpredictable world of political leadership and political conjuncture. Writing what the French call *l'histoire immédiate* is a hazardous business, and the speed of events will no doubt continue to outpace our judgements.

Part I

NATION AND IDENTITY: THEORY AND CONTEXT

1

NATION AND NATIONALISM IN CONTEMPORARY EUROPE

A theoretical perspective

Brian Jenkins and Spyros A. Sofos

The end of the Cold War and the demise of the bloc system in the late 1980s initially fuelled speculation about the advent of a 'New World Order'. The collapse of state-socialist regimes in Eastern-Central Europe, and then in the republics of the Soviet Union itself, raised expectations that liberal democracy and the market economy would establish themselves across Europe, and that economic and cultural globalisation would progressively promote this model worldwide.[1] In the process, it was argued, new opportunities for international cooperation would be opened up to tackle global issues like the environment and Third World debt, and to compensate for the declining autonomy of the nation-state in the field of economic and foreign policy. Indeed, what Hobsbawm has called 'the supranational restructuring of the globe' was seen by many to herald the slow demise of the nation-state, and by derivation the decline of national consciousness and of the viability of 'nationalism' as a political project.[2] The moves towards integration of the European Community through the Single European Act and the Maastricht Treaty, the recent enlargement of the European Union to fifteen members, as well as the prospects of further enlargement, seemed to confirm the beginnings of this process.

These expectations were severely dented in the early 1990s. The resurgence of so-called 'ethnic' nationalisms in post-communist Eastern and Central Europe, most tragically in what used to be Yugoslavia, and potentially with equal force in the territories of the former Soviet Union, threatens the dream of a 'common European home'. Furthermore, within Western Europe itself, the 'national question' has reasserted itself with a new vigour in a variety of different ways. Extreme right-wing forms of nationalism have re-emerged, with startling success in France, and with disturbing historical echoes in the reunified Germany and in Italy. The centrality of the issue of immigration in contemporary political discourse has raised questions about the rights of citizenship, the nature of nationality, the viability of a multicultural society, across the European Union. The rise of the Northern Leagues in Italy has challenged the integrity of the nation-state; the separatist 'micro-nationalisms' which flourished in the

1970s in old established states like Spain, Britain and France have stubbornly refused to disappear while new forms of particularism of diaspora and migrant communities have emerged.[3] Finally, events like the Gulf War and the Bosnian conflict have raised doubts about the efficacy of the EU, while the impact of the new recession has swollen the ranks of those who feel economically threatened by further transfers of sovereignty to 'Brussels'. Some of the momentum of European integration has been lost, and the traditional exponents of nationalist and ethnic/religious particularist rhetoric have found a new lease of life.

Of course, it may be argued, such developments are simply 'reactionary', a vain attempt to resist the inevitable process of globalisation. If nationalism no longer has any economic rationale, why should it long survive as a political project, whether of the Left or of the Right? Reason surely dictates otherwise? The process of growing economic and cultural interdependence is irreversible, and has already undermined the autonomy of even the strongest nation-states in Western Europe. The new 'Balkanisation' in the East is a historical throwback, a curious by-product of the collapse of the Soviet 'Empire', and the new states will sooner or later be forced by economic necessity to cooperate with one another, to federate, and to participate in European supranational structures.

Such hopes may be widely shared, but it should not be imagined that these predictions are new. The whole rationalist tradition of the Enlightenment, in both its liberal and socialist derivations, rests on the notion of a 'civilising process', a process of diffusion of a universalist democratic discourse of rights, radiating out in a linear fashion from its European core, breaking down parochialism and prejudice. As 'difference' was confined to the realm of the private, it was often assumed that, in this process, nations – seen primarily as cultural and/or economic entities – and nationalism would eventually be superseded by wider international solidarities and institutions. Of course, it may now be argued (as it has been before!) that the process has reached a critical stage, that the nation-state has fallen below some crucial threshold of credibility but equally it may be that this entire perspective is flawed.

Among the several attempts to explain the resilience and pervasiveness of nationalism in 'late modernity' Tom Nairn's analysis seems to provide an – at first sight – plausible link between nationalism and the dialectics of imperialism and the related process of economic globalisation the former sets in motion.[4] Rejecting the linear enlightenment model, he invoked a dialectical process driven by the global rationale of 'uneven economic development'; nationalism was identified as an ideology of economic modernisation, mobilising societies on the semi-periphery and periphery of the world system to resist imperialism and compete with the 'core' nations for economic resources. In their turn, the core nations were forced to respond. Nationalism had thus become the 'pathology of modern developmental history', ensuring that the battle between nation-states would supersede the Marxist concept of 'class struggle'.

Instructive though this approach may be, it remains rooted in a form of historical determinism and generalisation which we are anxious to avoid.[5] This volume does not aspire to erect an 'overarching theory' of this type. The complexity and diversity of the phenomenon which we are dealing with precludes such an ambition, though of course it has fuelled our debates, and will continue to do so. However, this is not to say that we have not established some 'common ground', though it would be pretentious to claim that this represents a 'theoretical framework'. Central to our shared position is the belief that 'nationalism' is essentially a 'political' phenomenon. This is not to dismiss economic, cultural and geographical factors as irrelevant to the subject of enquiry. But it does challenge the view that 'nationalism' is somehow the product of pre-existing socio-cultural entities called 'nations'. A starting point for the study of nationalism is not whether 'nation' exists; it is rather how the category operates in practice, that is, how nationalist logics and frames of reference are formulated and deployed. In a way similar to proposed conceptualizations of 'race',[6] we would argue that 'nation' should be conceptualized as 'an unstable and 'decentred' complex of social meanings constantly being transformed by political struggle. We would thus prefer to invert the relationship and regard nations as 'political' artefacts called into being by nationalist ideologies and movements.

Of course, the ideology of nationalism needs something on which to feed, some 'raw material' of collective identity. The potential ingredients of this are diverse – a common language, a shared history or culture, religious particularism, a sense of territorial, ethnic or 'racial' distinctiveness and/or assertion of opposition to other communities, or indeed the existence either in the past or in the present of some political identity – a state or subordinate administrative unit. However, such 'timeless' generalities detract from the fact that the concept of nationhood is a historically specific phenomenon, and a relatively recent one which has extended its influence across the globe only in the last two hundred years. From this point of view, more interesting than the 'raw material' of nationhood are the social-historical processes that have politically mobilised the former and promoted the proliferation of nations and nation-states.

In other words, nationalisms are the product of complex social negotiation, premised on the activation of social and cultural relationships and emotional investments among the – potential – members of the national community, as well as on strategies for the pursuit of interests, and attainment of power by individuals and collectivities. Their emergence, sustenance and demise are the outcome of conflict and negotiation at several levels of the 'social'. But it is the articulation of the 'national' to

11

political discourses and practices, the elevation of the nation to the status of a *political subject* that characterises nationalism.[7]

Benedict Anderson, in his remarkable book *Imagined Communities* locates the beginnings of this process in the decline of the religious 'imagined communities' in early modern Europe, the gradual replacement of Latin by the vernacular in the wake of the printing revolution, the secularisation brought about by the Enlightenment, the weakening of the great dynastic empires.[8] This, primarily cultural, perspective is a useful corrective to the economistic focus of classical Marxism, with its emphasis on the capitalist quest for wider markets, and the role of a common language as a vehicle for commodity exchange. The direct linkage thereby established between the rise of the 'bourgeoisie' and that of the nation-state has often proved problematic, for example when applied to the nationalisms of economically undeveloped Central and Eastern Europe in the nineteenth century, or indeed to the more recent national liberation struggles in the 'Third World'. None the less, the significance of socio-economic factors can clearly not be ignored.

The development of commerce and industry, the widening of markets, greater social mobility, urbanisation, the speeding up of communications especially with the railway revolution, all of these processes made it easier for people to 'imagine' their membership of a national community, though the level of this 'consciousness' was inevitably related to the degree of *societal integration* and to *social class*. Even in a country like France, already a prototype nation-state under the absolutist monarchy of the seventeenth century, and whose revolution launched the very principle of national sovereignty and the ideology of nationalism, peasants did not achieve a real sense of being 'French' until the closing years of the nineteenth century.[9]

However, while these cultural and economic processes clearly helped to prepare the ground for the emergence of 'national' identity, and subsequently helped to promote and to broaden it, they were not the key catalysts which brought nation-states and nationalism into being. The concept of nationhood is inextricably bound up with the notion of political legitimacy, with the location of sovereignty in the 'people'. As long as authority was deemed to derive from Divine Right, from hereditary succession, from a 'natural order' based on a society of graded estates, kings ruled over 'territories' not 'peoples', and the latter were 'subjects' not 'citizens'. It was in early modern Europe, and especially in the later part of the eighteenth and early nineteenth centuries, that the 'people' became a politically significant term, denoting initially a moral community.[10] In France, however, the revolutionary process drew the masses on to the political stage and associated the concept of the 'nation' with the powerful political symbolism of popular sovereignty.[11] The subsequent impact of these ideas on the rest of *Ancien Régime* Europe during the

Revolutionary and Napoleonic wars paved the way for the development of the 'nation-state' idea across the continent in the nineteenth century. This association of nationhood with the goals of democratic citizenship and social emancipation within a territorially bounded political community has been a powerful motor in the advent of political modernity virtually everywhere. It has characterised nationalist movements in diverse historical settings, from the first explosion of national sentiments in the European revolutions of 1848 to the era of post-war decolonisation, from the anti-fascist liberation struggles in occupied Europe to the contemporary autonomist aspirations of Scots, Bretons and Quebecois. However, it would clearly be perverse to suggest that nationalism is endemically associated with such 'progressive' ideals, or indeed that the proclamation of such ideas by 'nationalists' should necessarily be taken at face value. To do so would be to deny the ambiguity and political 'malleability' of nationalism.

NATIONALISM AND POLITICAL LEGITIMACY

The first key to understanding the contradictions of nationalism lies in the concept of political legitimacy. The popular movements of early modern Europe and especially the French Revolution challenged the traditional foundations of authority that underpinned the European 'Old Order', and ensured that states would increasingly need to invest themselves with the aura of popular consent. This was the driving force behind the gradual decline of the dynastic empires in nineteenth-century Europe, and growing aspirations to national self-determination and self-government. However, this process did not necessarily imply the adoption of 'bourgeois democracy' or, later, 'liberal democracy', let alone the radical forms of 'popular sovereignty' envisaged by the French revolutionaries of 1793. Indeed, in France the Bonapartist interlude was soon to prove that the imagery of the 'nation' and the 'general will' could be hijacked by a charismatic leader and an authoritarian plebiscitary dictatorship. This simply confirmed that the invocations of 'popular legitimacy' would not be the exclusive prerogative of democrats. The revolutions of 1848 did not secure the full democracy demanded by radical nationalists, but the more limited principle of constitutionalism. This in itself was seen to confer representative status, irrespective of the limitations imposed on the right to vote, on parliamentary powers or on civil liberties. It was the cautious liberalism of Cavour that eventually prevailed over the radicalism of Mazzini in the process of the Italian Risorgimento, while Germany was finally unified by Bismarck's *Junker* army. The 1870–1914 period was a crucial phase in the consolidation of the nation-state form in Western Europe, and in the development of what Hobsbawm calls 'state patriotism', but by the First World War few countries yet combined all the ingredients of a 'liberal democracy'. In this respect, it becomes difficult to sustain the argument that national self-determination is *necessarily* tied to a democratic project, whether 'bourgeois' or 'popular'. What can surely be said, however, is that nationalism is a product of the modern problematique of state legitimacy in the age of 'mass politics'. To be clear, nationalism is closely linked to the imagery of popular sovereignty, not necessarily to democracy. It articulates demands for expression of the national/popular/general will, without however necessarily linking them to the representation of particular social identities and interests. Its power therefore can be unifying, homogenising, as well as democratising as far as the national community is concerned. The way the nation is imagined is therefore crucial in exploring the relationship between nationalism and democracy.

IMAGINING THE NATION: CITIZENSHIP AND ETHNICITY

The crucial role of the French Revolution in the launching of nationalism is paradoxical in one important respect, namely that France was already, under the *Ancien Régime*, a prototype nation-state with well-established frontiers, a centralised administration, a standing army and a long history as a collective entity. Its revolution was 'national' in the sense that it conferred political identity on the 'nation' through the concept of citizenship. Since the geographical boundaries of the national unit were already defined, it did not need to be 'imagined' in territorial terms. In the sense that France was a 'state' before it became a 'nation' in the modern sense, it did not need to be 'invented' along those dangerous faultlines of language, religion and so-called 'ethnicity'. Of course, this is not to deny that many were wrongly stigmatised as traitors, were arbitrarily 'excluded' from the national community, were persecuted often unjustly for their social origins, religious convictions or political ideology. However, the cruelties of the revolutionary process did not detract in the long run from the principles of nationhood that were bequeathed to posterity; namely that the nation was a voluntary association of equal and free citizens, who enjoyed membership of the community by virtue of their residence on national soil, irrespective of their ethnic origins or religious beliefs. This model was, at least in theory, not only 'open' but 'universalist'; it bequeathed to all nations equal rights and status in the world community.

The export of these principles of national self-determination to a Europe still based on dynastic empires, petty principalities and statelets, and indeed in the East on feudal particularism, raised a different set of problems. In as far as the territorial divisions of the continent were ill-adapted to growing demands for constitutional and representative government, the revolutionary and Napoleonic legacy undermined the structures of the 1815 settlement. But the establishment of new units of government inevitably sought its rationale in non-associationist forms of collective identity. Whereas in France the 'state' had predated the 'nation', elsewhere the process was inverted. A sense of nationality had to be created as a precondition of state formation, hence the appeal to criteria of language, religion, a common history and culture and ethnicity, as a means of 'mapping' the future frontiers of self-government. In the case of Italy and Germany, this process took the form of unification of diverse kingdoms, principalities and statelets, on the initiative of an active core – Piedmont and Sardinia on the one hand, Prussia on the other. In Eastern Europe the process was one of secession from the great dynastic empires – Habsburg, Romanov and Ottoman – throughout the nineteenth and early twentieth centuries. In all of these settings, however, the 'nation' had to be defined as a socio-cultural entity before it achieved political reality as a state. The nationalism of the movements that assumed this role could not, therefore, rest on the French-inspired 'citizenship' model alone, with its essentially *associationist* emphasis on the nation as a voluntary (and therefore 'open') association, the product of political will, more akin to the type of social bond Ferdinand Tönnies called *Gesellschaft*. Hence the emergence of a second brand of nationalism, often identified as 'German' in its intellectual inspiration, which fed on the concept of '*Kulturnation*'. According to this, nations were 'communities of fate' bound together by seemingly objective qualities, such as history, language and culture and often, by connotation, blood ties. Rather than free associations based on residence, they were historically determined entities based on ancestry. By implication at least, they were 'closed' rather than 'open', particularist rather than universalist, based on an understanding of the nation as a less diffuse entity, as a 'natural', organic community whose existence is not the product of choice but has been determined by history and nature. If we are to use Tönnies' terminology once more, it could be argued that the *Kulturnation* is perceived or represented by advocates of this type of solidarity as an essentially *Gemeinschaft*-type community. However, as 'nations' are too large and complex to qualify for such a definition, it should be stressed that it is the type of perceived, 'imagined', bond among the nation's members, the desire to retrieve the feeling of intimacy and organic warmth associated with *Gemeinschaft* that is evoked by advocates of this brand of nationalism.

It would, however, be wrong to view this duality in an over-schematic way, to see nationalism in terms of simple dichotomies – 'good' and 'bad', 'open' and 'closed', 'Left' and 'Right', 'French' and 'German'. The reality is far more nuanced and complex, and in practice the two 'models' are not mutually incompatible. Cultural particularism often coexisted with genuine democratic aspirations in the nationalist movements of Central and Eastern Europe. And on the other side of the coin, in France itself the 'citizenship model' of nationhood was not immune to racial metaphors –

for example, the theme of the oppressed 'Gauls' governed by invading 'Franks' in republican nationalist imagery in the 1840s. While the polarity of these two models is a useful benchmark for distinguishing different types of nationalism, expressions like *Kulturnation* should not delude us into thinking that we are dealing with an objective social reality. Nations, on whatever principles they are conceived, are indeed 'imagined communities', social, cultural and political artefacts.

IMAGINING THE NATION: THE CLASS DIMENSION

Class and nation have often been juxtaposed as the two great competing loyalties of the modern age, and not surprisingly socialists have found the 'national question' particularly troublesome. Classical Marxism depicted nationalism as an ideological instrument of the bourgeoisie, and in the context of the established nation-state it would be hard to deny that the cultivation of national sentiments has been a powerful agent of social stabilisation. However, the claim that the nation-idea is endemically 'bourgeois' even in the gestation period which preceded state formation is much harder to sustain. Nationalist movements have often assumed a popular-democratic guise, and to suggest that they were simply the dupes of an ideologically manipulative and class-conscious bourgeoisie is to ignore social realities. A well-defined, self-aware and hegemonic capitalist class of this type arguably did not exist even in 1789 France, let alone in mid-nineteenth-century Central and Eastern Europe, or indeed in parts of the post-colonial world. To understand the popular appeal of nationalist movements in such settings, a different approach is necessary. While the traditional pattern of pre-industrial, pre-capitalist social relations was beginning to break down, the process of class differentiation typical of mature capitalism was not yet very far advanced, the nascent bourgeoisie was not in a position to impose class-conscious leadership, and nothing resembling an industrial proletariat had yet emerged. In this context, the concept of the *general will*, of the *people* (*peuple, popolo, Volk, narod*), of a socially undifferentiated 'citizenry', was ideologically sustainable as a rallying point for all those diverse conditions and estates that harboured grievances in the creaking edifice of the 'Old Order'. As Peter Burke points out:

> the term 'people', in opposition to that of the privileged classes, was common enough in political discourse in the Age of the French Revolution, ... [and] can occasionally be found still earlier. ... In the English Revolution of the 1640s, for example, the Levellers declared that 'all power is originally and essentially in the whole body of the people' ... [in] Germany in the age of Luther and the great Peasant War of 1525, a term in common use was 'the common man'.[12]

In the confrontation with narrowly based ruling élites, in societies with fluid class structures, the subaltern social groups, informed by popular mobilisations, forged oppositional, popular identities throughout early modern Europe. So indelible was the imprint of these identities upon the social imagery of European societies that elements of 'popular identity' or 'culture' have been incorporated to hegemonic political discourses – both democratic and authoritarian – ever since. Of course, this was a transitional phase in historical terms and eventually, in the wake of industrialisation, the bourgeoisie very often achieved hegemony, and shaped nationalist ideology to its own class-conscious purposes. In some cases, this shift from 'popular' to 'bourgeois' forms of nationalism preceded the formation of the nation-state, but it was above all in established states that the ideology came into its own as a vehicle of social integration and stabilisation. The corollary of this process was, of course, a growing sense of class consciousness among the 'dispossessed', and the emergence of an industrial 'proletariat'. Faced with bourgeois state nationalism, socialists from the 1880s onwards endeavoured to cultivate a sense of international working-class solidarity. However, even genuine 'revolutionaries' in the socialist and workers' movement were obliged to conduct their struggle primarily on 'national' terrain, and as a result their discourse frequently drew on the legacy of earlier 'popular democratic' nationalism as a source of ideological inspiration. Despite the aspiration to 'international' consciousness, they were constrained by the national framework within which politics was largely conducted.

To say this is to reaffirm the essentially 'political' character of nationalism. A deterministic Marxist approach to 'class' would, of course, argue that 'the workers have no fatherland', that the proletarian condition transcends 'nation'. However, political realities – the institutional and cultural difficulties of creating a genuinely 'international' socialist consciousness, the gradual acquisition by workers of citizen rights, the need for the socialist movement to compete for hegemony within the confines of the nation-state – militates against such assumptions. Socialists, most dramatically in the context of the two World Wars, have been obliged to consider their relationship with their 'nation' and to make difficult political choices.

A poignant illustration of how loyalties to class and to nation may interact in differing political circumstances is the policy of socialists with reference to the two World Wars. Their rationale for supporting the war effort in 1914 was essentially that their 'country' was worth defending against authoritarian and militaristic enemies. Throughout Europe, socialists succumbed to pressure to put national interests and pride first or to see them as a necessary condition for the achievement of their own political objectives, for as Hobsbawm points out:

17

All the major belligerents presented the war as defensive. All presented it as a threat from abroad to civic advantages peculiar to their own country or side; all learned to present their war aims (somewhat inconsistently) not only as the elimination of such threats, but as, in some way, the social transformation of the country in the interest of its poorer citizens.[13]

Thus, French socialists, for example, were drawn into a process of class collaboration by providing an ancillary justification for fighting the war (defence of workers' rights), but the real agenda was being set by the hegemonic classes and conservative forces whose war rationale and war aims had quite different bases. In the wake of the bloodbath, a tide of jingoistic and militaristic triumphalism returned the most right-wing French assembly this century, closing off any prospect of social reform. In contrast, the situation before and during the Second World War presented an entirely different picture. There was no national 'convergence' in the face of a common enemy, because Left and Right emphasised different external threats (Nazi Germany and the Soviet Union respectively), advocated different foreign policies, and were polarised around very different political value systems. In the context of the Nazi occupation and the Vichy regime, left-wing forces effectively captured the language of national liberation and social emancipation in the anti-fascist resistance movement.[14]

It is thus evident that the relationship between class and nationalism cannot be reduced to socio-economic determinism. The configuration of political and social forces at any particular historical conjuncture must be taken into account. Nationalism may be a vital instrument of social stabilisation, but 'bourgeois' interests transcend the 'nation' and may on occasions justify the sacrifice of national sovereignty. The extreme right-wing nationalism, anti-Semitic and exclusionist, which emerged in many established European states at the end of the nineteenth century (and which has often been regarded as 'proto-fascist') may have appealed primarily to a *petit-bourgeois* core, but its social constituency was in fact much wider than that. As for the working class, whatever the efforts of socialists to equip the labour movement with an international consciousness, concrete historical situations imposed difficult political choices which obliged left-wing forces to examine their relationship with their 'nation' and to present themselves as the bearers of key 'progressive' national values.

NATIONALIST MOVEMENTS AND NATION-STATES

To emphasise its political character implies that nationalism should be seen not as a merely 'cultural' phenomenon – an expression of a cultural or linguistic community; we would argue that in and through nationalism the (modern) political form of the nation-state and the longing for a 'more ancient and nebulous ... condition of belonging' – to use Timothy Brennan's words – are fused.[15] Nationalism is inextricably linked to political modernity, despite the often anti-modern elements of nationalist discourse, and to the forms of political subjectivity that this link entails. This means that nationalism constitutes a form of 'political imagination', a politicising force that transforms cultural communities and other collectivities into gestative political entities. Nations can be said to 'exist' only insofar as they have acquired, or have manifested some sort of aspiration to achieve statehood or some sort of recognition of sovereignty or *political subjectivity*.

It is necessary, however, to consider the distinction implied above – between the nationalism of existing sovereign states and that of nationalist movements – because implicit in much of the literature is a suggestion that this in itself may supply the basis of a typology. For example, Tom Nairn's recognition of the political ambiguity of nationalism leads him to contrast anti-imperialist liberation movements with the 'history of Italian fascism and the Japanese military state of the 1930s, ... the careers and personalities of General de Gaulle, General Amin and the Shah of Iran'.[16] It is tempting to see the struggles of aspirant nations, not only in the former colonial empires but also in nineteenth-century Europe and in some of the contemporary 'micro-nationalist' movements of Western Europe, as essentially progressive and democratic,[17] as opposed to the conservative, exclusionist or expansionist tendencies of nationalism in established states. The horrors of the ethnic conflict in former Yugoslavia are surely enough to invalidate this kind of simplification, though to say this is merely to underline a point made earlier. The 'democratic' aspirations of secessionist and liberationist movements have often gone hand in hand with the language of ethnic, cultural and linguistic exclusion. On the other side of the coin, within established nation-states left-wing forces have occasionally been able to seize the initiative and appropriate the language of nationalism in the process of articulation of progressive democratic values. Nairn's description of nationalism as 'Janus-faced' is indeed appropriate here – with a slight modification: the ambiguity of nationalism does not so much lay in the existence of both democratic and authoritarian, 'open' and 'closed' variants; it is the potential coexistence of both elements within every nationalist movement and ideology, the continuous tension and contradiction between them that renders nationalism ambiguous and malleable.

None the less, the passage of nationalism from 'movement' to 'statehood' has invariably had some ideological significance, as illustrated by the crucial phase of European history from 1870 to 1914. In Western Europe, these years saw the consolidation of the modern bourgeois state form. In some cases, like Britain and France, this occurred within long-established frontiers, whereas in Germany the political unit was a recent construction. But in general terms, the process involved the attempt to provide a degree of popular legitimacy for the relations of power crystall-ised in the nation-state, though the precise formula – extensions of the suffrage, representative institutions, social and educational reforms – varied from case to case. Common to all these settings, however, was the importance of nationalism, now refashioned from a revolutionary ideol-ogy partly inspired by democratic idealism into one which demanded loyalty to the nation-state. At one level, this may be seen simply as a conservative adaptation of the 'citizenship' model. The gradual extension of citizen rights to subordinate classes and subaltern social groups could serve to 'integrate' them within the social order and promote their loyalty to the established nation-state. Even the potentially 'revolutionary' indus-trial workers could be reconciled, in as far as they were offered a national framework within which to pursue their objectives – legalised trade unions and political parties, free elections, representative institutions. Everything was done to cultivate the image of a socially undifferentiated citizenry defined first and foremost by their membership of a 'nation'. To this end, states sought to foster a sense of national community; through the imposition of national literary languages, education and military conscription; through the symbolism of flags, anthems and ceremonial; through the *invention of tradition*.[18] Equally crucial, of course, in the long run-in to the First World War, was the identification of 'others' – external and internal, mainly enemy states whose hostility represented a threat to state sovereignty and national values.

However, this shift of nationalism from 'left' to 'right' was a much more tortuous ideological process than is suggested above. Earlier in the nineteenth century, conservative forces had rarely been over-concerned with the need to legitimate their rule by popular consent, preferring to rely on the deadweight of social deference and political passivity. 'National-ism' in its democratic guise had usually been regarded as dangerously subversive. What made nationalism a valuable weapon in the hands of the ruling classes within established nation-states was not just the new imperatives of mass politics, but the emergence at the end of the century of a hybrid form of popular and exclusionist nationalism which proved malleable to the dynamics of social conflict. Originally, this brand of nationalism far from being 'bourgeois' was anti-modern as far as its political rhetoric was concerned; indeed it often articulated popular resistance to capitalism and mobilised popular memories of the 'moral economy' of pre-modern Europe.[19] Although it was apparently hostile to both economic and political liberalism, its energy was directed mainly against liberal politicians and intellectuals rather than the capitalist system itself. Authoritarian and populist, 'social' rather than socialist, deeply

hostile to parliamentarism in favour of plebiscitary rule, its core constituency was *petit bourgeois*, though its appeal often extended more
widely to the *déclassés* of all social categories. Eric Hobsbawm has cogently
summarised the historical context within which this 'proto-fascist', populist form of nationalism emerged:

> The resistance of traditional groups threatened by the onrush of
> modernity, the novel and quite non-traditional groups now rapidly
> growing in the urbanising societies of developed countries, and the
> unprecedented migrations which disturbed a multiple diaspora of
> peoples across the globe . . . not to mention an international situation
> that provided plenty of pegs on which to hang manifestos of hostility
> to foreigners.[20]

Undoubtedly, this nationalism was fanned by inter-state rivalries, and
by the conviction that existing governments were congenitally incapable
of defending national interests thanks to the debilitating virus of liberalism
and parliamentarism. However, the real focus was more introspective – a
reformulation of the principles of nationality within established nation-
states on the basis, not of open citizenship, but of ethnic and cultural
determinism. This *closure* of national identity was manifested by the social
construction of internal 'others': hostility to foreigners, and above all to
Jewish immigrants fleeing the pogroms in Eastern Europe, was endemic
to this nationalism, but the list of 'internal aliens' extended further. Liberal
intellectuals, parliamentary democrats, international socialists – and a
little later the feminist movements, or 'sexual deviants'[21] – were stigmatised for dividing, subverting and betraying the 'nation', by espousing
'cosmopolitan' or 'decadent' ideals and undermining the middle-class
morality upon which most national cultures of the period were premised.

It was this latter component which proved most attractive to ruling élites
intent on preserving the bourgeois social order. If radical democrats, and
especially the leaders of the growing socialist and labour movement, could
be presented as traitors to the 'nation', this could serve to consolidate the
state. Of course, bourgeois state patriotism never entirely endorsed radical
right-wing nationalism, in either its internal or external manifestations. As
Hobsbawm writes: 'few governments, even before 1914, were as chauvinist as the nationalist ultras who urged them on'.[22] There was, however, an
undoubted ideological osmosis between the two.

So, just as movements struggling to achieve statehood often combined
democratic aspirations with ethnic particularism, so in these years a
similar contradiction emerged within many established nation-states. The
'citizenship model' fed on the process of social integration, and indeed on
a growing and largely apolitical sense of 'patriotism', and this implied an
open, voluntarist definition of nationality, based on residence. The other
version defined the nation in terms of ethnicity, culture and ideological

allegiance, and was inherently 'exclusive'. The merging of the two models meant at the very least that 'assimilation' to the hegemonic culture would be seen as a desirable condition of citizenship, and it raised the possibility that some might refuse to 'assimilate' or be deemed 'unassimilable'. The tension between these two principles is central to understanding the political malleability of nationalist ideology in established nation-states. At one end of the scale, the 'citizenship model' may provide the inspiration for radical democratic reform, respect for other nations, a multicultural society. At the other extreme lies the potential for chauvinism, militarism, 'cultural fundamentalism', fascism and 'ethnic cleansing'. In certain political circumstances, this kind of polarisation has indeed occurred. It would be wrong, however, to assume that nationalism can always be measured on a linear scale running from 'left' to 'right'. Both at the level of governments and political movements, and perhaps even more at the level of popular consciousness, the two sets of principles may become intertwined. It is this essential ambiguity that we will now address.

NATIONALISM AND NATIONAL CONSCIOUSNESS

Even in those countries where state frontiers were already well established (Britain, Spain, Portugal, France), large sections of the population, especially in remote rural areas, had limited geographical and social horizons and minimal political consciousness. The bearers of nationalist ideology, well into the nineteenth century in many areas, were essentially *minorités agissantes*, for all their claims to speak on behalf of 'the people'. Of course, to recognise this is also to understand that identification with something as large and 'abstract' as the 'nation' required an imaginative leap, an expansion of consciousness beyond the parochial level. If, today, national loyalties are often viewed as narrow and petty, this was not the case in the Europe of 1848, and this is another facet of the 'democratic' thrust of nationalism at that time.

However, a more important observation is that nationalism could not develop its full ideological appeal until the majority of the population had been integrated in the collective life of society. Many factors contributed to this process – the concentration of the workforce in industry and urban centres, the development of transport and communications, increasing social mobility, rising levels of literacy.[23] Political changes were equally vital – the growth of bureaucracy, education reform, military service, the extension of the suffrage. As indicated earlier, these processes were speeded up by the adoption of the nation-state form, as governments sought to secure legitimacy by actively promoting a sense of national identity. The spread of this model of political and social organisation worldwide has ensured that 'nation-talk', the 'national' idiom, permeates the political discourse of governments and political movements of almost every ideological shade. Even those that proclaim firmly internationalist principles (whether humanist or Marxist) have to make concessions to the 'national' dimension of popular experience and culture, and adapt their discourses accordingly. The effect on the wider community of this constant barrage of national symbols and references from every side is difficult to calculate. It undoubtedly helps to instil 'national sentiment', that sense of 'belonging' to a particular spatial and social environment, and this may amount to no more than a vague apolitical 'patriotism'. But may it not also lead to popular confusion, a failure to comprehend the differing signific-ance of rival nationalisms, a willingness to respond to the nationalist drum whatever the rhythm and whoever is beating it?

The answer to this question again seems to belong to the realm of politics. Political circumstances vary from country to country; they may produce clear ideological choices, or they may blur the picture in a variety of ways. But it should be recognised that popular loyalties to the nation are often politically amorphous and ambiguous, and therefore not only 'malleable' but also capable of subverting the intentions of those who attempt to mobilise them. Therein lies their danger. The 'nationalism' fostered by the British Labour Party against EEC membership in the 1970s may have sought its rationale in an anti-capitalist and democratic dis-course, but there can be little doubt that it also fed on popular chauvinism. Indeed, that was dramatically confirmed by Enoch Powell's influential intervention in the October 1974 British general election, when he called for a Labour vote because of that party's anti-EEC stance.

The saturation of political discourse with 'nation-talk' also raises a difficult conceptual problem. In an age where the language of patriotism has become a routine rhetorical device, how do we distinguish what is properly 'nationalist'? The term has little value as an analytical tool if it is used to refer to every ideology, movement or programme which makes some concession to the popular sense of 'belonging' to a particular community. To refer again to the British case: should we dub Margaret Thatcher as a nationalist because of her frequent (and often ineffectual) invocation of 'British interests' at EC summits, while all the time govern-ment policy favoured the internationalisation of the British economy, diplomatic and military subservience to the United States, and con-sequently an increasing loss of national sovereignty? This dilemma can only be resolved by once again insisting on the key relationship between 'nationalism' and the issue of state legitimacy in the modern age. On the one hand, the term may be applied to movements aspiring to create a sovereign state 'which will unite all individuals sharing a particular set of criteria of nationality (ethnic, cultural, historical) under a common regime based on the notion of popular sovereignty'.[24] On the other hand, within already established 'nation-states', the term may be applied to discourses that seek to secure the legitimacy of that state by creating or sustaining a sense of national identity, to political programmes that seek to protect or extend state sovereignty (defence in war, territorial expansion, economic protectionism, national autonomy in decision-making, etc.) or, finally, to attempts to form new political communities by creating new, or retrieving older, imagined communities.

This kind of definition allows us to avoid two extreme positions. The first is that of seeing 'nationalism' everywhere, and here Tom Nairn is a case in point.[25] As it has already been pointed out, identifying rather arbitrarily 'class' and 'nation' as opposites, he seeks a global explanation of the prevalence of national over class loyalties, in the process of 'uneven economic development'. In as far as national loyalties are seen as fundamentally inimical to the development of class solidarities, any movement or ideology that acknowledges them deserves the appellation 'nationalist'. A different position is developed by Eric Hobsbawm, whose writings on the subject began partly in response to Nairn's.[26] Reflecting the classical Marxist conviction that nationalism is essentially 'bourgeois', his much more restricted definition of 'nationalism', which he largely reserves for the process of European state-formation 1789–1918, and the nationalism of the established bourgeois nation-states of Europe from 1870 up to and including the period of fascism and the Second World War is not applied to movements normally deemed 'progressive' or associated with the Left. He skates over the democratic impulse that so often inspired the 'popular' state-aspiring nationalist movements of nineteenth- century Europe, focusing instead on their linguistic, religious or ethnic rationale. His use of the term in the twentieth-century context is equally selective. He is clearly right to distinguish the 'exclusive nationalism of states or right-wing political movements' from what he calls 'the conglomerate national/ citizen, social consciousness which forms the soil in which all political sentiments grow'. And indeed, as he continues, 'in this sense "nation" and "class" were not readily separable'.[27]

However, when he writes about the appropriation by the Left of patriotic sentiments during the anti-fascist resistance struggle in the Second World War, it is significant that he uses the word 'nationalism' in italics, and that he consistently emphasises that these liberation struggles were as much 'international' and 'social' as truly 'national'. This squeamishness about using the term 'nationalist' to describe movements of which he approves continues in his account of decolonisation; he argues that the anti-imperialist movements cannot be described as genuinely nationalist because they rarely coincided 'with a political or ethnic entity existing before the coming of the imperialists'.[28] He is even more reluctant to apply the term to the resurgent West European separatisms of the post-1968 period, which he sees primarily as reactions against centralisation and bureaucratisation 'wrapped in coloured banners'.[29]

From our perspective, however, each of these examples relates closely to the central dynamic of nationalism, namely the issue of political subjectivity, often in the form of a quest for state legitimacy, and illustrates the ambivalence of nationalism. Most of the European anti-fascist movements may have been engaged in an 'international' ideological war and in a 'domestic' social conflict, but they were 'nationalist' in the sense that in occupied Europe they were struggling to liberate national territory – in Britain to defend it, but in both contexts, the legitimacy of the pre-war state had been deeply undermined. Liberation and the defeat of fascism involved not just the restoration of national sovereignty, but also an attempt to redefine the social foundations of state legitimacy through the political mobilisation of national identity.

In the other two cases, Hobsbawm's conviction that some form of historical popular 'proto-nationalism' is at least desirable, perhaps even essential, for the formation of 'serious state-aspiring national movements' leads him once again to neglect the strictly political dynamics of nation-state formation. It is no doubt true that few anti-imperialist movements had a 'pre-colonial' ethnic or political foundation, that they were led by *minorités agissantes*, that it was largely *after* the achievement of statehood that the nation-building process began (though as Hobsbawm himself admits elsewhere, this is hardly unique: 'nations are more often the consequence of setting up a state than they are its foundations').[30] What counts is that the movements 'aspired' to nation-statehood (however 'imitative' this was of the European model, and however unpromising the 'raw material' of national identity). The key trigger mechanism again was a crisis of political legitimacy, the declining authority of colonial rule in both institutional and ideological terms and the struggle for political hegemony in the 'post-colonial' era .

Finally, as regards the rise of West European and Quebecois 'separatisms', the essence of Hobsbawm's case seems to be that further nation-state fragmentation is undesirable in the modern world, and that such states would anyway enjoy minimal sovereignty.[31] That argument has not, of course, prevented precisely such a process occurring in Eastern-Central Europe and the former Soviet Union, since 1989. Neither does it explain why such aspirations have developed even in long-established states like Britain, France and Spain. Ethnic solidarities hardly provide an explanation here, for until the post-1968 period the conventional wisdom was that these 'sub'-nationalities had been thoroughly assimilated. Once again, the trigger mechanism was political, namely a crisis of confidence in the legitimacy of state institutions. To dismiss these 'separatisms' as reactions to centralisation clothed in pseudo-nationalist garb is therefore to miss the point that 'nationalism' had often been associated with precisely such democratic aspirations. Discontent with the remoteness of 'big government', disillusionment with the regime in power at the centre, or indeed with the alternatives available in mainstream 'metropolitan' politics, may interact with a sense of cultural distinctiveness and provide the basis for a political movement after long years of hibernation.

Of course, Hobsbawm may be right in his secondary argument, namely that Scots, Basques and Corsicans are in fact less interested in full independent statehood than in more limited forms of autonomy, whatever their protestations. He may also be right that such movements may prove ephemeral, or that they may remain *minorités agissantes* with no substantial popular base. If so, that will merely prove that the crisis of established institutions was insufficiently profound to challenge the territorial integrity of the existing state.

CONCLUSION

This key relationship between nationalism and state legitimacy provides a broad framework for the analysis of its diverse manifestations in contemporary Europe. While the full ideological flavour of individual nationalisms will inevitably reflect specific national histories and cultures, their current revival cannot be separated from developments at the global level. These international processes have placed increasing strain on established state structures of Europe over the last two decades. Perhaps the most significant change of all, the end of the Cold War and the disintegration of the Soviet bloc, has produced the most dramatic resurgence of the nationalist phenomenon. It requires little perception to see the process of 'Balkanisation' in Eastern-Central Europe and the former Soviet Union as a direct consequence of the 'crisis of legitimacy' of the former communist states. The opening up of an 'ideological vacuum', which imported models of market economics and liberal democracy have largely failed to fill, combined with the frustration and societal insecurity that the social and ideological dislocations of the socio-economic transformation of Eastern-Central Europe is causing, has left space for nationalist movements whose 'democratic' rationale of self-government has often been infected by ethnic exclusionism (see Chapters 9–11). Of course, the precise historical legacy varies from case to case: previous existence of an ethnicity-based state, or of a frustrated national movement; the survival of a democratic political culture; the degree of federal autonomy tolerated under communism. However, to see the new nationalisms simply as the product of age-old ethnic rivalries is to accept nationalist myths and narratives uncritically.

The collapse of the post-war bipolar international system has had its repercussions on state legitimacy in Western European societies too. The unified Germany faces the task of redefining national identity, which for forty years had hinged on the complex, often antagonistic, relationship between the two German states (see Chapter 6). The rise of neo-nazism in part reflects the difficulty of reconnecting with the nation's previous history as a unified state. To an admittedly lesser extent, other West European states also drew part of their post-war national identity from their involvement in the bloc architecture of the 'free world' (NATO, EC, IMF, WEU, EFTA) and their opposition to communism. While the end of the Cold War opened the prospect of wider European cooperation, it also loosened existing alliances and removed a key component of the hegemonic discourse (anti-communism). An alternative scenario has therefore developed, namely the possibility of renewed inter-state rivalries in Western Europe, feeding on intensified economic competition, strategic uncertainties, and the need for governments to find new foreign targets as a focus for national cohesion (see Chapters 4–6).

Of course, the end of the Cold War was itself linked to another fundamental process whose political effects have become decisive in the last twenty years, namely the phenomenon of economic globalisation. The growing interdependence of the world economy, the increasingly trans-national character of economic activity, meant that it became impossible to insulate the command economies of the Soviet bloc from the competitive pressures of the international market. It has also proved more and more difficult to ignore such pressures in Western European societies, as the failure of the French Socialist government's 'Keynesianism in one country' confirmed in the early 1980s. State-interventionist economic policies have been widely called into question, as expensive, counterproductive, and indeed as no longer viable. This, more than any other single factor, has raised speculation about the long-term future of the nation-state form as the central focus of decision-making in the modern world. These pressures have been aggravated by the successive world recessions of the post-1973 period, and indeed by the slow decline of Western Europe as a techno-logical and industrial competitor in the 'new international division of labour'. In this context, while governments proclaim the virtues of the international market economy (or reluctantly acquiesce), it is hardly surprising to find that those who suffer the social consequences are increasingly disillusioned by apparent government indifference or impo-tence. It is in this climate of faltering state legitimacy and national self-doubt that separatist aspirations may flourish, tempted by the prospect of a more responsive and accountable micro-state. It is in this climate too that populist nationalism may take root, with its targeting of ethnic and other social and political minorities as scapegoats for the economic and social ills of the community.

This leads us finally to another great global issue, that of immigration, and especially the movement of peoples from the impoverished 'South' (and now 'East') into the advanced capitalist countries of Western Europe since the Second World War. While the buoyant economies of the 1950s and 1960s welcomed the arrival of 'guest workers', the social integration of those who had now become permanent residents became an increasingly difficult issue in the new recessionary climate of the 1970s and 1980s. Fears of unemployment, fears of 'contamination' by 'alien' cultures have created a fertile terrain for racism and cultural fundamentalism. The problem is exacerbated by the growing gap between rich and poor countries, which the increasing internationalisation of the market economy has done nothing to arrest. The build-up of economic and demographic pressures in Africa and the Asian sub-continent has created the spectre of an imminent 'invasion' from the south, hence the image of 'Fortress Europe': the supposed international idealism of European integration supplanted by the prospect of an embattled continent closed to the 'Third World' (see Chapter 3).

This raises again the issue of the fundamental ambiguity of nationalism: how membership of the nation is to be defined. As European nation-states established themselves in the period 1870–1918, the open 'citizenship' model (geared to social integration and stabilisation) was merged with an opposite set of principles, culturally or ethnically exclusive (and geared to the marginalisation of the 'unassimilable' and 'enemies of the state').[32] The tension between the two has remained, and according to historical circumstances the emphasis has shifted from one to the other. The 'exclusionist' model has enjoyed previous periods of ascendancy, notably at the turn of the century and in the 1930s. Indeed, it is tempting to draw analogies between the contemporary period and the era when this brand of right-wing nationalism first emerged, in the 1880s and 1890s. Then as now there was a combination of a recessionary economic climate combined with a phase of rapid economic modernisation, which threatened traditional classes with social extinction (today industrial workers rather than *petit bourgeois*), mass migratory movements providing ready scapegoats, a climate of international uncertainty and national introspection. This bred the societal insecurity, fear and pessimism on which populism feeds. However, the situation differed in at least one important respect. The earlier period was one in which the modern nation-state was first establishing itself, when a popular sense of nationhood often did not yet exist, when the nascent socialist and labour movement was still perceived as a revolutionary threat, when bourgeois state nationalism was still being invented as an ideology of social control. Today, however, we are faced with the curious paradox that the resurgence of diverse nationalisms has coincided with the declining credibility of the nation-state form, in a 'postmodern' context where the great competing ideologies or grand narratives of class society have lost their powers of mobilisation. Could it be that this is no paradox at all, that these nationalisms express a desperate resistance to the process of globalisation, filling a vacuum left by 'mainstream' pragmatic politics?

One important point remains to be made. While we have attempted to 'situate' contemporary nationalism in its historical setting, and to identify the processes which have promoted it, it is first and foremost a 'political' phenomenon, and therefore not 'fated' to happen. As we have indicated, the global changes to which we have referred also open up opportunities for genuine internationalism combined with a genuine multiculturalism, and in the current contingency, the viability of the nation-state as the primary focus of decision-making is indeed in question. Those who would oppose the more negative forms of nationalism that today appear to be in the ascendancy need, however, to adopt an appropriate strategy, based on a proper understanding of what they are dealing with. This involves recognition, first of all, that national sentiments are still deeply entrenched, and that they will not be transcended simply by a refusal to acknowledge them. Affection for one's social and spatial environment is not inherently negative, indeed it may be seen as a valuable source of cultural diversity in an increasingly homogenised world. Neither is it necessarily 'political' in its raw state, though as we have seen it is 'malleable'. It is necessary, therefore, to try and direct in its most positive and progressive direction, by insisting on a 'citizenship model of nationhood'. The notion of the national community as an open, voluntary association based on residence is compatible with humanist values and the spirit of international co-operation. Furthermore, by basing the 'nation' on the common exercise of citizens' rights (rather than on cultural exclusiveness), the foundations are laid for future transcendence of the nation-state. Indeed, the processes of post-modernisation and globalisation invite us to rethink and reformulate our notions of sovereignty, political subjectivity and citizenship: citizenship is not inherently 'national'; it implies democratic participation and accountability at diverse levels of decision-making. In a world of 'multi-layered' political communities comprising diverse overlapping global, transnational, national, regional, and local levels of political action,[33] the limits of the nation-state and of national sovereignty are manifest. To the extent that localities, regions and supranational institutions are empowered and achieve democratic legitimacy, national consciousness may be reduced to its proper place, as one of a set of 'multiple identities' where citizenship and politics are no longer confined within the boundaries of the nation-state.

NOTES

1 One of the most powerful affirmations of this can be found in F. Fukuyama, 'The end of history?', *The National Interest* 1989, no.16: 3–18; also in Fukuyama, *The End of History and the Last Man*, New York, Free Press, 1992; for a discussion of the issues raised by his *End of History* thesis, see J. Friedman, 'The new consensus', *Critical Review* 1989, 3: 373–410.

2 Different aspects of the decline of the nation-state are examined in R. Cox, *Power, Production and World Order*, New York, St Martins Press, 1987; M. Shaw,

'Theses on a post-military Europe; conscription, citizenship and militarism after the Cold War', in C. Rootes and H. Davis (eds), *A New Europe? Social Change and Political Transformation*, London, UCL Press, 1994; L. Starke, *Signs of Hope*, Oxford, Oxford University Press, 1990.

3 We are mainly referring here to the phenomenon of the 'restoration' of cultural or ethnic identities, or of the emergence of 'new ethnicities' by migrant and diaspora communities. See T. Modood, 'British Asian Muslims and the Rushdie affair', *Political Quarterly* 1990, 61(2): 143–60; S. Hall, 'Old and new identities, old and new ethnicities', in A.D. King (ed.), *Culture, Globalization and the World-System*, Basingstoke, Macmillan, 1991; S. Hall, 'New ethnicities', in J. Donald and A. Rattansi (eds), *'Race', Culture and Difference*, London, Sage, 1992.

4 T. Nairn, 'The modern Janus', in his *The Break-up of Britain*, London, New Left Books, 1977.

5 Nairn's account of the emergence of nationalism is indeed difficult to apply to the first development of nationalism in Europe and, more generally, is not applicable in the cases of several other colonial or post-colonial regions; see J. Breuilly, *Nationalism and the State*, Manchester, Manchester University Press, 1985, pp.26–8; A. Giddens, *The Nation-State and Violence*, Cambridge, Polity, 1987, p.213. Wallerstein, referring to the contemporary resurgence of nationalism seems to reach somewhat similar conclusions, as he argues that processes of *particularisation* such as the resurgence of ethnicity and nationalism, constitute an important aspect of the dialectic of globalisation, a form of resistance of nations and other collectivities to the erosion of their perceived autonomy. He, however, does not attempt to develop a theory of nationalism as Nairn seems to propose. See I. Wallerstein, 'The lessons of the 1980s', in his *Geopolitics and Geoculture*, Cambridge, Cambridge University Press, 1991.

6 M. Omi and H. Winant, *Racial Formation in the United States*, London and New York, Routledge and Kegan Paul, 1986, p.68.

7 Gellner (E. Gellner, *Nations and Nationalism*, Oxford, Blackwell, 1983) argues that nationalism creates nations, rather than the other way around, and Smith's analysis (A. D. Smith, *The Ethnic Origins of Nations*, Oxford, Blackwell, 1986; and *Theories of Nationalism*, London, Duckworth, 1971) points to a similar conclusion – nationalism is obviously involved in the transition from *ethnie* to *nation*.

8 B.Anderson, *Imagined Communities: Reflections on the Origin and Spread of Nationalism*, London, Verso, 1983.

9 E. Weber, *Peasants into Frenchmen*, London, Chatto and Windus, 1976, ch. 19. The same can be argued for Italian rural populations, see, for example, T. de Mauro, *Storia linguistica dell'Italia unita*, Milan, A. Guiffré, 1960.

10 E.P. Thompson, *The Making of the English Working Class*, London, Penguin, 1963.

11 There is some controversy as to which the 'first nation' was. It has been argued that 'England had been a nation' since the sixteenth century, whereas 'France' was transformed into a nation much later, well into the eighteenth century. For a powerful exposition of this argument see L. Greenfeld, *Nationalism; Five Roads to Modernity*, Cambridge, MA, Harvard University Press, 1992, pp.14–188. We would argue that throughout the seventeenth century, local and regional identities were slowly replaced by the emergence of the 'people' as a mainly 'moral' community. In other words, through the bread riots and other 'popular' mobilisations for the protection or restoration of the moral economy that was being eroded by the emergence of the political economy of capitalism, the 'people' defined itself as an entity premised on 'moral economy'-related rights, but not as a political subject.

12 P. Burke, 'We, the people: popular culture and popular identity in modern

Europe', in S. Lash and J. Friedman (eds), *Modernity and Identity*, Oxford, Blackwell, 1992, pp.199–230.

13 E.J. Hobsbawm, *Nations and Nationalism since 1780*, Cambridge, Cambridge University Press, 1990, p.89.

14 In the same period popular nationalisms of this sort emerged in Yugoslavia, Greece, France and to a lesser extent in Italy. For the cases of Yugoslavia, France and Italy, see the relevant chapters in this volume.

15 T. Brennan, 'The national longing for form', in H. Bhabha (ed.), *Nation and Narration*, London, Routledge, 1990, p.45.

16 Nairn, op. cit., p.347.

17 This was certainly a widespread view as far as the 'regionalist'/'micro-nationalist' movements in France, Italy, Spain and the UK of the 1970s and early 1980s were concerned. The cases of the nationalism of the Italian Leagues, or of the nationalisms which tore apart former Yugoslavia, or of some Western European regions (Catalonia, Austrian and Italian Tyrol, or Flanders, to name but a few) have been far more controversial as undemocratic or anti-democratic tendencies have been very much in evidence. Such an argument is developed regarding the case of the Italian *Lega Nord* (see Chapter 8, this volume). However belief in the democratic promise of contemporary 'micro-nationalisms' is still by no means negligible. See for example the special section on 'The Leagues in Italy', *Telos* 1991–92, 90, Winter; Dwayne Woods 'The crisis of the Italian party state and the rise of the Lombard League', *Telos* 1993, 93, Fall.

18 E.J. Hobsbawm and T. Ranger (eds), *The Invention of Tradition*, Cambridge, Cambridge University Press, 1983 and in particular, E. J. Hobsbawm, 'Mass-producing traditions: Europe 1870–1914' in Hobsbawm and Ranger, op. cit.

19 On the concept of 'moral economy' see E.P. Thompson, 'The moral economy of the English crowd in the eighteenth century', *Past and Present* 1971, no. 50: 76–136.

20 Hobsbawm, *Nations and Nationalism*, op. cit., p.109.

21 The exclusion of certain forms of sexuality and sexual behaviour from national culture and therefore of the groups associated with it from the nation is illustrated by the work of George Mosse. See G.L. Mosse, *Nationalism and Sexuality: Middle-class Morality and Sexual Norms in Modern Europe*, Madison, University of Wisconsin Press, 1985. Also, for a discussion of more contemporary forms of exclusion of sexual deviance from national cultures, see A. Parker *et al.* (eds), *Nationalisms and Sexualities*, New York, Routledge, 1992.

22 Hobsbawm, *Nations and Nationalism*, op. cit., p.122.

23 K.W. Deutsch, *Nationalism and Social Communication*, Boston, MA, MIT Press, 1966 and Anderson, op. cit., pp.40ff.

24 B. Jenkins and G. Minnerup, *Citizens and Comrades: Socialism in a World of Nation States*, London, Pluto, 1984, p.61.

25 T. Nairn, op. cit.

26 Hobsbawm, *Nations and Nationalism*, op. cit.

27 Ibid., p.145.

28 Ibid., p.153.

29 Ibid., p.178.

30 This statement, however, might need some modification; we suggest that it is *nationalism*, and not necessarily a state, that precedes nations.

31 Hobsbawn, *Nations and Nationalism*, op. cit., pp.163–83.

32 It should be stressed that enemies are not merely ethnic groups but also other social groups threatening the nation by deviating from the project of promotion of the national good.

33 H. Bull, *The Anarchical Society*, Basingstoke, Macmillan, 1977, pp.254–5.

SELECT BIBLIOGRAPHY

B. Anderson (1983) *Imagined Communities: Reflections on the Origin and Spread of Nationalism*, London, Verso.

E. Balibar and Immanuel Wallerstein (1991) *Race, Nation, Class; Ambiguous Identities*, London, Verso.

H. Bhabha (ed.) (1990) *Nation and Narration*, London, Routledge.

J. Breuilly (1985) *Nationalism and the State*, Manchester, Manchester University Press.

A. Giddens (1987) *The Nation-State and Violence*, Cambridge, Polity.

L. Greenfeld (1992) *Nationalism; Five Roads to Modernity*, Cambridge, MA, Harvard University Press.

S. Hall (1991) 'Old and new identities, old and new ethnicities', in A.D. King (ed.), *Culture, Globalization and the World-System*, Basingstoke, Macmillan.

—— 'New ethnicities', in J. Donald and A. Rattansi (eds), *'Race', Culture and Difference*, London, Sage.

E.J. Hobsbawm (1990) *Nations and Nationalism since 1780*, Cambridge, Cambridge University Press.

E.J. Hobsbawm and T. Ranger (eds) (1983) *The Invention of Tradition*, Cambridge, Cambridge University Press.

G.L. Mosse (1985) *Nationalism and Sexuality: Middle-class Morality and Sexual Norms in Modern Europe*, Madison, University of Wisconsin Press.

T. Nairn (1977) *The Break-up of Britain*, London, New Left Books.

A. D. Smith (1971) *Theories of Nationalism*, London, Duckworth.

—— (1986) *The Ethnic Origins of Nations*, Oxford, Blackwell.

2

LANGUAGES OF RACISM WITHIN CONTEMPORARY EUROPE

Martin Evans

> Cultural identity is inseparable from limits, it is always a boundary phenomenon and its order is always constructed around the figures of its territorial edge.[1]

> I believe that ideas about separating, purifying, demarcating, and punishing transgressions have as their main function to impose a system on an inherently untidy experience. It is only by exaggerating the difference between within and without, above and below, male and female, with and against, that a semblance of order is created.[2]

Antony Smith has outlined how national identity is a complex phenomenon, constructed out of a number of inter-related components – ethnic, cultural, territorial and legal-political. Each component, he argues, signifies bonds of solidarity which serve to bind together members of a national community.[3] Taking up Smith's ideas this chapter will argue that the articulation of national identity is premised upon the identification of symbolic boundaries. The demarcation of boundaries is central to the discovery of self-definition and location at the heart of any shared sense of national identity. Through such a mechanism members of a national community are able to mark out who they are, to differentiate between nationals and non-nationals, between insiders and outsiders, belonging and otherness. As such, national identity is produced through a process of negation, the creation of a coherent sense of self through explicit rejections and denials. It is a dynamic relationship, defined through the exclusion of groups deemed not to belong.

The identification of groups deemed not to belong is a central element of any nationalist movement of whatever political ilk. Thus the imagined German community of Nazi ideology was defined in terms of those it repudiated: Jews, communists, homosexuals, Slavs. At the opposite end of the political spectrum throughout the nineteenth century French Left nationalism, derived from the 1789 Revolution, presented itself as the true embodiment of the popular will, protecting the people against the enemies of the nation: the aristocracy, Roman Catholicism and international capital.

National identity, therefore, is neither natural nor stable. While un-doubtedly the repository of distinctive collective experiences, it is finally an invention, involving the establishment of opposites and 'others' which are used as yardsticks for self-definition. National identity is a fluid entity, where categorisation of 'self' or of 'other', inclusion and exclusion, is an arena of contest between competing groups and institutions within society.

Taking the above conclusions as a theoretical starting point the purpose of this chapter is to explore languages of exclusion in respect to one specific example: right-wing ethnic nationalist movements within contemporary Europe. My focus will be on the ways in which these movements have stigmatised particular immigrants and minorities as 'other' in order to arrive at a unified sense of national identity. What metaphors and cultural codes have they drawn upon to mark out these groups as different? What imagery have they deployed to scapegoat certain minorities as a threat to the nation? Throughout my concern will be with the particular shape of racist discourse, that is the manner in which minorities are denigrated and dehumanised. The first part of this chapter will explore theoretical ways of understanding the languages of racism; while the second part will concentrate on specific examples of racism within contemporary France and Germany.

THEORETICAL PERSPECTIVES

In *The Politics and Poetics of Transgression* Peter Stallybrass and Allon White have mapped out how identity is produced through the rejection of what is marked out as low, repulsive, dirty and contaminating.[4] For them this high/low opposition, in terms of representations of the human body, geographical space and the social order, is fundamental to mechanisms of ordering and sense-making in the European cultures. They show how historically high discourses of literature, statecraft and the church have been structured in relation to the low discourse of the urban poor, the working class and colonised peoples. Again and again, they argue, a sense of coherent identity is created through the repudiation of filth, chaos and hybrid states. However, they continue, this construction of identity is an unstable process. What they identify is a recurrent pattern of repugnance and fascination where the political imperative to reject the low conflicts unpredictably with desire for the 'other'. The demarcation of boundaries in order to unify the social collectivity, they argue, produces a mobile fusion of power and fear where what is socially peripheral returns to become symbolically central. In looking towards the margins the gaze of the centre is a fascinated gaze plagued by fear and anxiety about these areas of society. Thus within contemporary France Algerian immigrants play a symbolic role within the general culture out of all proportion to their actual social and political power. At the level of the imaginary French society is saturated with a whole network of fears about Algerians, where Algerian men are portrayed as predatory and criminal, Algerian women as erotic and sensual. In this sense it must be understood that racism, the transformation of human beings into abstract categories, is not only about violence and abuse, but also fascination and exoticisation.

Stallybrass and White are particularly interested in the carnival as a mode of understanding, and in this respect they see the work of Mikhail Bakhtin as a vital starting point. Within *Rabelais and his World*, written in the Soviet Union during the 1920s, Bakhtin describes how during the medieval period in Europe society was divided into two separate spheres, totally opposed to one another.[5] On one side there was the world of official medieval ideology and then on the other, folk humour. Official medieval ideology was embodied in sacred texts, religious rituals and festivals. Parallel to this was the world of folk humour grounded in carnivals, buffoon spectacles, comic fairs, oaths and curses. The latter constituted a world apart from official ideology and was a ritualised uncrowning of that ideology. Within the carnival official and hierarchic representations of the world were inverted. A clown would be disguised as a king; monks derided; church ceremonies parodied; the sacred profaned. All that was high, spiritual and abstract was systematically degraded. Bakhtin terms these two the classical body (official medieval ideology) and the grotesque body (folk humour). For Bakhtin the grotesque body is always in the act of becoming. Never finished, it is continually swallowing up the world or is in the process of being swallowed up. Shifting, incomplete, comic: the grotesque body emphasises those parts of the body which go beyond the its confines, such as the mouth, the phallus and the nose. Through these orifices the grotesque body interacts with the world, merging with animal forms and inanimate objects. Not only does the grotesque body tend towards lower bodily strata – knees, feet, genitals and anus – it is also multi-voiced in character where a plurality of languages interact to subvert hierarchies. Impure, heterogeneous, eccentric, collective, the focus of the grotesque body is on physical pleasure, in particular, eating, drinking, defecation, swallowing and dismemberment. In contrast the classical body is smooth and finished. Pure, symmetrical, harmonious, serious: it is a closed individuality which does not merge with other bodies. Protuberances are eliminated, orifices are closed. Single-voiced, the classical body emphasises the upper – the head, spirit, sky, air and mountains. As such it is always rational, hierarchical and monumental.

For Bakhtin the historical significance of Rabelais is that he transformed the function of folk humour. In *Gargantua and Pantagruel*, published in 1534, he drew upon the imagery of the grotesque body to parody the established order. Thus embodied in language forms, the grotesque body was dispersed across various discursive forms and practices. The categories of classical and grotesque now became part of a common stock of symbols by which people made sense of the world. Consciously or unconsciously body images were seen to 'speak' social relations and values with particular force. However, as the grotesque body was inscribed within the general culture it was transformed, becoming a distant echo of the one found within the popular-festival tradition. Within the carnival the grotesque body was always double-faced. Faeces and urine were seen to debase and destroy, regenerate and renew. They were blessing and humiliating at the same time. The communal, celebratory aspect of the grotesque was overlooked. Instead it became a mere negation, pursuing narrowly satirical aims.

In their study Stallybrass and White move beyond Bakhtin's formulations to consider carnival as one instance of the coding of high/low relations that occurs across the whole social structure. Hence the symbolic categories of grotesque realism located by Bakhtin can be rediscovered as a governing dynamic not only of the body and the household, but also the city and the nation-state. Stallybrass and White trace how the ideal of the classical body structured the high discourses of philosophy, statecraft and the law as they came to emerge from the Renaissance. These higher discourses, invariably associated with the dominant economic groups within society, existed at the centre of cultural power. Thus situated they gained authority by designating what is high and what is low, what is superior and what is inferior. From this perspective high discourse defined itself over and against what were seen as the vulgar practices of the populace, and here the imagery of the grotesque body was deployed to mark out the marginal, the low and the outside. Continually the popular classes were stigmatised as filthy, dirty and degenerate. Stallybrass and White then go on to outline how the symbolic categories of classical and grotesque characterised the great age of institutionalising during the nineteenth century with the establishment of asylums, prisons and mental hospitals. They chart how the outsiders-made-insiders – the mad, the criminal, the sick and the sexually transgressive – were constructed by the dominant culture in terms of the grotesque body.

Apart from Stallybrass and White this chapter will also be underpinned by the ideas of Floya Anthias and Nira Yuval-Davis outlined in *Racialized Boundaries*.[6] There they explain how the construction of a sense of national belonging is dependent upon the positing of specific boundaries. Symbolic boundaries, they argue, are the means by which human subjects are classified into those who can belong and those who cannot. Once in place, they represent categories of inclusion and exclusion which must not be transgressed. Anthias and Yuval-Davis describe how race, along with class, gender and sexuality, is a central component within the elucidation of these boundaries. They argue

Race is one way by which the boundary is to be constructed between those who can and those who cannot belong to a particular construction of a collectivity or population. In the case of race this is on the basis of an immutable biological or physiognomic difference which may or may not be seen to be expressed mainly in culture or lifestyle but is always grounded on the separation of human populations by some notion of stock or collective heredity of traits.[7]

They underline how the creation of boundaries in relation to belonging and otherness is a complex process ranging from the credentials of being born in the right place, through to conforming to cultural and symbolic practices, such as language and dress.

In this chapter the focus will be on the imagery used to mark out such boundaries. What stereotypes are utilised by right-wing nationalists within contemporary Europe in order to project as inferior, exclude and subordinate certain groups? How is the racist imagining of the 'other' expressed in concrete terms through party programmes and activism?

SCIENTIFIC RACISM IN THE NINETEENTH CENTURY

The opposition between classical and grotesque, outlined by Stallybrass and White, was an integral part of 'scientific racism' during the nineteenth century. The French racist theorist Arthur Comte de Gobineau continually invoked these symbolic categories to divide up the world into 'self' and 'other'. In his *Essay on the Inequality of Races*, published in 1853 and undoubtedly a key text in the development of racist theories, he constructs a hierarchy of races with the white race at the top and a number of inferior realms beneath it (Blacks, yellow races, hybrid races) which are characterised in terms of the symbolic repertoire of the grotesque body. For Gobineau this racial hierarchy is structured around the relationship to bodily functions. Thus, in Gobineau's opinion, the lower races are incapable of rational reflection. Fickle and easily led they are dominated by the demands of the lower bodily stratum. As he puts it: 'the brutish hordes of the yellow race seem to be dominated by the needs of the body'.[8]

Likewise the Mongolian tribes, according to Gobineau, see as their main aim material and physical enjoyment rather than spiritual or intellectual fulfilment. In contrast Gobineau presents the white race in terms of the classical body. For him what separates white people from other races is their capacity for rational evaluation. It is only among the white race, Gobineau argues, that it is possible to discover the level of intellectual reflection which makes it possible to talk about civilisation. Not surprisingly what Gobineau feared most of all was racial intermingling which would pollute the healthy stock of the white race and lead to social chaos. As Gobineau saw it miscegenation could only produce inferior, hybrid races leading to social chaos. In his opinion the clearest example of the consequences of such mixing was America. As he saw it, 'it is quite unimaginable that anything could result from such a horrible confusion but an incoherent juxtaposition of the most decadent kinds of people'.[9]

The imagery and ideas contained within Gobineau's 'scientific racism' exerted a powerful intellectual influence during the course of the nineteenth century. In Germany his ideas were taken up by Heinrich von Treitschke (1834–96). A member of the Reichstag from 1871 to 1884 and the intellectual leader of its pro-Bismarck faction, von Treitschke used his position of lecturer at the University of Berlin to propagate ideas which were avowedly nationalistic, imperialistic and racist. What he preached was an apocalyptic vision where history was determined by the struggle of race against race. Within his lectures and writings he assigned fixed racial characteristics to a wide variety of groups. Orientals were dismissed as effeminate, blacks as submissive, Latins as vacuous and shallow-minded. In contrast von Treitschke presented the Germanic peoples as natural warriors, characterised by beauty, nobility and higher spiritual yearnings, and he implored them to recognise their world-historical destiny. It was the role of Germans, he claimed, to overcome and subjugate inferior races and to this end he called on them to look to the east. Throughout his writings von Treitschke conjured up the image of a vast Slav threat, composed of subhuman peasants, who were poised to overwhelm not only the thinly scattered German settlements in the east but the whole of German civilisation. As a result Germany had a duty to expand eastwards and establish a vast German reserve. For von Treitschke this would be the first step towards his ultimate goal: the establishment of a world empire where Germany would dominate the globe.

Von Treitschke's arguments were indicative of a general trend at the end of the nineteenth century, namely the manner in which an assertion of national and racial superiority became closely intertwined with colonial expansion. Great stress was placed upon the superiority of European nations and their unquestioned right to impose their will on subject races, categorised as backward and inferior. Despite imperial rivalry the concept of European civilisation made for a certain affinity among different European countries, and this idea of European identity as a superior one in comparison to non-European cultures was instrumental in mapping out a particular world vision with Europe at the centre and the rest of the world at the margins. Clear lines now divided up the globe, separating the metropole from the colonies, superior races from inferior races, 'us' Europeans from 'those' non-Europeans. By the end of the nineteenth century these ideas had begun to penetrate popular culture across Europe, through cheap novels and popular comics, leading to a widespread acceptance of the notion of a racial hierarchy, with its crude equations between achieved levels of civilisation and innate racial characteristics.

Racist theories elucidated by Gobineau and von Treitschke were at the heart of the 'scientific' anti-Semitism which emerged at the end of the nineteenth century. Undoubtedly this new anti-Semitism adapted much of the age-old hostility to Jews which was deeply embedded within European culture. Already during the Roman Empire, because Jews refused to accept the deification of Roman emperors, they were viewed with suspicion as a people apart. Under the early Christian Church Jew hatred was reformulated and intensified. For the historian of anti-Semitism, Robert Wistrich, this theological hostility was explained by the fact that Judaism was viewed as a major religious rival which Christians had to fight against and overcome. For the latter Judaism came to be seen as the complete negation of their own beliefs. As Wistrich puts it:

> No other religion has so consistently attributed to them a universal, cosmic quality of evil, depicting them as the children of the Devil, followers of Antichrist or as the 'synagogue of Satan'. The fantasies concerning Jews which were developed in medieval Christendom, about their plotting to destroy Christianity, poison wells, desecrate the host, massacre Christian children or establish their world domin- ion, represent a qualitative leap compared with anything put for- ward by their pagan precursors.[10]

At the end of nineteenth century the new anti-Semitism signified another qualitative leap. Drawing upon pseudo-scientific biology and social Darwinism it projected Jews as a separate race with their own inherited characteristics. Jews, it was claimed, could never be assimilated because they had no concept of the national interest. As such they were parasites who always had one aim: the destruction of any host nation from the inside. Conspiracy theories of this nature, where Jews were presented as the prime movers behind a sinister international plot, took off in the last decade of the nineteenth century. The most famous example of this was the publication of the 'Protocols of the Elders of Zion' in Russia in 1905, a document purporting to give first-hand evidence of the existence of an international Jewish plot to dominate the world. Although later revealed to be a forgery fabricated by the tsarist secret police, the pamphlet was translated and widely disseminated throughout Europe. In Germany too the notion of a Jewish conspiracy began to circulate widely. Von Treitschke, for example, saw the hand of the Jew everywhere. The Jews, he argued, were responsible for liberalism, socialism and the revolutions of 1848. To combat this growing influence he supported calls to restrict Jewish civil rights, curb Jewish immigration and set quotas on Jewish participation in government, teaching and law. Not surprisingly von Treitschke's ideas were enthusiastically taken up by the Nazi regime and used to legitimise their own race war against the Jews.

Important as well, was the way anti-Semites, at the end of the nineteenth century, began to make an explicit link between the 'Jewish spirit' and capitalism. The prominence of Jews within big business and high finance, in particular the House of Rothschild, was singled out as evidence of a shadowy Jewish world government. And to this end the stereotype of the fat, bloated Jewish capitalist living off the fat of ordinary people now became a central element of anti-Semitic discourse. However, the main impetus for the new anti-Semitism was the westward migration of Yiddish-speaking Jews fleeing the pogroms in eastern Europe and Russia during the 1880s and 1890s. Foreign in religion, language and customs, this influx of poor Jewish migrants created a moral panic and unleashed a wave of anti-Semitism within certain sections of Western European society. The new Jewish migrants became the focus of a whole series of fears and phobias, not least the notion that they were prone to various types of crime, and to this end grotesque imagery was mobilised again and again to stigmatise them as outsiders. Dirty, smelly, fundamentally alien: for anti-Semites, Jews were an 'inferior' race who now threatened to swamp European civilisation. In this respect the imagery associated with illness was to become a recurrent trope within anti-Semitic discourse. As Susan Sontag has argued the military metaphor in medicine first came into wide use in the 1880s, with the identification of bacteria as agents of disease. Bacteria was said to 'invade' or 'infiltrate'; it was also said to 'destroy' and 'pollute'. Loaded language of this nature was now taken over by anti-Semites and applied to the newly arrived Jewish migrants.[11] The latter were presented as carriers of disease, in particular syphilis, whose 'invasion' posed grave health risks to the peoples of Western Europe. At the same time the disease metaphor was used to underline the spiritual threat posed by the Jewish race. Capitalism, liberalism, socialism, communism: all of these were presented as specifically Jewish credos which threatened to undermine traditional European society. Now the Jew came to be seen as the symbol of the threat of modernity whereupon urbanisation, democracy, and the advance of mass society were seen as outside forces foisted upon Europe by the Jewish race.

The new anti-Semitism was particularly virulent within France. Here the principal propagandist was Edouard Drumont who seized upon the uproar caused in 1882 by the failure of the bank, the Union General, to mount a popular anti-Semitic campaign. He argued, incorrectly as it turned out, that the bank was owned by Jews and that this was concrete evidence of a wider Jewish conspiracy against French national interests. Thereafter his aggressive rhetoric, combining populism, Catholicism and racism, as well as nostalgia for a pre-1789 France, began to win a growing audience. His book the *Jewish France* (*La France juive*) became a best-seller, selling over 100,000 copies on its publication in 1886. Within it he characterised the Jews as a rootless people whose only motive was profit. Throughout, he used high and low imagery to define the racial characteristics of the Jew. In contrasting the Aryan and the Semite Drumont proclaimed:

> The Semite is mercantile, covetous, scheming, subtle and cunning. The Aryan is enthusiastic, heroic, disinterested, frank and trusting to the point of naiveté. The Semite is earth-bound with scarcely any concern for the life hereafter; the Aryan is a child of heaven who is constantly preoccupied by higher aspirations. One lives in the world of reality, the other in the world of the ideal.[12]

He then went on to propose the theory that the Jews had used the 1789 Revolution to seize power in France. When the Revolution emancipated the Jews, Drumont declared, it had created a nation within a nation whose express aim was the subjugation of the ordinary French masses. Since then, he argued, they have been engaged in a secret, subterranean plot to extend their political and economic influence. Slowly but surely they have gained control of key institutions, using their wealth to buy off corrupt republican deputies. Throughout the book Drumont made clear his hatred of modern life. The rootlessness of urban existence was, in his opinion, testament to the growing Jewish influence, and he called for a return to the simplicity of the pure, uncorrupted countryside, the repository, he argued, of real French values. Parallel to this he condemned all racial mixing between Jews and French people since this would undermine the health of the true French stock. In 1889 he established an anti-Semitic league and in 1892 he founded the daily *La Libre Parole*, which he used as a platform to attack what he characterised as the 'Jewish Republic'.

A few years later the Dreyfus affair, when Captain Alfred Dreyfus was arrested on false spying charges, provided an opportunity for a renewal of anti-Semitism in France. Stripped of his rank in January 1895, in the courtyard of the Ecole Militaire, the guilt of Captain Dreyfus, who was one of the few Jews on the General Staff, was quickly attributed by anti-Semites to a Jewish conspiracy. The most prominent anti-semitic movement was Action française, whose leading ideologue, Charles Maurras, was vitriolic in his denunciation of the Jews. Nomadic and cosmopolitan, the explicit purpose of the Jew, Maurras claimed, was to sow disorder and chaos within France. Only the army and the Church, he went on to claim, were invulnerable to their poisoning influences. The recurrent image used by Maurras was to present the French nation as a house which Jews were in the process of squatting and vandalising. To put an end to the insidious process, Maurras repeatedly called for the establishment of an authoritarian regime. Once in place Maurras made it clear that this regime would have one explicit aim: to exclude Jews from French public life.

The ideas of Action française continued to exert a powerful influence during the 1920s and 1930s. As with Maurras the anti-Semitic press of this period drew upon the categories of the grotesque body to stigmatise Jews as different. In the *Jewish Invasion*, published in 1927, Henri-Robert Petit characterised Jews as 'oriental lepers and the real vermin of the world'. He warned French people to watch out for 'hooked noses, fleshy lips, crinkly hairstyles, the owners of which jargonise in their native Yiddish' and who had escaped from the ghettos of eastern Europe to take French jobs and money.[13] French anti-Semitism was to reach its apogee with Marshal Petain's Vichy regime of 1940–4 when the latter introduced a detailed series of measures which reduced Jews to second-class citizens. Inspired by Maurras's slogan of 'France for the French' the aim was to cleanse the nation of Jewish influence. Thousands of Jews were dismissed from political and civil service posts, and strict quotas put upon Jewish participation in banking, finance and the professions. Similarly, thousands more were deprived of their French citizenship, interned in transit camps and handed over to the SS for extermination in Nazi death camps.

RACISM WITHIN CONTEMPORARY EUROPE

Racism within contemporary Europe must not be understood as a simple throwback to the nineteenth century. Contemporary racism is not the racism of the colonial period or the racism of Nazi Germany. It has been modified in the light of the current historical context, even if what is often striking about the new structures of exclusion and violence is the persistence of past stereotypes and prejudices. Racism is not a static phenomenon. Rather it is a concept open to constant reformulation whose particular thrust will vary according to different times and to different places.

The distinctive content of contemporary racism is evident in respect to anti-Semitism within eastern and central Europe. As Paul Hockenos has underlined in a recent study of the extreme Right, although the new anti-Semitism has much in common with what has gone before, the evil of Jewry is now invoked under new historical conditions and with a content specific to those circumstances.[14] In eastern and central Europe the acute pace of economic and social change since the end of communism has produced fear and uncertainty. Post-1989 the sense of expectation was very great, as it was widely believed that the introduction of free-market capitalism would lead to a dramatic improvement of living standards. When this failed to materialise large numbers of people became bitter and disappointed, creating a volatile atmosphere in which the search for scape-goats has become very strong. It is in this context that groups throughout the former communist bloc have begun openly to assert a renewed anti-Semitism, targeting Jews as the force responsible for the current economic ills.

Perhaps the clearest example of this renewed anti-Semitism is the Russian nationalist movement Pamyat' (Memory). Pamyat' is an umbrella organisation, bringing together a variety of disparate groups, all of which stress their anti-Jewish platform. As a movement it first came to public prominence in 1985 when it asserted the authenticity of the 'Protocols of the Elders of Zion'.[15] Since then Pamyat' has never ceased to peddle the belief in a Jewish conspiracy as the primary cause of the economic and political crisis. Within Pamyat' propaganda Jews are vilified as alien, rootless and fundamentally anti-Russian. This image is then contrasted with the supposed qualities of Russian rural life, stressed as healthy, pure and uncorrupted. As the move towards the free-market economy has accelerated under Boris Yeltsin since 1991 Pamyat''s anti-Semitic rhetoric has been given a new twist. The International Monetary Fund, which has encouraged the introduction of liberal economic principles, is stigmatised as a Jewish plot directed from Israel. What is continually promoted is the notion of an innocent Russian people being duped by a greedy Jewish lobby who wish to enslave Russia to America. In this way Jews are crudely associated with imported Western values, capitalism, democracy, pop music, homosexuality, AIDS, all of which are construed as a threat to the spiritual health of the Russian nation.

Anti-Semitism of this nature is not limited to Russia, one powerful indicator of this being the way in which the 'Protocols of the Elders of Zion' now freely circulates within every post-communist country. The Patriotic Grunwald Association in Poland, the National Patriotic Front in Hungary, the weekly papers *Europa* and *Romania Mare* in Romania; all of these groups subscribe to Pamyat'-style anti-Semitism. In each case Jews are caricatured as bloodthirsty predators taking over the political, economic and cultural centres of power. Continually the juxtaposition is made between 'us', the real people, and 'them', the Jews, whose hidden hand is selling out the national interest to international capital.

Like the Jews the Roma (gypsies) have also been subjected to renewed hostility. In common with anti-Semitism, anti-Roma racism is deeply embedded within European culture. Traditionally the Roma have been reviled as vagrants and thieves whose nomadic culture has marked them as outsiders. Such hostility intensified with the rise of the nation-state during the nineteenth century. In the context of modern nationalism the Roma were viewed as a non-people whose urge to move was incomprehensible because it defied the logic of national parameters. Again like anti-Semitism the persecution of the Roma reached a chilling climax under national socialism. Nazism identified the Roma as 'rootless parasites' who threatened the purity of the New Order. Within occupied Europe the Nazis established a policy of extermination which led to the death of more than 250,000. The defeat of Nazism did not bring about an end to anti-Roma racism which continued to persist across the continent. However, the period since 1989 has seen a heightening of the phenomenon, especially among ethnic nationalist groups within eastern Europe. This is because ethnic nationalism of this nature is predicated upon two assumptions. First, the attachment to territory within clearly defined boundaries; and second, the desire to control this territorial space with the explicit aim of producing an homogenised society according to specific criteria. For right-wing nationalists, the Roma are an object of loathing because their transitory existence disrupts these assumptions. Their whole existence is viewed as a threat, undermining ethnic purity. As a result, Romani refugees have been targets of mounting far-Right violence, particularly in the Czech and Slovak republics and Germany. In the summer of 1992, German neo-Nazis orchestrated a campaign of anti-Roma racism. Within pamphlets and posters neo-Nazis differentiated between the German people on the one hand and the Romani refugees on the other, likened to a 'dirty plague' contaminating German society.

IMMIGRATION AND RACISM

Since 1989 Europe has witnessed a rising tide not only of anti-Jewish and anti-Roma, but also anti-immigrant racism. The reason for this increased racism is threefold. First, there has been a huge increase in the numbers of immigrants, asylum seekers and illegal entrants wishing to come to Western Europe. The economic crisis in the Third World; greater awareness of the possibilities of escape; improved travel facilities; the existence of a sophisticated forged documents industry: all of these factors explain the intensification of migratory flows since the late 1980s. Second, the end of the Cold War has left Western Europe with the feeling that it is exposed to the threat of human movement not just from the South but also from the East. The disintegration of the Iron Curtain means that the European Union's eastern border is no longer sealed, and this has fuelled fears of a large-scale migration from the former communist countries. Third, an awareness of immigration and the external pressures on Europe has been heightened by the emergence of far-Right nationalist parties who are explicitly racist and who see immigration as a threat to their national identity. Although these parties have remained relatively marginal in terms of electoral support, there is little doubt that, particularly in France and Germany, they have set the mainstream political agenda, making immigration a dominant issue within West European politics.

Undoubtedly a fortress mentality is a central element of the current anti-immigrant racism. The racist rhetoric promoted by the National Front in France or the Republican Party in Germany lacks the expansionist element of nineteenth-century imperialism: there is no notion of France or Germany expanding outwards to dominate the world. Instead the key question is the permeability of their own national borders, and how to secure them against the influx of immigrants and refugees. In generalising about immigration in this way the far Right draws upon an emotionally charged imagery. In the first instance their idea of immigration is highly racialised. Immigrants are portrayed as dark-haired Muslims who do not speak the language properly. Immigrants are denigrated as dirty and unclean whose whole way of life is incompatible with European values. Immigrants are talked about as an invading horde; they are the enemy within whose actions are controlled by foreign forces. Immigrants are criminalised as pimps and drug pushers whose anti-social behaviour is responsible for the general breakdown in law and order. And finally immigrants are characterised as 'spongers' and 'scroungers' whose presence represents a threat to the living standards of the white population. In using such rhetoric the National Front and the Republican Party want to advance the notion that immigrants are non-citizens who, because ethnically they do not belong, must not be granted any rights. At the same time they want to underline the idea that their own respective national identities are under attack from outside. It is the French and Germans, they argue, who are being discriminated against; it is they who are being abused by people of non-European origin. In each case they cast themselves in a defensive role whose purpose is essentially twofold: to stop the 'immigrant invasion' and to reassert the political and economic rights of the white population.

Cultural separatism

Another new dimension within the language of the National Front in France and the Republican Party in Germany is the theme of cultural separatism. Cultural separatism represents a major rethink which further differentiates contemporary racist discourses from those of nineteenth-century colonialism or Nazism. Through the advocacy of racist differentialism, it claims to respect all races and cultures. In making such a claim, the differentialist position is apparently premised on the appreciation of difference, of the right of each culture to develop freely, of the right to a homeland and to a national identity. In short, everyone has the right to a national identity and to the development of their own culture just as long as they exercise these rights in their own country. Stressing his adherence to the principles of cultural separatism, the contemporary racist/nationalist Right flatly rejects the charge of racism: Jean-Marie Le Pen argues for example that he does not preach hatred or extermination, but difference and a stop to immigration. Indeed, Le Pen has often claimed his appreciation of North African culture. However, his argument is that North Africans must understand that they have no place in France because their 'markedly different' way of life and culture can only flourish and reach their full potential within the cultural and geographical boundaries of the Maghreb. As such, Le Pen argues, the anti-racists are the real racists because their espousal of multiculturalism will destroy racial dis-tinctiveness.

Nevertheless, for all its apparent novelty, cultural separatism is still underpinned by assumptions derived from the nineteenth century. De-spite the talk of equality there is still a clear belief in the superiority of Europe in respect to non-European cultures.

Max Silverman has outlined how since 1945 the pattern of migration to France has seen a significant increase in ex-colonial migrants, especially from North and Sub-Saharan Africa.[16] This means that the lines of the colonial hierarchy separating France from the colonies have become increasingly blurred as ex-colonial immigrants settling in France have come to occupy the same geographical space as French people. What many French people find disconcerting, Silverman argues, is the close proximity of these ex-colonial subjects. The notion of the colonial legacy, Silverman continues, is important if it is understood not simply as a straightforward reproduction of colonial structures, but as a confrontation between, on the one hand, the legacy of those structures, and then on the other, the post-colonial migration of people and products. The new racism in France is different from colonial racism in that it is the product of this collision. It is the result of decolonisation and the breakdown in the colonial hierarchy. Immigrants from Africa generate so much anxiety in France because by living in France they are seen to be transgressing the boundary between 'here' and 'there', overturning the spatial relations between centre and periphery which colonialism established. This is why the new racism puts so much accent upon place and space, belonging, frontiers, mixing, inclusion and exclusion; it also explains why the new racism reserves so much hatred for the hybrid and multicultural. This is because the latter disrupts notions of a fixed national identity; it challenges easy definitions of what it means to be French in the late twentieth century. Similar anxieties are evident within the far Right in Germany. They are obsessed by the idea that Turks and Slavs, races which they categorise as backward and inferior and whose place, in their opinion, is elsewhere, are swamping Germany. They are fearful that, as they see it, the presence of Turks and Slavs will inaugurate an inevitable process of miscegenation which will undermine the ethnic composition of the German people, resulting in the creation of a 'mongrel' race.

Given the geographical position of Germany it has become the point of arrival for huge numbers of migrants not only from eastern Europe but also for those fleeing the conflict in former Yugoslavia. At the same time the reason the German government was willing to accept such a large intake of people, in marked comparison to other countries such as Britain where very tight restrictions have always been maintained, was because it operated a liberal policy on political asylum as well as an open-door policy towards ethnic Germans. The combination of these factors means that within the context of Western Europe Germany became the focus of overwhelming demographic pressures. In 1992 alone, 123,000 asylum seekers arrived in Germany from former Yugoslavia, 104,000 from Romania and 231,000 ethnic Germans arrived from eastern Europe.[17] Immediately the far Right seized on these figures to generate an anti-immigrant campaign which made considerable political inroads. In April 1992 the Republican Party (REP) took nearly 10.9 per cent of the regional vote in Baden-Wurttemberg, while the even more extreme German People's Union (DVU) scored 6.6 per cent in Schleswig-Holstein.

In electoral terms the most important party on the far Right in Germany is the Republican Party. Formed in 1983 out of Christian Social Union (CSU) dissidents who were disenchanted with what they saw as the pro-GDR policies of Franz Joseph Strauss, the Republican Party is led by Franz Schönhuber, a war veteran unrepentant about his membership of the SS. Anti-immigrant rhetoric is a central platform of the REP. AIDS, crime, unemployment: for the Republican Party immigration is the root cause of all of Germany's problems. Political propaganda produced by the REP portrays Germany as a boat overflowing with immigrants who are sucking the German economy dry. 'Germany cannot accept any more foreigners because the boat is full' proclaims an REP poster.[18] It goes on to explain that all Turks must be repatriated because they do not conform to German standards of behaviour. In making these crude connections between immigration and the economic crisis the Republican Party advances the notion of *Volksgemeinschaft*, the defence of German rights. Using the explicitly Nazi concept of living space Schönhuber argues that Germany must be restricted to Germans. As he puts it: 'We're not a welfare office for the Mediterranean. . . . We want to protect the German people's ecological living space against foreign infiltration.'[19]

For the REP Germans belong to a closed ethnic community whose coherence is threatened by unrestricted immigration. At the June 1992 party convention delegates called on Germans to rise up and defend their national identity. The combative mood of the convention was underlined by the way in which party members passed motions demanding the total rejection of a multicultural society; the protection of the purity of the German language; and the return of the Eastern territories. The more extreme DVU echoes many of the themes of the REP. Founded in 1971 by Gerhard Frey, in September 1991 the DVU won 6.1 per cent in the Bremen state elections and 10 per cent in Bremerhaven. Six months later it took 6.3 per cent of the regional vote in Schleswig-Holstein. In each campaign the creation of anti-foreigner sentiment was central. DVU activists distributed posters portraying hordes of foreigners pushing open a gate. Through such imagery the DVU set out to ram home a simple message: that immigrants and asylum seekers are sucking ordinary Germans dry. In particular, the DVU peddled the image of oversized Turkish families 'sponging off' the social security system. Here, Turkish women were scapegoated in specific ways: fat, ugly, unhygenic; DVU propaganda presented them as passive objects who 'reproduced like rabbits'. In the eyes of the DVU immigration is the most prominent example of a general battle for German purity, where the issue is not only the influx of foreigners, but also prostitutes, homosexuals, criminals and the general breakdown of society. According to the DVU all of these groups are enemies of the people who must be cleansed from the nation.

For the DVU anti-immigration rhetoric is closely linked to an anti-Left stance. It is the Left, the DVU tells supporters, which is encouraging uncontrolled immigration as part of a subterranean plot to destroy German national identity. In this way the DVU presents itself as a national liberation movement whose aim is the creation of an ethnically pure state. To underline this message the electoral success in Schleswig-Holstein was celebrated as a 'victory for the righteous cause of the German people'.[20] Now, it was emphasised, the DVU had a base from which to conduct a campaign of national renewal and in the ensuing months DVU motions in the Schleswig-Holstein parliament called for a clampdown on bogus asylum seekers, as well as the purification of 'school books of anti-German dirt and trash'.[21] In June 1992 DVU activists began to agitate in Rostock on the Baltic coast of the former GDR against Romani refugees and guestworkers. Pamphlets distributed by the DVU stigmatised these groups in familiar ways. Romani refugees were attacked as non-conformist nomads, part of a general 'gypsy plague' engaged in the systematic harassment of ordinary citizens; immigrants were portrayed as a 'flood' or 'invasion' whose separate culture was threatening to 'swamp' that of Germans; while African guestworkers from the former GDR were characterised as a health threat, infecting the German nation with AIDS. DVU propaganda went on to urge German citizens to take the 'immigrant problem' into their own hands, and there is little doubt that the DVU played a key role in the large-scale anti-foreigner pogrom on 24 August 1992 when a guestworker hostel was burnt down.

The Rostock pogrom is significant in that it indicates how far the extreme Right has succeeded in creating a climate of hatred, a trend already clearly discernible in 1991 when there was a tenfold increase in recorded racist attacks compared with the previous yearly average.[22] There is little doubt that the imagery peddled by the REP and DVU, of a beleaguered national identity under threat from outsiders, has made inroads within a wider consciousness, legitimising violence against those minorities which the far Right rejects.

All of the anti-immigrant imagery advanced by the REP and DVU is echoed by the National Front in France. Like their German counterparts the National Front have used the immigrant issue to construct a particular definition of the French people. North African immigrants, the National

Front claims, cannot be integrated into France. Their way of life is incompatible with civilised French values. North Africans, it is maintained, are dirty and unhygienic; prone to criminality; while their religion, Islam, is militantly opposed to white Christian values. For the National Front the presence of North African immigrants is symbolic of a general process of decay, intimately linked to the issues of law and order, permissiveness, and a pervasive sense of national decline. AIDS, drug trafficking, rising crime, delinquency: all are projected as imported phenomena, the direct result of this immigration 'invasion'. And here what Le Pen constantly reiterates is the demographic explosion taking place in the Third World. At the moment the population of North Africa stands at 50 million; by the year 2000 it will have reached over 100 million. The image Le Pen conjures up is one of this population literally spilling over to submerge France in what he calls a 'wave of Third World misery'.[23]

In characterising the immigrant issue Le Pen makes continual use of biological metaphors. North African immigration he likens to a virus weakening the healthy body of the French nation. When confronted with such a virus, he argues, the body can only take so much. Inevitably there is a limit at which point the body will react to protect itself. In making this parallel Le Pen presents the National Front as a natural defence mechanism which has sprung forth to protect French identity. Continuing with the biological metaphor Le Pen stigmatises North African immigrants as parasites whose presence is an unbearable burden, dragging France down to the level of a Third World country. They have, for example, retarded the French economy. Cheap immigrant labour was damaging because in the short term it allowed businesses to ignore the need to modernise French industry. Immigrants, Le Pen never tires of telling people, have 'stolen' French jobs. In this sense the summary removal of immigrants is conjured up as a realistic solution to unemployment.[24] Immigrants are an affront to Le Pen's sensibilities because they are undermining the purity of the French nation. He is vehemently opposed to all racial mixing which he terms 'le melting potism'. What multiculturalism will lead to, he argues, is the disintegration of French identity. To combat such moves Le Pen calls for a re-establishment of racial hierarchies. North Africans must go back to North Africa; the cultural superiority of Western Europe must be reaffirmed; all intermingling must stop: in short there must be a return to the colonial order of things.[25]

Like the German far Right Le Pen uses the concept of 'living space'. He warns French people:

> We must act ... by occupying our vital space, because nature has a horror of space and if we do not occupy it, others will occupy it in our place.[26]

Through such language the world is couched in terms of races and cultures struggling for survival. Again and again Le Pen talks in terms of military metaphors. To counter the 'immigrant invasion' Le Pen calls for a reconquest of national identity where French people are once again proud of their history and civilisation. In schools, he argues, French people must be taught French culture; in respect to housing and employment priority must be given to nationals over non-nationals.[27] Quite simply France must be reserved for French people and here Le Pen underlines the particular threat posed by Islam. By language, custom and race the North African population is not French. Most of all it is their religion, whose beliefs are presented as the antithesis of French Catholic values, which marks them as outsiders. Drawing upon deeply held prejudices within European culture, Le Pen demonises Islam as an intransigent religion whose aim is the eventual domination of France.[28] As the pro-Le Pen paper *Minute* put it in 1985:

> The spiritual emptiness within France is incapable of resisting the establishment of a religion which is intolerant and intransigent. The battle-axe has not been buried ... the holy war, which aims to submit the whole world to the faith of Mohammed, remains a duty for a Muslim.[29]

Imagery of this nature combines to confront French people with an apocalyptic scenario. For the National Front the French national identity has two choices: either it will survive or it will be replaced by Islam, there is no in-between.[30] Through the notion of an Islamic plot the National Front makes explicit links between immigrants and other internal enemies. It is the Left, Le Pen claims, which has deliberately encouraged immigration as a way of destroying French national identity. Similarly Le Pen uses immigration to attack homosexuality as anti-national. Interviewed by a gay radio station in 1984, Le Pen claimed that, since the gravest threat to the world is the exploding birth rate in the Third World, homosexuality in France, if it was allowed to continue, would lead to the end of the world.[31] For Le Pen homosexuality is morally and physically repulsive. It is deviant behaviour which, because it threatens the family unit and hence the continuation of the French race, is indicative of the way French people have lost the will to survive. Only by returning to family values, he argues, will France produce enough babies to defend its living space against the rising immigrant population.

The language of racism mobilised by the National Front is closely related to the language of class. North African immigrants and their descendants are seen as the basis of the new poor, the core of a dangerous underclass which is the root cause of the breakdown within the inner-cities. Again and again this underclass is presented as a threat to middle-class France, the repository of anti-social values which, unless contained, will spread outwards to the rest of society.

Within National Front discourse the construction of the immigrant threat is also highly gendered. The image of the North African immigrant mobilised by the National Front is closely tied to colonial stereotypes of Arab masculinity as a dark, uncontrollable force. Under the colonial order of things the Arab male was classified as a creature of instinct, controlled by sexual passions, incapable of the refinement to which the white races had evolved. Contemporary National Front discourse is infused with this imagery. For the National Front Arab masculinity is a predatory threat, a focus of fear and foreboding. Animalistic, violent, highly sensual: the attributes of the Arab male are presented as other to the values of French civilisation. North African men, it is claimed, are rapists threatening 'our women'; they are muggers, pimps and drug pushers contaminating 'our society'. In this way Le Pen has created a moral panic, presenting people with a set of polarised choices: immigrant versus French, 'good' versus 'evil', civilised and uncivilised standards, anarchy or order. What Le Pen constructs is the image of a nation under siege from a rampant Arab masculinity. Above all, it is French women, as the biological reproducers of the nation, who must be insulated from the predatory instincts of North African men. If the purity of French women is not upheld, Le Pen warns, the French race will sink into disorder. Likewise, National Front discourse stereotypes North African women as fecund. Their passive nature, it is claimed, leads them to 'breed like animals'. Through such imagery, the National Front conjures up a demographic menace, whereby a galloping immigrant birthrate will mean that by the end of the next century, the French population will have been replaced by a North African one. To protect white society from this alien threat Le Pen proffers a simple solution: the repatriation of all immigrants. Only through such action, Le Pen argues, can the ethnic and spiritual homogeneity of the French nation be preserved.

Within *The Holocaust and the Liberal Imagination* Tony Kushner under-lines the need to learn the lessons of the Holocaust.[32] What Kushner calls for is the establishment of a global and inclusive 'universe of obligation' which, as he sees it, was so lacking in respect to the ethnic, religious and sexual groupings targeted by the Nazis. The examples of nationalism discussed within this volume raise the issue of obligations towards immigrants and minorities within the new Europe. Since 1989 Europe has witnessed the resurfacing of ethnic nationalism within which the articu-lation of languages of inclusion and exclusion have been central. Through-out the continent the identification of otherness has created the basis for racist violence and ethnic cleansing. If 'civilisation' is the goal, then nationalism must be judged according to the quality of life it offers to those on its margins. Within contemporary Europe what must count is the protection afforded by the majority to its minorities. Never has the need to go beyond dehumanising stereotypes and establish the common bonds of humanity been so great or so compelling.

NOTES

1 Peter Stallybrass and Allon White, *The Politics and Poetics of Transgression*, Methuen, London, 1986, p.8.
2 Mary Douglas, *Purity and Danger*, Routledge, London, 1966, p.4.
3 Antony Smith, *National Identity*, London, Penguin, 1979, p.91.
4 Peter Stallybrass and Allon White, op. cit.
5 Mikhail Bakhtin, *Rabelais and his World,*, MIT Press, Cambridge MA, 1968.
6 Floya Anthias and Nira Yuval-Davis, *Racialized Boundaries*, London, Routledge, 1992.
7 Ibid., p.2.
8 A. Gobineau, *Selected Political Writings*, Cape, London, 1970, p.27.
9 ibid, p.35.
10 Robert Wistrich, *Anti-Semitism: the Longest Hatred*, Methuen, London, 1991, p.xviii
11 Susan Sontag, *Illness as a Metaphor*, Penguin, London, 1983, p. 70.
12 Edouard Drumont quoted in J S McClelland, *The French Right: from de Maistre to Maurras*, Jonathan Cape, London, 1970, p.92.
13 Quoted in Paul Webster, *Petain's Crime*, Macmillan, London, 1990, p.22.
14 Paul Hockenos, *Free to Hate*, Routledge, London, 1993. On the subject of anti-semitism in contemporary Europe see also Neil Landsman, 'Anti-Semitism in Eastern Europe', *Journal of Area Studies*, 1994, no. 4: 159–71.
15 On the role of Pamyat' within contemporary Russian nationalism see the chapter by Paul Flenley in this volume, 'From Soviet to Russian identity: the origins of contemporary Russian nationalism and national identity'.
16 Max Silverman, *Deconstructing the Nation: Immigration, Racism and Citizenship in Modern France*, Routledge, London, 1992.
17 Figures from Andrew Marshall, 'So, where are Mr Wardle's immigrants?', *Independent*, 14 February 1995.
18 'The boat is full' was an REP poster slogan used in the April 1992 regional elections.
19 Franz Schönhuber, quoted in Michael Schmidt, *The New Reich*, Hutchinson, London, 1993, p.179.
20 DVU pamphlet, May 1992.
21 Quoted in Michael Schmidt, *The New Reich*, op. cit. p.181.
22 Alec G. C. Hargreaves, 'Migration controls and European Unity', *Journal of Area Studies*, 1992, p.77.
23 Jean-Marie Le Pen, *Les Français d'Abord*, Carrere-Michel Lafond, Paris, 1984, p.99.
24 During the 1984 European elections the slogan advanced by the National Front was: 'Two million unemployed is two million immigrants too many'.
25 For example Le Pen has written: 'We believe in the superiority of European civilisation, in the necessity of its world authority, tempered by Christian charity and European humanism', *Les Français d'Abord*, p.73.
26 Jean-Marie Le Pen quoted in Edwy Plenel and Alain Rollat, *L'effet Le Pen*, La Decouverte, Paris, p.29.

27 Interestingly here Le Pen likens himself to the Native American leader Sitting Bull. As Le Pen sees it he has come out of his reserve to defend the rights of his people.
28 For an analysis of Western perceptions of Islam see Edward Said, *Orientalism*, Routledge & Kegan Paul, London, 1978. Within it Said shows how Islam has a special place within the European experience providing Europe with one its deepest and most traumatic images of the 'other'.
29 Comment la Gauche veut Arabiser la France', *Minute*, 18–24 May 1985, p.11.
30 The fact that the National Front has supported the Islamists in Algeria must not be seen as a softening of the National Front position. For the National Front the Islamists are potential allies because if the latter got into power they would want to bring back all Algerian immigrants who they fear are being corrupted by western values.
31 Interview with Radio Libre Frequence Gaie, 11 June 1984.
32 Tony Kushner, *The Holocaust and the Liberal Imagination*, Blackwell, London, 1995.

SELECT BIBLIOGRAPHY

Anthias, F. and Yuval-Davis, N. (1992) *Racialized Boundaries*, London, Routledge.
Hockenos, P. (1993) *Free to Hate: The Right in Post-Communist Eastern Europe*, London, Routledge.
Kushner, T. (1995) *The Holocaust and the Liberal Imagination*, Oxford, Blackwell.
Lewes, B. and Schnapper, D. (eds) (1994) *Muslims in Europe*, London, Pinter.
Said, E. (1978) *Orientalism*, London, Routeldge & Kegan Paul.
Schmidt, M. (1993) *The New Reich*, London, Hutchinson.
Silverman, M. (1991) *Deconstructing the Nation: Immigration, Racism and Citizenship in Modern France*, London: Routledge.
Wistrich, R. (1991) *Anti-Semitism: the Longest Hatred*, London, Methuen.

3

IMMIGRATION, CITIZENSHIP AND THE NATION-STATE IN THE NEW EUROPE

Mark Mitchell and Dave Russell

ACROSS EUROPE: THE CHANGING PICTURE

One of the most striking features of the New Europe is the extent to which the late 1980s and the 1990s have seen concerted efforts by Western European governments to develop new and tougher forms of immigration control. Among the member states of the European Union in particular, there have been attempts to harmonise national policies relating to matters of immigration and asylum as a consequence of the creation of the Single Market and the potential that this has brought about for increased labour mobility across the European Union (EU). In the 1987 Single European Act, the then-European Community was defined as an area without internal frontiers. To make this a reality, the Act envisages the progressive abolition of all internal border controls to permit free movement within the Community. Although there is still some way to go before this goal is fully realised, a substantial degree of policy harmonisation has occurred and there is now in place a framework of policies, administrative rules and procedures that is applied with increasing consistency across the EU.

However, the real impetus for the growth of this nascent European immigration regime lies not in the creation of the Single Market itself but in changes in the patterns of migration across the EU over the past ten years and the potential consequences of these for EU member states in a situation where internal border controls are diminishing. Three dimensions of the changing pattern of European migration are particularly important in this respect.

First, although the inflow of migrant workers has declined sharply since the 1950s and 1960s, this should not be taken to imply a complete end to 'primary' immigration by guest workers. Although France, Germany and the UK – the major recipients of primary immigration in the period up to 1970 – have all but ceased to admit new primary immigrants from non-EU countries, this is not the case with all EU member states. In particular, Italy, Portugal and Spain, traditionally countries of emigration, have in recent

54

years become net recipients of third-country migrants as their economies have begun to grow. A substantial number of these are believed to be illegal immigrants with estimates for 1991 showing 600,000 'illegals' in Italy and 300,000 in Spain.[1]

Second, the late 1980s and early 1990s saw a substantial increase in the number of asylum seekers applying to reside permanently in Europe. This was due in part to the migratory pressures created by the disintegration of the communist regimes in Eastern Europe and the escalation of the conflict in the former Yugoslavia. Germany alone received nearly 450,000 new applications for asylum in 1992, an eightfold increase over a five-year period. Similarly, the UK saw its number of asylum seekers rise to nearly 60,000 in 1991 from under 5,000 in 1986. Although the increases in numbers seeking asylum in other EU countries were less spectacular, it is the case that from the mid-1980s to the early 1990s there was a substantial increase in applications from asylum seekers across all EU and most EFTA countries.[2] The fall in the overall number of asylum applications over the past two years has come about largely as a result of the introduction of tougher measures of control by member states. The repeal in 1993 of the clause in the German constitution that granted the right of asylum to all those suffering from political persecution was a major factor in effecting this reduction. What is also apparent is that this and other measures have been introduced as part of a concerted attempt by the governments of EU member states to crack down on the number of asylum seekers.

Third, there has been concern at the growth in the number of so-called illegal immigrants entering Western Europe in recent years. In 1991, the International Labour Organization estimated that around 14 per cent of the foreign population of Western Europe – approximately 2,600,000 people – were illegal residents, with Germany and Italy having the largest number of 'illegals'.[3] There is nothing particularly new in the phenomenon of illegal migration to Western Europe, which has been widespread throughout the post-war period. However, a combination of weak immigration controls, the close proximity of the Maghreb and the existence of a large informal economy has made the countries of southern Europe a prime target for illegal migration in recent years.[4]

The creation of the Single Market has meant that the issues of immigration and asylum are now transnational European problems. Although the Single European Act allows for the free mobility of labour only for those holding full citizenship of an EU member state and for the free movement of individuals only for those who are either citizens or who are legally resident non-EU nationals, in a situation in which border controls are being progressively reduced, the restrictions on the cross-EU mobility of 'illegals' becomes impossible to enforce. It is for this reason that the immigration policy of any single EU member state is now of direct and immediate interest to others within the EU.

The simultaneous strengthening of external border controls between the EU and the outside world and the reduction of cross-border controls between member states has often been referred to in terms of a strategy to create a Fortress Europe.[5] This metaphor, while it may have a superficial appeal, inadequately represents the complexities of the changing nature of the EU's relationships with the outside world, particularly the post-communist states of Central and Eastern Europe. Fortress Europe presents an over-simplistic view of an attempt to build a secure barrier around the EU with the gates on its eastern and southern fronts firmly closed.

In fact, the geopolitical reordering of the New Europe in the form of overlapping systems of cooperation, both formal and semi-formal, between a wide range of nation-states in Western, Northern, Central and Eastern Europe through a variety of transnational organisations implies the need for a more complex model to represent the attempts to regulate and control migration into Europe in recent years.[6] If we are to continue to make use of the Fortress Europe metaphor, then we must recognise that the various forms of economic, political, military and cultural cooperation across Europe are creating a shifting complex of bulwarks, ditches and ramparts in which the outer defences in particular are constantly being reshaped. The establishment of formal links between Germany and members of the Visegrad group, linking the return of 'illegals' and asylum seekers to the provision of aid to assist with the development of cross-border policing, illustrates the ways in which non-EU countries are becoming enmeshed in the EU's attempts to regulate migration.[7]

Finally, it is important to note that the contemporary arguments about immigration across Europe are not, and never have been, solely about numbers! It is not the ethnic Germans, the British patrials or other 'returnees' from colonial outposts in Africa, Asia or the Americas that are believed to constitute a 'problem' for the individual states concerned. Indeed, these groups are rarely if ever referred to as 'immigrants'. Rather, it is migrants and asylum seekers from so-called Second and Third World countries who are identified as problematic by the potential 'host' countries of Western Europe. Not only do these groups lack the necessary cultural capital to enable them to participate in the accepted ways of living in the countries concerned and to share and enjoy its values and traditions; they frequently lack any interest in acquiring these cultural values and thus represent, in the eyes of many, a potential challenge to the integrity of the nation and to the maintenance of a strong sense of national identity. This has been underscored in recent years by the growth of Islamic fundamentalism and the perceived threat that this poses to Western Europe with its predominantly Christian traditions. The apparent dysfunctions posed by the continued migration to Western Europe of Muslims from Turkey, the Middle East, the Indian sub-continent and the Maghreb, coupled with events such as the Gulf War, the escalating crisis in Algeria and the Salman Rushdie affair, have served to amplify fears of 'cultural swamping' and to reproduce unitary and undifferentiated concepts of national/cultural identity that some commentators have argued are an inappropriate foundation for post-industrial societies of the late twentieth century.[8] We will return to these issues in the later sections of this chapter.

TOWARDS A EUROPEAN IMMIGRATION REGIME

Over the past ten years, the introduction of an array of policy initiatives, legal and constitutional reforms and administrative changes has created a comprehensive, if not yet completely coherent, system of immigration controls across the New Europe. Taken together, these changes represent the growth of a new European immigration regime that is far more complex than is suggested by the Fortress Europe metaphor.

As yet, there is no common EU policy on immigration and asylum, with policies varying across member states who have been unwilling publicly to cede their sovereign powers over these matters. Although granted some additional powers under the Maastricht Treaty, the formal authority of the European Commission in the sphere of immigration remains extremely limited. Nevertheless, a variety of inter-governmental initiatives over the past decade has *de facto* produced a significant degree of policy convergence across the EU and beyond in the sphere of immigration. Multilateral agreements such as the Schengen Accord as well as transnational initiatives emanating from the Working Group on Immigration are, in effect, producing an emergent European immigration regime of policies, rules and procedures governing both the policing of Europe's external borders and the gradual reduction of internal cross-border controls within the EU.

However, it is necessary to look beyond the EU to other geopolitical areas in order to identify more fully the edifice of a new immigration regime. This evolving regime is based on a form of international governance to which treaty organisations such as the European Free Trade Association, the European Economic Area and the Nordic Union also make a significant contribution. The internationalisation of migration management has also been extended by the growth of a range of Re-admission Agreements between various Western and Eastern European states, facilitating the return of assorted unwanted immigrants in exchange for compensatory aid packages for countries accepting returnees and asylum seekers in transit. Such agreements have also had the effect of extending the geographic reach of the emergent immigration regime eastwards as well as helping to create a 'buffer zone' between 'inner' and 'outer' Europe.[9]

The growth of a nascent system of international governance in the sphere of immigration can be seen as a means through which the nation-state continues to exercise some control and influence over these matters. Within this emerging system, the nation-state and the ideas of the national interest and national sovereignty are central elements in the current politics of immigration. Rather than denoting a weakening of the nation-state, the creation of an international immigration regime and institutions of cooperation to regulate migration represent a response to a situation in which individual European states no longer have the capacity to exercise complete control over policies relating to migration. The partial loss of legal sovereignty is the price that must be paid for maintaining a measure of state autonomy in the face of mounting migration pressures.[10]

Across Western Europe, recognition of the need for a concerted response to these pressures has led to a range of policy changes, some emanating from the EU itself, some resulting from inter-governmental collaboration and others from initiatives taken by individual governments. Together, these interrelated policies form the basis of the emergent European immigration regime.

EUROPEAN COMMUNITY INITIATIVES

To date, it is the restrictive measures introduced by individual governments or through inter-governmental collaboration that have provided the impetus for the development of a European immigration regime, rather than the top-down imposition of supranational migration policies. Nevertheless, the EU institutions have gradually become more involved in the control and regulation of migration, despite the concern of nation-states to protect their sovereignty and promote subsidiarity.[11] Although in a weak position to implement the goals of the Single Market and to guarantee the free movement of labour, the European Commission has found itself increasingly drawn into immigration matters. The Maastricht Treaty fuelled this tendency by giving the Community, for the first time, limited formal competence in the area of immigration and asylum. Along with security and judicial cooperation, immigration became a 'third pillar' issue of the European Union under the Treaty. In practice, this has given the EU powers relating to the harmonisation of visa policies and the regularisation of internal controls on the movements of non-EU nationals. Although only a relatively small step towards supranational transcendence, the accretion of power to Brussels in this area clearly curtails national sovereignty. For instance, the UK is now required to abolish the preferential arrangements which allow citizens of most Commonwealth countries the right to visit the UK without a visa.[12] In effect, member states will not be allowed to operate their own visa policies.

Post-Maastricht, new structures have emerged which have begun to incorporate and harmonise the work of inter-governmental bodies such as the Trevi Group and the Ad Hoc Group on Immigration. This clearly illustrates the extent to which the EU has begun to play a more active role in this field.[13] Immigration and asylum matters are progressively becoming subsumed within an organisational structure consisting of a Council of Interior and Justice Ministers of the EU, a permanent secretariat for handling all 'third pillar' issues, along with a K4 Committee of member state representatives and a Working Group on migration.[14] Under these new arrangements, the EU has assumed new competencies though it is still not permitted to issue directives. How far this change will facilitate a more open scrutiny of decisions hitherto made in secret ministerial conclaves remains to be seen.

Indirectly, the European Commission has become more involved with immigration matters as a result of its responsibilities in the broad area of social policy as, in practice, significant aspects of immigration policy interface with the Commission's social policy competences.[15] As a result, conflicts have occurred between national and EU law. The UK government has run into difficulties with its 'primary purpose rule' concerning the legitimacy of marriages between British nationals and non-EU nationals which, it has been suggested, are often arranged to secure migration to the UK. The role of the European Court of Justice has been important in upholding the principle that the right to free movement for EU nationals should not be undermined by obstructive national legislation relating to their spouses or dependants.[16] However, member states such as the UK continue to resist EU jurisdiction over these matters. Conditions for family reunification have been further restricted by member states and by an inter-governmental resolution adopted in June 1993, specifying which categories of family members are entitled to the right of reunification. The EU has not yet proved itself capable of developing transnational legally binding instruments in this or other areas of migration policy. Two areas have been identified by the European Commission as priorities: harmonising approaches to defining who is a refugee and developing minimum standards for asylum procedures.[17] However, to date, the Commission has been able to suggest only the device of a convention to address the differences between member states and is, at present, unable to do more. Similarly, measures proposed by the Commission as part of a 'tough and tender' approach to combat racial discrimination seem unlikely to secure the necessary unanimous support of the Council. The current campaign for a 'Starting Line' directive in favour of Union-wide anti-discrimination legislation in response to the rise of racial extremism across Europe also seems unlikely to obtain sufficient support. Nor are member states likely to endorse the proposed legislation to penalise employers who give jobs to illegal immigrants. Altogether, it is the case that many immigration and immigration-related issues have become part of a supranational agenda and discourse at the European level.[18] In addition to matters related to entry and residence, these include a range of social policy issues such as employment and working conditions, social security and pensions, family reunification, anti-discrimination legislation and the education of immigrant children. The agenda may have expanded, but these new policy concerns remain outside the formal decision-making mechanisms of the EU and the role of the Commission is only to offer advice and to make policy recommendations. Overall, while the Maastricht Treaty gives the Commission new responsibilities in the area of migration policy, the individual member states retain the upper hand.

Inter-governmental initiatives

For the last decade and more, inter-governmentalism has been the preferred approach of member states seeking to take coordinated action in controlling migration flows. National governments have come to recognise that their immigration and asylum policies cannot be considered in isolation, since measures taken in one country are always liable to affect migratory movements in another. Inter-governmental processes have developed largely under the auspices of the European Council but outside the legal competence of the EU. Various *ad hoc* agreements have emerged through these processes, often influencing legislative changes within member states and usually involving the harmonisation of rules and procedures. Before Maastricht, the most important inter-governmental policy developments occurred as a result of the deliberations of the Schengen and Trevi groups, together with the Ad Hoc Group on Immigration. These initiatives have had a decisive impact in shaping the emerging European immigration regime. The original Schengen Accord, signed in 1985 by France, Germany and the three Benelux countries, was aimed primarily at the dismantling of internal border controls. The subsequent 1990 Schengen Convention, signed by all member states except Denmark, Ireland and the UK, focused more on the need to control external frontiers, to harmonise the powers of exclusion and to improve the cross-border policing of refugees, illegal immigrants and other unwanted aliens. It commits the participants to the establishment of a common administrative structure and to a progressive pooling of national resources in order more effectively to control the flow of refugees and illegals. In particular, this has involved the creation of the Schengen Information System, a computerised management information system based in Strasbourg and designed to share police intelligence on criminals, refugees and illegal immigrants. The Trevi Group of Justice and Home Affairs ministers is similarly concerned with criminal surveillance issues and the security problems posed by asylum seekers and illegal immigrants, although its original brief involved serious crimes with an international dimension such as terrorism and drug running. Together, these two groups have been critically important in shaping a new European internal security system with respect to immigration matters which, once it is in full operation, will enhance considerably the effectiveness of the policing of migrants and asylum seekers across Europe. It is also liable to criminalise arbitrarily, without adequate means of defence, an increasing number of economic and political migrants.[19] However, the implementation of the Schengen system has been delayed due to various matters of dispute between the Schengen states such as the reconciliation of different national policies on data protection and the possession of soft drugs.[20] This demonstrates the extent to which inter-governmental co-operation can be thwarted by difficult-to-reconcile national policies. The impact of internal political disputes within member states over immigration controls also seems likely to delay the full implementation of the Schengen agreements. In June 1995, the French government, concerned at the successes of the far-Right parties in the municipal elections, decided to reintroduce internal border controls following their elimination for a three-month trial period. Under the terms of the Schengen Convention, France, Germany, Spain, Portugal and the three Benelux countries had been due to end all cross-border controls on 1 July 1995 following the three-month trial.

The Dublin Convention on the right of asylum was signed in 1990 by all member states except Denmark. Its major objective was to prevent asylum seekers submitting multiple applications for asylum to several member states simultaneously. In addition, asylum seekers whose applications had been rejected by one member state were to be returned to their country of origin, rather than having their applications routed to other EC countries. The Dublin Convention attempted to define the criteria for the country responsible for dealing with an asylum application, the thrust of which was to allow an asylum seeker to make only one application in the Community. The harmonisation process was further advanced in November 1992 through another inter-governmental agreement reached by EC immigration ministers meeting in London under the auspices of the Ad Hoc Group on Immigration. This agreement aimed to hasten the repatriation of asylum seekers through the development of accelerated procedures to deal with so-called 'manifestly unfounded' applications. The arrangement was that asylum seekers would be sent back to the first safe haven or 'third host country' that they had passed through on their way to the Community. In effect, this agreement has helped to create a kind of ring fence around the EU, beyond which exists a 'buffer zone' made up of 'safe countries' of transit where it is believed that unsuccessful asylum seekers face no serious risk of persecution.[21]

Finally, it is worth noting that the Corfu Summit of EU Foreign Ministers in June 1994 established an anti-racism commission to develop ideas for 'encouraging tolerance and understanding of foreigners'. The French and German governments, concerned at the growing incidence of acts of racist and xenophobic violence, were behind this initiative. The preliminary report of this commission is expected to call for the 1996 revision of the

Maastricht Treaty to empower EU institutions to combat discrimination on the grounds of race, ethnic origin and religion. But although this initiative represents a positive, if modest, response to the problems of racial violence and far-Right extremism across Europe, it can hardly be seen as indicative of a major inter-governmental drive against racial discrimination and hostility to foreigners. Indeed, it is the very same set of concerns, linking the rise in migration to the growth in popularity of the politics of racial hatred and violence, that has provided the principal justification for the cross-European coordination of ever-more restrictive immigration and asylum policies.

Individual government initiatives

Tougher anti-immigration policies have been developed in recent years by national governments, partly in response to the resurgence of the extreme Right, particularly in France and Germany. Most notably, the electoral success of the Front National in France was used by the Interior Minister Charles Pasqua to justify the announcement in June 1993 of an intention to pursue a policy of 'zero immigration'.[22] Pasqua's tough reform package included measures to slow down family reunions, to hasten expulsions and to give the police extra powers in dealing with illegal immigrants and refugees. The proposed reforms met with some resistance and provoked the threat of a constitutional crisis but the majority had been enacted in a modified form by January 1994.[23] Electoral support for the Front national was an important political catalyst in shifting immigration to the centre of the French political agenda, thus opening the door to Pasqua's hard-line stance. The build-up of pressures across the political spectrum for tighter immigration controls has served to compromise France's historic record on asylum and its established provision for refugees.

Both France and Germany have tried to legitimise stricter immigration controls and tighter restrictions on refugees by emphasising the need to harmonise European policy and to implement the Schengen Accord. The reality is that a combination of internal and external pressures has pushed both countries towards more restrictive influx control measures. In both, the asylum question has been at the centre of the politics of immigration and in 1993, Germany responded to its own particularly acute asylum problems by repealing the liberal laws on asylum that were enshrined in its constitution.

During the early 1990s, it became widely accepted within mainstream German political opinion that support for the neo-Nazis would continue to rise and ethnic violence continue to increase unless the influx of foreigners was halted. There was a widespread belief that the country's liberal asylum laws were being abused by 'economic refugees' from Eastern Europe and the Third World. The need to crack down on the 'misuse of asylum' was first articulated by Chancellor Kohl and the coalition parties led by the Christian Democratic Union (CDU), but it was only when the opposition German Social Democratic Party (SPD) changed tack and fell into line behind the Government that the constitutional changes were introduced. In effect, the right to asylum has been removed since asylum seekers entering Germany via another EU country or arriving from 'safe third countries' such as Poland or the Czech Republic are to be immediately returned. These constitutional changes were seen by many in Germany as a capitulation to the far Right and to xenophobic violence. However, the response from mainstream politicians has been to emphasise the extent to which these changes have brought Germany more into line with other EU member states.

For some time, the UK has presented itself as the EU country which has taken the toughest stance on immigration. An earlier build-up of anti-immigration pressures in Britain sparked a significant tightening of immigration controls during the 1960s and 1970s, and the limited electoral success of the neo-fascist National Front in the mid-to-late 1970s prompted the passage of the 1981 British Nationality Act, introduced by the first Thatcher government. The UK continued to set the pace in the immigration field with the 1987 Carriers' Liability Act and the 1993 Asylum and Immigration Appeals Act. In each case, the UK government incorporated into national legislation provisions within the Schengen Agreement while, at the same time, refusing to risk a 'levelling down' of immigration controls by signing up to Schengen. The 1993 Act also authorised the fingerprinting of asylum seekers to prevent multiple asylum applications and benefit fraud, thus ensuring that asylum seekers are treated like suspect criminals on arrival. Subsequently, the first steps have been taken by the Interior and Justice Ministers to establish an EU-wide computerised fingerprinting scheme known as Eurodac, which will facilitate the exchange of information about refugees and unwanted immigrants.[24] This demonstrates well the interaction that has taken place between individual government and inter-governmental initiatives in the development of a European immigration regime.

Other important features of this policy process have been the changes in immigration policy initiated by aspiring or new member states either as a prelude to, or a consequence of, joining the EU. Spain presents a case in point. In preparation for full entry into the EC the following year, Spain passed the 1985 Foreigners Law which forms the basis of Spanish immigration policy.[25] Prior to joining the Schengen system, the Spanish government, as part of an 'active immigration policy', introduced a requirement on nationals from the Maghreb to obtain a visa before entry into Spain.[26] Most importantly, a regularisation campaign was initiated to deal with the growing number of illegal immigrants, with preferential access to work and to residence permits offered to migrants from Latin America, the

Philippines, Portugal and Gibraltar on the grounds of 'cultural identity or affinity'.[27] Immigration is a relatively new phenomenon and has not been a contentious political issue in Spain. Unlike in France and Germany, the extreme Right has been politically insignificant in recent times. Instead, a major pressure for change has come from membership of the European Community itself and its collective concern with controlling the entry of migrants at the southern borders of Europe. To alleviate concern within the Community over its liberality towards 'economic refugees', the Spanish government in 1992 modified its Law of Asylum and Refuge, collapsing the distinction between the two categories and abolishing the automatic right of entry. As with Italy, however, illegal immigration remains a problem and an issue of concern for other member states fearing a drift northwards of clandestine North African and non-EU Hispanic nationals.

The movement towards common immigration practice at the European level has increasingly involved the imitation by new immigration countries of immigration rules and procedures established by the old countries of immigration. In fact, there has been a tendency for different governments to implement policies which have proved to be effective elsewhere, thus changing national practices in line with wider European conventions and norms.[28] The emergent European immigration regime is not simply an aggregate of multilateral agreements such as the Schengen Convention and transnational initiatives emanating from the Working Group on Immigration. Indirectly, it is also the product of a complex variety of individual government initiatives flowing from shared discourses and normative standards.

CITIZENSHIP AND NATIONALITY: TOWARDS A POLICY CONVERGENCE?

Significant national variations persist across Europe regarding the regulations governing the acquisition of citizenship for immigrants and their dependants. These differences have diminished since the first phase of mass migration into Western Europe prior to the 1970s. This has led some observers to claim that 'there has been a convergence of policies in European countries: the former colonial countries have become more restrictive, while the former guestworker countries have become less so'.[29]

There is some truth in this claim. Most clearly, the initial 'open-door' system which allowed Commonwealth immigrants freely to enter the UK with full and equal citizenship rights as British subjects has long since ended. More recently, the Portuguese government curtailed the automatic right of Brazilian migrants to opt for Portuguese nationality, with accompanying full rights as EU nationals.[30] On the other hand, elsewhere in Europe there has been a trend towards the gradual extension of citizenship rights for migrants.[31] In Germany and elsewhere, long-established immigrants have undergone a transition from the status of temporary foreign workers to permanent settlers with some limited rights.

In many ways, however, the process of convergence is more apparent than real. Fundamental differences remain despite the development across Western Europe of similar forms of immigration control. In terms of access to citizenship rights and nationality, the position of immigrants and their descendants varies considerably across different countries. A comparative analysis of the situation in France, Germany and the UK, for instance, reveals that fundamental differences exist in relation to: the acquisition of legal, political and social citizenship rights by non-EU citizens and illegal immigrants; policies towards naturalisation; and the willingness to tolerate or encourage a plurality of cultures as part of the development of a multicultural society. A look further afield across Europe reveals even more diversity over matters of citizenship and nationality, reflecting the continuing significance of deep-rooted national traditions, differences in political culture and ideology and fundamental divergencies over the significance of cultural conformity for the maintenance of national identity. Nevertheless, as a consequence of continuing large-scale migration in an era of growing European integration, citizenship rights are being recast, though not on any coherent basis.[32] As yet, there are relatively few signs of harmonisation across the EU: the principle of subsidiarity clearly prevails over any notion of European citizenship.

Citizenship of the European Union, introduced following the adoption of the Maastricht Treaty, is entirely dependent on a conception of national citizenship, since EU citizenship can only be acquired by individuals holding citizenship in one of the member states.[33] As a result, the link between nationality and citizenship is, in the main, reproduced rather than undermined by the current conception of European citizenship. Broadly, there is a threefold differentiation of the population into citizens, quasi-citizens and foreigners, founded on the basis of national citizenship.[34] EU nationals who migrate to another country in the Union enjoy important employment, residence and social welfare rights, but they are not full citizens as they are granted only limited political rights. Further, the position of these quasi-citizens is usually different to that of a variety of non-EU nationals resident within Europe who have far more limited citizenship rights. However, even among these 'third country' nationals, there are significant variations. Permanently settled foreigners or *Ausländer* of Turkish nationality in Germany have acquired legal and social rights of citizenship which stop short of the entitlement to vote; legally resident aliens in some countries like Sweden, Denmark, the Netherlands and Ireland have local voting rights; while a vast array of illegal immigrants, asylum seekers and temporary workers have few, if any, rights at all. It is evident that various forms of 'citizenship' exist within the different member states of the EU alongside an increasing incidence of dual citizenship.[35] The growth in numbers of denizens and the uneven development of citizenship rights for resident aliens is a significant feature of the New Europe. More important, it complements the near-total exclusion from citizenship rights of a growing number of 'extra-communitarian' migrants or 'margizens' drawn largely from the less developed world, either as temporary contract workers or illegal immigrants.[36] While, according to Martiniello, a nationalist logic places limitations on the further development of citizenship rights for EU nationals, it can be argued that there is a racist logic to the systematic exclusion of 'cultural aliens', deemed to be non-European, from citizenship rights. The marginalisation of this growing category and their deteriorating status is a logical extension of the hostile and unwelcoming attitude towards immigrants which is the hallmark of the European immigration regime.

However, within this broad picture, there are variations in the degree to which immigrants are integrated and accepted in different nation-states that are the products of different national traditions and political cultures. Primarily, the acquisition of citizenship and nationality is shaped by the way in which the nation is defined within the different discourses on nationality and national identity in different countries. Although Western European countries have moved closer to each other, the deeply embedded nature of national traditions and national identities seems likely to preserve existing differences, thus delaying the long-term incorporation of migrants into full citizenship.[37] Recent changes in citizenship policies and in the rules for acquiring various forms of citizenship in different countries amount to changes at the margins, rather than any fundamental shift in the established conventions of citizenship.

Across Europe at the present time, the countries of immigration can usefully be divided into three categories based on different ideal types of citizenship.[38] First, there is an exclusionary or ethnic model of citizenship which defines the nation in terms of ethnicity and deep-rooted ties of culture and language. Within this model, minorities are excluded from citizenship or allowed only limited legal and social rights. Citizenship is acquired at birth through parental nationality and naturalisation is extremely difficult since immigrant settlers and their dependants are ethnic outsiders who can never become an accepted part of the nation. Germany, denying within official discourse that it is a country of immigration, offers the closest fit with this model. Immigrants and their children who have settled in the country remain marginalised foreigners. The possibility of full integration for Turkish nationals and others is denied since, culturally, they do not belong to the German nation. In contrast, 'ethnic Germans' born and living in another territory have full rights to German citizenship and nationality. Although these arrangements have come under increasing pressure in recent years, nevertheless they remain largely intact.

Second, most closely associated with France, there is the republican or 'civic' model of the nation. In sharp contrast to the ethnic model, the nation is represented as a political community of free and equal citizens who have acquired citizenship rights by virtue of their residence on national soil irrespective of their ethnic origins.[39] Membership of the nation and participation in the nation-state is not dependent on ethnicity, religion or language. Immigrants can be fully incorporated into the nation if they are willing to accept its political rules and identify with, and participate in, the national culture. Naturalisation is relatively easy and *jus soli* or citizenship by birthplace is the norm for descendants.[40] Although this appears to be a more open model of citizenship and nationality than that based upon *jus sanguinis*, a logic of assimilation clearly underpins this ideal type. Cultural assimilation is the price that must be paid by minority ethnic groups for their integration into the political community as full citizens. In effect, there is no place within this model for long-term cultural and ethnic diversity.[41]

Conversely, a third alternative multicultural model of citizenship and the nation does allow scope for the maintenance of cultural and ethnic differences. As with the republican model, naturalisation is relatively easy and full citizenship is acquired as of right by the descendants of first-generation migrants. However, cultural assimilation is not required as a *quid pro quo* and the right of immigrants and their children to remain ethnically distinct and to continue to pursue their traditional customs and practices is accepted, within the framework of the law. The clearest examples of this model can be found beyond Europe, in countries of immigration such as Australia and Canada. In these countries, the development of cultural pluralism has long been an accepted feature of the process of nation-building. A variety of groups of immigrants with ethnically diverse backgrounds has been rapidly incorporated into the nation with the right to remain culturally different. For example, in contrast to most European countries, Canadian immigration policy has become increasingly selective and immigrants possessing capital and entrepreneurial skills have been admitted irrespective of their cultural origins or commitment to cultural conformity. Inside Europe, the multicultural model has been most actively pursued by Sweden, although its implementation has become more problematic with the growth in the numbers of political refugees that has arisen partly as a consequence of Sweden's more humanitarian stance on matters of immigration and asylum. Sweden's liberal multicultural immigration policy is also in transition as a consequence of the need to bring Swedish policies and practices into line with those of its new EU partners.[42]

A complex variety of pressures for change has highlighted tensions and has led in practice to some blurring of the differences between these models. Significantly, the established ties of nation and identity, differently inscribed in the competing exclusionary and assimilationist models, have become more difficult to sustain in each case. Furthermore, multi-cultural issues and debates have become more prominent in all the immigration countries across Europe to a greater or lesser extent.[43] The permanent settlement across Europe of a variety of minority ethnic groups and the growing pluralisation of Western European societies has served to transform multiculturalism into an ideological battleground and has encouraged the growth of 'identity politics' across Europe. Expressions of concern about the so-called threat to the nation and the dilution of national identity in different Western European countries have taken the form of moral panics, in which 'genuine fears' about the growth of multi-culturalism are voiced.[44] This, in turn, has inhibited the translation of ethnic diversity and cultural hybridity into effective and substantial forms of multicultural citizenship. Reactionary ethno-nationalist ideologies have been mobilised against multiculturalism and have enjoyed some success in undermining its political legitimacy in different countries.

Among the leading immigration countries in Europe, the UK has probably moved closest to embracing the multicultural model. There has been a radical shift away from the old 'imperial model' of citizenship which prevailed in Britain until 1962 and gave rights of entry, along with formal equality, to citizens of the British Empire.[45] Since 1962, UK immigration policy has been progressively shaped by the idea of ex-clusivity whereby the principles of birthplace and lineage determined citizenship entitlements. The adoption of the 'patriality' clause in the 1971 Immigration Act moved the UK significantly towards the German ethnic model in at least one key respect.[46] On the other hand, Britain has subsequently implemented a number of policy initiatives that are based on the principles of multiculturalism and have been influenced signifi-cantly by the US approach towards legislating for equality. Most notably, the 1976 Race Relations Act departed significantly from the principles of formal equality and equal treatment for different ethnic groups. The introduction of the concept of indirect discrimination, in effect, gave legal recognition to the right to cultural difference. Although limited in appli-cation, this provision identified the possible adverse impact on minority ethnic groups of treating all individuals in the same manner, irrespective of ethnicity. The UK anti-discrimination legislation, by allowing for cultural and ethnic differences, introduced a modest measure of positive action into statute and legalised certain forms of separate provision catering for the social needs of minority ethnic groups. Leaving aside questions concerning the efficacy of its implementation, the UK anti-discrimination legislation stands out as one of the clearest legislative expressions of multiculturalism across Europe.

An official policy stance in favour of a limited form of multiculturalism has been augmented within recent legislation by a symbolic commitment to race equality and ethnic diversity across a variety of areas of social welfare provision such as housing, community care and education. Furthermore, in the 1980s and 1990s at the sub-central government level, a range of local service providers and professional practitioners have, with mixed success, sought to develop multicultural forms of provision.[47] In turn, there has been a hostile reaction from some sections of the press and the political Right against anti-racism and multiculturalism. Without question, there remains a deep-rooted hostility among some of the population to the idea of Britain as a multicultural country.[48] Perhaps this was most clearly revealed in the clamorous outcry against the Muslim community sparked by the Salman Rushdie affair in the late 1980s. Over and over again, the complexity of the subject matter was reduced to the issue of the cultural incompatibility of Islam with Western liberalism and British national identity. The overwhelming inference drawn by substantial sections of the press and by a wide range of political commentators has been that all Muslims subscribe to one position or speak with one alien voice. They could not, or did not want to, belong to the British nation. Similar sentiments concerned with cultural separateness have kindled a number of schooling controversies linked to the apparent 'threat' posed by the alien presence of too many Muslim children in some classrooms.

Altogether, it is obvious that, in Britain as elsewhere in Europe, there exist opposed racialised discourses that present radically different views about the integration of minority ethnic communities and the desirability of cultural diversity. An unresolved tension exists between assimilationist arguments that link citizenship rights to the duties of cultural conformity and multicultural arguments where the right to be culturally distinct and to have cultural traditions and practices recognised and respected is seen as an important prerequisite to the attainment of a wider range of citizenship rights. Nevertheless, it is evident that official discourse and mainstream élite opinion in Britain supports a broad policy stance in favour of cultural pluralism and a 'race relations' perspective, with allowance made for minority group rights. Furthermore, a significant degree of political space has been opened up for the mobilisation of a group perspective on identity and rights. For example, in the last decade 'separatist' minority demands concerning controversial issues like same-race adoption and separate schooling have occupied a more prominent place on the policy agenda and achieved some degree of legitimacy, particularly at the level of the local state.[49] While these proposals may have engendered fierce opposition, both from outside and within minority ethnic communities, the actual existence and toleration of such demands illustrates the extent to which such issues have a serious place within the politics of race in Britain.

In many ways, the situation in France is very different. Clearly, both Britain and France bear traces of the 'imperial model', in that each has incorporated into the nation former colonial subjects and their descendants with full political and civil rights. However, the UK has developed a definition of citizenship and an understanding of nationhood which is some way removed from that which exists in France. In contrast to the more ideological French approach, Britain has, since the 1970s, attempted pragmatically to combine elements of both the ethnic and multicultural models into a revised definition of nationality and citizenship. France has managed largely to preserve its uniquely expansive system of citizenship law, although some modest change in nationality law took place in 1993.[50] Furthermore, despite growing opposition from across the political spectrum, an assimilationist understanding of nationhood has continued to prevail alongside a commitment to universalist principles and individual rights. There remains a deep-seated resistance towards the recognition of minority group rights in France and little scope exists for the formal recognition of cultural difference among French citizens. All the same, it is still relatively easy for immigrants to acquire French citizenship.

Political opposition to French citizenship law has centred on the problem of migrants from North Africa, especially Algerian immigrants and their descendants. It is important to note that the attack on *jus soli* and the ideology and practice of assimilation has found support since the mid-1980s from both the extreme Right and the liberal Left in France. As it became a major force in French politics, Le Pen's Front National made much of the running in the campaign for a more restrictive definition of French nationality. In taking a hard-line anti-immigration position, Le Pen campaigned against the automatic acquisition of French citizenship by children born in France of foreign parents. Strong objections were raised to the straightforward acquisition of citizenship by spouses of French citizens and to the laxity of control over naturalisation. Citizenship should only go to those with French hearts and minds. To be French you had to feel French and earn the right to be treated as such.[51] Le Pen's nationalist rhetoric also played on the notion of the cultural incompatibility of Muslim beliefs and way of life with French culture and society. An essentialist, undifferentiated characterisation of Islam served to support representations of Muslim immigrants as unassimilable. Crucially, Le Pen's strong anti-assimilationist position advocated the exclusion and repatriation of cultural aliens from the Maghreb since they could not – nor in practice did they really wish to – be incorporated into the French nation.[52]

Opportunistically, the extreme Right drew on the 'differentialist' rhetoric advocated previously by the French Left which made the case for the 'right to be different'. This anti-assimilationist argument challenged fundamentally the requirement for cultural conformity as a condition of citizenship. It also pointed to the growing gap between the rhetoric and reality of assimilation. Creeping multiculturalism in French schools and elsewhere was seen to indicate a decline in the assimilatory powers of French institutions. Assimilation was both undesirable and impossible.[53]

Voices on the Left also expressed opposition on behalf of second-generation Algerian immigrants to the way in which French citizenship and allegiance to the French state was involuntarily imposed on them. In this respect, the Left are more concerned with the manner of access to French citizenship than the degree of openness and the apparent ease of acquisition of citizenship rights which preoccupy those on the Right.[54]

The emergence of citizenship and national identity as a highly contested issue in French politics led, in 1986–7, to a failed attempt by the Centre Right Chirac administration to restrict access to French nationality. Despite evidence of popular support for nationality reform, the strength and effectiveness of political opposition led the government and mainstream Right parties to back down on a commitment to remove *jus soli* from French citizenship law.[55] The government's reform proposals were never put to a vote in the French parliament. Instead, in an attempt to defuse the issue, an independent commission was established to consider at greater length the reform of the French Nationality Code. Subsequently in 1993, a new Centre Right coalition government finally introduced some limited reforms, removing the right to the automatic acquisition of French nationality for children born of alien parents. However, this hardly represents a fundamental erosion of the liberal system of access to citizenship based on *jus soli*, since the acquisition of nationality remains open to second-generation 'immigrants' who can show a desire to become French. As such, it reaffirms an underlying commitment both to forced assimilationist principles and an inclusive view of citizenship.

The position of second- and third-generation 'immigrants' in Germany remains very different, with an exclusionary model of nationhood continuing to prevail and the formal frontiers of German citizenship still sharply defined. While 'ethnic Germans' have immigration rights and an automatic entitlement to full citizenship, non-German immigrants and their descendants still have only limited access to citizenship. Reunification prompted a heavy inward flow of ethnic German migrants from Eastern Europe after 1989, facilitated by a reaffirmation of the German ethno-cultural view of nationality.[56] A traditional commitment to the principle of *jus sanguinis* and an historic 'law of return' has granted German patrials an inalienable right to acquire German citizenship. However, a substantial increase in the numbers of ethnic Germans migrating from Poland, Romania and the countries of the former Soviet Union has led to a tightening of controls since 1990 and to the imposition of informal quotas to restrict the rate of migration.[57] In sharp contrast to the expansiveness shown towards *Aussiedler*, a restrictive policy stance on non-German immigrants has been maintained even though, over time, many 'foreigners' from southern Europe have been transformed from temporary labour migrants into permanent settlers. The process of settlement has produced a growing number of 'foreigners' – over a million –

born in the Federal Republic but denied access to German citizenship.[58] While the anomaly of settlement without citizenship has been acknowledged by the mainstream German political parties, little or no progress has been made in altering the citizenship status of second- and third-generation foreign 'immigrants'.

In 1990, there was some relaxation of the naturalisation rules whereby persons brought up and educated in Germany could no longer be denied an opportunity to become naturalised citizens. However, a renunciation of original citizenship was required from such persons and the possibility of dual citizenship was ruled out.[59] This strict renunciation requirement has effectively deferred many qualified foreigners from seeking naturalisation. There remains an unwillingness to allow dual citizenship, even for third-generation immigrants. In 1986, a proposal by the SDP for the introduction of *jus soli* for third-generation immigrants was defeated by Christian Democratic political forces.[60] More recently in November 1994, the liberal FDP, in its negotiations on a government programme for Chancellor Kohl's new Centre Right coalition, compromised on its central demand that Germany's settled immigrant communities, and especially the 1.8 million Turks, should be granted the right of dual nationality.[61] Instead, a diluted form of civic incorporation was agreed which will give limited citizenship rights to third-generation immigrants, provided that their parents have been domiciled in Germany for more than ten years and at least one was born there.[62]

Evidently, it is likely to remain immensely difficult for 'foreigners' to acquire German nationality and become members of the nation for the foreseeable future. The idea of the nation in German political discourse remains essentially concerned with ethnic and cultural identity and parental descent. As a result, in order to acquire German citizenship, it is necessary for an individual to become German in more than a legal sense.[63] Furthermore, naturalisation can only be conferred upon individuals who must apply in person for their citizenship. There is no scope for any form of collective incorporation for minority ethnic groups.[64]

Across the EU, German citizenship law is still exceptional in its restrictiveness and stringency. The difference between French and German citizenship policies remains the sharpest but, overall, the requirements for citizenship acquisition continue to vary enormously across the EU. In contrast to the degree of convergence which characterises immigration policy across the New Europe, moves towards convergence in citizenship policies have been extremely limited, with few signs of serious movement towards transnational European citizenship. With this in mind, Brubaker has cogently argued that 'in the European setting citizenship is a last bastion of sovereignty; states continue to enjoy a freedom in this domain that they increasingly lack in others.'[65]

RACE, NATION AND IDENTITY IN THE NEW EUROPE

In many respects, there is nothing particularly new in the virulent expression of hostility towards immigrants and their descendants that has been such a significant feature of the New Europe in the 1990s. From the earliest days of post-war migration, immigrants have had to face anger and resentment from the indigenous population, particularly over competition for scarce resources in the spheres of employment and housing. However, what is new about today's expressions of racism and xenophobia is that anti-immigrant campaigns tend to be legitimised by presenting immigration as a threat to the integrity of the nation. In this sense, the problem of migration has been transformed from a labour or housing market problem to an identity problem. Immigration is seen to be one of the principal causes of the so-called crisis of national identity that is apparently endemic to many Western European societies.

However, on closer examination, the arguments over the erosion of national identity and its associated political and social consequences can be seen to take different forms and to work at different levels of analysis. At the most general level, this crisis is seen as an expression of post-modern existence itself, where certainties have vanished and everything is in a state of permanent flux. The impact of 'globalisation' on economic, social and cultural processes that increasingly transcend national boundaries is emphasised. The weakening of the nation-state, which is no longer able to control or direct the interconnected complex of economic and geo-political systems that characterises the post-modern world, has undermined its capacity to meet the electoral demands of its citizens. States are less and less able to secure desired policy outcomes and this in turn promotes dissatisfaction and a 'crisis of legitimacy' which, in turn, threatens to undermine national identity.[66] In this vein, Wallace has recently argued that 'there is an underlying crisis of national identity in most European states expressed in different forms of popular disillusionment with established institutions and élites'.[67]

This is a sweeping claim that is difficult to substantiate. As a theoretical approach, it provides an insufficient understanding of the particular conditions and circumstances which may be engendering a sense of 'identity panic' within particular societies.[68] What is needed is a conjunctural analysis which identifies the specific factors that have encouraged the growth of ethnic exclusionist attitudes in different European countries in recent years and examines the conditions under which the political Right has been able to mobilise sentiments concerning the apparent threat to the integrity of the nation posed by 'others'. However, it is also important to avoid over-simplifying the wide variety of racist and xenophobic responses that have emerged across Europe in recent years.

73

Although it is the case that many European countries have experienced a growth of hostility towards minority ethnic communities in the form of racial harassment and violence, limited forms of electoral success for far-Right political parties and a general intolerance of 'outsiders', it is our contention that these and related phenomena should not be subsumed under the blanket heading of European racism.[69] Of course, the existence of a network of extreme right-wing political activists across Europe is well known. However, the far Right is known for its internal schisms and factionalism and serious differences in political strategy and outlook continue to prevent effective collaboration of the far Right in Europe.[70] More important, the existence of racism is far deeper and more pervasive across Europe than is suggested by the size and influence of far-Right political groupings which, in many EU countries, enjoy minimal electoral support.

However, if what is implied by the term 'European racism' is the increasing hostility manifested across all EU member states in recent years towards asylum seekers and 'illegal' migrants with black and brown skins seeking to gain the right of permanent residence in Europe, then this again presents a one-sided and limited view of racism. In particular, it ignores the fact that racism has as its target millions of EU citizens of non-European descent as well as non-EU citizens who are more or less permanently domiciled in Europe. Racism in Europe is not simply a knee-jerk reaction to the perceived threat of further mass migration from the South and East.

In reality, the situation is more complex than this and cannot be explained by reference to the all-embracing idea of European racism. There exist across Europe different ideological/political assumptions concerning national identity and citizenship that are deeply embedded within political and commonsense forms of discourse in the societies concerned. In recent years, all EU member states have moved to harmonise their rules and procedures governing immigration and asylum. The attempts to implement policy changes in these areas in order to introduce a degree of standardisation over systems of immigration control across the EU have required different sets of policy adjustments in different countries. These adjustments have, in turn, stimulated a variety of political disputes within the individual societies due to the existence of deep-rooted historical divergencies on these matters. This has engendered a variety of hostile reactions which have led to disagreements over the implementation of these changes that respect or take account of the cultural traditions and political conventions of the countries concerned. The gradual extension in scope of the European immigration regime has provoked a range of different political disputes across Europe as the requirements of this regime have conflicted with the ideas of nationhood and national identity in different EU countries. The resulting political debates on race, ethnicity and migration have been conducted in different ways across Europe. This has generated not a monolithic Euro-racism, but various forms of racism and racist discourse in different European countries.

In Germany, the restrictive system of access to citizenship based on the principles of *jus sanguinis* has been combined with a reasonable degree of tolerance on the part of the majority of Germans towards the maintenance of cultural differences by non-nationals. The reunification of Germany and the profound impact that this has had on the 'backward' economy of the former GDR, has helped to produce a dramatic change in the nature and intensity of racist hostility and violence towards 'foreigners'. But it is important not to overemphasise the significance of the neo-Nazi skin-heads and their racist violence that, overwhelmingly, have been concentrated within the territory of the former East Germany.[71] This tends to deflect attention away from the fact that racism has been present for many years in West Germany. The ethnic nationalism that formed the basis of the constitution of West Germany did, as we have seen, prevent migrants who are unable to demonstrate German ancestry from acquiring full German citizenship. At the same time, the Federal Republic often claimed, with some justification, that its migrant workers and asylum seekers have been more generously treated than elsewhere in Europe, even though they have had no realistic prospect of eventual naturalisation. In terms of legal rights and access to welfare benefits, this would seem to have been the case, even down to the present day. Although this dominant form of ethnic racism has helped to produce the conditions under which the neo-Nazi fringe can recruit among the disaffected youth of the Eastern states, it is not in itself identical to the extreme forms of racism that have been so prominently portrayed in the media in recent years. Moreover, as it becomes increasingly obvious that the 'myth of return' for millions of non-nationals will never become a reality, so the major political parties have started, somewhat hesitatingly, to debate solutions that will offer to Turkish migrant workers and their dependants the prospect of eventually achieving full political as well as legal and social citizenship.[72]

Similarly in France, the hostility shown by the Front National and its supporters towards minority ethnic groups, and particularly towards migrants and their families from the Maghreb, does not encompass the totality of racism within contemporary France. Settlers and their dependants have traditionally been able to acquire French citizenship relatively easily, on condition that they demonstrate a willingness to assimilate to the French way of life. Cultural pluralism and group rights have been identified as contrary to the French republican tradition where one's rights as an individual citizen are conditional upon acceptance of established political and cultural rules and conventions. This monocultural racism has been the dominant form of racist discourse in France, though increasingly it has been at variance with the reality on the ground, where the lack of cultural compliance on the part of some minority ethnic groups has been increasingly obvious. This, in turn, has provided a rich ideological vein for the Front National who have been able to maintain that, since cultural assimilation is an impossibility, the principles of *jus soli* do not apply and therefore migrants from the Maghreb should be repatriated.

The situation in the UK is again different, with the emergence of a consensus across much of the political spectrum in favour of the idea that multiculturalism provides both a means of winning the hearts and minds of minority ethnic groups and a policy framework for achieving their progressive integration into society with minimal loss of cultural identity. However, the hegemony of multiculturalism has only ever been partial in the UK and influential insiders, particularly on the Right of the Conservative Party, have been able to limit its impact by ensuring that key pieces of legislation have been framed on the basis of monocultural ideas.[73]

What has become increasingly obvious since the mid-1980s is that, within British political discourse, multiculturalism is a moveable feast – it can mean all things to all people! Consequently, it has become something of a 'hurrah word' – mention it and everyone across a wide spectrum of liberal-Left opinion gives three cheers! However, the feel-good factor that surrounds multiculturalism has served to mask a set of serious shortcomings at the very heart of its philosophy. By focusing on the more exotic elements of minority ethnic cultures, multiculturalism tends to distract attention away from the harsher realities of racism in contemporary Britain. Concentrating as it does on food, on dress, on music and the like, multiculturalism tends to downplay the importance of unemployment, of sub-standard housing and of racial harassment and violence. Thus, while the idea of inculcating respect, tolerance and understanding of cultural differences undoubtedly resonates with a substantial section of the British population, as a basis for the establishment of an alternative model of citizenship and nationality in contemporary Europe, the multicultural model has some serious weaknesses. Nevertheless, in comparison to the exclusionist model that operates in Germany and the assimilationist model applied in France, the multicultural model that has emerged in the UK has one distinct advantage. It recognises the importance of 'difference' as being at the very core of contemporary citizenship. In their varying ways, the other two models imply a simplistic and unilinear connection between citizenship and nationality and assume an undifferentiated concept of national identity that, in reality, cannot be sustained.

In the final analysis, all discussions of national identity tend to rely on an essentialist definition of what are ultimately and irreducibly the core characteristics of being British, French, German, etc. Today in our postmodern world, we more and more exhibit multiple identities that exist in fractured and non-contiguous forms. To attempt to 'read off' one's national identity from such characteristics as which cricket team one supports or whether or not one is prepared to die for one's country simply misses the point.[74] Our identities are no longer shaped – if they ever were! – by a common set of shared experiences that are circumscribed by a national boundary and are hermetically sealed from external contamination. The theoretical foundation for a form of citizenship appropriate to the New Europe of the twenty-first century may not yet be entirely clear. However, what is certain is that this will have to reflect the contemporary reality of cultural differences and multiple identities. There can be no return to the simplistic assumption that citizenship rights are dependent upon either ethnic purity or cultural homogeneity.

NOTES

1 W. Böhning, 'Integration and immigration pressures in Western Europe', *International Labour Review* 1991, 130: 445–58.
2 Figures on numbers of asylum seekers are taken from SOPEMI, *Trends in International Migration*, Paris, OECD, 1992.
3 Böhning, op. cit., p.450.
4 M. Baldwin-Edwards, 'Immigration after 1992', *Policy and Politics* 1991, 19: 199–211.
5 We have used this concept in an uncritical way in an earlier article. See M. Mitchell and D. Russell, 'Race, citizenship and "Fortress Europe"', in P. Brown and R. Crompton (eds), *Economic Restructuring and Social Exclusion*, London, UCL Press, 1994, pp.136–56.
6 M. King, 'Fortress Europe', Occasional Paper no. 6, University of Leicester, Centre for the Study of Public Order, 1994.
7 G. Kolankiewicz, 'Consensus and competition in the eastern enlargement of the European Union', *International Affairs* 1994, 70: 477–95. See also King, op. cit.
8 See, for example, S. Castles, 'Migrations and minorities in Europe. Perspectives for the 1990s: eleven hypotheses', in J. Wrench and J. Solomos (eds), *Racism and Migration in Western Europe*, Oxford, Berg, 1993, pp.17–34.
9 King, op. cit.
10 See A. McGrew, 'A global society?', in S. Hall, D. Held and A. McGrew (eds), *Modernity and its Futures*, Oxford, Polity Press, 1992, especially pp.86–92, for a discussion of the distinction between the sovereignty and autonomy of the nation-state.
11 A. Butt Philip, 'European Union immigration policy: phantom, fantasy or fact', *West European Politics* 1994, 17: 167–91.
12 J. Carvel, 'Europe to force visa laws in UK', *Guardian*, 8 January 1994.
13 T. Bunyan, 'Trevi, Europol and the European state', in T. Bunyan (ed.), *Statewatching the New Europe*, Nottingham, Statewatch, 1993, pp.15–36. See also King, op. cit.
14 King, op. cit.
15 Butt Philip, op. cit.
16 Ibid.
17 European Commission, *Background Report on Immigration and Asylum Policies*,9 April 1994, European Commission London Office.
18 Y. Soysal, 'Immigration and the emerging European polity', in S. Anderson and K. Eliassen (eds), *Making Policy in Europe: the Europification of National Policy Making*, London, Sage, 1993, pp.173–88.
19 Ibid.

20 Butt Philip, op. cit.
21 King, op. cit.
22 P. Webster, 'Pasqua aiming for zero immigration', *Guardian*, 2 June 1993.
23 R. Cohen, *Frontiers of Identity: the British and Others*, London, Longman, 1994, p.179.
24 J. Carvel, 'Scheme to fingerprint aliens bolsters fortress mentality', *Guardian*, 21 June 1994.
25 S. Ellwood, 'Spain is different', unpublished paper presented to conference on Racism, Ethnicity and Politics in Contemporary Europe, held at the European Research Centre, Loughborough University, 24–6 September 1993.
26 Butt Philip, op. cit.
27 Ellwood, op. cit.
28 Soysal, op. cit.
29 S. Castles and M. Miller, *The Age of Migration: International Population Movements in the Modern World*, London, Macmillan, 1993, p.199.
30 Butt Philip, op. cit.
31 Z. Layton-Henry (ed.), *The Political Rights of Migrant Workers in Western Europe*, London, Sage, 1990.
32 Butt Philip, op. cit.
33 M. Martiniello, 'Citizenship of the European Union: a critical view', in R. Bauböck (ed.), *From Aliens to Citizens*, Aldershot, Avebury, 1994, pp.29–47.
34 Castles and Miller, op. cit.
35 T. Hammar, *Democracy and the Nation State: Aliens, Denizens and Citizens in a World of International Migration*, Aldershot, Avebury, 1990.
36 Martiniello, op. cit.
37 D. Cinar, 'From aliens to citizens. A comparative analysis of rules of transition', in Bauböck, op. cit., pp.49–72.
38 Castles and Miller, op. cit.
39 A. Smith, 'National identity and the idea of European unity', *International Affairs*, 1992, 68: 55–76.
40 M. Baldwin-Edwards and M. Schain, 'The politics of immigration: introduction', *West European Politics* 1994, 17: 1–16.
41 Castles and Miller, op. cit.
42 A. Ålund and C. Schierup, *Paradoxes of Multiculturalism: Essays on Swedish Society*, Aldershot, Avebury, 1991.
43 Castles and Miller, op. cit.
44 C. Husbands, 'Crises of national identity as the "new moral panics": political agenda-setting about definitions of nationhood', *New Community* 1994, 20(2): 191–206.
45 The imperial model of citizenship defined 'belonging to the nation' in terms of being a subject of a ruling imperial power, thereby securing the integration of different peoples within multi-ethnic empires. See Baldwin-Edwards and Schain, op. cit., p.11, for a brief discussion of the imperial model.
46 The 1971 UK Immigration Act defined patrials as people with substantial personal connections with the UK through birth or descent. As such, they were free from immigration controls and entitled to British citizenship. To qualify, it was sufficient to have had at least one grandparent who was a British citizen.
47 M. Mitchell and D. Russell, 'Race and racism', in P. Brown and R. Sparks (eds), *Beyond Thatcherism*, Milton Keynes, Open University Press, 1989, pp. 62–77.
48 Husbands, op. cit.
49 Mitchell and Russell, *Race and Racism*, op. cit.
50 P. Weil and J. Crowley, 'Integration in theory and practice: a comparison of Britain and France', *West European Politics* 1994, 17: 110–26.

51 R. Brubaker, *Citizenship and Nationhood in France and Germany*, Cambridge, MA, Harvard University Press, 1992, p.179.
52 M. Silverman, *Deconstructing the Nation: Immigration, Racism and Citizenship in Modern France*, London, Routledge, 1992, p.167.
53 Brubaker, op. cit., p.148.
54 Ibid., p.160.
55 S. Wayland, 'Mobilising to defend nationality law in France', *New Community* 1993, 20: 93–110.
56 Brubaker, op. cit., p.171.
57 D. Thränhardt, 'Germany: an undeclared immigration country', *New Community* 1995, 21: 19–36.
58 Brubaker, op. cit., p.172.
59 Ibid., pp.173–4.
60 Ibid., p.177.
61 A. Tomforde, 'Kohl's partners in brave show of unity', *Guardian*, 15 November 1994 and also 'Kohl's allies duck citizenship issue to preserve coalition unity', *Guardian*, 12 November 1994.
62 Ibid.
63 Brubaker, op. cit., pp.183–4.
64 Ibid.
65 Ibid., p.180.
66 McGrew, op. cit. Also P. Schlesinger, 'Europeanness: a new cultural battle-field?', in J. Hutchinson and A. Smith (eds), *Nationalism*, Oxford, Oxford University Press, 1994.
67 W. Wallace, 'Rescue or retreat? The nation state in Western Europe, 1945–1993', *Political Studies* 1994, 42: 74.
68 E. Balibar, 'Es gibt keinen Staat in Europa: racism and politics in Europe today', *New Left Review* 1991, no. 186: 5–19.
69 For a discussion of the concept of European racism, or Euro-racism, see: Balibar, op. cit.; A. Sivauandan, 'Editorial', *Race and Class* 1991, 32: v–vi; and F. Webster, 'From ethnocentrism to Euro-racism', *Race and Class* 32: 11–18.
70 For example, the far-Right parties in Germany and Italy have been unable to reach agreement on a political strategy for the South Tyrol. It is for this reason that the Italian far-Right members of the European Parliament have refused to join the Technical Group of the European Right, the formal grouping of far-Right MEPs.
71 C. Wilpert, 'The ideological and institutional foundations of racism in the Federal Republic of Germany', in Wrench and Solomos, op. cit., pp.67–81.
72 In the aftermath of the 1994 election, the victorious Christian Democrats proposed to extend the possibility of acquiring German citizenship to third-generation descendants of Turkish migrants. However, this proposal was subsequently shelved due to opposition from within the ruling coalition, especially from the Bavarian CSU.
73 For example, the 1988 Education Reform Act prescribes that pupils should take part in a daily act of collective worship at school that is wholly or mainly Christian in character.
74 These have been suggested as criteria for assessing 'Britishness' by, respectively, Norman Tebbitt and Enoch Powell.

SELECT BIBLIOGRAPHY

Baldwin-Edwards, M. and Schain, M. (eds) (1994) *The Politics of Immigration in Western Europe*, London, Cassell.

Baubök, R. (ed.) (1994) *From Aliens to Citizens: Redefining the Status of Immigrants in Europe*, Aldershot, Avebury.

Brubaker, R. (1992) *Citizenship and Nationhood in France and Germany*, Cambridge, MA: Harvard University Press.

Castles, S. and Miller, M. (1993) *The Age of Migration: International Population Movements in the Modern World*, London, Macmillan.

Cohen, R. (1994) *The Frontiers of Identity: The British and Others*, London, Longman.

Collinson, S. (1995) *Europe and International Migration*, London, Pinter.

Husbands, C. (1944) 'Crises of national identity as the "new moral panics": agenda-setting about definitions of nationhood', *New Community* 20, 191–206.

Lewes, B. and Schnapper, D. (eds) (1994) *Muslims in Europe*, London, Pinter.

Miles, R. and Thränhardt, D. (1995) *Migration and European Integration: the Dynamics of Inclusion and Exclusion*, London, Pinter.

Silverman, M. (1992) *Deconstructing the Nation: Immigration, Racism and Citizenship in Modern France*, London, Routledge.

Smith, A. (1991) *National Identity*, Harmondsworth, Penguin.

Waever, O., Buzan, B., Kelstrup, M. and Lemaitre, P. (1993) *Identity, Migration and the New Security Agenda in Europe*, London, Pinter.

Wrench, J. and Solomos, J. (eds) (1993) *Racism and Migration in Western Europe*, Oxford, Berg.

Part II

NATIONHOOD AND NATIONALISM IN WESTERN EUROPE

4

RECONSIDERING 'BRITISHNESS'

The construction and significance of national identity in twentieth-century Britain

Kenneth Lunn

All the England players whom I would describe as foreigners may well be trying at a conscious level, but is that desire to succeed *instinctive*, a matter of biology? There lies the heart of the matter.[1]

This concluding sentence in Robert Henderson's article in *Wisden Cricket Monthly* sparked off a fierce debate not simply within the confines of the cricketing fraternity but on a number of related issues concerned with national identity. Henderson's piece, ostensibly an analysis of recent failures by the English cricket team, had focused on the selection of 'non-English' players (i.e. those born outside Britain or who were of Commonwealth descent), and suggested that they might lack the necessary commitment to achieve the highest success on the field. Henderson's conclusion, however, that 'Englishness' was something innate or even genetic, produced accusations of racism and heated discussion about the implications of his ideas beyond the cricket field.[2]

Henderson himself widened his discussion by introducing the notion of 'post-imperial myths of oppression and exploitation', which he felt may have influenced those 'foreign-born' English players and the general tone of his argument drew attention to the construction of national identity and of so-called national loyalty. Over the last twenty years, such questions have been foregrounded on a number of occasions. The Falklands War and the Gulf War have been well-documented locations for the employment of a rediscovered sense of 'national' triumph, which has at times spilled over into xenophobic and racist rantings. However, the longer-term trend has been the inexorable decline of Britain's status as a world power, in political and diplomatic circles. The break-up of the Eastern bloc and the relative eclipse of the Soviet Union has not noticeably created space in which Britain's political power has been resurgent. Participation within a

European context still remains a hotly contested issue, both within the controlling Conservative Party and among other political groupings. Fierce critics on the political Right may have created local difficulties within Conservatism but there has been a groundswell of support for the line of argument which they produce. Great concern is frequently expressed about the loss of British sovereignty which seems implicit in a greater acceptance of European integration. One writer in *The Salisbury Review* referred to 'Maastreachery'[3] – the signing-away of British independence by acceptance of measures of European legislation. Paul Johnson, a somewhat individualistic writer in terms of traditional political location, has seen the European issue as similarly reflecting the betrayal of British sovereignty and identity by 'the Vichy regime in Westminster and Whitehall'.[4] Publicly expressed fears of 'Europeanisation' have focused attention very powerfully on the impact of such a political direction and has clearly indicated the political potential of support for such a perspective.

It is also clear that, alongside this diplomatic and political decline, there is a shrinking of the financial and manufacturing role for Britain within the global economy. Despite protestations by successive Conservative governments, the economic realities of changes in the worldwide structures are well rehearsed. The impact of this has certainly been felt in the restructuring of the British economy, which has now been 'trimmed' to meet what has been defined as the new economic reality for Britain. The political and social tensions of this restructuring remain a constant divisive factor and have raised new questions about the coherence of British society in the light of the very wide economic, cultural and social gulfs which have been added to by this economic experience.

In addition, fears about the dilution of British stock have re-emerged as a significant political issue. As with concern about Britain's political and economic status, this is hardly a feature unique to the late twentieth century. Similar voices were raised at the turn of the century over Jewish immigration and, since the 1950s, concerning 'New Commonwealth' settlers. However, the breaking down of European frontiers has, as in other states on the Continent, provided political space for right-wing Tories and others to raise alarms about the threat of illegal immigration, ostensibly in terms of the drain on economic resources but also in terms of the cultural threats of an increasingly multi-ethnic society towards the British 'way of life'. Such views about the impact of 'New Commonwealth' immigration are already commonplace and thus are reinforced by this newly perceived threat caused by closer ties with Europe.

Not only has immigration and/or ethnic origin been defined as a challenge to British national identity but there is also a sense in which the very nature of 'Britishness' has come under question. In part, this stems from the recent electoral political configuration of the United Kingdom where, as David Marquand has pointed out, Conservative hegemony no longer exists outside England. Scotland, Wales and now Northern Ireland have all rejected the particular brand of Conservative politics which is currently on offer.

> The Tories' historic vocation as the party of an imperial state and United Kingdom is now exhausted. The Union still exists, of course, and the Tories still defend it. But the more vigorously they fight for it, the less they embody it.[5]

Detailed consideration of the forces lying behind Scottish and Welsh voices of separate identity and drives towards forms of independence and devolution must lie with other commentators. The work of Morgan and Williams on Wales and McCrone *et al.*[6] on Scotland are some of the best examples of such analyses. Above all, what has emerged in the last twenty years is further evidence of the cultural and political divisions long present within the geographical concept of Britain and a reflection of the growing politicisation of that fragmentation. Indeed, as part of a reaction to the rejection of Conservative values outside England, there has been a reassertion of calls for English nationalism. These have been largely from the radical Right of the political spectrum. Thus, in *The Salisbury Review*, Raymond Tong called for a declaration of English independence, partly as a response to the political situation outlined above but also as a reaction to the perceived devaluing of English patriotism over the course of the twentieth century.[7] Similar sentiments were advanced by Paul Johnson's argument that 'There is no such thing as Britishness'.[8] His response to calls for schools to instruct pupils with a sense of Britishness was to focus on the different forms of national identity within Britain. In a somewhat idiosyncratic way, he labelled Scottish and Welsh nationalism as 'natural' phenomena, forged out of 'alien oppression'. In contrast, 'Englishness' was indefinable, often indescribable, felt rather than constructed. Until recently, Johnson maintained, 'Englishness' was also uncelebrated but contemporary events were now bringing out more overt declarations of English pride and identity.

It is not necessary to agree with the political posturing of Johnson in order to recognise the significance of social and economic fragmentation of British society. The concept of national identity has been shaken by events both within Britain and outside and its value as a political symbol, often unstated, has once more become publicly contested. Much of the contemporary sociological and political analysis of what constitutes 'Britishness' has been concerned with the underlying tensions of the concept and at the exclusion clauses, written or unwritten, which accompany any notion of national identity. One major failing, however, of the general nature of much of this writing is its use of 'history'. Reference is frequently made to the historical formation of national identity and to the use of the past in contemporary constructions of Britishness. These are, however, often uncritical assumptions about that history, about the imagery of the past which is so frequently drawn upon to help create the present. It is, like 'Englishness', taken for granted. What we need to recognise is that national identity has always been a constructed identity and that we need to move beyond a simplistic evocation of historical identity to acknowledge the constancy of active formation and reformation. Furthermore, it was always selective. Paul Johnson's recipe for teaching Englishness to schoolchildren was to make them read more history. 'It is all there, in Holinshed and Clarendon, in Macaulay and Carlyle, in Trevelyan and Arthur Bryant'.[9] But clearly, it is not all there; the writers listed provide nothing like a comprehensive history of England and Englishness. They contribute towards the mythology of identity which draws on a particular version of the past.

Thus, we need a much more thoughtful perspective on the processes of the construction of national identity, both for contemporary Britain and for the past. It is vital to see 'the past' as the location of dynamic processes and to help formulate an understanding of current debate about perceived crises of national identity through the perspective of historical exploration.

Before looking more specifically at historical construction of national identity in Britain, it is salutary to examine the language and imagery of much of the defensive rhetoric of Englishness in contemporary debate. In perhaps the most often cited phraseology, designed particularly to reassure those who feared a swamping of British culture as a result of European integration, Prime Minister John Major offered his vision of an England (albeit defined as Britain) which would always exist. He spoke of warm beer, of cricket on the village green, of spinsters cycling to evensong and other particularly rural images which represented, at least for his particular political purposes, the vision of the England he wished to protect. There is also a feeling among commentators within a particular age group that there has been a significant change in the nature of British identity. As Alison Light notes, there is a 'farewell tone' in much of the contemporary political analysis.

> Is it because we are really at the end of that Englishness, that voice and grammar which drew so much on histories of imperialism and whose modern transformations, which carried such authority between the wars, are now finally exhausted? . . . Is indeed the very idea of an English nationality . . . inevitably tinged with the elegiac? Is it because we are watching the collapse of so many of the sodalities and solidarities which this century has created, and of the epistemological frameworks which gave us collective forms of belonging and belief, that even a history of conservatism must become an epitaph?[10]

For Light, the personal sense of loss, even of an unacceptable form of Englishness, colours the way in which political analysis is constructed.

Whatever the particular nature of the angst which leads to such pondering of national identity, the link with an historical imagery is apparently unavoidable. Responses to the political crises have sought to draw upon a specific version of the past in order to attempt to make sense of the present. This approach inevitably calls to mind vividly the analysis of Eric Hobsbawm and Terence Ranger.[11] As Hobsbawm points out, 'invented traditions' seek to establish continuity with a suitable historic past.

> It is the contrast between the constant change and innovation of the modern world and the attempt to structure at least some parts of social life within it as unchanging and invariant, that makes the 'invention of tradition' so interesting for historians of the past two centuries.[12]

John Major's attempt to resurrect a particular version of an England in order to occupy a political position in a contemporary debate is merely one recent effort in what has become a tradition in its own right.

From these strands identified above, it is clear that public versions of 'Britain' are constructions, achieved in a number of ways and using a variety of social, cultural and political techniques. They are significant in that they operate at a series of levels and fulfil a range of functions. They work not merely at the level of identifying and stereotyping a particular image of Britain and Britishness but, in the process, they actively exclude other possibilities, other versions of Britain. This can take a number of forms.

The use of the term 'English' as a synonym for 'British' is more than just a slovenly application of the word. It represents a series of assumptions about the natural right of England to speak for Britain and, by the imposed silence, the inability of Welsh, Irish and Scottish voices to challenge effectively those assumptions.[13] It reproduces the imperial philosophy in which the mother country represented the greater whole. The imagery need not be produced in an overtly conscious way. As Colls and Dodd suggest in ironic fashion, 'The English do not need nationalism and do not like it; they are so sure of themselves that they need hardly discuss the matter.'[14] However, as Linda Colley and others have recently shown,[15] there are complex processes behind this apparently effortless façade. In order for the English swan to glide serenely across the water, a considerable amount of furious beneath-the-surface paddling is required.

We can also locate the ways in which images of Britain sought to challenge the reality of social and economic divisions within the country. Clearly, this is not a revelation in theoretical terms but it does provide a valuable exercise to determine the nature of the ways in which images are selected, presented and then exclude other versions of that identity. For a social historian, it is the fragmentation of British society which is often the focus of analysis; the powerful rhetoric of national unity is, therefore, conspicuous by its articulation and needs to be related very firmly to the context within which it is developed.

The more usual approach to the study of these themes is to highlight the construction of these very positive and clear views of Britain in time of crisis. Reference has already been made to the Falklands conflict of the 1980s. Equally, we could refer to the literature on both World Wars and the formal attempts by the State to create a propaganda of unity to better implement the war effort.[16] Other conflicts, such as the 1956 Suez Crisis, have, no doubt, a similar significance in terms of the restructuring and restatement of British identity. However, the deconstructing of such public images is already taking place. Angus Calder's *The Myth of the Blitz* goes a considerable way to unpacking the cosy images of war-time consensus. If this can be done for the period in which the full range of state apparatus was brought to bear on the process of presenting a united front, then similar critical analysis ought to be applied to other eras.

In this case, it is to the 1930s, a period of what has been fashionable to identify as an age of political and social tranquillity, despite the traumas of unemployment, depression and earlier characterisation of ideological conflict that attention is directed. Having first established that the decade reveals a complexity of divisions, attention will then focus on the way in which certain perceptions came to be foregrounded more than others. Little of what is presented in this piece can be said to represent path-breaking new research. What it does offer is an attempt to draw together a range of material and interpretations on images of Britain in the 1930s. These concentrate on images created for public consumption, on what is not offered as well as what is. In this way, it is intended to reflect the cultural, political and social diversity of British society and to indicate the significance of attempts to homogenise those experiences.

Discussions on the nature of inter-war British society have tended in recent years to revolve around the optimistic/pessimistic approaches. Recent historiography has veered towards the former; major revisions to the gloomy picture of the Depression years seem to have developed first in the field of economic history, with an emphasis on 'new' industries and aggregate statistics. This encouraged a rethinking of the social and political dimensions of Britain in the 1930s with fairly consistent attempts to stress the overall lack of conflict during these years. Emphasis has been placed on the moves towards a standardised and homogeneous culture, rising living standards and wider patterns of consumption for the majority and on the political marginalisation of 'extremes' – communism and fascism.

In such a debate, the previous foregrounding of certain contemporary commentators has also become marginalised. In these writings, attention had been drawn to the inequalities between different groups. Gaps between the employed and the unemployed, status differences within the middle classes, regional variations in terms of identity and culture were all stressed. Particular focus was directed on the impact of long-term and structural unemployment, the decline of staple industries and the localised impact of such economic patterns. The writing was often emotive but then such situations produce these kinds of passionate response. Perhaps with some validity, the dominant historiography now questions the validity of these sources as a major element in any analysis of the inter-war years. It seeks to highlight other sources which refer to improved living standards for those with regular incomes and other positive indicators of the optimistic school's interpretation.

Thus, writers like J.B. Priestley and George Orwell, along with a host of other commentators and survey compilers, have been neglected by many historians writing in the 1980s and 1990s. This reflects a tendency to neglect an analysis based on 'multiple identities', in spite of its fashionability in theoretical terms, and to emphasise the 'British' experience and the drive towards homogeneity. In truth, of course, few historians pursue one or other of these routes exclusively but as an overall shift of emphasis, the notion of a British identity and its construction in the 1930s has been a concern of history-writers since the early 1980s.

It is, therefore, appropriate to return to sources such as Priestley and Orwell to remind ourselves of their arguments, since these may have become lost in the revisionist scramble. We also ought to recognise the relative scarcity of certain kinds of critical analysis for the inter-war years. Light has drawn attention to the disinterest of many literary figures in the Britain of the 1930s. British life was seen as unchallenging and emasculated. 'Abroad' was exciting and contrasted with the mundanity of Britain. 'Driven into exile, many modernist prophets and minor cognoscenti lament both the proletarianisation and the domestication of national life.'[17] However, it is still useful to re-evaluate the analyses which were produced at the time.

Priestley's *English Journey*, published in 1934 following his travels of the previous year, has often been cited as a yardstick of social and economic differences in 1930s Britain. His reflections on the existence of three Englands and on the complexities of Englishness have been powerful testimony for many historical analyses. These three nations – the first, 'Old England, the country of cathedrals and minsters and manor houses and inns, of Parson and Squire; guide-book and quaint highways and byways England',[18] the second, 'the nineteenth-century England, the industrial England of coal, iron, steel, cotton, wool, railways'[19] and the third, 'the new post-war England, belonging far more to the age itself than to this particular island'[20] – in turn comprised the mosaic of British life which could be held up against the uniform image sometimes presented.

Priestley also noted, however, the power of forces within the 'New' England driving towards conformity, homogeneity and a lack of spontaneity, all aspects of modernism which he clearly despised, often in somewhat patronising tones. Significantly, he also suggested that patriotism had become a force which could disguise or push to one side the significance of the social and economic divisions he had identified. What he called 'Big Englanders' – 'red-faced, staring, loud-voiced fellows, wanting to go and boss everybody about all over the world, and being surprised and pained and saying, "Bad show!" if some blighters refused to fag for them'[21] – were the objects of his scorn. He felt that their championing of a British identity, often constructed in opposition to 'abroad' and to 'foreigners' was at the expense of more critical review of British society, and expresses the view, 'I wish their patriotism began at home, so that they would say – as I believe most of them would if they only took the trouble to go and look – "Bad show!" to Jarrow and Hebburn'.[22]

Orwell also identified a fragmented Britain, at least in terms of economic divisions, but noted that a sense of national identity could preclude its impact. In *The Lion and the Unicorn*, he was very clear about the vast discrepancies in economic terms.

> There is no question about the inequality of wealth in England. It is grosser than in any European country, and you have only to look down the nearest street to see it. Economically, England is certainly two nations, if not three or four.[23]

However, the passage continues with an indication of the powerfulness of a sense of common national identity.

> But at the same time the vast majority of the people feel themselves to be a single nation and are conscious of resembling one another more than they resemble foreigners. Patriotism is usually stronger than class-hatred, and always stronger than any kind of internationalism.[24]

Orwell made much of the 'unconscious' aspects of this patriotism and the instinctive nature of what he defined as English characteristics. He felt that 'the intellectuals' of the time had not been able to analyse successfully this instinct and thus had been unable to challenge it. He made political assessments about the 1930s based on this 'naturalistic' approach.

> However much one may hate to admit it, it is almost certain that between 1931 and 1940 the National Government represented the will of the mass of the people. It tolerated slums, unemployment and a cowardly foreign policy. Yes, but so did public opinion.[25]

This unproblematic approach to 'public opinion' may be contested, but what Orwell's writings do is identify the importance of any construction of national identity in an understanding of the social and political history of the period.

One recent area of research of relevance to a discussion of public opinion must surely be the cinema. Given its well-documented impact on the Britain of the 1930s, with massive audience figures for weekly attendance, careful analysis of output by film companies and distributors and assessments of audience demand and responses, conclusions about the role of the cinema in the construction of a particular British identity ought to be forthcoming. However, in any analysis of the role played by the cinema in constructing images of Britain, it is vital to identify the different components. Considerable attention has been given in the academic literature to the documentary movement, which has often been seen as the creator of a social realist series of images of Britain.

In the arts, it was very much an era of realism – of the Left Book Club and committed left-wing poetry, of Mass Observation and massively detailed social realist novels like those of J.B. Priestley, A.J. Cronin and Winifred Holtby. The only intellectually respectable area of the cinema was the documentary movement.[26]

The verdict of the 'left-wing British film culture'[27] of the 1930s reflects an evaluation of the main products of commercial cinema in Britain. A significant element of criticism was the British cinema industry's failure to project any realistic visions of Britain. As J. Richards says, '[i]f there was one thing that critical opinion was agreed about in the 1930s, it was the almost total absence of the reality of contemporary British life from the mainstream British cinema'.[28]

Richards provides ample evidence of the extent to which this realist element was lacking until 1938 or 1939. Even then, films like *The Citadel*, *The Stars Look Down* and *The Proud Valley*, all set in industrial South Wales and attempting to engage with the realities of economic and social life in that setting, left out elements of contemporary political debate. There is little or no reference to nationalisation or union activity, for example.[29] In addition, they reinforced a very stylised and limited characterisation of the Welsh which gave no attention to the nature of Welsh society. As Stead comments, '. . . much of the dialogue and characterisation are hopelessly stylised and provide an early example of the caricatured way Welshness was to be depicted in British films for the next twenty years'.[30]

The contemporary criticism was not simply that few attempts were made to portray the 'real' Britain but that feature films rarely made any effort to promote aspects of British life at all. Sir Stephen Tallack, Secretary of the Empire Marketing Board, produced in 1932 a pamphlet, 'The Projection of England', calling for 'a fitting representation of England' to be presented and then provided a check-list of the elements of this 'acceptable face'.

At one end of the spectrum are to be found, I suppose, such national institutions and virtues as:

The Monarchy (with its growing scarcity value)
Parliamentary Institutions (with all the values of a first edition)
The British Navy

The English Bible, Shakespeare and Dickens
In international affairs – *a reputation for disinterestedness*
In national affairs – *a tradition of justice, law and order*
In national character – *a reputation for coolness*
In commerce – *a reputation for fair dealing*
In manufacture – *a reputation for quality*
In sport – *a reputation for fair play*

At the other end of the spectrum might be found such events as *The Derby* and the *Grand National, The Trooping of the Colour, The Boat Race, Henley, Wimbledon, Test Matches* and the *Cup Final*. But between these two extremes comes a medley of institutions and excellencies, which every man may compile for himself according to his humour and his ingenuity. My own list would include:

Oxford and *St Andrews*
Piccadilly, Bond Street, Big Ben and *Princes Street, Edinburgh,*
The English countryside, English villages, the English home and *English servants*
The Lord Mayor of London
The Times, Punch and the *Manchester Guardian*
The Metropolitan Police and *Boy Scouts*
The *London omnibuses* and *Underground Railways*
Football and Foxhunting
English bloodstock and *pedigree stock*
The arts of *gardening* and of *tailoring*.[31]

As Richards notes, this was a 'class-biased image', reinforcing the notion of an absence of social realism. But, as he also suggests, this vision of a 'sympathetic and patriotic depiction of British institutions and British character' received general support in both the popular press and the popular film press, who endorsed this kind of output. Thus, when British films did focus on British themes, they tended to reinforce a particular set of values and identity, often far removed from the series of multiple identities which could be said to exist in Britain at this time.

There is one further area of cinema output which is often neglected in the consideration, and that is newsreels. Considerable attention has been devoted to the impact of cinema output, including newsreel, in Nazi Germany and, to a lesser extent, fascist Italy, in terms of constructing a political consensus but the theoretical and critical approaches have not been applied in any significant way to British newsreels. And yet, as Nicholas Pronay wrote over twenty years ago:

They are important historical evidence which deserves study. Not as records of events, but as records of what a very large, socially important and relatively little documented section of the public saw and heard, regularly from childhood to middle age.[32]

His general thesis is that newsreels produced in the 1930s actively sought to promote particular images of Britain, ones which reinforced what the companies felt much of the audience wished to see. Specifically, Pronay sees the newsreels as supporting a vision of Britain which was 'decent'. In so doing, they tended to emphasise what might be termed a consensus view of Britain:

> The newsreels laid stress on the points of similarity, identity of outlook and interest between the world of the government and that of their working-class regulars. Above all, they stressed the points of consensus rather than the points of conflict. The majority of newsreel editors, it should be added, did so by inclination as well as necessity.[33]

What was offered to the viewing public was not, however, 'real':

> The newsreels made much of their depiction of actuality and competed with each other to be as up-to-date as possible: signature tunes, background music, very official-sounding commentators and bold captions were all used to heighten the tension and to create a sense of journalistic urgency and yet, in reality, they hardly dealt with contemporary issues at all.[34]

A brief survey of newsreel production of the later 1930s gives a very clear idea of exactly how this was attempted. Above all, the newsreels sought to counter the impression of a depressed Britain and one which had lost its place in the world order. Thus, emphasis was placed on British successes, at sport, in economic terms and in both domestic and international politics.

In the sporting world, British triumphs in tennis, motor-racing, swimming, golf and cricket in particular were consistently paraded in front of the viewers. Occasionally, a note of triumphalism was directed at opponents from other nations who had been defeated. Thus, in the coverage of the 1934 Derby, the British winner defied 'foreign invasion'. Motor-racing, particularly the numerous attempts on the land-speed record by Malcolm Campbell, was a major element of the coverage. Indeed, it was Campbell's charismatic image which led to his appointment as editor of British Movietone News in 1935, where he displayed the 'bravery, technical know how and gentlemanly conduct of the Englishman'.

In economic terms, the newsreels sought to promote the images of British technical and industrial achievement and to repulse notions of decline. The stress was also upon industrial peace and cooperation, with examples of improved working conditions such as new canteens and leisure facilities at work and on the growing impact of paid holidays for many workers.

Politically, as has already been suggested, it was consensus rather than conflict which was the overwhelming emphasis. This effect was often achieved by highlighting the tensions and conflict abroad with the alleged calm of British domestic politics. 'Politically, the newsreel companies contented themselves with support for the king and his government and with general remarks about the British genius for avoiding confrontation.'[35] In this project, newsreel companies and politicians were as one. There has been some debate as to the party-political bias displayed by the newsreel companies. Both Gaumont British and British Movietone are commonly cited as being particularly sympathetic to Conservative aims in the 1930s and it does seem clear that the Conservative Party saw the usefulness of the cinema as a medium of political propaganda.[36] However, as with much propaganda, the more effective communication was through the less overt articulation of a wider political conception, which happened to meet immediate party needs as well.

For example, in the later 1930s, with a constant stress on war in Spain and Palestine, conflict in Central Europe, the contrast with a peaceful and stable British scene was vividly presented by the newsreels. Prime Minister Stanley Baldwin echoed this approach in a November 1936 special message for newsreel showing. Having identified the problems 'abroad', he noted the tranquillity of British society where the 'people as a whole have never been more prosperous, better cared for and more contented'. Although admitting that, in 'certain districts', there were still some difficulties (presumably a reference to massive regional unemployment in the 1930s), the social services were said to be expanding all the time. This assumption that the economic dislocation of the inter-war years could be reduced to a little local difficulty and dealt with by 1930s welfare provision certainly does not correspond to much of the historical analysis of the period, although the creation of such an image was an important aspect of consensus politics at this time.

It is at this stage that we can note the linkages between this kind of emphasis in a particular newsreel presentation and the emergence of a new version of British/English identity in the post-First World War years. Alison Light has identified what she calls 'conservative modernism',[37] a phenomenon which was neither the 'overtly politicised high Toryism' nor 'the supremacist glorification of nationhood which had inspired the imperialist endeavour in the late nineteenth century'. What was emerging was a more inward-looking form of Englishness: a notion of the English as 'a nice, decent, essentially private people'.[38] This new form of identity need not conflict with the older perspectives identified above. Indeed, it was their interaction, the process of reforming of identity, which was important in this period.

Baldwin's role in the construction of a 'conservative' vision of England has been acknowledged by various commentators. He first appeared in newsreels in 1923[39] and made a number of contributions drawing on a vision of England and Englishness which contributed towards a particular political construction. 'The constant harping on England and the English character in his speeches was gradually assimilated into a more general argument in favour of the national government.'[40] Thus, as Ramsden argues:

> This verbal picture of a sensible and moderate people united behind their government, true to their historic traditions, was one that Baldwin put across at every opportunity. In the gloomy Britain of the thirties it was no doubt a reassuring message, and one that many of the electorate accepted, but it was also greatly reinforced by the sight and the sound of Baldwin himself, almost the incarnation of this simple, no-nonsense message.[41]

Similarly, Malcolm Smith has claimed that Baldwin was, on newsreel, 'the bluff country squire' who 'lauded the commonsense of the British way, condemned the politics of division and the extremism of other countries, congratulating a weekly cinema audience of anything up to seventeen million on being British'.[42] Smith goes on to suggest that what he calls 'newsreel Toryism' was 'suprapolitical' but such an approach gives too much focus on 'political' as a party concept. The use of such imagery is very much part of a wider political agenda, where the impression of non-sectarianism is skilfully woven into a particular discourse, the aim of which is to disguise social and economic divisions. This vision of a 'commonsense' conception of Englishness/Britishness, one which had little need of explanation or analysis, was clearly an effective political strategy, both in the party-political sense and in a wider hegemonic process which sought to eclipse any attention on the internal divisions within the nation-state.

What is still lacking, however, in the conventional historiography is any significant attempt to explain the ways in which Conservative (and conservative) hegemony operated in the 1930s. Explanations tend to rest on the deficiencies of other parties and some tacit notion about the essential commonsensical political or, perhaps more appositely, non-political character of 'the British'.[43] Little space has been given to the positive ways in which such notions were constructed and reconstructed. As Light argues, 'conservatism, of the lower-case variety, has been even more unaccounted for (than the ideological constructs of the Conservative Party)' and calls it 'one of the great unexamined assumptions of British cultural life'.[44] Given the centrality of the idea of nationhood in conservative values, it is clearly important in this context to challenge such an assumption.

As part of this attempt to evaluate, the importance of the label 'non-political' needs to be established. This explanation, if it can be called that, for the effectiveness of a conservative and Conservative hegemony deserves closer attention, more than this current study can offer. As illustrated, the impact of Baldwin's vision of England was enhanced by its apparent non-sectarian or party identity. For such an approach to be effective, it has to be reinforced by wider social attitudes and responses to the concept of 'political'. Contemporary commentators remarked upon the decline of a political consciousness. Priestley was among those who perceived such a trend, saying '[a] great proportion of the English electorate is probably becoming less and less politically minded. . . . People are beginning to believe that government is a mysterious process with which they have no real concern.'[45]

One could question whether there ever had been the kind of politicised nation on which such a comparison was based but his essential point about a lack of overt political challenge to a status quo is worth pursuing. Priestley himself could carry the argument even further.

> Monotonous but easy work and a liberal supply of cheap luxuries might between them create a set of people entirely without ambition or any real desire to think and act for themselves, the perfect subjects for an iron autocracy. There is a danger of this occurring in the latest England. Unlike nineteenth-century England, it is not politically minded.[46]

Again, it is not necessary to accept all the implications of Priestley's comments but they do focus on particular aspects of inter-war Britain which are hardly challenged by the more mundane historical analysis of that period.

It is possible to see a change in the emphasis of British identity in this new conservative mould but also to recognise its continuities with the past. Nowhere is this more apparent than in the evocation of an historic past and an idealised future which lay in the pastoral vision. While the images of Britain promoted in the newsreels were sometimes industrial, as has already been indicated, when the full force of patriotism was being enthused, the tendency was to return to a more mythical vision. The associations of justice, military defence, politicians and monarchy were held to constitute the core values of a British identity. However, the actual images which bound these core elements bore little resemblance to the 'social realist' Britain. 'This England', produced by Gaumont British in April 1939, as an introduction to coverage of the war budget, is perhaps the most extreme example of this presentation. It opened with St George, mounted on a charger, across the introductory titles and the commentary highlighted the yearly miracle of Spring and the 'quiet and gentle beauty' of the British countryside. The idyllicism continued with reference to the metaphoric calm, 'so rooted in the sanity of the solid earth'. Specifically, it was to rural Kent that the newsreel first turned, with its leafy winding lanes, where the only traffic noise was the creak of a farm cart, 'challenged by the impetuous chatter of a stream'. The audience is then transported to

Shakespeare country, Anne Hathaway's cottage and Shakespeare's school, again symbolic of 'this England that we hold so dear'. Shots of children dancing on a village green and Union Jacks being unfurled to the tune of 'Jerusalem' played by a brass band then cut to footage of a misty river scene and then a stately country home. The whole of this rural idyll quite blatantly draws on an imagery of Britain which has immensely powerful evocations for much of the audience and which has served as a very effective counter to 'abroad' but also to the other 'Britains' which were in existence in those years.

The emphasis on the 'rural' in the inter-war years has in some senses been very clearly identified. Stevenson and others have drawn attention to the concern with the leisure and health potential of the countryside, with the establishment in 1926 of the Council for the Preservation of Rural England (CPRE) and the growth of leisure pursuits like cycling, hiking, camping and youth hostelling in the inter-war years.[47] 'Hiking and rambling boomed, particularly in the 1930s, when they combined a cult of healthy athleticism with the deep-seated fondness for the countryside which operated powerfully in British culture.'[48] However, the focus on the countryside in these years is a more complex phenomenon than the mere provision of a safety-valve for anxieties about the unhealthiness of urban living. It came to serve as the symbol of British historical identity. As Patrick Abercrombie, whose pamphlet 'The Preservation of Rural England' led to the establishment of the CPRE, wrote, 'the greatest historical monument that we possess, the most essential thing which is England, is the Countryside, the Market Town, the Village, the Hedgerow Trees, the Lanes, the Copses, the Streams and the Farmsteads'.[49] Such an image also provided a counterbalance to the increasingly apparent social and economic divisions in Britain. This notion of a British/English identity has been very clearly articulated by Alun Howkins' work:

> Since 1861 England has been an urban and industrial nation. The experience of the majority of its population is, and was, that of urban life, the boundaries of their physical world defined by streets and houses rather than fields or lanes. Yet the ideology of England and Englishness is to a remarkable degree rural. Most importantly, a large part of the English *ideal* is rural.[50]

However, as Howkins suggests, this ideal was not simply a vision of the idyllicism of the countryside, it also represented a model of society: 'an organic and natural society of ranks, and of inequality in an economic and social sense, but one based on trust, obligation and even love – the relationship between the "good Squire" and the "honest peasant"'.[51] For Howkins, this model was particularly powerful during the First World War, when it may have served very effectively to draw together the fighting forces of officers and men across the class divide but it could equally be said to represent the ways in which such imagery might be promoted to breach the social divisions of inter-war Britain.

What seems to emerge, then, from this somewhat peremptory sketch of national identity and its significance is a recognition first and foremost of the power of any notion of Britishness in this period. Its particular construction in these years may well have produced significant changes in emphasis, as Light's work on 'conservative modernism' has suggested, and further work on other aspects of the processes whereby a sense of Britishness was asserted as part of a dominant but discrete political discourse is clearly required. What is also suggested, however, is that, even while this modernisation of national identity was under way, there were retreats into the age-old symbolism of rural Britain, where fewer questions about the sense of identity and its origins were required.

Indeed, it seems remarkable that, at the end of the twentieth century, and following an intense period of radical political and economic change instituted by successive Conservative governments, the image of English-ness evoked remains significantly rural and replicates the hierarchical values of previous societies. It raises all kinds of questions about the depth and impact, in ideological terms, of what has become known as 'Thatcher-ism'. In the last twenty years, at times of particular economic or political crisis, it was these deep-seated and mythological images which provided the kind of security and justification for the political direction which had become apparent in the inter-war years. While it would be naive to make direct comparisons between the 1930s and the 1980s and 1990s, there are interesting parallels in the dialogues over national identity. What is clear are the ways in which a dominant sense of Britishness is a manufactured product, engineered to appeal to something far more profound and deep-seated than much of the parliamentary rhetoric and party frothings. The retreat in the 1990s to a vision of England and of Englishness which are in many senses mythological is an indication not merely of the barrenness of contemporary political discourses in dealing with concepts of national identity but of the powerfulness of the historical making of what passes for that identity.

NOTES

1 R. Henderson, 'Is it in the blood?', *Wisden Cricket Monthly* 1995, July 10.
2 "'Unequivocally English"'', *Runnymede Bulletin* 1995, no. 287 July/August: 3.
3 *Salisbury Review* 1993, 12 (1): 16–17.
4 P. Johnson, 'Being English is getting a lot of laughs when others would merely see oddness verging on lunacy', *Spectator*, 5 August 1995: 21.
5 D. Marquand, 'Flagging fortunes', *Guardian*, 3 July 1995.
6 K.O. Morgan, *Wales 1880–1980: Rebirth of a Nation*, Oxford, Oxford University Press, 1982; G.A. Williams, *When was 'Wales': a History of the Welsh*, Harmonds-worth, Penguin, 1985; D. McCrone, S. Kendrick and P. Straw (eds) *The Making*

of Scotland: Nation, Culture and Social Change, Edinburgh, Edinburgh University Press, 1989.

7 'The English Dimension', *Salisbury Review* 1994, 13 (1) September: 14–17.

8 Johnson, op. cit., p.21.

9 Ibid.

10 A. Light, *Forever England: Femininity, Literature and Conservatism between the Wars*, London, Routledge, 1991, p.19.

11 E. Hobsbawm and T. Ranger (eds), *The Invention of Tradition*, Cambridge, Cambridge University Press, 1983.

12 Ibid., p.2

13 See H. Cunningham, 'The Conservative Party and patriotism', in R. Colls and P. Dodd (eds), *Englishness: Politics and Culture 1880–1920*, Beckenham, Croom Helm, 1986, pp.283–307.

14 'Preface' in ibid.

15 L. Colley, *Britons: Forging the Nation 1707–1837*, New Haven, CT, Yale University Press, 1992. See also K. Robbins, *Nineteenth-Century Britain: England, Scotland, and Wales: The Making of a Nation*, Oxford, Oxford University Press, 1988.

16 See, for example, the recent study, D. Morgan and M. Evans, *The Battle for Britain: Citizenship and Ideology in the Second World War*, London, Routledge, 1993.

17 Light, op. cit., p.7.

18 J.B. Priestley, *English Journey*, London, Heinemann, 1934, p.397.

19 Ibid., p.398.

20 Ibid., p.401.

21 Ibid., p.416.

22 Ibid.

23 G. Orwell, *The Lion and the Unicorn: Socialism and the English Genius*, London, 1941, Penguin edition, 1982, p.48.

24 Ibid.

25 Ibid., p.51.

26 J. Richards, *The Age of the Dream Palace: Cinema and Society in Britain 1930–1939*, London, Routledge, 1984, p.4.

27 Ibid.

28 Ibid., p.245.

29 P. Stead, 'Wales and film', in T. Herbert and G. E. Jones (eds), *Wales Between the Wars*, Cardiff, University of Wales Press, 1988, pp.168–71.

30 Ibid., p.172.

31 Quoted in Richards, op. cit., p.249.

32 N. Pronay, 'British newsreels in the 1930s: 2. their policies and impact', *History* 1972, 57: 72.

33 Ibid., p.67.

34 Stead, op. cit., p.163.

35 Ibid., p.165.

36 See, for example, T. Hollins, 'The Conservative Party and film propaganda between the wars', *English Historical Review* 1981, 96: 359–69.

37 Light, op. cit., p.11.

38 Ibid.

39 J. Ramsden, 'Baldwin and film', in N. Pronay and D. Spring (eds), *Propaganda, Politics and Film, 1918–45*, Basingstoke, Macmillan, 1982, p.127.

40 Ibid., p.140.

41 Ibid., p.142.

42 M. Smith, *British Politics, Society and the State since the Late Nineteenth Century*, Basingstoke, Macmillan, 1990, p.129.
43 See, as an example of such an approach, J. Stevenson and C. Cook, *The Slump*, London, Cape, 1977. Even the more recent K. Laybourn, *Britain On the Breadline: A Social and Political History of Britain between the Wars*, Gloucester, Allen Sutton, 1990, offers little definitive analysis of Conservative hegemony. M. Pugh, *The Tories and the People 1880–1935*, Oxford, Blackwell, 1985 has less than twenty pages on the period 1914–35.
44 Light, op. cit., p.14.
45 Priestley, op. cit., p.44.
46 Ibid., p.405.
47 On this theme, see S. Jones, *Workers At Play: A Social and Economic History of Leisure 1918–1939*, London, Routledge, 1986; F. Gloversmith (ed.), *Class, Culture and Social Change: A New View of the 1930s*, London, Harvester Wheatsheaf, 1980; A. Rogers, 'People in the countryside', in G. Mingay (ed.), *The Rural Idyll*, London, Routledge, 1989, pp.103–12.
48 J. Stevenson, *British Society 1914–45*, Harmondsworth, Penguin, 1984, p.392.
49 Quoted in P. Lowe, 'The rural idyll defended: from preservation to conservation', in Mingay (ed.), op. cit., p.121
50 A Howkins, 'The discovery of rural England', in Colls and Dodd (eds), *Englishness*, op. cit., p.62.
51 Ibid., p.80.

SELECT BIBLIOGRAPHY

Anderson, B. (1983) *Imagined Communities: Reflections on the Origin and Spread of Nationalism*, London, Verso.

Calder, A. (1992) *The Myth of the Blitz*, London, Pimlico.

Carter, E., Donald, J. and Squires, J. (eds) (1993) *Space and Place: Theories of Identity and Location*, London, Lawrence and Wishart.

Colley, L. (1992) *Britons: Forging the Nation 1707–1837*, New Haven, CT, Yale University Press.

Colls, R. and Dodd, P. (eds) (1986) *Englishness: Politics and Culture 1880–1920*, Beckenham, Croom Helm.

Corner, J. and Harvey, S. (eds) (1991) *Enterprise and Heritage: Cross Currents of National Culture*, London, Routledge.

Fulbrook, M. (ed.) (1993) *National Histories and European History*, London, UCL Press.

Light, A. (1991) *Forever England: Femininity, Literature and Conservatism between the Wars*, London, Routledge.

Samuel, R. (ed.) (1989) *Patriotism: The Making and Unmaking of British National Identity* (3 volumes), London, Routledge.

Samuel, R. and Thompson, P. (eds) (1990) *The Myths We Live By*, London, Routledge.

5

NATION, NATIONALISM AND NATIONAL IDENTITY IN FRANCE

Brian Jenkins and Nigel Copsey

France was a 'state' long before it became a 'nation'. The image of an historic community of native Gauls and Franks, contained within 'natural' frontiers and conscious of their collective identity since the time of Clovis, is a retrospective myth. In fact it was only through a long process of conquest and annexation that the Capetian and Valois kings gradually extended their realms beyond the Parisian heartland of the Ile de France into Normandy, Aquitaine, Burgundy, Provence, and Brittany. By the mid-sixteenth century, they had incorporated most of the territories of the modern 'hexagon', with the exception of Basque and Catalan enclaves in the south-west, Nice and Savoy in the south-east, and Alsace-Lorraine in the east. Even then, however, France remained a loose amalgam of provinces with long and vulnerable land frontiers, a semi-feudal patch-work of local customs and loyalties, geographically and linguistically diverse, riven by religious and social wars. It was only with the emergence of the absolutist monarchy of the seventeenth and eighteenth centuries, with its centralised royal bureaucracy and professional standing army, that the process of nation-building truly began.

STATE AND NATION

In one respect, absolutism may be seen as a necessary compensation for France's ethnic and cultural heterogeneity. The centralised royal state set out to unify and defend a fragile territorial 'empire'. For all its organ-isational defects, the administrative and judicial apparatus was, in the context of the time, vast and tentacular, extending its influence to every corner of the realm and attempting to regulate religion, language, artistic expression, business and access to the professions. As de Tocqueville famously argued,[1] 'the Great Revolution failed to dismantle this cen-tralised edifice, and instead inherited it, bequeathing it in turn to Napoleon who gave it its definitive modern shape. In the nineteenth century it survived wars, revolutions, and changing regimes, and with the eventual victory of liberal democracy in 1870 achieved popular sanctity as the 'one and indivisible French Republic.'

This centralising tradition was sustained by a continuing sense of the fragility of French nationhood. A history of war and foreign invasion engendered constant anxiety about the vulnerability of borders and the centrifugal tendencies of peripheral regions. Similarly, France's geographical and cultural diversity was further compounded by the political and ideological divisions of the Revolution, and successive regimes saw the centralised state as a necessary antidote to the disintegrative forces at work in civil society. The omnipresence of central administrative power, both civil and military, and the tutelage it exercised over local government through the office of the *préfet*, made the French state an increasingly important reference point in the lives of ordinary people.

However, the identification between 'state' and 'nation' could not be accomplished until the mass of the population felt involved in the public life of the collectivity. The beginnings of this process are, of course, commonly located in the revolutionary decade (1789–99), which undoubtedly drew huge numbers of peasants and townsfolk into sustained political activity for the first time, and raised the ideal of popular citizenship. Nevertheless, as one author has recently observed, 'sovereignty was transferred from the king, whose powers were in many respects fictional, to the nation, whose very definition was no less a work of political imagination'.[2] From this perspective, the political battles of the first seventy years of the nineteenth century were essentially contests for control of the state between rival *minorités agissantes*, urban rather than rural, Parisian rather than provincial, leaving large swathes of the 'backward', parochial countryside untouched.

As we shall see, this is an unwarranted generalisation, but it underlines a further historical characteristic of the French state, namely its emergence as a primary channel for social advancement. The origins of this process are again to be found in the absolutist state which, in Colin Mooers's formulation, offered the nobility an economic alternative to seigneurial rent in the form of office-holding financed by royal taxation.[3] The rising bourgeois middle classes were equally tempted by this avenue of social promotion, and the status conferred by public service deflected energies away from the capitalist transformation of 'civil society' well into the nineteenth century. This in turn left large sections of the rural population trapped in a subsistence economy, socially and culturally isolated from the mainstream of 'national' life.

By the same token, however, the activities of the centralised state apparatus were truly 'national' in scope, and thus it was precisely among the wealthy and educated ranks of office holders and place seekers that a rudimentary sense of 'nationhood' began to take root. And when the absolutist system entered its period of financial crisis in the 1780s, and was no longer able to satisfy bourgeois demands for a dwindling supply of titles and offices, it was in these same circles that the great Enlightenment debates were launched about the nature of political authority, about the state's relationship with the 'social orders', and eventually its relationship with the 'nation'.

Precocious ideological 'modernity' thus coexisted with relative economic 'backwardness', and this is crucial to understanding the character of nation-state formation in France. The process was predominantly a *political* one involving the gradual penetration of civic values into the countryside where the mass of the population lived. Initially, under the Restoration and Orleanist monarchies (1815–48) this was largely the work of *minorités agissantes* inspired by republican or indeed Bonapartist ideals, struggling to dislodge habits of rural deference and passivity. But once the masses gained permanent access to the political process, with the granting of universal male suffrage in 1848, the state itself began to play a more active role in the integration of these new 'citizens' and the cultivation of national unity.

The decisive phase came with the establishment of the Third Republic, a liberal parliamentary democracy which finally gave substance to the exercise of political and civil liberties. In a regime based on the social compromise of bourgeois and peasant property rights, and which significantly increased the representative weight of rural and provincial France, the age of mass politics truly dawned. It is against this background that the 'nationalising' influences of mass schooling, military conscription and the 'delayed' railway revolution played such a decisive role, turning 'peasants into Frenchmen' in Eugen Weber's famous phrase.[4] By 1914, only 3 per cent of conscripts could neither read nor write, and the use of standard French was ruthlessly imposed by primary schools and other state agencies at the expense of local dialects and languages. The teaching of civic (and, for boys, military) virtues replaced religious education, and the symbolism of tricolour, *Marseillaise* and Bastille Day reaffirmed the identity of the 'citizen' nation. Finally, growing national sentiments were inevitably sharpened by memories of defeat in the 1870–1 Franco-Prussian war, by bitterness at the loss of Alsace-Lorraine, and by the hope of eventual *revanche*, feelings which the Republic turned to good effect in pursuit of national unity.

There were, of course, limits to this process of assimilation. The *bourgeois* character of the Republic prevented it from fully integrating the interests of the industrial working class, as reflected in the regime's meagre record in the field of social welfare and labour legislation before 1914. This left many workers feeling excluded from the national community, despite their possession of *formal* citizen rights. Arguably, it was only with the social reforms that followed the Liberation in 1944 that the working class truly developed a sense of membership of the 'nation'.[5] An even more glaring domain of 'exclusion' was the denial of political, and indeed some civil, rights to the female half of the population. The gender history of French nationhood remains to be written, but inevitably women's confinement to a domestic role made them more parochial and traditional in their political attitudes, and the eventual granting of the suffrage in 1945 was only the first stage in their conquest of citizenship. In this respect their situation is analogous to that of many non-European immigrants who, having gained citizen status through the relatively liberal 1945 nationality code,[6] none the less find their formal rights undermined by social prejudice and economic disadvantage.

This last point underlines the limitations of a largely political and state-induced sense of nationhood. There is the danger that it will remain something of an abstraction, imposed from above and therefore potentially alienating, unless reinforced by deeper processes at work in 'civil society'. In France, formal citizenship was achieved in a country where the relatively slow pace of capitalist transformation had left local and regional loyalties deeply entrenched. It is, of course, true that France's economic 'retardation' was indeed only 'relative'; that urbanisation, industrialisation and the transport 'revolution' changed the lives of millions of French people in the course of the nineteenth century; that peasant smallholders were increasingly drawn into commodity production. But the fact remains that in 1911 56 per cent of the nation still lived in the countryside, and 42 per cent of the working population were still engaged in farming. And though by then 'peasants' had allegedly been turned into 'Frenchmen', rural and urban society often remained culturally distinct, and Paris remained for many provincials the distant embodiment of an invasive and meddlesome 'state'.

A second danger of politically defined nationhood is its capacity to *divide*. Of course, the practice of citizenship may produce no more than a bland 'state patriotism' (Hobsbawm's phrase), that growing popular sense of 'having a stake in the country' which developed in Western Europe before 1914, and which tragically allowed the 'citizen-masses' to be plunged by the ruling classes into the 'mutual massacre of World War I', in the belief that they were thereby defending hard-won civic rights.[7] However, this 'integrationist' perspective must be qualified by other considerations. In a country where history has been as divisive and conflict-ridden as that of France, it is likely that even the most 'innocent' national sentiments may become politically 'charged'. National identity has long been a contested area, where rival ideologies define the 'nation' in radically different ways. And while this more politicised discourse – the realm of *nationalism* proper – has usually been the preserve of *minorités agissantes*, it may gain a wider popular resonance in moments of crisis when the very legitimacy of the State is called into question. In a history punctuated by revolution and war since 1789, France has known many such moments, and has seen the language of nationhood appropriated successively by Left and Right.

NATIONALISM: IDEOLOGY AND CONFLICT

The great dates in France's revolutionary calender – 1792, 1848, 1871 – confirm the resilience of a popular democratic tradition, fostered by the radical republican movement, which first linked the concept of 'nation' with the sovereign rights of the 'people', and in its name challenged both 'traitorous' domestic élites and the 'reactionary' powers of *Ancien Régime* Europe. Of course, whatever the mobilising power of such appeals to *la volonté générale* in times of crisis, the notion of a socially undifferentiated 'Third Estate' was already illusory in 1789, and was even more so in 1848 as France's uneven capitalist development increasingly divided the interests of workers, middle classes, and peasants.[8] But the powerful association between radical democratic aspirations and the defence of national sovereignty survived this process of class differentiation. In 1871, the largely working-class Paris Commune claimed to embody the 'nation' in its patriotic opposition to the armistice signed with the victorious Prussians, and its demands for a popular 'social' democracy. And seventy years later, in the resistance struggle against the Nazi occupation and Vichy collaborationism, communists and socialists effectively recaptured the language of nation from its long association with the Right, and again wedded it to a vision of democratic renewal and social justice.

Of course, the Great Revolution eventually gave birth to a different brand of nationalism, in the form of Bonapartism, which survived Napoleon's fall in 1815 and enjoyed a dynastic 'second coming' with Louis Napoleon's 1851 *coup d'état*. Both 'Empires' followed periods of intense revolutionary upheaval and division, and are normally seen as an 'exceptional' form of authoritarian state, capitalising on political deadlock and exhaustion, and seeking to reconcile conflicting social interests in a period of 'consolidation'. In this context, the unity of the 'nation' was incarnate in the plebiscitary authority of the leader and a dynamic modernising state. The quest for national 'glory' (whether military or economic) replaced mass political participation as a mobilising theme, and social egalitarianism was expressed through a meritocratic technocracy rather than through representative institutions.

However, despite the significant differences between these two traditions, they were both viewed as anathema as by the Catholic royalist élites which dominated France under the Restoration and Orleanist monarchies (1815–48). Both radical republicanism and Bonapartism were associated with 'dangerous' egalitarian ideas, and with a war-threatening challenge to the European settlement of 1815. The traditional Right was thus deeply suspicious of the whole concept of 'nation', and its power to mobilise the political aspirations of the 'masses', preferring instead to rely on the traditional patterns of social deference and political passivity which persisted in much of rural France.

The great sea-change which saw nationalism shift from Left to Right in the closing years of the century must be set in its broad historical context. The impact of socio-economic change and the advent of mass politics under the Third Republic had undermined the traditional social hierarchy in the countryside, and weakened the hold of deferential values associated with royalism and Catholicism. The conservative Right was thus forced to compete more actively for mass support and to seek a clearer ideological identity. At the same time, with the establishment of the Republic, democratic nationalism lost much of its mobilising power on the Left to become an 'integrative' ideology associated with the consolidation of the republican state.[9] The growing socialist and labour movement increasingly abandoned the language of 'nation' in favour of an appeal to the international solidarities of class. In this respect, ideological 'space' was opened up for a conservative reworking of nationalist discourse.

Initially, however, this new nationalism was born not in conservative circles, but in the populist challenge mounted against the Republic in the late 1880s by the so-called *Boulangist* movement.[10] Opportunistically backed by royalists, the social foundations of General Boulanger's campaign were essentially urban, *petit bourgeois* and plebeian. It fed on the fears bred by economic insecurity, on frustrated hopes of *revanche* against Germany, and its appeal was eclectic, addressed to all those who felt marginalised by the political and economic liberalism of a 'bourgeois' parliamentary Republic. Its ambiguous blend of aggressive militarism, political authoritarianism and social egalitarianism not surprisingly attracted the rump of the Bonapartist movement, but it also won temporary support among radical-republicans and socialists.

In the course of the 1890s, however, this body of ideas became more firmly anchored on the Right. While the theme of *revanche* provided a powerful external focus, the essence of the new nationalism lay in its redefinition of membership of the national community. The inclusive territorial notion of open citizenship was replaced by the concept of an ethnic homeland defined by culture and race. Anti-Semitism was a central mobilising theme, fuelled by the recent wave of immigration from Eastern Europe. But the language of exclusion encompassed all those whose political or religious affiliations were deemed a threat to the unity of the 'nation' – Protestants, free-masons, liberal intellectuals, 'international' socialists. This 'proto-fascist' nationalism established an ideological tradition which has resurfaced in different guises according to historical circumstance – the leagues of the 1930s, the Vichy regime, the 1950s Poujadist movement, the Front national.[11]

The broad ranks of the traditional Right were not immediately amenable to this kind of populism, and indeed they would never entirely endorse its more radical features. However, for Catholic conservatives who had accepted the Republic only grudgingly, and who had never entirely embraced the democratic ideal, the theme of national unity provided a powerful new discourse for discrediting their enemies on the Left. In the divisive era of the Dreyfus Affair, radicals and socialists would be berated for undermining the authority of two key institutions of French national identity, the Army and the Church. And in the run-up to the First World War, liberals, pacifists and international Marxists would be accused by an increasingly bellicose conservative Right of dividing and weakening the nation in the face of the 'hereditary enemy'.

By 1914, therefore, every political tradition from extreme Left to extreme Right had at some time or other presented itself in nationalist colours, and the elements of an historical pattern become visible. On the Left, revolutionary democratic nationalism was watered down into the integrative consensus-building ideology of the liberal bourgeois Republic, which claimed to have completed the work of 1789 and to have established equal citizenship. On the Right, the new 'integral' populist nationalism was adapted into a distinctly conservative ideology, which remained hostile to the 'excesses' of parliamentary democracy and anti-clericalism, more attached to the 'real' France of traditional rural values than to the 'legal' France of the Republican state, but none the less increasingly implicated in the institutions of the regime.

On both Left and Right, therefore, nationalisms that were developed in opposition to the established political order were appropriated and transformed to purposes of social integration and stabilisation. What still divided them was often more symbolic than real, feeding on historical enmities rather than on substantive policy differences. The separation of Church and State in 1905, and the growing acceptance by much of the moderate Right of the parliamentary Republic, should logically have effected a reconciliation. There was little to separate the Centre Left radicals from conservatives in their willingness to go to war in 1914, and both were equally committed to the defence of bourgeois property rights against the growing challenge from the socialist and labour movement. In this respect there was a convergence of these two 'state nationalisms' in their joint insistence on the primacy of 'national' loyalties over those of 'class'.

However, the ideologically charged climate of the 1930s reasserted the Manichean divide between Left and Right, and increasingly evacuated this centre ground. The twin threat/temptation of communism and fascism, and growing disaffection towards the parliamentary Republic, led to a genuine crisis of national identity, as rival ideologies battled to appropriate France's past. And when the regime collapsed in 1940 in the wake of military defeat, the core values of Left and Right were reasserted with extraordinary force by the minorities who actively collaborated or resisted.

The nationalism of the Vichy regime blended a profoundly anachronistic nostalgia for the pre-democratic, pre-industrial France of *Travail, Famille, Patrie* with the anti-Semitic populism of the extreme Right, while the Resistance movement revived the revolutionary-democratic tradition of national liberation and social emancipation last exemplified in the Paris Commune of 1871.[12]

NATION AND NATIONALISM IN THE POST-WAR ERA

The question of state legitimacy would never be posed in quite such dramatic terms again, nor would the issue of national identity ever again be so sharply and clearly polarised between Left and Right. Vichy's *Révolution nationale* was quickly disowned by its erstwhile devotees, and while the Resistance Charter inspired the post-Liberation social and economic reforms, it never fulfilled its dream of a great united, independent, egalitarian democracy. In the post-war period, France faced a profoundly changed and changing world in which its role and status were uncertain. These new international realities transcended the traditional ideological battles of *la guerre franco-française*, and blurred the classic distinctions outlined in the previous section. The rebuilding of Europe, the onset of the Cold War, the implications of bloc politics, the decolonisation process, created multiple divisions within the French political community and contributed to the destabilisation of the Fourth Republic.

Nationalism in the 1950s was largely driven by responses to external events, and fed on the frustrated hopes of national regeneration born in the Resistance and Liberation. The Gaullism of the RPF (1947–53) may have recalled the authoritarianism and anti-parliamentarism of the Boulangist tradition, but it was also a product of its time, and of its leader's very personal vision of national *grandeur* and independence. The French Communist Party was equally keen to exploit its new patriotic Resistance credentials, increasingly equating its 'class' aspirations with the struggle to free the French 'nation' from its dependence on 'international capitalism'. Despite their mutual antagonism, these two forces converged around the themes of anti-Americanism, resistance to European 'supranationalism' and opposition to German rearmament. They were later joined on the terrain of nationalism and hostility to the Fourth Republic by the Poujadist movement (1954–8), whose defence of small-business interests reflected above all a nostalgic attachment to a traditional France threatened by rapid economic and social modernisation.

However, across the middle ground of Fourth Republic politics – conservatives, Christian democrats, radicals and socialists – the nation-state became a less important ideological reference point in the new climate of the Cold War. Here, anti-communism (whether 'capitalist' or 'democratic' in its rationale) denoted an alignment with 'the free world', support for the supranational bloc architecture of the Western Alliance, and France's increasing integration into the free-market structures of the Western economy. The 1950s debates on European institutions and on German rearmament thus tended to unite the nationalist 'extremes' against the pro-European and Atlanticist 'centre'.[13] In this respect, the ideological specifics of rival nationalisms were less salient than the policy issues which drew them together, and the common theme that France was increasingly losing control of its own destiny.

On the other great external issue of the time, France's relationship with its colonial empire, neat ideological distinctions are equally problematic. While in both the Indo-China and the Algerian wars there was a degree of polarisation between Right and Left, between proponents of a 'military solution' and advocates of a negotiated settlement, all sections of France's mainstream political community found it hard to accept the legitimacy of national liberation movements in the colonies. Indeed, it was a socialist-led government in 1956 which intensified the military pacification effort in Algeria, and while communists opposed the war, their attitude to the cause of the Algerian national liberation movement remained highly ambivalent. The notion that France had a 'civilising mission' in the world, that 'citizenship' of the French empire offered colonial peoples their best hope of emancipation, was widely shared across the political spectrum, as was the belief that holding on to Algeria was crucial to the maintenance of national status.

The various 'nationalist' positions adopted in the 1950s thus confirmed the existence of a common core of beliefs which transcended the differences between nationalisms of Right and Left – namely the conviction that France was an exemplary nation with a world role. It was on this basis that, with the advent of the Fifth Republic, de Gaulle was able to construct a synthesis which neutralised many of the classic contradictions between Left and Right views of the nation. His reputation as a conservative and anti-communist disarmed the opposition of many who would otherwise have resisted his granting of Algerian independence, and his endorsement of state-led economic and social modernisation. And his pursuit of an independent foreign and defence policy within the broad framework of the Western Alliance and the EEC gave a measure of satisfaction both to convinced Atlanticists and Europeanists, and to those like the communists who welcomed de Gaulle's occasional flourishes of anti-Americanism.

Internally too, de Gaulle laid the foundations for a broad constitutional consensus, thereby reducing the ideological ferocity of *la guerre franco-française*. By bringing rebellious elements of the French Army in Algeria under civil control between 1958 and 1962, he effectively ended the Army's intermittent role ever since Boulanger, as an institutional pole of attraction for those who opposed the authority of the French Republic. More significantly, he created a presidential regime which neutralised the traditional anti-parliamentarism of elements on the Right, and which eventually proved sufficiently 'democratic' to reassure most of its opponents on the Left.

With the consolidation of the Fifth Republic, therefore, it seemed that French national identity had become more consensual and less problematic than ever before. The political symbolism of nationhood had lost much of its power to divide, and France appeared to have come to terms with its status as a middle-ranking power. That introspective obsession with national decline, which had so often fuelled the nationalism of both Left and Right, had been replaced by a view of France's role in the world which was both more optimistic and more realistic.

Similarly, the profound social changes wrought by France's post-war economic modernisation appeared to have created a more homogeneous national community. Rapid urbanisation and industrialisation, the extension of mass education, the communications 'revolution' and the advent of a secular 'consumer society' might be expected to have ironed out cultural differences based on region, class and religion.[14] The presidentialism of the Fifth Republic was widely seen as the apotheosis of this modernisation process, the final stage in the 'nationalisation' of political life.[15]

Towards a new crisis of national identity?

However, the synthesis achieved under de Gaulle has proved fragile in the light of subsequent developments. Gaullist 'nationalism' was built on something of a contradiction, in the sense that although its objectives may have been pragmatic (to reconcile the French people to a changed world order), it achieved this rhetorically by exaggerating the degree of autonomy enjoyed by the French state. The discourse of national *grandeur*, the symbolism of the 'independent' nuclear *force de frappe*, and the self-assertive idiosyncrasies of Gaullist foreign policy, tended to disguise the realities of 'super-power' politics and the constraints imposed by France's alignment within the 'bloc' system. Similarly, de Gaulle's determined use of the state as an agency for economic modernisation and for the defence of French business interests obscured the fact that the national economy was becoming increasingly integrated into the structures of world capitalism, through the liberalisation of trade and the increasingly transnational character of financial and industrial operations.

If this latter process was well under way in the 1960s, it accelerated in the 1970s under the impact of the world recession. In all advanced capitalist countries, the efficacy of state economic planning was further undermined by international uncertainties, and the spiralling costs of the public sector became unsustainable – the so-called 'crisis of big government'. Keynesian-style interventionism was increasingly challenged by new neo-liberal and monetarist doctrines, whose adoption in turn hastened the processes of economic internationalisation. Of course, the attendant social tensions kept protectionist and interventionist reflexes alive, but only in France did they bring into power a government of the Left with a distinctly nationalist programme of economic regeneration.

George Ross has described this programme as 'Chapter Two of the Resistance Charter',[16] and it certainly shared many of the priorities of the Liberation reforms – nationalisation, the commitment to social welfare and workers' rights, economic planning, the promise to 'liberate' France from its dependent status within the new 'international division of labour'. The attempt to recreate the discourse of the previous phase of socialist–communist collaboration in power (1944–7) always lacked conviction, and it is doubtful how far the Resistance-style rhetoric of national liberation (and the equation of Giscard's economics with 'Vichyite' defeatism) still had any real popular resonance. The failure of this so-called 'Keynesianism in one country', and the speed with which the socialists embraced a more liberal market-oriented policy in line with international constraints, quickly revealed the illusions of this nationalist posture.

The proven irrelevance of this Left version of nationalism confirmed something that was already becoming evident in the heyday of Gaullist nationalism some fifteen years earlier. Namely there was a widening gap between what was *promised* in the name of national self-assertion, and what could actually be *delivered*. Furthermore, the tendency in both versions (as in so many other variants of nationalism in French history) to equate *nation* with *state* meant that the perceived decline in the autonomy and influence of the state had profound repercussions on national identity itself. The effects of economic globalisation, of the widening realm of supranational decision-making, of France's integration into the burgeoning structures of the European Union, have imposed external constraints on an increasing number of policy areas. And while the end of the Cold War has created new sources of tension between nation-states, it has also removed some of the classic reference points for nationalist ideology. The anti-communism which traditionally underpinned right-wing nationalism has lost all credibility, while the anti-Americanism on which both Left and Gaullist nationalisms fed has only a residual cultural appeal in the 'new world order'. In short, the dwindling autonomy of the nation-state has weakened the credibility of national*ism* as a political programme.

The problem is exacerbated by the decline of other collective solidarities through which a sense of nationhood was mediated. Institutions like the Catholic Church and the army, which used to embody key national values for many on the Right, have lost much of their status and influence, and this is mirrored on the Left by the dwindling mobilisational appeal of the trade unions, the Communist Party, or indeed the secular *Ecole republicaine*. The weakening of identities based on class or religion, formerly so divisive, might be seen as contributing to a more comfortable sense of nationhood, based on pluralism and tolerance.[17] However, the process is equally likely to involve atomisation and growing *anomie*, an ethos of individualism whose victims feel socially marginalised and excluded.

This brings us back to the dangers of a state-led process of nation-formation, which under different regimes sought to impose the prevailing state ideology on to a recalcitrant 'civil society'. This reluctance to accept the cultural diversity of the nation, this 'assimilationist' instinct with its emphasis on universal values, may in the past have served to cement national loyalty. However, this centralising tradition becomes a handicap when the political credibility of the nation-state is itself called into question. The status of *regional* identity in France is a case in point. In as far as the republican state sought to eradicate regional particularism in the interests of a homogeneous national political culture, the danger is that once the legitimacy of the central state is weakened, the cultural 'cement' which held the nation together will disintegrate. The Jacobin tendency to see regional and local sentiments as inimical to national loyalties, rather than as essential components of nationhood, ultimately becomes counter-productive in this new setting.

However, the emphasis placed by most historians on the leading role of the state in the process of French nation-formation needs to be qualified in certain respects. Regional identity, far from having been eradicated, remains resilient, and may comfortably coexist with wider loyalties. Caroline Ford has recently argued in a case study of Brittany, that an acute sense of cultural difference, and a strong regional attachment to Cath-olicism (often deemed 'anti-national'), did not in the long run work against the development of a sense of nationhood.[18] Through a process of negotiation with the Centre, national allegiances were resisted, then appropriated and transformed in line with regional values. This argues in favour of a different conception of the 'nation', seen less as a culturally homogeneous unit shaped by state ideology than as a 'framework' for political action, based on a multiplicity of identities (class, region, religion, ethnicity, gender). Sometimes, these other solidarities may conflict with or transcend national loyalties. On other occasions, they may be sub-ordinated to them. More often, however, this issue of 'choice' between competing allegiances will not arise.[19]

The events of May 1968 arguably gave expression to precisely this kind of pluralism. The essence of the May movement has often been seen as a challenge to centralisation and bureaucratisation, and it is no accident that, in its simultaneous rejection of the Gaullist state and the French Commun-ist Party, May 1968 targeted the two main contemporary incarnations of the Jacobin (and Bonapartist) tradition. And while the May events were linked, in George Ross's words, to 'a powerfully individualistic and anti-authoritarian cultural liberalism',[20] they also raised the prospect of new forms of *collective* solidarity. The rise in the 1970s of the so-called 'new social movements' (feminism, ecology, Third Worldism and, indeed, regionalism), the *autogestionnaire* theme of workplace democracy, the new vigour of *la vie associative*, all testified to the strong *communitarian* impulse of the May movement.

It is, of course, true that this optimism (some would say utopianism) has now been largely dissipated. The socialist programme of the early 1980s 'recuperated' many of these themes, but the reforms introduced (decentralisation, women's rights, worker representation, etc.) were too moderate to carry conviction. Indeed, the socialists' endorsement after 1983 of the cult of enterprise and the ethos of the market suggested that for them as much as for the Right, 'civil society' was above all the domain of economic individualism rather than that of social cooperation.

The effect has been to 'demobilise' civic activism, to sanction those consumerist forces which encourage the 'retreat into private life', and to promote that growing disillusionment with mainstream politics denoted by the so-called contemporary 'crisis of political representation'. Voting patterns in the late 1980s and early 1990s confirm this worrying trend – the unconvincing electoral performance of the main contenders for power,[21] the success of anti-system parties like the Front national and the Greens, the proliferation of electoral 'lists' based on local personalities and single-issue campaigns, the surges of support for political eccentrics like Philippe de Villiers or for media personalities like the entrepreneur Bernard Tapie and the tele-philosopher Bernard-Henri Lévy.[22] While the process has some way to go before it begins to resemble Italy's systemic crisis (see Chapter 8 in this volume), it would be complacent to ignore the symptoms.

GLOBALISM AND NATIONALISM

Here we come to the core of the 'post-modernist' analysis of the nation-state and its contemporary crisis. The nation-state is, in Touraine's words, 'the political expression of modernity', a complex system of cultural values and institutionalised norms 'oriented towards rational action'. Today, however, we are witnessing a growing disjunction between the institutional capacity of the nation-state to achieve rational objectives, and the continuing 'cultural' need for people to feel some sense of collective 'belonging'. On the one hand, identification with the 'nation' is being undermined by 'the internationalisation of mass production and mass consumption', and on the other individual and collective actors seek to defend 'a memory, a cultural heritage, and try to enhance personal freedom and creativity'.[23]

The potential dangers of this process are all too evident – on the one hand a descent into the ruthless 'rational' individualism of the international marketplace, and on the other a retreat into an 'irrational' collective counter-culture based on religious or ethnic exclusion. Touraine's solution reflects his conviction that 'there is no contradiction between national identity, European integration, and minority or regional rights'. As he puts it, 'we can no longer concentrate all aspects of our social and cultural life at the national level', rather we must learn 'to live simultaneously at various levels of political and social organisation'.[24]

This perspective, voluntarist rather than truly pessimistic, none the less acknowledges that the decline of the nation-state is fraught with dangers. Only five years earlier, Eric Hobsbawm had been more sanguine about this process, which he welcomed as possibly heralding the demise of nations and nationalism.[25] The contrast between the two viewpoints is not only a philosophical one, it also reflects a change of mood in the intervening period. The end of the Cold War, the revolutions in Eastern Europe, and the collapse of the bloc system were certainly dramatic confirmations of what Hobsbawm called 'the supra-national restructuring of the globe'. But the initial optimism which saw these events as opening the path to a 'common European home' and a 'new world order' has proved tragically misplaced. Rather than peaceful convergence around the themes of liberal democracy and market globalism, we have seen a process of destabilisation which has given the forces of 'nationalism' a new lease of life. While the effects have been most dramatic in the disintegrating state systems of former Yugoslavia and the former Soviet Union, within the European Union too there is a new scepticism about the efficacy of supra-national institutions and growing resistance to some of the implications of 'economic globalisation'.

In the case of France, adaptation to the realities of the post-1989 'new world order' has been particularly problematic.[26] The much-vaunted 'independence' of French foreign and defence policy was geared to the mechanisms of the Cold War, which allowed France to exploit the 'space' between the rival blocs. The collapse of this world system therefore threatened to expose the limitations of French claims to great-power status, and thereby to undermine a key component of France's restored 'national identity'. Of course, ever since the mid-1980s Mitterrand had embraced the cause of European integration, which provided France with an alternative vision of '*grandeur*' as the leader of an emerging new 'bloc', and in some respects the events in Eastern Europe vindicated this perspective. The collapse of communism nurtured the old Gaullist dream of a Europe 'from the Atlantic to the Urals', while the strengthening of the European Union appeared all the more necessary to contain the might of a reunified Germany.

However, the 'consensus' that seemed to be emerging around the European idea in the early years (1988–92) of the second Mitterrand presidency proved vulnerable. Opposition focused on the tensions between 'enlargement' and 'integration', on the choice between a wider 'confederal' *Europe des patries* and a closely integrated federal Union, on the so-called 'democratic deficit' of a bureaucratic Europe and the threatened loss of national sovereignty. This reflected growing unease at the prospect of German hegemony within the European Union, the fear that France's 'political' clout (the bomb) no longer measured up to Germany's 'economic' muscle (the mark) and growing political assertiveness. But it also reflected a phenomenon that has been more widely felt across the European Union in the wake of the new economic recession, namely the increasing resistance of the most vulnerable social groups to the forces of economic globalisation, and to a European supranationalism which threatens to remove the protective shield of the nation-state.

The 1992 referendum campaign on the Maastricht Treaty vividly recorded this shift in popular attitudes, as public enthusiasm for endorsement melted away through the summer to provide the barest majority (51.04 per cent) at the polls in September. Even more worrying was the gap that opened up between voters and politicians (in the June 1992 Congress of Parliament a mere 8 per cent of deputies and senators had voted against), and the gulf was particularly wide in the case of Jacques Chirac's neo-Gaullist party, whose electorate largely voted 'no' (67 per cent). The pattern that emerged over both Maastricht and the 1994 GATT negotiations was of a political mainstream (the conservative RPR–UDF coalition, the socialists) which is essentially 'globalist' (by resignation as much as conviction) and a disparate opposition represented by the Communists, the Greens and the Front national.[27] However, the pressures on the new president Jacques Chirac to placate his own electorate were already evident in his campaign commitments to a degree of economic interventionism,[28] in the hints of 'Euroscepticism' over progress to a single currency, and indeed in his early decision (July 1995) to resume French nuclear weapon tests in the South Pacific.

Populist flourishes like these, with nationalistic overtones, will no doubt continue to be part of the government's repertoire. So to, indeed, will policies designed to appease racist attitudes, as already indicated by the approach of both the Chirac (1986–8) and Balladur (1993–5) governments to the policing of immigrants and to the nationality code. Of course, it is not only the conservative Right that has succumbed to such pressures, nor can the trend be presented simply as a cynical attempt to steal the clothes of the Front national. The so-called 'ethnicisation' of social problems predates the rise of the Front national, and implicates not only the Giscard presidency (1974–81) but also the parties of the Left.[29] The temptation of a dangerous populism linking nostalgia for French *'grandeur'* with ethnic intolerance is ever present.

However, globalist pressures will continue to constrain policy options and impose pragmatic solutions. For this reason, 'nationalism' is no longer a credible basis for a political programme, but the decay of the nation-state will not be a comfortable experience. Hobsbawm may be right that nations and nationalism are 'no longer a major vector of historical development',[30] but until alternative institutional focuses for both political action and social identity are developed, the current pattern of deepening popular dis-illusionment with political leaders and processes is likely to continue. And this context, identified by Touraine and others as 'post-modernist', provides an appropriate framework for the analysis of that most virulent contemporary form of French nationalism represented by the rise of the Front national.

THE FRONT NATIONAL IN CONTEXT

Since its initial breakthrough in the 1984 European elections, the Front national (FN) has established itself as a resilient political force command-ing the support of 10–15 per cent of the French electorate. It is difficult to avoid the verdict that the resurgence of the extreme Right in France has resulted from a multi-faceted causal process involving, in the words of Hainsworth, 'a complex alchemy and conjuncture of variables'.[31] While it is tempting to agree with most commentators that no single factor accounts for the rise of the Front national, the danger of such an approach is that it may fail to locate the emergence of the FN in a manageable frame of reference.

Advantageously, the 'post-modernist' thesis avoids this pitfall by pro-viding a distinct context in which the revival of right-wing extremism in France can be conceived. To be fair, a number of commentators[32] have attempted to contextualise the FN in terms of the sociological framework of anomie. However, although this has been linked to a process of social and cultural 'deregulation' and 'disintegration', surprisingly little effort has been made to link this anomie concept to post-modernity.

It goes without saying, of course, that 'post-modernism' is a contentious term that elicits the most dissenting of voices. Its value, however, is that it serves to emphasise a significant transition in contemporary social, economic and political conditions. The expression 'post-modernism' will be used in this chapter to refer to an amalgam of features implicit in the terms 'post-industrialism', 'post-socialism' and 'post-colonialism'. Per-haps 'post-materialism' should also be added to this compound since it draws attention to plurality and to the emergence of 'new values' (even though 'post-materialist' values paradoxically chastise the crass con-sumerism of 'post-modern' society). The term 'post-modern' does not necessarily have to imply a decisive and comprehensive break with modernity as some protagonists in the debate suggest. Instead it could be taken as a transitional extension of modernity incorporating a series of unique transformations. Thus, in France, these transformations have contrived to produce a 'micro-crisis' of 'community consciousness' and individual identity, alongside and encapsulated within an overarching 'macro-crisis' of nation-state and national identity.

This 'micro-crisis', predominantly urban and finite, reflects a growing fragmentation of social life where the domain of the 'collective' has been deregulated by socio-economic change. The structural transformations associated with the advent of 'post-industrial' society – the decline of manufacturing, the rise of services and new technologies, mass un-employment and labour insecurity, the decay of working-class culture and institutions – have progessively eroded 'community', that subjective feeling of commonality based on shared meanings.[33] Consequently, a sense of identity, belonging and meaning must be sought elsewhere, and in the post-modern condition this universal need has to be largely satisfied through consumerism. However, this is problematic, not least because consumerism is typically competitive and divisive. Even if commodities can provide meaning, identity and prestige, as Baudrillard has alleged, this does not rule out the possibility that consumerism can be dysfunctional. Indeed, Baudrillard himself detects the potentiality of fatigue with con-sumerist demands leading to 'anomie in the society of abundance'.[34]

If we use Anderson's formula of nations as 'imagined communities', where the nation is subjectively conceived in terms of 'deep, horizontal comradeship',[35] then it is understandable why a crisis of 'community consciousness' in post-industrial France could make a revival in extreme Right nationalism possible. By default, the lack of alternative sources of communal identity (class, religion, occupation, kinship, etc.) necessarily strengthens the hand of nationalism. Significantly in France, this dis-solution of 'community consciousness' occurred at a time when, ironically, mainstream nationalisms were losing credibility. Fortuitously for Le Pen, the potentiality for nationalist mobilisation remained undeveloped by mainstream Right or Left as nationalist discourses of the Gaullist or 'Resistance-Liberation' type lost relevance in the early-to-mid 1980s. As these discourses withdrew from the foreground of French politics, space opened up for extreme Right nationalist mobilisation.

However, this still does not sufficiently account for the emergence of the Front national, because it is also significant that the urban areas of advanced industrial decline where the FN has enjoyed its greatest success are also multiracial constituencies (the Nord, Paris and its environs, Alsace-Lorraine, Lyon and the Mediterranean littoral). Here, 'post-industrialism' has combined with the effects of 'post-colonialism'. The term 'post-colonialism' refers to an inversion of the previous colonial relationship, where immigration replaces colonisation. As a result, as Silverman points out,[36] the old boundary distinction between 'here' and 'there' is broken down; 'there' is now 'here', and 'the other' (i.e. the 'enemy') is now within. Once this national boundary had been breached, the ideological dynamics of the 'colonial legacy' alongside the crisis of 'community consciousness' ensured that new symbolic boundaries were formed to delineate social space and create 'distance'. So in due course, the *bidonville* and the *ghetto* were packaged within the neo-racist symbolic discourse of the *seuil de tolérance*.[37]

This 'threshold of tolerance' theory, which posited that large concentrations of non-European immigrants should be avoided, achieved wide currency in the 1980s. It drew attention to the 'non-assimilable' difference of non-European immigrants and negatively equated such concentrations with a host of social problems. This 'problematisation' of non-European immigration fuelled anxieties about the effects of non-integration on social cohesion, and was translated into an introspective concern with 'safeguarding' French national identity from 'immigrant invasions'.

Significantly, this eagerness to 'preserve' French national identity, recently exacerbated by the collapse of Soviet communism, has redirected the confrontational axis from East–West to North–South, towards possible new adversaries on Europe's southern Islamic periphery. This directional shift draws sustenance from the perceived cultural distinctiveness of Islam and the emergence of fundamentalist forms. Internally, this confrontational axis defines attitudes at the neighbourhood level, where the dominant fear is that local 'immigrant invasion' will hasten the ongoing process of social fragmentation. Not surprisingly, it is often the case that FN voting is greatest on the periphery of the highest immigrant concentrations and this encirclement, which has been termed the 'halo-effect',[38] reinforces the anomie thesis and confirms that fragmentation of community is a prevailing anxiety. In such areas, 'micro-national' defence mechanisms at local level serve to compensate for the perceived weakness of nation-state boundaries. And in these areas where, typically, structural change has stripped away traditional solidarities, the creation of new boundaries based on 'ethnicity' provides a ready and accessible source of meaning and belonging. At the same time, however, resistance to immigrant 'incursions' reinforces the isolation of high immigrant clusters and this militates against future integration into French society.

This brings us to an essential point. The anomie engendered by post-industrialism and post-colonialism has been radicalised further by a 'macro-crisis' of the nation-state. Initially put under strain by mass migratory movements, the formal parameters of the French nation-state now appear to have depreciated further as a consequence of the transfer of political power, above to supranational institutions, and below to decentralised authorities. This fragmentation of power has produced a growing disjunction between nation-state and society, which has been aggravated further by post-socialist economic globalisation. With the definitive global victory of the market model, the function of the nation-state now becomes 'optimal insertion in the global economy'.[39] To achieve this, the nation-state reorientates itself towards inculcating society with an ethos of competitiveness. Yet, paradoxically, although this reorientation seeks to advance 'security' by maintaining and increasing living standards, in reality it induces insecurity by making employment precarious and by threatening social welfare. This was certainly borne out under Edouard Balladur's conservative coalition government (1993–5), whose economic measures (continuation of the 'strong franc' policy, economic restructuring, renewed attempts at privatisation, the miscarried plan to reduce the minimum wage for young workers, etc.) confirmed the political reorientation of the nation-state towards this global competitive role.

What we are left with is a post-modern phenomenon of a 'society without a shell'[40] where nation-state and society are being 'decoupled'. This 'parting of the ways' between society and nation-state means that the protective shelter provided for the former by the latter is dissolving. Society still expects the nation-state to 'deliver the goods' but its institutional capacity to meet this demand is being progressively undermined by the multiple processes of post-modernity. The reduced capacity of the nation-state to control and protect society engenders a crisis of national identity as society becomes exposed to diverse cultures, commodities, lifestyles and values which, in turn, threaten to overwhelm and dissipate indigenous cultural reproduction. Clearly, this 'decoupling effect' is a succourless development for those individuals affected by anomie. Having lost the security of intermediary sources of community (kinship, religion, class, etc.) this crisis of the nation-state and national identity can only reinforce the prevailing 'anomic' crisis of individual identity.[41]

In this environment, 'anomic' individuals may well countenance extreme authoritarian solutions of the kind promulgated by the Front national. In the eyes of the FN, it is all too obvious that the nation-state is neglecting its essential duties, that the boundaries of the nation-state must be forcibly reconnected to the 'French people', to a 'traditional', natural and homogeneous society uncomplicated by social and cultural diversity. This 'traditionalist' discourse (which perhaps conceals a more revolutionary, fascist agenda) is arguably the key to the FN's attraction in the post-modern context. By reasserting fundamental regulatory ties like family, morality, religion and nation in a society where such ties appear to have been dispersed by a heterogeneous post-modern culture, the FN provides structure, security, meaning, a collective sense of belonging. This traditionalism, which Taguieff has termed the 'ideology of the concrete', serves to counter *anomie* through 'the restoration of a natural order, such that civil society is once again a hierarchically ordered totality in which each person is finally in his legitimate place'.[42]

In another respect, it could be useful to conceive this quest for new 'concrete identities' in terms of a form of right-wing post-materialism. This, of course, runs counter to Ronald Inglehart's classic, though very narrow, contention that 'post-materialists' align themselves with the Left.[43] Commentators like Ignazi argue that the Front national represents an authoritarian rejection of (leftist) post-materialist values such as feminism, multiculturalism, participation and tolerance.[44] Yet attitudinal surveys of Front national voters have consistently shown that its electorate also seems to possess what can conceivably be described as 'post-materialistic' characteristics.

Observers frequently highlight quasi-obsessional material concerns in FN cohorts such as unemployment and physical insecurity (law and order), inextricably tied to immigration. This however appears to conceal vital non-material (or post-material?) 'anomic' concerns, especially the threat immigrants allegedly pose to identity, community, culture, moral values and environment. It seems probable as well that the FN's greatest appeals are to those fatigued by the rise of competitive, materialist-consumerist society. Far from being simply a materialistic reaction, it may in fact be argued that the FN offers its own type of right-wing post-materialist value system and in this way acts as a protest alternative, or 'counter-culture', to the 'new politics' and post-modern pluralism of the Left.

This counter-culture has been assisted by a general loss of faith in the ability of the 'political class' to repulse the processes of post-modernity. The failure to resolve social and cultural disintegration (itself indicative of the restrictions placed upon the nation-state by globalisation and the fragmentation of power) has ominously given rise to a diffuse political 'dissensus', expressed not only through abstentionism but also through support for the anti-system Front national.

Interestingly, the Front national offers its rejoinder to the post-materialist agenda of the Left by reviving and revising traditional currents in French political culture. It mixes populism with nationalism, coated with pre-industrial values such as community, morality, obedience, religion, discipline and social order. Alongside this traditionalist value-system, which recalls the conservative authoritarianism of the old royalist Right, there is a populist appeal to the sovereignty of the people expressed through a 'Popular Initiative Referendum' and the need to 'cleanse' France of decadence, mismanagement and corruption – an echo of the right-wing brand of Jacobinism which emerged in the wake of the Boulanger Affair.[45]

What Taguieff calls the 'fluctuating syncretism' between these two traditions[46] has been central to the fortunes of the French extreme Right for the last 100 years, and movements have enjoyed their greatest success when they have managed to 'synthesise' the two and thus widen the 'spectrum' of their appeal. However, there are dangers in insisting too heavily on these historical continuities. The first is that by exaggerating the specificity of the French extreme Right, by overemphasising the conservative 'counter-revolutionary' elements in the FN's ideology, the potential resemblances with 'fascist' movements are obscured. Taguieff's use of the term 'national-populist' to describe the eclecticism of the FN[47] avoids systematic consideration of the nature of fascist ideology, itself 'spectral-syncretic' in Eatwell's phrase.[48] And Taguieff also fails to recognise that, by constantly invoking historical traditions, the FN may well be trying to hide revolutionary, fascist ideology at the core in an insidious 'crypto-fascist' style.

Ideological debates to one side, even if the FN does echo earlier authoritarian nationalist traditions, the context in which it has developed its appeal belongs to 'this day and age', rather than to previous times. Of course, the cyclical view of history may offer some interesting insights. Hobsbawm's analysis of the conditions which favoured the emergence of radical right-wing nationalism in late nineteenth-century Europe certainly invites contemporary analogies: dramatic shifts in social class structure, mass migratory movements, the resistance of social groups threatened with marginalisation.[49]

However, while periods of rapid social transition (like revolutions) may display certain mechanical similarities, history moves on. What Hobsbawm calls the 'onrush of modernity' – the coming of age of mass politics, industrial society and the modern State – has a century later been replaced by the apparent decay of that same model of social and political organisation. The rise of the Front national must be historically contextualised within this overarching post-modern configuration. The convergence of post-industrialism, post-colonialism, post-socialism and post-materialism provides a manageable frame of reference which takes as its starting point a finite crisis of 'community consciousness' and then interweaves this 'micro-crisis' with a 'macro-crisis' of nation-state and national identity. Emerging with the transition from modernity, it thus follows that the Front national should be interpreted as a 'transitional' (though not necessarily transitory) phenomenon, as a vain response to the contemporary 'anomic' pressures of post-modernity and the increasing limitations of the French nation-state.

NOTES

1 A. de Tocqueville, *The Old Regime and the French Revolution*, New York, Doubleday, 1955.
2 H. Lebovics, 'Creating the authentic France: struggles over French identity in the first half of the twentieth century', in J. Gillis, (ed.), *Commemorations: The Politics of National Identity*, Princeton NJ, Princeton University Press, 1994, p.239.
3 C. Mooers, *The Making of Bourgeois Europe: Absolutism, Revolution and the Rise of Capitalism in England, France and Germany*, London, Verso, 1991, p.56.
4 E. Weber, *Peasants into Frenchmen: The Modernization of Rural France 1870–1914*, Stanford, CA, Stanford University Press, 1976.

5 The degree to which workers were 'integrated' into the institutions and value-system of the Republic at an earlier stage (before 1914) is the subject of lively historical debate. For a useful discussion, see R. Magraw, *France 1815–1914: The Bourgeois Century*, London, Fontana, 1983.

6 The 1945 Nationality Code allowed French nationality *at birth* to anyone born in France one of whose parents were also born on French territory (which included Algeria until 1 January 1963). It also automatically gave French nationality *at the age of majority* to those born in France of foreign parents, unless they explicity chose not to adopt it. The Balladur government (1993–5) introduced significant amendments restricting access.

7 E. Hobsbawm, *Nations and Nationalism since 1780*, Cambridge, Cambridge University Press, 1990, p.89.

8 For further discussion of this 'class' dimension of nationalism, see B. Jenkins, *Nationalism in France: Class and Nation since 1789*, London, Routledge, 1990.

9 This process was not restricted to France. The State's role in cultivating national loyalties in European countries 1870–1914 is analysed in E. Hobsbawm and T. Ranger (eds), *The Invention of Tradition*, Cambridge, Cambridge University Press, 1983.

10 Some historians see Boulangism as the true birthplace of French nationalism, and it is certainly true that only in the 1890s did a political movement emerge that specifically defined itself as 'nationalist'. See R. Tombs (ed.), *Nationhood and Nationalism in France: From Boulangism to the Great War*, London, Harper-Collins, 1991.

11 The theme of the ideological continuity of the French extreme Right has been promoted primarily by René Rémond's classic and influential *Les droites en France*, Paris, Aubier-Montaigne, 4th edn, 1982.

12 See B. Jenkins, op. cit., pp.129–52.

13 This alignment was exemplified above all by the debate on the proposal for a European Defence Community (1950–4).

14 See H. Mendras and A. Cole, *Social Change in Modern France*, Cambridge, Cambridge University Press, 1991.

15 This well-established argument is, perhaps, most succinctly developed in M. Duverger, *La République des citoyens*, Paris, Ramsay, 1982.

16 G. Ross, 'Adieu vieilles idées: the middle strata and the decline of resistance-liberation Left discourse in France', in J. Howorth and G. Ross (eds), *Contemporary France: A Review of Interdisciplinary Studies*, vol. 1, London, Frances Pinter, 1987.

17 See H. Mendras and A. Cole, op. cit.

18 C. Ford, *Creating the Nation in Provincial France: Religion and Political Identity in Brittany*, Princeton, NJ, Princeton University Press, 1993.

19 As Hobsbawm points out, 'Men and women did not choose collective identities as they chose shoes, knowing that one could only put on one pair at a time.' It was only when these multiple identities/loyalties conflicted directly with one another 'that a problem of choosing between them arose'. E. Hobsbawm, op. cit., pp.123–4.

20 G. Ross, op. cit., p.64.

21 At the 1993 legislative elections, the main contenders for power (the socialists and the conservative RPR–UDF coalition) together attracted only 56 per cent of the vote. At the June 1994 European elections, these mainstream parties won less than 40 per cent. At the 1995 presidentials, the three candidates identified with these parties pooled only 60 per cent (as against over 70 per cent in 1981 and 1988).

22 Levy and fellow intellectuals launched a *'Sarajevo'* list for the June 1994 European elections, which registered 12 per cent in the opinion polls before collapsing at the end of May. Tapie's list for the same elections eventually won 12 per cent of the vote, as indeed did the list led by Philippe de Villiers.

23 A. Touraine, 'European countries in a post-national era', in C. Rootes and H. Davis (eds), *Social Change and Political Transformation*, London, UCL Press, 1994, pp.13–26.

24 A. Touraine, op. cit., p.22.

25 E. Hobsbawm, op. cit., pp.161–83.

26 A. Chafer and B. Jenkins (eds), *France: from the Cold War to the New World Order*, London, Macmillan, 1996.

27 D. Hanley, 'France and GATT: the real politics of trade negotiations', in Chafer and Jenkins, op. cit., pp.131–51.

28 P. Fysh, 'Gaullism and the New World Order', in Chafer and Jenkins, op. cit., pp.181–92.

29 Giscard suspended inward labour migration from non-EC countries (1974) and later planned the mass repatriation of Maghreb immigrants as a remedy for unemployment. The PCF notoriously supported the demolition of an immigrant hostel in its Vitry-sur-Seine municipality in December 1980. Socialist ministers blamed strikes by immigrant workers in the French automobile industry (1982–3) on Islamic fundamentalists, despite the absence of any supporting evidence. See A. Hargreaves, 'Immigration, ethnicity and political orientations in France', in Chafer and Jenkins, op. cit., pp.207–18.

30 E. Hobsbawm, op. cit., p.163.

31 P. Hainsworth 'The extreme Right in post-War France: the emergence and success of the Front national', in P. Hainsworth (ed.), *The Extreme Right in Europe and the USA*, London, Frances Pinter, 1992, p.41.

32 H. Le Bras, *Les Trois France*, Paris, Odile Jacob, 1986. P. Perrineau, 'Le Front national 1972–1992', in M. Winock (ed.), *Histoire de l'extrême droite en France*, Paris, Seuil, 1993. E. Todd, *The Making of Modern France: Politics, Ideology and Culture*, Oxford, Blackwell, 1991.

33 See A. Cohen, *The Symbolic Construction of Community*, London, Routledge, 1993.

34 D. Kellner, *Jean Baudrillard: From Marxism to Postmodernism and Beyond*, London, Polity, 1989, p.17.

35 B. Anderson, *Imagined Communities: Reflections on the Origin and Spread of Nationalism*, 2nd edn, London, Verso, 1991, p.6.

36 M. Silverman, *Deconstructing the Nation: Immigration, Racism and Citizenship in Modern France*, London, Routledge, 1992, p.111.

37 See N. MacMaster, 'The seuil de tolérance: the uses of a "scientific" racist concept', in M. Silverman (ed.), *Race, Discourse and Power in France*, Aldershot, Avebury, 1991.

38 P. Perrineau, op. cit., p.264.

39 O. Waever and M. Kelstrup, 'Europe and its nations: political and cultural identities', in O. Waever, B. Buzan, M. Kelstrup and P. Lemaitre (eds), *Identity, Migration and the New Security Agenda in Europe*, London, Frances Pinter, 1993, p.88.

40 Ibid., p.70.

41 See H. Le Bras, op. cit.

42 P-A. Taguieff, 'The doctrine of the Front national in France' *New Political Science* 1989, 16–17: 51.

43 R. Inglehart, *The Silent Revolution*, Princeton, NJ, Princeton University Press, 1977.

44 P. Ignazi, 'The silent counter-revolution: hypotheses on the emergence of extreme right-wing parties in Europe', *European Journal of Political Research* 1992, 22(1): 3–34.

45 According to Zeev Sternhell, Paul Déroulède's *Ligue des patriotes*, a key vehicle of Boulangism, set the traditionally left-wing Jacobin clientele 'against the Republic' for the first time – Z. Sternhell, 'Paul Déroulède and the origins of French nationalism', in J.C. Cairns (ed.), *Contemporary France: Illusion, Conflict and Regeneration*, New York, New Viewpoints, 1978.

46 Taguieff, op. cit., p.56.

47 Ibid. See also Hainsworth, op. cit., and M. Winock, *Nationalisme, anti-Semitisme et fascisme en France*, Paris, Seuil, 1990.

48 R. Eatwell, 'Towards a new model of generic fascism', *Journal of Theoretical Politics* 1992, 4(1): 161–94.

49 Hobsbawm, op. cit., p.109.

SELECT BIBLIOGRAPHY

Chafer, A. and Jenkins, B. (1996) *France: from the Cold War to the New World Order*, London, Macmillan.

Hainsworth, P. (1992) 'The extreme Right in post-war France: the emergence and success of the Front national', in P. Hainsworth (ed.), *The Extreme Right in Europe and the USA*, London, Frances Pinter, pp.29–60.

Hoffmann, S. (1974) *Decline or Renewal? France since the 1930s*, New York, Viking.

Jenkins, B. (1990) *Nationalism in France: Class and Nation since 1789*, London, Routledge.

Ross, G. (1987) 'Adieu vieilles idées: the middle strata and the decline of resistance-liberation Left discourse in France', in J. Howorth and G. Ross (eds), *Contemporary France: A Review of Interdisciplinary Studies*, vol. 1, London, Frances Pinter.

Silverman, M. (1992) *Deconstructing the Nation: Immigration, Racism and Citizenship in Modern France*, London, Routledge.

Tombs, R. (ed.) (1991) *Nationhood and Nationalism in France: from Boulangism to the Great War*, London, HarperCollins.

Weber, E. (1976) *Peasants into Frenchmen: The Modernization of Rural France 1870–1914*, Stanford, CA, Stanford University Press.

6

POST-WAR NATIONAL IDENTITY IN GERMANY[1]

Gerd Knischewski

The so-called 'German question' is deeply rooted in both German and European history. The eighteenth and nineteenth centuries saw the advent of the modern nation-state in Europe as the predominant entity for the execution of political and economic power. Germany, however, deeply fragmented into a multitude of smaller states since the Holy Roman Empire (Heiliges Römisches Reich Deutscher Nation), and, especially in the east, with uncertain boundaries, no clearly defined territory, and an ethnically mixed population, found it difficult to organise and establish itself as a nation-state.

Historically, the 'German question' was in fact made up of a number of questions. First, how should the outer boundaries of a unified Germany be defined? Second, who was deemed a German anyway? And what status should be granted to Germans outside and aliens within the territory of a German state? Finally, what should be the inner constitution, and hence democratic justification, of the German nation-state?

These questions have persisted throughout the history of Germany. In recent years, a new dimension has been added as the concept of national identity appeared on the agenda. This can be analysed first of all in terms of collective perceptions of the outside world, and feelings of belonging to a nation. Both of these aspects can be assessed by means of statistics and empirical evaluation, although this is fraught with considerable methodological problems.[2] Second, the analysis may focus more narrowly on the political attitudes and actions of political protagonists and the public with regard to 'national issues'.

A BRIEF HISTORY OF THE PROBLEM

Historically, the meanings allocated to the concept of nation were different in Germany and France. According to French understanding, the nation is equated with the (democratic) state.

Due to its fragmentation into many small states, the 'belated nation'[3] of

125

Germany did not exist as a political entity, but only as a territorial and cultural concept. Debates about how to achieve a unified state centred on the questions of which of the German regional states should be part of a future nation-state, and how were the many Germans to be dealt with, especially in eastern Europe, who traditionally lived outside the boundaries of what was perceived as German territory.

Another difficulty was posed by what von Krockow describes as 'the lack of a national milieu' in Germany.[4] Unlike other nation-states, Germany was not united by a common, or at least dominant, literature and religion, but on the contrary had been deeply divided by the rift between Catholics and Protestants since the Reformation and the ensuing Thirty Years War (1618–48). Territorial particularism had even prevented the development of an undisputed capital.

As, in Germany, the nation could not establish itself as a political community of free citizens, the developing movement for unity proclaimed, with recourse to the philosophers Herder and Fichte,[5] the idea of the nation as a community with homogeneous ethnic and cultural roots and a common language, though parts of the movement still combined its demand for unity with that for parliamentarisation and a democratic constitution.

Thus, whereas in the 'French model' it was the universalist declaration of the citizen-state which became the dominant characteristic of modern political nationality (*Staatsbürgernation*), the 'German model' stressed the particularist characteristics of an ethnic community of common origin and descent (*Volksnation*) which revealed itself in the national spirit (*Volksgeist*) and its language, culture (*Kulturnation*) or even landscape. The opposition to the French version of the national idea was intensified by the fact that the German national movement reached its first peak during the anti-Napoleonic liberation wars in 1813–15.

Formally, it was Napoleon's military victory in 1806 which marked the end of the Holy Roman Empire. However, the first Reich of the Germans had long before ceased to be of any importance in terms of power politics. In this vacuum, a new power dualism evolved between the two German states of Austria and the 'newcomer' Prussia.

In order to prevent a concentration of German power in Europe, the Congress of Vienna in 1815 did not permit the first German Reich to reestablish itself. This led to a kind of nostalgic Reich patriotism which later demanded the restoration of the Reich. The Holy Roman Empire was superseded by the German Confederation (Deutscher Bund) consisting of thirty-nine sovereign German states and with only extremely weak central institutions. The fact that the German Confederation also included vast areas with a predominantly non-German population would prove a continuous source of political conflict. The internal climate was characterised by social tensions between the industrialising and increasingly liberal west and the agrarian and autocratic east which prevailed until far into the twentieth century.[6]

In terms of power politics, the Confederation was a latent great power in a transitional stage which lacked social and political unity. The breakdown of the bourgeois revolution in 1848 weakened the position of the German liberal bourgeoisie which in turn slowed down the process of parliamentarisation and constitutionalism. It also made the bourgeois classes susceptible to ideas advocating a non-democratic single statehood. Moreover, the failure of the revolution and thus of the concept of a liberal unified state further intensified the power struggle for Germany between Austria and Prussia.

In this situation, the Prussian prime minister and *'Realpolitiker'* Bismarck took the initiative. His realistic assessment of the power constellations in Europe allowed him to wage three successful wars against Denmark, Austria and France during the years from 1862 to 1871 and enabled him to found a federal German state which excluded Austria and ensured Prussian dominance. The Prussian king became 'Kaiser' (emperor) of the newly established 'Deutsches Reich'. But even in this new German state, political borders and the borders of German settlement were not identical, and the new German Reich was additionally burdened by the annexation of Alsace-Lorraine. However, the decisive question was how the new great power was to determine its place within the European balance of power.

In conceptual terms, the new nation-state saw itself in the tradition of the medieval empire. Instead of the black, red and gold which had been the colours of the liberal movement for unity, the Prussian black, white and red tricolor was chosen as the national flag – colours which have retained their symbolic value as an expression of a right-wing conservative nationalism to this day. The new German state showed little tolerance towards national minorities living within its territory. The Polish population in the Prussian provinces was put under pressure to 'germanise', and Alsace-Lorraine was given an inferior administrative status.[7]

This exclusive and aggressive definition of what constituted the German nation also prevailed in domestic politics. The government had taken it upon itself to fight 'the enemies of the Reich', namely political Catholicism and social democracy. Given these social and political tensions, it is hardly possible to speak of a common national identity. Surges of industrialisation had created a number of victims of modernisation among the bourgeoisie who, supported by Bismarck, regarded themselves as the national-conservative core of the nation and formulated an increasingly aggressive nationalism.[8]

This nationalism was expressed in the foundation of a number of associations and societies and was based on two ideological principles. The first of these, essentially *volksdeutsch* (ethnic German) in character, aspired not only to align German borders with those of German settlement, but also claimed the national (i.e. racial) superiority of the German people. This self-elevation of the German nation was reflected in an increased anti-Semitism and delimitation of non-Germans which was based on the assertion that 'German culture' was of higher value than 'Western civilisation' (i.e. democracy) – a belief which was to become known as the German *Sonderweg* (special path). The second ideological influence was imperialism, which demanded the role of a world power with colonies for the German Reich. This aspiration, too, was latently racist.

The foundation of the Deutscher Flottenverein (German naval association) in 1898 and the Deutscher Wehrverein (defence association) in 1912 bears witness to the fact that German nationalism became increasingly militaristic which in turn explains the enthusiasm which greeted the outbreak of the First World War. It also shows that some central elements of National Socialism had been prepared both in ideological and organisational terms during the period of the Kaiserreich.

The First World War was a militaristic attempt to realise the expansive and aggressive aims of German nationalism. The German defeat ended in the peace treaty of Versailles under which Germany lost territories in the east and west, was refused the right to unite with Austria, was partly demilitarised, was made to pay reparations and accept sole responsibility for the war. In its aftermath, the revision of the Versailles Treaty became the goal of many, extending far beyond the circles of right-wing nationalists.

Germany became a democratic republic for the first time, though it retained the name Deutsches Reich. This Weimar Republic (so-called after the place where its constitution was passed), however, proved too weak to defeat the aggressive and expansionist nationalism of the late Kaiserreich. On the contrary, the right-wing nationalists kept their strong positions in the armed forces, legal system, administration and academia. They contributed to the destabilisation of the democratic system, and in the final stages of the Weimar Republic took an active role in the process that led to Hitler's installation as chancellor.

The reasons for the failure of the first German republic were manifold. One of the main factors, however, was that the National Socialists succeeded in using an economic and political crisis situation to develop a mass movement whose nationalist programme and actions gained widespread support. In a number of ways, National Socialism took up the fundamental historical problems connected with the German question and provided them with radical solutions. Initially, the issue of Germany's borders was posed as a necessary revision of the Versailles Treaty. Hitler's popularity after 1933 was partly a direct result of his successes in 'wiping out the humiliation of Versailles': the occupation of the demilitarised

Rhineland, the return of the Saarland and the Sudetenland into the Reich, the annexation of Austria in 1938 (this latter act recalling the revolutionary 1848 vision of a unified Germany).[9]

However, this revisionism marked only the beginning of an imperialist expansionism which was directed towards the east. Eastern Europe, including the Soviet Union, was to be enslaved and become dependent territory in order to create new living space for a 'people without space' ('*Volk ohne Raum*'). Consequently, the Deutsches Reich was renamed Großdeutsches Reich (Greater German Reich) during the Second World War. The ideological justification of this claim to hegemonic status in Europe was clearly racist. The National Socialist definition of nation was not based on statehood or citizenship but exclusively on biological descent. An aggressive and expansive nationalism was justified as an act of self-defence by the supposedly superior German (Aryan) race against the subversive influence of the allegedly inferior Slavonic and Jewish races. From this social-Darwinist perspective, the 'racial war against the east', and the genocidal 'final solution of the Jewish question' had a grimly conclusive logic.

The racially motivated war against the east was accompanied on the domestic front by the elimination of the 'enemies of the people'. The Marxist labour movement, homosexuals, the physically and mentally handicapped (i.e. 'genetically inferior people'), Jews and gypsies were excluded from the nation in a process of increasing discrimination which in many cases culminated in physical annihilation.

National Socialism was the second, and more radical, attempt at attaining a hegemonic position for Germany. Like the first one, it ended in military defeat. However, the more radical aims of National Socialism in turn produced more radical consequences.

THE SITUATION AFTER 1945

In the immediate aftermath of the Second World War, Germany found itself completely defeated in political, military and economic as well as moral terms. Until 1949, Germany was under the legislation of the four occupying allied forces, and the old nation-state had ceased to exist. German territory was split up into four occupied zones (i.e. American, British, French and Soviet), and about one-third was divided off and put under 'Polish or Soviet administration'.

In 1949, when cooperation between the occupation forces had given way to the emerging Cold War, two new German states were founded, the Federal Republic of Germany (FRG) comprising the three western occupied zones, and the German Democratic Republic (GDR) on the territory of the Soviet zone. Between the war and 1964, about 12 million refugees and expellees left their homes in the east of the former German Reich or fled the Soviet zone/GDR.[10] Nonetheless a considerable number of ethnic Germans stayed despite the difficulties they had to expect.

Neither of the two German states was granted full state sovereignty. In 1955, both states were allowed to re-establish armed forces, but only within the framework of the opposing military alliances of the North Atlantic Treaty Organization (NATO) and the Warsaw Pact. Even after 1955, there formally existed residues of allied authority in West Germany, which were reduced in 1968 when the Federal Republic passed its highly controversial Emergency Laws, and were finally removed only in 1990 when the four allied powers and the two German states signed the 'Treaty on the Final Settlement with Respect to Germany' (the so-called 'Two-plus-Four Treaty') which smoothed the way for German unification at the international level.

Discussion of the lessons to be drawn from National Socialism and its war, and the possibility of a 'fresh start' for Germany on a West German basis, was confined to a small élite of intellectuals who were not burdened by guilt for Nazi atrocities. The vast majority of Germans, on the other hand, were politically apathetic and, until well into the 1950s, preoccupied with day-to-day material survival. Intellectuals demanded a radical rejection of the old anti-Western and nationalist German *Sonderweg* with regard to both culture and politics, and the abandonment of negative German traditions such as militarism and nationalism. The 'nation', it was claimed, had lost on moral grounds its potential to serve as an integrative ideology enjoying absolute priority over any other loyalties. Hence Germany had to adopt the political values of liberalism, representative democracy and the rule of law, and come to terms with a new role as a peaceful member of the family of nations. The idea of a United States of Europe was greeted with enthusiasm.

National consciousness

Although national issues, such as occupation and lack of sovereignty, European integration, rearmament, the loss of eastern territories, the problem of refugees, and German reunification, were to play an important and polarising role in party-political debates until about 1960, German national identity in both senses (i.e. collective perceptions of the world on the one hand, and the identification with the nation on the other) was considerably more defensive and distinctly different from that of other Europeans. In the collective consciousness, seeing and defining oneself openly as German was regarded as highly problematic in the context of Nazi atrocities, the total defeat of Germany, the accusation of the collective guilt of all Germans, and the allied occupation. In the view of Alter, this marks the beginning of a change of national consciousness which laid the foundations for a 'post-national' identity which is still visible in Germany today.[11]

The most obvious sign of this transformation was, and still is, the relatively low national pride of Germans, as compared to other European nationalities, especially among the younger generations. In 1990, about 40 per cent of Germans declared that they felt indifferent towards the German flag.[12] On the other hand, Germans of all generations identify to a remarkable extent with the country's economic achievements, and in particular the social security system. Since the experience of the 'economic miracle' in the 1950s and early 1960s, West Germans have become extremely 'welfare-conscious'.[13]

Another important aspect of German collective consciousness is a pronounced need for security, or, to put it less positively, a fixation on crises and anxieties (*Angst*). Surveys have often shown a discrepancy between people's positive evaluation of their own situations and their negative assessment of the general state of affairs. Fears for the future in the shape of inflation, nuclear war and environmental disasters figure prominently not only in the media, but also among the general public.[14] This pessimism, and the restraint towards national symbols, may well reflect the psychological after-effects of a turbulent history, which has seen at least four radical changes to the political system in little more than seventy years (1918–90).[15]

Nationalism

After 1945, the possibility that the national idea might develop into an aggressive German nationalism could almost be excluded. Although it is true that the population was initially indifferent to the new democratic constitution of the Basic Law, this general attitude changed and became increasingly positive as a result of economic prosperity. However, it was only in the early 1970s that surveys confirmed an acceptance of democratic principles and institutions.[16]

In contrast with the first German (Weimar) republic, the social and political élites this time behaved as supporters of the system. Part of the price to be paid for this loyalty was a (too) swift rehabilitation of collaborators of the Nazi regime. Integration of the élites into the new order was aided by the fact that, in view of the Cold War, the process of denazification was soon discontinued. However, although surveys carried out by the Allies revealed that Germans still supported the ideas of National Socialism to an alarming extent,[17] any attempts at establishing an openly aggressive and nationalistic culture were doomed to fail. In 1952, the right-wing extremist Socialist Reich Party was banned by the Federal Constitutional Court, and other right-wing splinter groups were absorbed by the governing conservative parties, the Christian Democratic Union (CDU) and the Christian Social Union (CSU).

Although the refugees' and expellees' organisations maintained their political claims to a 'correction' of the German borders in the east, they committed themselves in a charter published in 1950 to non-aggression and to mutual recognition of the 'right to a homeland'. Initially these organisations exercised considerable influence on the parties, which, however, decreased the more successful the integration of expellees and refugees into West German society became.

Right-wing extremist parties were only able to regain some influence as late as the 1960s, when in some elections at local and regional level the National Democratic Party (NPD) managed to gain over 5 per cent of the vote which is the prerequisite for entering parliament in the FRG electoral system. This success turned out to be short-lived when in 1969 the NPD failed to achieve the same at the national (FRG) level by a very narrow margin. Their campaign slogans had been: 'Stop immigration' and 'Abandonment [of the eastern territory] equals treason'.[18] Nationalist right-wing extremist parties had to wait until the late 1980s to be re-elected to local and regional governments, this time in the guise of the German People's Union (DVU) and the Republikaner. However, an extra-parliamentary militant neo-fascism has existed at least since the late 1970s. In 1980, thirteen people died at the Munich Oktoberfest as a result of a right-wing bomb attack. In 1981, the methodologically controversial study by the social sciences research institute SINUS was published which claimed that 13 per cent of West Germans had a right-wing extremist world view.[19]

National symbolism

When the West German state was founded in 1949, Bonn was chosen as its capital; a cosy, idyllic town which is neither awe-inspiring nor representative. On the whole, national symbols and rituals were used extremely sparingly. Until 1952, the FRG did not even have a national anthem. Only then did the conservative Chancellor Konrad Adenauer, in the face of resistance from the Federal President Theodor Heuss, restore the 'Deutschlandlied'. This had been the German national anthem since 1922 but had been discredited by its adoption by the National Socialists. However, only the third verse invoking unity, justice and freedom was considered fit for official use; public singing of the first verse ('Deutschland, Deutschland über alles') remained banned.

The national holiday of the FRG was changed twice between 1949 and 1990. From 1950 to 1953, the anniversary of the first plenary session of the federal parliament, on 7 September 1949, was officially celebrated. From 1954 to 1990, the uprising of workers in the GDR on 17 June 1953, which was interpreted by the West as an indication of the East German people's desire for reunification and officially named the 'Day of German Unity', was the West German national public holiday.[20] Since 1990, 3 October, the day on which the GDR officially became part of the FRG, has been the new 'Day of German Unity' and national public holiday, the official cele-brations for which are held by annual rotation successively in each of the sixteen federal states (Bundesländer) that constitute the FRG.

Until the early 1970s, the GDR officially maintained the aim of reunifi-cation. Not until 1974 was the constitution changed and the corresponding passages deleted. However, throughout the existence of the GDR, the two German states competed on both a national and international level for moral superiority and thus recognition as the only legitimate German state.

This competition also took place in the arena of national symbols. Among others, the flags of the FRG and the GDR were identical, apart from the GDR symbol 'Hammer and compasses in a garland of corn' as a pointer to the 'state of the workers and peasants'. In 1949, the GDR had declared, against the Western interpretation of allied agreements, (East) Berlin its capital which then gained a privileged status, corresponding to its representative importance for the state. Also in 1949, the GDR had created its own national anthem, the lyrics of which, however, were not sung after 1974 as they contained a reference to the aim of reunification ('Germany, united fatherland').

The answer of the GDR to the many religious bank holidays in the FRG was a plethora of political anniversaries, which were normal working days. The most important of these was 8 May (VE Day), which was celebrated as the 'Day of the Liberation from Fascism' in the GDR but until the 1980s was not commemorated in the FRG at all.

The FRG constitution and German unity

The FRG regarded itself as a provisional arrangement in political and constitutional terms. The preamble to the Basic Law demanded the re-unification of Germany as well as a united Europe. With regard to its past as a nation-state, the FRG saw itself as standing in continuity and as legal successor of the German Reich within the borders of 1937 (i.e. before the annexation of Austria). This claim was supported by a ruling of the Federal Constitutional Court of 1973 in which it defined the FRG as (geographically) 'partially identical' with the Reich. With regard to its future, however, this West German core of the Reich was incomplete. 'Middle' and 'East' German territories (the GDR) and the areas in the east which had been placed under 'Polish or Soviet administration' as a result of the Potsdam Agreement between the allied powers were still seen as part of Germany and subject to reunification. In the beginning, all parties had subscribed to the slogan *'Dreigeteilt? Niemals!'* ('Divided three ways? Never!').

The dominant figure in West German post-war politics, Federal Chancellor Adenauer (1949–63) of the Christian Democratic Union (CDU), had always rejected the dominance of Protestant Prussia in the German Reich, being himself a Catholic from the Rhineland. His priorities were to regain German sovereignty and firmly to establish the FRG in the West. Reunification could only be achieved on this basis. Adenauer knew that to this end he had to make concessions to the Allies and convince them that the Germans had ultimately parted with nationalism.

Ironically, in the early years of the FRG the oppositional Social Democrats were mainly responsible for the revival of traditional, national patterns of argument and appealed to national feelings in Germany. They insisted on German interests and on the primacy of reunification and even dubbed Adenauer 'chancellor of the Allies' for his Western integration policy. The conservative politics of rearmament in 1955 and the ambition to become a nuclear power in 1957 were interpreted by the SPD as proof of a resurgence of German militarism and nationalism.

The official policy of the conservative-led federal governments with regard to Germany as a whole consisted of a series of aggressive legal titles: non-recognition of the GDR, claim to sole representation of Germany by the FRG, continuing existence of the Deutsches Reich, Allied responsibility for all Germany and Berlin, final establishment of borders in a peace treaty. The aim of these legal titles was to isolate the GDR and thus precipitate its collapse.[21]

Substitute identities

Due to the external conditions of the Cold War and economic development, the national idea increasingly lost priority in favour of Western-style democratic statehood. The shadow of the Nazi past and the deterrent effect of the GDR led to a general attitude in which the national imperative figured less prominently than freedom and welfare.

On an institutional level, European integration presented itself as a substitute for national identity. Nowhere else was the European idea greeted as enthusiastically as in (West) Germany. Although this general enthusiasm was primarily psychologically motivated, it has to be emphasised that the shrewd politician and dedicated anti-nationalist Adenauer had realised that only by passing on parts of state sovereignty to supranational bodies, such as the European Coal and Steel Community (ECSC) in 1952 and the European Economic Community (EEC) in 1957, could this same state sovereignty be regained, with the re-establishment of its own army and its integration into NATO being the decisive step. Moreover, Western integration had the additional effect of psychologically rehabilitating Germany.

Restrictions on German sovereignty remained most effective in the military realm. The West European Union (WEU) Treaty of 1954 denied the FRG the right to own ABC weapons. In the eventuality of a war, the contingent of the West German army, the Bundeswehr, was placed under NATO (i.e. American) supreme command. The 'Two-plus-Four Treaty' of 1990, which lays down the foreign policy conditions for German unification, confirmed Germany's renunciation of ABC weapons.

Due to the total integration of the FRG into the West and the world market, its foreign policy developed both its visionary European idea and its pragmatic focus as an extremely successful 'trading state'[22] which made use of its growing power only economically by 'employing the cheque-book'.[23] From the perspective of power politics, the FRG was most often described as 'an economic giant but a political dwarf'. The fact that for historical reasons the FRG was confined, and later confined itself, to multilateral decision-making processes within alliances made German solo actions an impossibility where foreign policy was concerned.[24]

Another important dimension of the West German collective substitute identity was (and still is) anti-communism which, though it regarded the East Germans in the GDR as 'brothers and sisters' in the 'Soviet zone' who were to be pitied, prohibited any contacts at state or official level. The GDR served as a negative backcloth for comparisons and thus had a positive 'system-stabilising' effect on the FRG.[25] For a long time, the foreign relations of the FRG were dominated by the 'German question', namely the division of Germany. The so-called Hallstein Doctrine of 1955 threatened any third state which recognised the GDR with the breaking off of diplomatic relations. In the General Treaty of 1955, which accompanied the entrance of the FRG into NATO, the Western allies supported the FRG's claim to sole representation and assured it of their support for reunification under the terms of the FRG. On the domestic front, 'socialism' was equated with 'communism' and thus labelled as the 'enemy within'. How much Adenauer used this as national rhetoric even against the Social Democrats is illustrated by the fact that he denounced them in his election campaign of the 1950s as 'Moscow's fifth column'.

Additionally, the USA became a partner and protector and for the West Germans and not only let them forget their moral guilt for the war and German atrocities but also invited them to a new 'crusade against the enemy in the East'. Ideological bloc thinking served as another source of identity.

But the USA not only provided security and political orientation. It became more and more a cultural model which was enthusiastically adopted at least by parts of West German society. Although in the early years, many Germans still preferred idyllic, sentimental *Heimat* films, the 'Americanisation' of popular and everyday culture could not be halted, and soon, the American example of a consumer society was to determine mass consciousness. The car boom which was copied from the USA 'stamped the national perception of the 1950s in just the same way as the railways had made the "economic nation" of the 1850s'.[26]

Especially in the media and the jargon of the youth, the influence of the English language has increased enormously since 1945.[27] Kaase speaks of a 'socio-cultural diffusion' which made the development of a specifically German state of political awareness or specifically German modes of thinking only to a very limited extent possible,[28] a diagnosis which is shared and commented on with equal concern by both the Left and the Right.

CHANGE IN THE 1960s AND 1970s

The 1960s and early 1970s were characterised by far-reaching economic crises and modernisation processes in many areas. The end of the post-war economic boom and the structural change in traditional industries led internationally to an expansion of the public infrastructure, especially of the educational system.

In 1968, many countries in both East and West witnessed strong student and left-wing extra-parliamentary movements whose general concern was for peace and democratic reforms. However, in Germany the struggle took on an additional dimension: the Nazi past of the 'father generation' which had been insufficiently dealt with and remnants of which were still present in the society of the FRG.

The battle for history

Historical identity (i.e. a positively evaluated historical continuity) is an important, maybe the most important, component of national identity. The lack of this was probably the biggest obstacle for the development of a strong, self-confident and positive national feeling in Germany. The vast majority of FRG citizens had cut out German history from their self-definition. In particular, the National Socialist past was a taboo subject for politics and society alike.[29] Psychoanalysts interpreted the unwillingness to confront the Nazi past as a guilt complex which the Germans tried to resist by repressing it on both a moral and a psychological level.

The accusation of repressing the recent past exacerbated the generation conflict of the 1968 student revolt (the extra-parliamentary opposition, or 'APO' in German), which marked a break in consciousness and national identity in many ways. The silent generation of parents who refused to confront the past was unable to hand down a positive image of 'Germanness'. It became impossible for many of the younger generation who had grown up in a prosperous and consumption-oriented society to identify with their silent parents, with the horrific German past, with a state which, albeit democratic, was still shaped by authoritarian values, institutions and behaviour, and with the notion of the continuous existence of one

German nation. The Left saw themselves as internationalists (and developed a lasting partiality towards foreign, mostly 'revolutionary' models and folklore, e.g. Cuba, Vietnam, Chile, Nicaragua).

The APO reinstated, but clearly defined as negative, the continuity of German history. Instead of repressing the past, they insisted that any interest in history should focus on National Socialism, a concept which was widely put into practice in schools in SPD-governed federal states of the FRG. In political education, a clear change in paradigm ensued, in which the aim of 'anti-fascism' replaced that of 'German unity'. By the same token, the totalitarianism theory which put National Socialism on a par with GDR socialism was rejected. The demand for reunification soon became regarded as a conservative, revisionist concern. The intellectual Left managed to achieve cultural hegemony in parts of the media and the education system for a considerable time.

The new Deutschlandpolitik

A further break in national self-definition was marked by the new *Ost-* and *Deutschlandpolitik* of the Social–Liberal coalition government which had come into power in 1969. Forced to adjust to the new detente bilateralism of the USA and the USSR, the FRG confirmed in treaties with Poland and the Soviet Union its acceptance of the existing borders. Although the FRG insisted that a final settlement be left to a peace treaty between Germany and the Allied Powers, this meant in fact that for the time being claims to the former eastern territories were abandoned. The politics of isolation and confrontation with regard to the GDR, which had been based on aggressive legal titles, was also changed. In a treaty of 1972, the FRG recognised the state sovereignty of the GDR. Although the treaty stated that on the national question its parties agreed to disagree, for the time being reunification had clearly been wiped off the political agenda. *Deutschlandpolitik* was redefined as a policy for improving (bilateral) German–German relations. The concept behind this 'treaty politics of small steps' was based on the assumption that by integrating the GDR into a process of European detente and thus securing its existence, the system would finally be reformed and liberalised by the ruling Socialist Unity Party (SED) itself. The German Socialist Democratic Party (SPD) politician Egon Bahr, the mind behind this policy, believed in the possibility of 'change through rapprochement'.[30]

On the level of society, it was hoped by the Social–Liberal government that an increase in communication between Germans on both sides of the border would help to maintain or even intensify the feeling of all Germans for the 'unity of the nation'. In return for diplomatic recognition and extensive Deutschmark revenue, the GDR had to commit itself to accrediting Western journalists and easing travel restrictions, which in actual fact amounted to accepting a certain degree of Western influence. As visitors from the FRG in effect 'imported' Western standards (i.e. confronted GDR citizens with Western freedom and consumer goods) the GDR found it increasingly difficult to justify its system, and reacted with a number of measures of national delimitation. In 1974, the aim of reunification was taken out of the constitution, and the idea of the continuing existence of one German nation, on which there was consensus among all main political parties in the West, was countered by the claim to a 'socialist nation of German nationality'.

In order to hold up the notion of one German nation, the FRG promoted a concept of nation according to which it was united by a common culture and consciousness. From 1968 onwards, a 'Report on the State of the Nation' was published which tried to measure by statistical means and on the basis of a communication theory approach how the common consciousness of the Germans had developed. It was assumed that an increase in letters, telephone calls and travel from East to West and vice versa equalled an increase in common ground.

However, in 1994, even Egon Bahr described this approach as illusory as it had failed to overcome the differences in mentality between East and West Germans.[31] On the contrary, surveys showed that, while contacts increased, so at the same time did alienation. Although reunification was still supported by many interviewees, it was no longer given priority, and its actual possibility was seen as almost nil.[32]

To say farewell to the idea of an all-German identity, indeed to question the concept of nation itself, became an important characteristic of the political Left as a whole. The Green and 'alternative' movements generally shared this attitude. Even national-oriented SPD politicians such as Egon Bahr accepted the divided statehood as almost irreversible, and, as late as 1988 Willy Brandt, who had always maintained the unity of the nation, described the aim of reunification as 'the self-deceit of the FRG'. To hold to the unity of the nation and to reunification became more and more a defining characteristic of the conservatives and the political Right in general. The Left countered the anti-communist, anti-detente and anti-GDR politics of conservative reunification supporters with an anti-anti-GDR stance which in a way stood up for the other German state and had stopped questioning its existence or its shortcomings on human rights issues.

The less reunification was perceived as a realistic political objective, the more it became apparent that 'German identity' could no longer be equated with a unified German state. It was obvious that, with the recognition of the GDR (and hence the status quo) which found its most symbolic expression in the admission of both German states to the United Nations in 1973, the question of how the FRG defined itself in terms of national identity had to be reconsidered.

Even when the conservatives resumed office in 1982 under Chancellor

Helmut Kohl (CDU), they continued de facto the Social–Liberal *Deutsch-landpolitik*, and in 1987 gave the East German leader Erich Honecker a full state reception with all the rituals due to a foreign head of state when he became the first leader of the GDR to visit the FRG in an official capacity. The question had to be raised as to whether it was not more honest for the FRG to abandon the quest for state unity altogether and finally recognise itself as a state. Did not the aim of lasting inner stability require the FRG to develop its own West German democratic identity, even a West German patriotism, with which its citizens could identify?

To this end, in 1979 the political scientist Dolf Sternberger, and later the philosopher Jürgen Habermas, promoted so-called 'constitutional patriotism'[33] as a post-national alternative to a traditional all-German national identity. The majority of the Left and liberal camp adopted this concept. The Germany of 'constitutional patriotism' consciously confined itself to the FRG.[34] It was now the stance towards the principles of Western democracy that became crucial for the 'German question' and German identity. 'Nation' became identical with the West German state which was understood as a citizen-state. Thus West German identity was defined less as German than as democratic.

The process of modernisation, which in *economic* terms is, among other things, characterised by the trend towards a service-dependent economy, results in *sociological* terms in social changes and the evolution of new sets of values. Old 'social milieux' break up to be replaced by an increasing 'individualisation' and 'pluralisation of life-styles'. Post-material values which emphasise the right to self-fulfilment are on the increase. The younger generations are especially affected by changes in values.[35] In 1989, 34 per cent of all West Germans in the age-group ranging from 14 to 35 years regarded the East Germans as a different nation and did not see the GDR as part of Germany.[36]

'Meaning' is seen as something individual rather than collective. Younger generations increasingly find their identity not in large units such as the nation, state or ethnic group, but within smaller ones such as peer-groups, local communities, regions or *Heimat*. From a national perspective, the sense of collective identity and national solidarity is on the decline. From a functional point of view, the political system is in danger of dissolving under the strain of individual interests.[37]

THE RENAISSANCE OF 'NATION' AND 'HISTORY' IN THE 1970s AND 1980s

Parts of the Left rediscovered the 'national question' of German unity within the context of the peace movement of the early 1980s which had gained its main impetus from the NATO 'Dual Track Decision' of December 1979. In a new Cold War climate they saw West and East

Germany as the potential battlefield for a nuclear clash between the superpowers USA and USSR and revived old concepts of a confederate and neutral united Germany in the heart of Europe.[38]

Both German governments, in spite of the early 1980s debate surrounding the superpowers' modernisation of nuclear armaments, were interested in safeguarding their 'mini-detente'. Therefore, they maintained that the Germans shared a common responsibility for peace ('Never again must a war be started from German soil') and to a certain degree returned to the traditional definition of the one German nation.

During the 1970s and 1980s, a number of crises were diagnosed, such as the stagnation of the European project ('*Eurosclerosis*'), the end of social democratic reform politics and a 'change of tendency towards the right' ('*Tendenzwende*') in the FRG, the increase in tensions between the superpowers, and the deficits of industrial societies as revealed by ecological disasters and economic depressions. These crises also posed a threat to some of the Germans' (substitute) identities which up to then had proved reliable. The FRG was flooded with publications on the problem of identity in general, and of national identity in particular. Ever sensitive to such 'crises of meaning', the Germans went again in search of new orientations.[39]

Waves of nostalgia swept over Germany. In 1984, the *Heimat* TV series by Edgar Reitz gripped the whole nation, and mushrooming flea markets provided the bric-à-brac and flavour of the past. There was also an increased interest in history. Exhibitions on the *Staufer* (Swabian aristocracy) in 1977 and on Prussia in 1981 achieved record numbers of visitors. This interest in history even led to a 'Hitler wave' ('*Hitlerwelle*') which produced an abundance of publications and films, including the publication of the 'Hitler diaries' in 1983 (which turned out to be a hoax) in the respected German magazine *Stern*.

Rather than being an expression of traditional national or nationalist attitudes, the quest for identity in the national past was probably more deeply rooted in a general philosophy of life which implied a critical or pessimistic view of culture and modern civilisation.[40]

The promotion of 'national identity' gained additional impetus when Helmut Kohl became Chancellor of a CDU-led government in 1982. Kohl, however, with a PhD in history and a notoriety for invoking 'history' in every possible situation, stood for a more traditional concept of the nation. He created a kind of all-German language policy which, while continuing the detente-oriented *Deutschlandpolitik* of the former SPD-led government, rhetorically subsumed the GDR into the all-German nation. Reviving the term of 'fatherland', he frequently spoke of 'our German fatherland', 'our compatriots in the GDR', and 'two states in Germany' (rather than 'two German states').

Kohl's remedy for the 'spiritual and moral crisis' he had identified in

Germany was an increased use of national symbols such as the anthem and the flag and a 'rehabilitation' of German history. He initiated the building of two national History Museums in Bonn and Berlin and the setting up of a National Memorial in Berlin. In a number of symbolic political acts, he tried to relieve German history of the burden of National Socialism. The most famous examples of this were pointed gestures of reconciliation with the French President Mitterrand in Verdun in 1984 and US President Reagan at a German war cemetery in Bitburg in 1985. This attempt at a history policy was supported by conservative historians and journalists who tried to historicise National Socialism and thus relativise it as the most important paradigm for German historical consciousness.[41]

The most famous academic example of conservative attempts at historical revision was the so-called 'historians' debate' ('*Historikerstreit*') which was held in the print media from 1986 onwards. It was the conservative historian Nolte who had initiated the debate with the following revisionist thesis: that Hitler had accomplished an 'Asian deed' as a reaction to a threat posed by Stalin, who was the true inventor of the totalitarian model. As a result, National Socialism loses its singularity in history.[42]

This neo-conservatism in the interpretation of history did not remain unchallenged. Since the 1980s, there have been fierce arguments between the Left and Right about the importance, implications and interpretation of the period of National Socialism for the national identity of the Germans. The Left still demand a continuous and intensive *Vergangen-heitsbewältigung* (a uniquely German term meaning 'coming to terms with the past') in the form of discussions about the specific responsibilities that result for Germans from National Socialism, and a *Gedächtnisarbeit* (a labour of remembrance) in order not to forget the crimes committed in the name of the German people. This *Gedächtnisarbeit* materialises in many local history initiatives which try to unearth the traces of National Socialism and anti-fascism in their local communities. With regard to National Socialist memorials, the 1980s saw a development which can almost be described as a boom in commemoration to which a vast number of new local memorials bear witness.[43]

The demand for the commemoration of National Socialism had increasingly to be met by official functions. In the 1980s, public commemoration of the anniversaries of important events of the war and the Nazi regime was subject to fierce arguments between the Left and the Right. On the fortieth anniversary of the end of the Second World War (8 May 1985), the then President of the FRG, Richard von Weizsäcker (CDU), in a widely acclaimed and publicised speech described the day as one of liberation for the Germans. For this he was harshly criticised by members of his own party, but even more so by the Bavarian Christian Social Union (CSU) which would have preferred a greater emphasis on the total devastation of Germany, the loss of the *Heimat* in the east and the start of the division of Germany. The same debate was to arise again ten years later, but this time the conservative Right took the initiative by launching a campaign *Gegen das Vergessen* (Let us not forget) in which they stressed the loss of *Heimat* and the beginning of communist rule in East Germany.

GERMAN UNIFICATION[44]

After unification, the debate about German national identity was dominated by two questions. First, is the new Germany really united, or are there now two German identities: an East German, and a West German? Second, is the united, bigger Germany again threatened by the inner forces of nationalism?

Unification and unity

The leadership of Mikhail Gorbachev resulted in a number of reforms not only in the Soviet Union itself but also in other states of the Eastern bloc. These reforms bypassed the GDR, but nonetheless provoked a mass exodus of GDR citizens to the FRG via Hungary and Czechoslovakia on the one hand, and increased the activities of democratic opposition groups on the other. In October 1989, the protests against the rigid stance of the government culminated in mass demonstrations which challenged the self-definition of the state as a 'people's democracy' with the slogan 'We are the people'. When after the opening of the Berlin Wall in November 1989 the demonstrations continued, the slogan 'We are *one* people' emerged and soon drowned out the earlier version. This marked a transition from a politico-democratic to an ethnic concept of nation and put the single nation-state back on the agenda.

The fundamental question as to whether the Germans should aspire to a single nation-state soon polarised the cultural élites in both East and West Germany. The supporters of state unity maintained that the German people and culture had remained intact and had now regained the opportunity to blossom. Many observers regarded the East Germans' desire to achieve swiftly a level of welfare and consumption comparable to that of the West Germans as the main motivation behind the wish to reunite, a wish many East German intellectuals saw as a betrayal of the right of the GDR to reform itself. Both Eastern civil rights activists and dedicated communists favoured only a confederation of the two German states in which both could develop independently. They hoped for a reformed socialism or the synthesis of a 'third way' between capitalism and socialism. The famous West German author Günter Grass rejected a unified nation-state for historic reasons: for him, Auschwitz prohibited a resurrection of the German nation-state. Most of the West German Left who saw themselves as 'post-national Europeans' argued that the nation-state had passed its sell-by date and was functionally obsolete. This opinion was voiced among others by the SPD politician Oscar Lafontaine, who was later to challenge Helmut Kohl for the post of Chancellor in the first all-German elections in 1990.[45]

This controversy continued when the issue in question was no longer *whether* to achieve unity, but *how*. The Basic Law of the FRG allows in Article 23 for the accession of new members to the federation, and in Article 146 for a reunification of Germany which has to be sealed by the drafting of a new constitution. The Left favoured the latter possibility, as in their eyes only a new constitution approved by a referendum could give the unified nation-state its democratic legitimation as the state of all its citizens. The way actually chosen for unification, however, was based on Article 23 and a formal process of concluding treaties (i.e. the 'Treaty on Economic, Currency and Social Union', and later the 'Unification Treaty'). This was criticised by the Left as giving the FRG absolute dominance over the GDR, and was even labelled an annexation of the GDR by the FRG.

The opponents of unification, especially within the civil rights movement and the Party of Democratic Socialism (PDS) which is the successor organisation of the former ruling Socialist Unity Party, found their scepticism confirmed by the actual transformation process which many describe as colonisation.[46]

The current public debate focuses on the differences rather than the common ground between the East and West Germans. Over decades, the political cultures and mentalities have grown apart. West Germans were moulded according to the liberal, democratic Western model which cherishes the critical faculty of the individual while in the East authoritarian values have prevailed. Thus the East Germans are faced with a lengthy (and one-way) adjustment process which is to 'bring them up to West level'. If national identity is defined as a system of (consciously) shared (political) values and beliefs, such a common value-system can only to a very limited extent be assumed to exist after a division of forty years.

Different understandings of history also contribute to the conflict between East and West Germans.[47] Psychologically, most East Germans find themselves in a permanent defensive position as the West threatens to reinterpret and debase their individual biographies acquired in a state which did not act under the rule of law.

But it is not only different pasts that split the Germans. While, prior to unification, they claimed to be 'united though divided' ('*Spaltung in der Einheit*'), they are now threatened with becoming 'divided by unity' ('*Spaltung durch die Einheit*'). This alludes to the so-called 'wall in the heads' ('*Mauer in den Köpfen*'), a psychological 'wall' which has replaced the physical wall that split Berlin in two for over twenty-eight years. The East Germans feel treated as second-class citizens by the arrogant West Germans, the so-called '*Besserwessis*' (a pun derived from *Besserwisser* (know-all) and *Wessis* the East German term for people from the West). The West Germans counter this by describing the East Germans as *Jammerossis* (whingeing Easterners).

The asymmetrical economic, social, legal, cultural and political trans-formation processes following unification have left different traces in the east and west. Although there are certainly a number of positive changes, it is mainly the East Germans who have to change, adjust, reappraise and 'suffer'. Unemployment, which was unknown in the GDR but has now reached a peak of up to 30 per cent (if hidden unemployment is included), weighs especially heavily on the East Germans. The pressure of the transformation process is translated by some into nostalgia for the GDR which becomes positively transfigured. A specific East German identity partly expresses itself in a changed consumer behaviour which more and more reverts to produce and products familiar from GDR times.[48] The rapidly decreasing birthrate in East Germany since unification points to enormous social uncertainty and fear of the future. In surveys, the number of East Germans who define themselves as East Germans or former GDR citizens rather than Germans has grown.[49]

The most obvious expression of a distinct East German identity with regard to political attitudes is the success of the Party of Democratic Socialism (PDS) in national, regional and local elections in the east. Though burdened with the legacy of the past, the PDS has managed to establish itself in the east as a populist protest party which even enjoys the support of some prominent figureheads of the GDR opposition, while in the West it is still marginal. In the perception of the majority of West Germans, on the other hand, unification has not resulted in major changes apart from an increase in taxes, a cut in public spending, and repeated appeals to solidarity with East Germany of which they have soon grown tired.

A new nationalism?

Since 1990, the rise in racially motivated attacks, especially on asylum seekers and other foreigners, together with the growth in number and increasing public presence of neo-fascist organisations gives cause for concern.[50] This is underlined by the considerable, though not constant, gains of right-wing extremist parties in local and regional parliamentary elections. A most frightening incident occurred in 1992, when a group of young 'hooligans' set fire to an asylum seekers' hostel in Rostock/East Germany, their actions approved and even applauded by adult by-standers. On the other hand, it was only in West Germany that right-wing extremist parties such as the German People's Union DVU and the *Republikaner* succeeded in getting enough votes to take up seats in the parliaments of some of the federal states. And two surveys published in 1991 saw no signs of a rising German nationalism but testified rather to a 'pragmatic national consciousness'[51] or 'nationalist attitudes to a lesser degree than in other countries'.[52]

There are many possible, partly contradictory and exclusive, explanations for the evolution of militant right-wing extremism in Germany. Hostility towards foreigners in general and asylum seekers in particular is seen by some as a defence mechanism of an economic 'DM nationalism' which would like to reserve Germany's material wealth for the Germans: 'Germany to the Germans'; 'Germany first'; 'Foreigners go home!'. This attitude could help to explain why the hostility also encompasses 'ethnic Germans' from eastern Europe, some of whom have also become targets of violent attacks. Such an attitude can be found in other Western countries, too. In this context, the rejection of foreigners is sometimes also based on supposedly cultural grounds: 'Foreigners are criminals and fail to adjust to their new environment.'

However, it cannot be overlooked that, especially from the neo-Nazi camp, there are also attacks on members of the political Left and the disabled (i.e. people who, according to Nazi ideology, are 'un-German' or 'biologically worthless'). This constitutes a direct link to National Socialist racial theory. In the eyes of Weissbrod, this nationalism, which she considers to be widespread, is due to the fact that, despite all ideological claims to the continuing existence of one German nation, two distinct national identities have developed during forty years of separation. As there are no common (democratic) values and traditions on which a national identity could be based, a number of Germans have recourse to historical (i.e. ethnic/biological) patterns, and define their 'Germanness' by means of national delimitation.[53]

This process was reinforced by a dangerous public debate about a restrictive reform of Germany's asylum law. Anxieties that asylum seekers posed a threat to the German culture and welfare system were demagogically instrumentalised in party-political campaigns for federal state elections. In 1993, the asylum law was tightened, an official political act which could be interpreted as a late justification for right-wing violence. Dual citizenship for 'guest workers' is still rejected by the government. That these 'foreigners' are not seen as part of the citizen-nation of the FRG is illustrated by the fact that, when people grew more and more conscious that the term 'guest workers' had become inaccurate and, in fact, obsolete, politicians came up with the substitute expression 'our foreign co-citizens' ('unsere ausländischen Mitbürger'). What seems to be an embrace, actually marks them off as not belonging.

The debate on the 'nation'

The Left's concept of a multicultural society which is not founded on a common identity based on a common past and culture but on 'constitutional patriotism' has since unification been countered by the Right with the revival of the idea of the 'people's nation' as a community united by solidarity and a common fate (*Schicksals- und Solidargemeinschaft*). The leader of the CDU parliamentary group in the German national parliament, Wolfgang Schäuble, hopes that political, economic and social crises can be dealt with more effectively when the population is emotionally tied to the nation.[54] The political Right promotes, and appeals to, values such as the willingness to make sacrifices for the national cause in order to alleviate the antagonism between East and West Germans and to make Germany more competitive and attractive to industrial investors by means of 'deregulation' and the 'flexibilisation' of its workforce. This environment has created a climate in which parts of the Left have concluded that the concept of 'constitutional patriotism' on its own might not be sufficient to counter the 'people's nation', but needs to be extended to include a positive Left concept of nation and patriotism.[55]

In the quest for a common national identity, the interpretation of, and attitude towards, history still seems to be crucial. The debate on history which started in the 1980s has been resumed. On a political level, the attempt to relativise, if not rehabilitate, Nazi history by symbolic acts continues. To his chagrin, Kohl was not allowed to participate in the ceremonies commemorating the fiftieth anniversary of D-Day in Normandy; in the official farewell ceremonies to the Russian troops from Berlin in September 1994, Kohl, unlike Boris Yeltsin, omitted any reference to the crucial role Soviet troops had played in the military defeat of National Socialism. To an even greater extent, Nazi history is being disposed of in the 'Central Monument for the Commemoration of the Victims of War and Tyranny' which was officially opened in 1993. This controversial monument commemorates *all* victims at the same place and at the same time: Germans and Jews, soldiers and civilians, victims of National Socialism and GDR socialism.[56] These are only some of the attempts to turn Germany into a 'normal' state, liberated from its Nazi stigma.

This process of 'renormalisation' is helped by the current concentration on the Stasi-files, that is, the files of the omnipresent GDR secret service on many citizens of the former GDR. The second *Vergangenheitsbewält-igung*, namely that of the GDR, could serve to drive out and finally close the book on the first *Vergangenheitsbewältigung*, that of National Socialism. This is at least the aim of the political Right. The totalitarianism theory which equates GDR socialism and National Socialism is experiencing a successful comeback.

Moreover, conservative historians and journalists have started a critical re-evaluation and reassessment of the history of the FRG for which the model of the first German nation-state under Bismarck serves as a yardstick.[57] The last few years have given rise to an intellectual 'new Right' who not only reject the negative fixation of German history on the National

Socialist regime, but who also start to question the Western orientation and integration of the FRG.[58] This new Right regards itself as 'advocate of the German nation'[59] which is not to be equated with the old FRG. New issues are put on the agenda: Should not the old FRG be described as an abnormal intermediate stop, a kind of superimposed *Sonderweg*, a satellite state under Anglo-American influence? Is it not time to put an end to German self-hatred and self-accusation in the aftermath of Hitler? Was the SPD detente policy not just wrong, but even a betrayal of the nation? Is it not time to get rid of the anti-authoritarian legacy of the extra-parliamentary opposition and to revive old historical models such as the Prussians? Is it not time for the FRG to pursue its own national interests in a more self-confident way, after forty years of power-political self-denial? Has Germany's centre not traditionally been more to the east than the west?

Foreign policy after unification

In order to assess to what extent official policies have already been shaped by the 'national discourse' a deeper analysis of, for example, 'the national interest' in German foreign policy since 1990 would be necessary. None the less, a few observations can be made to highlight the new situation after unification.

Immediately after unification, Germany supported the initiative of French President Mitterrand for a European economic and currency union which was subsequently outlined in the Treaty of Maastricht. The official European policy of the German government still steers towards supranational integration. However, a German rejection of the French wish to integrate the new and bigger Germany further and more firmly into Europe would have raised suspicion and might have led to anti-German alliances. That Germany is perceived as a real threat could be observed in the wake of the French referendum on the Maastricht Treaty in 1992, during which both supporters and opponents of the treaty used the fear of a German dominance over Europe as one of their main arguments. In the meantime, scepticism about the concept of a currency union has also arisen in Germany, mainly on the Right of the political spectrum and especially from the conservative CSU. In their eyes, an independent European central bank shaped after the model of the Bundesbank is an indispensable precondition. The CDU politicians Lamers and Schäuble in 1994 published a discussion paper which shows that the conservatives are prepared to pursue the idea of a two-tier European integration, with Germany and a few selected other countries as its core.[60] Among the German population, enthusiasm for European integration has dwindled since unification.[61]

The restraint German foreign policy had exercised after the Second

World War was for the first time interrupted in 1991 when, during the Yugoslavian conflict, Germany pressed its partners on the diplomatic recognition of Slovenia and Croatia. This German attitude gives rise to old fears of German hegemonic status in Eastern-Central Europe. The conservative German press, for example the *Frankfurter Allgemeine Zeitung*, has criticised Britain and France's perceived lack of hostility towards the Serbs, and interpreted this as a sign of support for an overtly anti-German power in the Balkans.

In 1994, the German Federal constitutional court gave its permission to an out-of-area deployment of the German army, the Bundeswehr. Thus for the first time since the Second World War, a military option has been made available as a means to pursue German national interests. However, the German public is deeply divided over this issue.

The German federal government supports Poland, Hungary and the Czech Republic in their applications to join the EU and NATO as this is in line with German economic and security interests. None the less, suspicions have arisen that Bonn is interested in establishing a special relationship between Germany and Russia, and German restraint in criticising Russia in the Chechen conflict has been taken as proof of this. With regards to the German-speaking minorities in eastern Europe, a latent potential for conflict cannot be overlooked although it has not yet found its way into a new nationalist discourse.[62]

In conclusion it is clear that German reunification in the context of the new Europe and the 'new world order' has created new strategic options which have provoked a considerable degree of apprehension among Germany's allies. However, despite some tentative flexing of the political muscles it appears that German foreign policy has still not fully come to terms with the new options available. The title of A. Bahring's book *Deutschland, was nun?*[63] (*Germany, what next?*) seems to spotlight this new situation for united Germany.

NOTES

1 The author of this article is west German and argues mainly from the perspective of the 'old' FRG.
2 H. Honolka, *Schwarzrotgrün. Die Bundesrepublik auf der Suche nach ihrer Identität*, Munich, C.H. Beck Verlag, 1987, pp.59–63.
3 H. Plessner, *Die verspätete Nation. Über die politische Verführbarkeit bürgerlichen Geistes*, Stuttgart, Kohlhammer, 1974.
4 Ch. von Krockow, 'Zur Anthropologie und Soziologie der Identität', *Soziale Welt* 1985, 2: 142f; cited in Honolka, op. cit., p.87.
5 J.G. Fichte, 'Reden an die deutsche Nation', in *Fichtes Werke*, ed. by I.H. Fichte, Berlin, 1971, vol. 7, pp.359, 374f; J.G. Herder, *Ideen zur Philosophie der Geschichte der Menschheit*, Berlin, Weimar, R. Löwit, 1965, vol., 1, p.368f.
6 I. Geiss, *Die deutsche Frage 1806–1990*, Mannheim, Leipzig, Vienna, Zurich, BI-Taschenbuchverlag, 1992, p.6.

7 O. Dann, *Nation und Nationalismus in Deutschland 1770–1990*, Munich, C.H. Beck Verlag, 1993, p.162.

8 O. Dann, ibid, p.187

9 I. Geiss, op. cit., p.73

10 P. Glotz, *Die deutsche Rechte*, Munich, Heyne Verlag, 1992, p.152.

11 P. Alter, 'Nationalism and German politics after 1945', in J. Breuilly (ed.), *The State of Germany. The National Idea in the Making, Unmaking and Remaking of a Modern Nation-State*, London, Longman, 1992, pp.154–76.

12 P. Merkl, 'A new German identity?', in G. Smith *et al.* (eds), *Developments in German Politics*, Basingstoke, Macmillan, 1992, pp.327–48.

13 U. Liebert, 'Kein neuer deutscher Nationalismus? Vereinigungsdebatte und Nationalbewußtsein auf dem "Durchmarsch" zur deutschen Einheit', in U. Liebert, and W. Merkel (eds), *Die Politik zur deutschen Einheit. Probleme, Strategien, Kontroversen*, Opladen, Leske und Budrich, 1991, pp.51–94.

14 Ch. von Krockow, 'Die fehlende Selbstverständlichkeit', in W. Weidenfeld (ed.), *Die Identität der Deutschen*, Bonn, 1983, pp.154–69.

15 Imperial Germany (founded in 1871) was superseded by the Weimar Republic (1918) which was transformed into the Third Reich (1933), the defeat of which resulted in allied occupation (1945) which in turn led to the division into the separate states of the FRG and the GDR (1949) which were finally united to form the new FRG (1990).

16 H. Rausch, 'Politisches Bewußtsein und politische Einstellungen im Wandel', in W. Weidenfeld (ed.), *Die Identität der Deutschen*, op. cit., pp.119–53.

17 Ibid.

18 This alluded primarily to the *Ost- und Deutschlandpolitik* of the Social Democratic party (SPD).

19 *5 Millionen Deutsche, 'Wir sollten wieder einen Führer haben ...'. Die SINUS-Studie über rechtsextremistische Einstellungen bei den Deutschen*, Reinbek, Rowohlolt Verlag, 1981.

20 However, a survey conducted in 1994 by *Der Spiegel* magazine revealed that about a third of the German population had no idea what had taken place on 17 June 1953 (*Der Spiegel* 1994, 51: 109).

21 Ch. Hacke, 'Die Deutschlandpolitik der Bundesrepublik Deutschland', in W. Weidenfeld and H. Zimmermann (eds), *Deutschland-Handbuch. Eine doppelte Bilanz 1949–1989*, Munich, Vienna, Carl Hanser Verlag, 1989, pp.535–50.

22 V. Rittberger, 'Die Bundesrepublik Deutschland – eine Weltmacht? Außenpolitik nach vierzig Jahren', *Aus Politik und Zeitgeschichte. Beilage zur Wochenzeitung Das Parlament*, Bundeszentrale für politische Bildung, Bonn, 1990, vols 4–5, pp.3–19.

23 This was still the case during the Gulf War in 1991 where Germany was reproached by its NATO partners for not deploying troops but offering high financial contributions instead.

24 H.P. Schwarz, *Die gezähmten Deutschen. Von der Machtbesessenheit zur Machtvergessenheit*, Stuttgart, Deutsche Verlagsanstalt, 1985, provides an example that this restraint was criticised even prior to German unity when he denounced German foreign policy as being 'oblivious to power'. This criticism sees the German people and their political élites as sunken into an idyllic dreamland ('swissification') which knows neither conflict nor war. The FRG, it is claimed, has hidden behind its Western partners and enjoyed the security of not having to make controversial decisions. Only German unification has revealed the falseness of this situation and put a stop to its continuation.

25 M.R. Lepsius, 'Die Teilung Deutschlands und die deutsche Nation', in L. Albertin and W. Link (eds), *Politische Parteien auf dem Weg zur parlamentarischen*

Demokratie in Deutschland. Entwicklungslinien bis zur Gegenwart, Dusseldorf, Droste Verlag, 1981, pp.417–49.

26 H. James, *A German Identity 1770–1990*, London, Weidenfeld & Nicolson, 1989.

27 S. Barbour, 'Uns knüpft der Sprache heilig Band. Reflections on the role of language in German nationalism, past and present', *Stuttgarter Arbeiten zur Germanistik*, 1993, 280: 313–32.

28 M. Kaase, 'Bewußtseinslagen und Leitbilder in der Bundesrepublik Deutschland', in W. Weidenfeld and H. Zimmermann (eds), *Deutschland-Handbuch*, op. cit., pp.203–20.

29 W.J. Mommsen, 'Wandlungen der nationalen Identität', in W. Weidenfeld (ed.), *Die Identität*, op. cit., pp.170–92.

30 R.H. Brocke, 'Deutschlandpolitik der SPD', in W. Weidenfeld and K-R. Korte (eds), *Handwörterbuch zur deutschen Einheit*, Frankfurt/Main, Campus Verlag, 1992, pp.216–28.

31 'Wie gehts, Egon Bahr?', interview by U. Esterer, in *Vorwärts* 1994, 12: 47.

32 M. Kaase, op. cit., pp.202–20.

33 D.Sternberger, 'Verfassungspatriotismus', *Frankfurter Allgemeine Zeitung*, 23 May 1979.

34 K.R. Korte, 'Deutschlandbilder. Die deutsche Frage in den siebziger und achtziger Jahren', in W. Weidenfeld (ed.), *Politische Kultur und deutsche Frage. Materialien zum Staats- und Nationalbewußtsein in der Bundesrepublik Deutschland*, Colonge, Verlag Wissenschaft und Politik, 1989.

35 M. Kaase, op.cit.

36 H.A. Winkler, 'Nationalismus, Nationalstaat und nationale Frage in Deutschland seit 1945', in *Aus Politik und Zeitgeschichte. Beilage zur Wochenzeitung Das Parlament* 1991, 40: 12–24.

37 This supposed trend to 'de-nationalise' identity is still prevailing among younger people, even four years after unification. In a recent survey conducted by the magazine *Der Spiegel*, only about one in three of all 14- to 29-year-olds regarded themselves primarily as Germans, and even these showed parallel local, regional and European identities. Only 52 per cent are proud to be German, 57 per cent express indifference towards the German flag, 31 per cent do not have any thoughts in connection with the nation, and for 21 per cent it is an old-fashioned term. Over 60 per cent maintain that the day the Berlin Wall came down was not a 'key experience for a new national feeling'. On the other hand, the same survey unearthed some attitudes from which the survival of traditional national identities may be inferred: 87 per cent regard themselves as superior to the Polish people, 24 per cent think that without the war Hitler would have been a great statesman ('Die Eigensinnigen. Selbstporträt einer Generation', *Spiegel special*, 1994, vol. 11).

38 R. Stolz (ed.), *Ein anderes Deutschland. Grün-alternative Bewegung und neue Antworten auf die Deutsche Frage*, Berlin, Verlag Clemens Zerling, 1985.

39 K.R. Korte, op. cit., pp.112–31.

40 Ch. Fenner, 'Das Ende des Provisoriums Bundesrepublik. Reaktionen einer postnationalen Gesellschaft auf die Anmutung des Nationalen', in W. Süß (ed.), *Die Bundesrepublik in den achtziger Jahren*, Opladen, Leske & Budrich, 1991, pp.307–20.

41 Ch.S. Maier, *Die Gegenwart der Vergangenheit. Geschichte und die nationale Identität der Deutschen*, Frankfurt, New York, Campus Verlag, 1992.

42 E. Nolte, 'Vergangenheit, die nicht vergehen will', in *Historikerstreit. Die Dokumentation der Kontroverse um die Einzigartigkeit der nationalsozialistischen Judenvernichtung*, Munich, Piper Verlag, 1987, pp.39–48.

43 B. Eichmann, 'Denkmäler: Grabsteine für Denkprozesse? Wie wir es versäumten, mit NS-Geschichte umzugehen', *Das Parlament* 1986, 20–1: 3.

44 The use of the terms 'unification' or 'reunification' in itself divides the political camps. While the Right favour 'reunification', the Left tend to refer to the accession of the GDR to the FRG as 'unification'.

45 U. Liebert, op. cit., pp.51–94.

46 Ibid.

47 F.P. Lutz, 'Verantwortungsbewußtsein und Wohlstandschauvinismus: Die Bedeutung historisch-politischer Einstellungen der Deutschen nach der Einheit', in W. Weidenfeld (ed.), *Deutschland. Eine Nation – doppelte Geschichte. Materialien zum deutschen Selbstverständnis*, Cologne, Wissenschaft und Politik, 1993, pp.157–74.

48 R. Gries, 'Der Geschmack der Heimat. Bausteine zu einer Mentalitätsgeschichte der Ostprodukte nach der Wende', *Deutschland Archiv* 1994, 10: 1041–58.

49 E. Noelle-Neumann, 'Wird sich jetzt fremd, was zusammengehört? Der Allensbacher Monatsbericht', *Frankfurter Allgemeine Zeitung*, 19 May 1993.

50 K. Bullan, J. Bischoff and R. Detje, *Nationalismus und Neue Rechte*, Hamburg, VSA Verlag, 1993.

51 W. Weidenfeld and K.R. Korte, *Die Deutschen – Profil einer Nation*, Stuttgart, Klett-Cotta, 1991.

52 E.K. Scheuch, *Wie deutsch sind die Deutschen? Eine Nation wandelt ihr Gesicht*, Bergisch Gladbach, G Lübbe Verlag, 1991, p.85.

53 L. Weissbrod, 'Nationalism in reunified Germany', *German Politics* 1994, 3: 222–32.

54 W. Schäuble, *Und der Zukunft zugewandt*, Berlin, Siedler, 1994.

55 S. Berger, 'Nationalism and the Left in Germany', *New Left Review* 1994, 206: 55–70.

56 In my opinion, the fact that for the monument a Christian symbol (i.e. the Pietà) has been chosen is in itself an indication that the claim 'death has eradicated all differences', that is, the unwillingness to differentiate between different groups of victims and different degrees of victimisation, goes hand in hand with total indifference and ignorance towards the feelings of survivors of the Holocaust.

57 K. Weißmann, *Rückruf in die Geschichte*, Frankfurt, Berlin, Ullstein, 1992.

58 R. Zitelmann, K. Weissmann and M. Grossheim (eds), *Westbindung. Chancen und Risiken für Deutschland*, Frankfurt, Berlin, Propyläen, 1994.

59 H. Schwilk and U. Schacht (eds), *Die selbstbewußte Nation. 'Anschwellender Bocksgesang' und weitere Beiträge zu einer deutschen Debatte*, Frankfurt, Berlin, Ullstein, 1994.

60 Tactics won't save Britain from the essential decision', interview with K. Lamers by V. Smart in *European*, 10–16 February 1995, p.10.

61 Abschied von Europa?', survey by *Die Woche*, 30 June 1995, p.19.

62 G. Knischewski, 'Is the German Question finally solved?', *Journal of Area Studies. Perspectives of German Unification*, 1993, 3: 79–93.

63 A. Bahring, *Deutschland, was nun?*, Berlin, Siedler Verlag, 1991.

SELECT BIBLIOGRAPHY

Breuilly, J. (ed.) (1992) *The State of Germany. The National Idea in the Making, Unmaking and Remaking of a Modern Nation-State*, London Longman.

James, H. (1989) *A German Identity 1770–1990*, London, Weidenfeld & Nicolson.

Journal of Area Studies (1993) *Perspectives on German Unification*, no. 3 – special issue.

Smith, G. *et al.* (eds) (1992) *Developments in German Politics*, Basingstoke, Macmillan.

Part III

STATE, NATION AND REGION IN SOUTHERN EUROPE

7

MULTIPLE NATIONAL IDENTITIES, IMMIGRATION AND RACISM IN SPAIN AND PORTUGAL

David Corkill

Problems of nation and identity and the relationship between the state and the nation have been central to the history of Spain and Portugal for centuries. The Iberian neighbours are interesting case studies because they reveal the contrasting fortunes of attempts to forge collective identities at a national and regional level. Interestingly, after twenty years of democracy, issues of nation and identity are still very much at the centre of political discourse despite the perceived wisdom that credits Spain with having dealt successfully with the problem of regional nationalism and accommodated different identities as part of the transition process. Nevertheless, Spain is regarded as 'a laboratory for what a new Europe of regionalisms might be'.[1] At the same time, the Iberian nations, who both became members of the European Union in 1986, have demonstrated acceptance of, even enthusiasm for, European political union and the pooling of sovereignty. Indeed, it may be argued that Iberia demonstrates that centre and periphery nationalisms can coexist with supranationalism in the form of plural identities.

Spain and Portugal are among the oldest of the European states. Portugal lays claim to be the oldest nation-state in Europe, usually dated from as early as 1139. Unity in the Iberian peninsula was initially imposed during the Roman occupation of Hispania and later by the Spanish monarchy. Spain was under unitary monarchical rule from the early sixteenth century, although it remained only 'a dynastic union, a kind of confederation of kingdoms'[2] coexisting with strong basic identities (local and religious) underpinned by special privileges and legal peculiarities. Spanish unity, under an adminstratively weak state, was largely artificial until the late nineteenth century. In consequence, nationalism did not act as a force for social cohesion. No national flag existed before 1843, national monuments were few and the national anthem dates from the twentieth century. However, the centuries of struggle to remove the Arabs (*los moros*) from Spain forms part of the Spanish collective memory and is remembered in religious, cultural and folk ceremonies. That is why the recent increase in migration from North Africa touches a nerve (Maghrebi immigrants are known as *moros*) and reawakens fears of a threat emanating from across the Straits of Gibraltar. Both Spain and Portugal were pioneer imperial powers and the empire was an essential ingredient in attempts to forge a national, as distinct from local, identity. The imperial era all but ended for Spain in 1898, although Franco had ambitions to resuscitate the imperial dream, but the Portuguese empire endured until 1974. In fact the Salazar dictatorship employed the full weight of its propaganda machine and educational system to equate the concept of the Portuguese nation with the possession of a colonial empire.

Since the Napoleonic invasions there have been no major external security threats to the peninsula and, crucially, Spain did not become directly involved in the two World Wars while Portugal remained neutral during the 1939–45 conflict. However, internal differences were exacerbated by civil wars which further undermined the legitimacy of the Spanish state. According to Stanley Payne: 'in no other European country has nationalism been weaker than in Spain prior to 1936'.[3] The nation-building process was delayed by the self-criticism in the aftermath of the disastrous defeat and loss of the remaining major imperial possessions in the 1898 Spanish–American war. Spain lost its empire at the very time when other European powers were engaged in imperial expansion. Elsewhere in Europe nationalism was linked to modernisation. However, both Spain and Portugal were latecomers to industrialisation (large-scale industrial development does not get under way seriously until the 1960s in some parts of the peninsula) and therefore the forces of centre nationalism were correspondingly stunted. The distinctive feature is that industrial development occurs on the periphery in Catalonia and the Basque country while the capital, Madrid, artificially located at the geographical centre, had no industrial base to underpin its political-administrative hegemony. The same is true to a lesser extent in Portugal where the original industrial heartlands were located around Oporto in the north, while Lisbon remained a political and administrative centre.

Both countries endured long-lasting dictatorships for the best part of the twentieth century. From the 1920s to the 1970s there were no democratically elected governments (apart from the ill-fated Spanish Second Republic 1931–6). The authoritarian regimes that exercised power were contemporaneous with European fascism but both the Franco and Salazar regimes are more appropriately classified as clerico-conservative and reactionary, rather than fascist. Consequently, racism was not an important component in their ideology and programmes. In fact the dictators cultivated the myth of 'multicultural empires' based on the claim that the Spanish and Portuguese were less racist and more tolerant than other Europeans – it helped justify Salazar's retention of the African colonies long after other imperial powers had retreated from empire.

It is useful to distinguish between the period up to the mid-1970s and the post-transition period when democratic government was installed. The new democratic order provided the challenge and opportunity to restructure and develop a new framework within which the problems of national and regional identity could be readdressed. It is inevitable that more attention is devoted to the Spanish case when dealing with issues of national identity. Portugal's clearly defined borders and the absence of ethno-linguistic cleavages ensured that regional and local conflicts and tensions were muted, although traditionally based local identities remain strong. When separatist tendencies did surface, as among disgruntled settlers in Portugal's African territories during 1974–5, they were short-lived.[4]

DICTATORSHIP AND RIGID CENTRALISM

The unity of the Iberian peninsula is compromised by geographical factors. Brassloff[5] writes of 'the fragmented nature' of Spain which encouraged the growth of local identities. During the late nineteenth century what Payne[6] calls 'regional micronationalism' developed on the periphery as 'a centrifugal protest against the manifold frustrations attending the process of modernization and ... a reaction against the relative failure of nine-teenth-century liberalism in Spain'. There were two principal components to this nationalism. First, a cultural and ethnic basis and, second, a resentment at the inequitable distribution of economic and political power.

The foundations for the type of centralised nationalism associated with the Franco years were laid in the 1920s. During the Primo de Rivera dictatorship the ingredients of a centralising, authoritarian and develop-mental state were put in place. One of its major features was a cultural nationalism closely identified with the Catholic Church. In the 1930s an authoritarian centre nationalism was forged in response to the threat from the Left. It was essentially reactive against the forces of collectivisation, secularisation, and the federalism as outlined in the Catalan (1932) and Basque (1937) Statutes and the unfulfilled promises made to Galicia. The centralising nationalists were a politically heterogeneous group com-prising Catholic right-wing corporatists (CEDA), Carlist traditionalists, Falangist fascists and right-wing authoritarians united by a common fear of the Balkanisation of Spain. The army, a pillar of the new regime, regarded safeguarding the unity of Spain as one of its major duties. Franco used force to impose a centre-based conformity by ruthlessly suppressing expressions of regional identity and, in particular, linguistic differentiation. Catalan and Galician were dismissively categorised as 'dialects'. In its place he imposed a Castilian hegemony glorifying 'España' and its 'sacred and indestructible unity'. Francoist nationalism was not integrative, rather it sought to Castilianise, by replacing all traces of Spain's liberal past with an intolerant, anti-secular, anti-intellectual, anti-foreign Catholic conservatism. In so doing he created lingering feelings of resentment and injustice. In the 1960s the implicit offer to trade economic growth and privileges in return for political and cultural subordination was made by the regime in an attempt to renegotiate the bases of its legitimacy. Inevitably under an authoritarian, corporatist political order, the concept of social citizenship failed to take root in Spain and the development of civil society was consequently stunted.

Spanish nationalism was severely compromised by its links with the dictatorship, encapsulated in Pérez-Díaz's summation:[7]

> Francoism exhausted the whole gamut of standard Nationalist topics and emotions. The very concept of Spain had become tainted by association with notions of grandiloquent and vacuous imperialism, enforced Catholicism and centralized and authoritarian unitarism.

By the 1970s centre nationalism had few supporters and was compromised by its association with a deeply unpopular regime. Opposition to Franco became synonymous with regionalist politics. The regime's knee-jerk response to urban guerrilla violence, such as the shootings and bombings perpetrated by the Basque terrorist group ETA (Euskadi Ta Askatasuna – Basque Homeland and Freedom), had been to increase the level of state repression. The heavy-handed response of the state security forces served only to stir up opposition among the Basques and other nationalist movements and confirm that an inflexible regime still relied on coercion to maintain itself in power. As a consequence large numbers of Spaniards do not identify with 'España', and avoid using the term, preferring instead to refer to the 'Spanish state' or 'the peninsula'.[8]

The Salazar dictatorship in Portugal based its claim to legitimacy on the contention that democracy and representative government were incompatible with 'national unity'.[9] Expressions of opposition to centralist controls were countered by a combination of repression and propaganda to promote national myths which mixed the fictions that Portugal remained a great power with a unique civilising mission in Africa. Defiant assertions that the country stood *orgulhosamente só* (proudly alone) were reinforced by the revival in national Catholicism which was centred on the promotion of the *Fátima* cult. But, above all, Salazar relied on depoliticisation, traditionalism and non-political icons (the famous *'football, fado and Fátima'*) as both a validating mechanism and to engender a sense of national identity.

NATIONALISM IN A DEMOCRATIC CONTEXT

Although the Iberian dictatorships both terminated in the mid-1970s the transition processes followed different trajectories. In Portugal the military overthrew Salazar's successor Marcelo Caetano and a period of upheaval followed (1974–6) during which short-lived regional tensions surfaced. They took the form of a south (radical, leftist)–north (conservative, moderate) divide as the military tried to forge a government alliance with the communists. A potentially explosive situation was diffused when constitutionalist elements within the military asserted themselves and threw their weight behind the pluralist, West European democratic model advocated by the political parties and leaders like Mário Soares.

It is generally agreed that in the Spanish case there could have been no successful transition without addressing the devolution question. When constructing the new political order the historic nationalisms had to be accommodated and offered some form of self-government. As Pérez-Díaz points out[10] the political class felt no attachment to centre nationalism but did feel a sense of historical guilt that legitimate claims had been repressed for so long. The 'politics of consensus', a pragmatic approach skilfully managed by Adolfo Suárez and endorsed by all the major political forces, produced a compromise. The resulting 1978 Constitution, referred to the 'insoluble unity of the Spanish nation' but also guaranteed 'the right to autonomy of the nationalities and regions which form it' in an attempt to find a balance between centralism and localism and to avoid antagonising either Right or Left. Significantly the right to form autonomous communities was granted to all parts of Spain and 'what had initially been proposed as an answer to the problem posed by nationalist causes became a general formula for the structure of the Spanish state'.[11] The three 'historic' nationalisms (Basque, Catalan and Galician) were put at the head of the queue because they claimed to have the characteristics associated with nationhood – language, history, culture and collective identity. This was the basis of their claim for autonomy and, from some quarters, for their independence. However, some regions resented their treatment as inferior to the historic autonomies and ultimately an improvised, *ad hoc* solution emerged which, despite containing 'limitations and inconsistencies',[12] did win general approval in the short term.

By 1984 the Spanish territory had been divided into seventeen autonomous communities, each with its own statute of autonomy and regional assembly. Clearly very little logic existed in the arrangements:

- the communities differed greatly with respect to the strength of local nationalism;
- some communities comprised several provinces, others only one;
- the powers initially devolved to each community varied considerably. This led to accusations that a two-tier autonomy process existed in practice;
- another layer of government was inserted into an already heavily over-bureaucratised structure;
- and Madrid remained the main source of finance for the communities.

The Basque provinces illustrate the confusion: Basque nationalism is based on a language (*Euskera*), historic devolved legal and financial rights (*fueros*) and, in some versions, notions of ethnic and racial superiority. Born in the 1890s as industrialisation drew migrant labour to the north from other parts of Spain it received a new impetus following the influx of thousands of non-Basques in the 1960s. The territorial meaning of the nation is ambiguous in the Basque case because it incorporates provinces where little Basque is spoken. It is interesting not so much because of ETA violence and continued nationalist demands but for its role in democratic consolidation under a pluralist, quasi-federal structure. While the Basque nationalists were critical of the constitutional settlement (less than 50 per cent actually voted in favour) it has gradually become more widely accepted over the years. In part this can be explained by the gradual transfer of resources to the new tier of government. The share of expenditure controlled by the regional authorities rose from 13.5 per cent in 1983 to 44.2 per cent in 1994.[13] Violence, which has claimed 800 lives in twenty-five years of terrorism, has declined and ETA has been marginalised. Two approaches are identifiable within Basque nationalism: 'the moderates' who assert Basque identity within the Spanish state, like the regional president, José António Ardanza and the Basque Nationalist Party (PNV); and 'the radicals' typified by ETA and Herri Batasuna (HB or Popular Unity). It did appear that the moderate PNV had become domesticated and posed no challenge to the legitimacy of the Spanish state. However, there is recent evidence that the Basques may be leaning towards rejectionism. During the campaign for the October 1994 regional elections the Centre Right PNV leader, Xavier Arzalluz, made a series of controversial statements:

> I'd take a black man who speaks Basque before a white man who doesn't. We are not loyal to the Constitution. If some of our youths have been out shooting it is because they [the Spanish nationalists] have imposed their law with arms.[14]

Arzalluz's rhetoric and the orchestration of support for independence can be interpreted as part of an effort not to be outflanked by HB. The PNV was struggling to come to terms with the realisation that the notion of the Basque nation had become increasingly outdated by the late 1980s and early 1990s. The problems arose because the party continued to stress its Catholicism in an increasingly secular society and continued to be identified with outdated cultural and social mores. Some were satisfied with the concessions already won on autonomy. Not surprisingly the PNV quickly embraced the concept of 'a Europe of Regions' (or even 'Europe of the Cities') – in which the nation-state is downgraded – as a non-violent means to achieve greater autonomy within a unified Europe and resist domination by core regions and international forces. The creation of the Committee of the Regions (CR) in March 1994 enabled the PNV and Catalan leaders like Jordi Pujol to argue that the Basques and Catalans can become European regions on a par with Spain. In its 1993 election programme the PNV included a section on 'Euzkadi: a nation in Europe', but far more attention was paid to the problems caused by declining traditional industries and calls for further transfers of the powers outlined in the Basque statute.[15]

Catalonia provides an illustration of the important role that language plays in national identity where it has become a symbol for nationalist aspirations as well as the links between identity and territoriality ('portable identity', in particular) generated by migration. It is estimated that approximately one quarter of the Spanish population speak a regional language either singly or bilingually and Catalan is recognised by the EU as a working language. Although regarded as 'moderate' in the pursuit of its aims Catalonia responded to mass migration into the region and the threatened dilution of its identity by insisting on 'linguistic immersion' in order to promote monolingualism. Instead of treating them as outsiders the Catalan regional government, the Generalitat, has pursued a policy of integrating newcomers into Catalan culture and society – in part this reflects the traditional distrust of bilingualism. When it was announced that children up to the age of eight would be taught entirely in Catalan at school the large population of *castellanohablantes* (Castilian Spanish speakers) reacted angrily, accusing the Catalan authorities of wishing to eradicate Spanish against the wishes of the parents and behaving 'like Franco, but in reverse'.[16] Feelings ran particularly high in provinces like Tarragona which has a large Spanish-speaking population. Eventually legal action led the high court to rule that the Generalitat had violated the law by denying primary education in their own language to Castilian speakers, but this did not deter the Catalan authorities from introducing strict new laws in 1994 to discourage bilingualism. It is also worth recognising that problems have arisen when language planners have tried to impose their version of linguistic 'normalisation'. Traditional Galician speakers from the rural hinterland have resisted attempts to introduce a 'Castilianised' orthography.[17]

Devolution may have involved the transfer of administrative and political power from Madrid to the regions, but it has been counterbalanced by a concentration of economic power at the centre. Ironically, as the capital began to rival Catalonia in its ability to attract foreign investment it came closer to being 'the true metropolis of the national economy'.[18] In contrast, the autonomous tier of government has, broadly speaking, drawn resources from the centre. The tilting of the political balance back in favour of the regional nationalists is the product of Spain's political evolution under the consolidated democracy. Following the 1993 parliamentary elections the government headed by Prime Minister Felipe

González did not enjoy a majority in the Cortes and was dependent on the votes of nationalist deputies to keep it in power. As a result González has been forced to make some concessions to nationalist calls for greater autonomy. In late 1994 the prime minister, speaking in a debate on the autonomous communities, agreed to consider reform of the senate with a view to increasing regional representation. He also promised to improve the allocation of funds, grant the regions more say in European policy, give consideration to reform of the Spanish constitution, and streamline the civil service.

It is interesting to note that while Spain debated the exact form devolution would take, a new focus for national unity was being forged. To the surprise of many, the monarchy played a key role in the transition to democracy. King Juan Carlos's commitment to democracy and in particular his unwillingness to back the right-wing coup attempt in 1981 won the monarchy considerable public esteem and respect, even from among former republicans. Events during 1992 ('The Year of Spain') helped to consolidate further the sense of national belonging. The attention focused on Spain during the 500th anniversary celebrations of Columbus's voyage to America (Expo '92 in Seville and the Olympic Games in Barcelona) raised questions about how Españolised the events should be. During the Olympic Games the potential conflict was skilfully mediated by a judicious balancing of symbols and practices during the eleven-day event. Equal status was given to the national and Catalan flags, Catalan featured among the four official languages used and the Catalan national hymn and sardana (a folk dance symbolising Catalan culture) were integrated into the opening and closing ceremonies. The prominent role played by the monarchy and the royal family enhanced the prestige of the Spanish state (which benefited also in economic terms) and the ability to avoid conflict confirmed that Spain had become a mature, pluralist democracy.[19]

IMMIGRATION

Spain and Portugal have gone from being major labour exporters during the 1960s to become 'new immigration centres' in the 1990s.[20] Traditionally Iberia has welcomed immigrants from the Spanish and Portuguese-speaking countries in Latin America and seasonal labour from North Africa. However, by the 1980s fears were being expressed that the Straits of Gibraltar were becoming A 'European Rio Grande' or 'Europe's sluicegate'. Indeed, the term *espaldas mojadas* or 'wetbacks' is used to describe migrants attempting to escape from poverty and political persecution in Africa.[21] There are a number of reasons why Iberia became so attractive to potential migrants:

- the growing prosperity and integration into the European Union;
- the traditional North European importers of labour imposed tight controls on immigration (which they were pressing southern Europe to replicate);
- Iberia was regarded, at least temporarily, as the 'soft underbelly' located on Europe's southern frontier geographically contiguous with the migrant's point of origin where war and famine acted as 'push' factors;
- the removal of internal barriers allowing for the free movement of labour have made Spain and Portugal ideal entry points for migrants seeking work and economic betterment in the EU.

The official (if not very reliable) figures for foreign residents in 1987 showed that Spain (335,000) and Portugal (90,000) lag far behind the major recipients Germany (4.6 million), France (3.6 million) and the UK (1.7 million). However, the significant feature of recent years is the accelerating migratory trend into Iberia. In the process the proportion of 'marginal' migrants (unskilled, work seeking) has overtaken 'élite' migration (retirement). In tandem with this development geographical concentration has become more marked. The number of immigrants from the Maghreb countries entering Spain doubled in the late 1980s. The majority of this new wave of immigrants comprised Berbers from the Rif mountain region in Morocco. Many of them exchanged their savings for a hazardous journey on a fishing vessel transporting illegal immigrants across the Straits. The illegal workforce in Spain grew substantially to an estimated 170,000–260,000 in 1989. To the Portuguese total must be added 60,000–70,000 irregular migrants.[22] The geographical concentration is even more marked than in Spain. The majority originate in the PALOP (*Países de Língua Oficial Portuguesa*) or Portuguese-speaking former colonies which comprise the Cape Verde Islands, Angola, Guinea-Bissau, Mozambique and São Tomé. The vast majority of the irregular migrants find work in Portugal's growing informal economy. Male migrants enter the construction industry and female migrants find employment as domestics in family service. In general they suffer acutely poor housing and working conditions, low wages, and insecure employment.

Despite the influx (only recently curtailed by restrictions on both sides of the Straits) immigrants make up only 2 per cent of the total population in Spain compared to 9 per cent in Germany and 7 per cent in France. This has not prevented some politicians, abetted by the media, playing up the link between immigration and crime and, in particular, the rise in drug dealing, prostitution, begging, etc. Recent surveys show that the vast majority of the Spanish public support 'government restrictions on immigrants seeking employment' even though immigrants comprise only 0.7 per cent of the total labour force. Despite their self-perception as a tolerant, assimilationist people the Portuguese appeared in first place in a European-wide survey[23] on intolerance towards minority groups. Discrimination appeared to be particularly visible in such areas as education and housing. Clearly, although the combination of poverty, authoritarian repression and a desire to make good abroad are recent in the Iberian memory, the Spanish and Portuguese show little sympathy or understanding for today's immigrants.

FORTRESS IBERIA

Two much-reported incidents illustrate the new tensions over immigration. The first flashpoint was the murder in November 1992 of a Caribbean immigrant from the Dominican Republic, Lucrecia Pérez, and the subsequent trial of four men, including a policeman. The police found fascist propaganda and flags with swastikas during a search of the policeman's apartment. What became widely regarded as Spain's first racist murder prompted a great deal of introspection and questioning. It was accompanied by the appearance of street graffiti proclaiming 'Stop immigration! Spaniards first!'. It provided evidence that racism and intolerance are probably more prevalent than previously thought, justifying the low pay and often appalling working conditions which immigrant labour suffers. Indeed, Ellwood[24] links the two phenomena in her study of the Spanish Right which, somewhat cautiously, stresses that social marginalisation was probably a more significant factor than race.

The second flashpoint was Lisbon's Portela Airport in January 1993 when eight Brazilians were deported despite having their passports in order, return tickets and sufficient money with them. The incident served as a touchstone for an anguished debate about Portuguese attitudes to foreigners. Apparently the police at the airport asked the Brazilians 'If Brazil is so big, why do you have to invade our country, which is so small?'[25] (*Cambio*, 16 March 1993). It highlighted Portugal's new role as a 'gendarme' for the European Union. To compound matters the Portuguese ambassador to Brazil referred to the expelled in disparaging and racist terms as *vagabundas* (prostitutes) and mulattoes. Not surprisingly emotions ran high and the Brazilians reacted swiftly to what they regarded as an affront. The Brazilian President Itamar Franco recalled his ambassador in Lisbon and rescinded laws to assist Portuguese settlement in Brazil, where one and a half million are already resident. Politicians and the press trawled through the long history of relations between the two Portuguese-speaking *povos irmoes* (brother peoples) recalling that in the past when Portugal experienced a crisis Brazil willingly opened its doors to welcome immigrants.

Immigration policy has evolved in parallel with the closer alignment between northern and southern Europe. The Portela incident indicated that the government was stumbling towards the formulation of an immigration policy. It reflected in part the response to pressure from Europe on the Iberians to tighten up their migration and asylum laws, but it also appears to meet with public approval. Opinion polls indicate that a majority are in favour of curbs on foreigners and 'economic refugees' in particular. In one survey three-quarters of those polled agreed that Portugal should limit the entry of job-seeking immigrants. In a parallel move the *Lei de asilo* (Asylum Law) has also been modified to take account of the prevailing mood. Opposition to the restrictive measures was expressed by the Portuguese President, Mário Soares, himself a former political exile under the dictatorship. The authorities gave illegal residents time to regularise their status, but the period proved to be too short (October 1992–February 1993), there was an information deficit and fear prevented many from doing so in case they were given the threatened 'one-way ticket' back to their country of origin.

In response to a perceived increase in xenophobia and racist incidents the Camara Municipal de Lisboa (Lisbon Council) established the Conselho Municipal de Comunidades Imigrantes e Minorias Etnicas (Municipal Council for Immigrant Communities and Ethnic Minorities) in July 1993 to stimulate a dialogue with the minority communities and to promote social integration. The Portuguese themselves were reminded just how vulnerable immigrant communities can be when the French government toughened its attitude to jobless illegal immigrants during 1994. It was decided that if a foreign worker from the EU is unemployed for more than twelve months, continued residence in France will only be granted for one extra year. If not then in work the immigrant faces expulsion. The measure was introduced to deal with the increased number of Portuguese and other foreigners entering France, where 12 per cent of the workforce is un-employed, in search of work. The new migration wave is directly attrib-utable to the crisis in Portuguese agriculture generated by entry into the European Community and the direct effects of the Common Agri-cultural Policy.

Portugal has no national identity problem comparable to that of its neighbour. It is certainly true that Portugal possesses one of the European 'cultures of the world' with an historical and literary tradition dating back many centuries. However, it has been necessary to redefine the nature of that identity during the last two decades. Portugal's place in the world is at the centre of this questioning as its identity has been transformed from one based on empire to a regional entity inside the European Union. It is a debate that is taking place against the background of the gradual erosion of nation-state sovereignty from above and below by the twin processes of Europeanisation and regionalisation. Portugal, along with its European partners, is coming to terms with a more limited and shared sovereignty and the adjustments associated with 'identity transference'.[26]

A survey conducted by the University of Lisbon's Institute of Social Science revealed that the Portuguese people possess considerable national pride (68.8 per cent, compared to 49 per cent for Spain and 38 per cent for Europe as a whole). However, the majority identify first with their region before their country or Europe. Interpretations of these findings suggest that these attitudes are associated with a traditional existence and are felt most strongly among the religious, rural and old. Interestingly, European integration was not viewed as a threat to national sovereignty. Over 65 per cent felt that EU membership had produced tangible benefits, but qualified their Euro-enthusiasm by reserving the right of national government to have the last word on vital matters.[27] Braga da Cruz, in his study on 'Nationalism and patriotism in contemporary Portuguese society', concluded that 'the Portuguese have a strong sense of national identity, a consistent national unity, and a deep sense of national sovereignty'.[28] However, the author warned that the forces unleashed by the modernisation process threatened to undermine this national cohesion.

A central feature of Portuguese national identity is the emigrant. Indeed, Brettell[29] regards the emigrant (over 1 million left Portugal to work abroad during the 1960s) as a core symbol in the Portuguese cultural system and a vehicle. for the nation's 'imagined community'. According to this interpretation today's emigrants are symbolic transformations of the Portuguese *navegadoes* (explorers). While abroad they carry with them markers of national identity and a strong link with a *terra* – their homeland.

> The emigrant is a pilgrim, a journeyer, and emigration is Portugal's national rite of passage ... the emigrant feels his Portugueseness once he is abroad and confronted by the other.[30]

In a reworking of Salazarist propaganda it is argued that Portugal is something more than a mere nation: it is *um povo peregrino* – a pilgrim people. Through travelling and working abroad the emigrant serves an important function in helping counteract the sobering reality that Portugal is *um pais pequeno* – a small, marginal country. Nevertheless, this is counterbalanced by the fact that Portuguese is the seventh most spoken language in the world, used on three continents by around 200 million people. This has given new impetus to efforts that led to the creation of the Comunidades de Paises de Lingua Portuguesa (CPLP), a forum established in 1994 to promote cooperation among Portuguese-speaking countries and communities around the world.

The poet Luís de Camões, author of the national epic *Os Lusíadas*, has come to be regarded as a synthesis of the national heritage. Following the 1974 Revolution the official national day was the 'Day of Camões and the Portuguese Communities'.[31] The poet proved to be such a potent symbol of national identity because he died in the year (1580) that Portugal lost its independence to Spain (restored sixty years later). In the nineteenth century the Romantic Movement promoted the memory of Camões as part of their efforts to construct and affirm the myths and symbols of Portugal's neglected imperial past.[32]

THE FAR RIGHT IN POST-AUTHORITARIAN IBERIA

Iberia has not proved to be fertile soil for the far Right which is, to all intents and purposes, politically marginalised and not perceived as a threat to the new order, despite events like the Tejero coup attempt to dislodge Spain's fledgling democracy in 1981. The explanations for this conclusion are partly historical and, until recently, the absence of issues that can be effectively exploited. The evidence to support this argument is strong, although there are signs that the situation may be undergoing modification in the 1990s.

Electorally the far Right has made a negligible impact on democratic politics in Spain. It is fragmented and suffers from a dearth of charismatic and strong leaders. The principal reason for this failure is the electorate's rejection of anyone associated with the old order and a discredited past.

1977 the far Right polled 105,000 votes, less than 1 per cent;
1979 400,000 votes, 2.2 per cent;
1982 the largest far-Right party, the UN, won only 100,899 votes;
1987 Frente Nacional (FN) received 123,000 votes in the European poll;
1989 The FN's 59,783 votes and the Falange's 23,500 votes left the far Right without a seat in the parliament (Cortes).

Participation in democratic elections taught the far Right an uncomfortable lesson: 'neither today nor in the 1930s had they won the hearts, minds, wallets or ballot papers of more than a handful of Spaniards'.[33] At the heart of this weakness is fragmentation – there were over 400 small, mainly skinhead, groups in the mid-1980s comprising little more than 'a tiny nuclei of adolescents'.[34] Their lack of resources, organisation and followers means that they are reduced to painting graffiti and attending commemorative demonstrations. Crucially the far Right has failed to find a leader to rally around. The best-known figure on the far Right, Blas Pinar, leader of the Fuerza Nueva and its successor the neo-fascist Frente Nacional, is unable to serve as a rallying point because he lacks the necessary credentials having spent the Civil War abroad. Another important factor is that until recently no racial element existed to focus on as a scapegoat for the large-scale and rising unemployment problem. Furthermore the Left does not pose the threat it did in the 1930s and no longer serves as a recruiting sergeant for the Right. The socialist and communist parties have abandoned Marxism for reformism and managing the capitalist system. Finally, the economic and social élite feel that their interests are best protected by the political status quo. A further explanation for the far Right's inability to exploit the immigration issue is that the socialist administrations since 1982 led by Felipe González have adopted a relatively harsh line, epitomised by the *Ley de Extranjería* (Law on Foreigners) and other immigration legislation.

A further complication for the far Right in Spain is provided by regionalism. The Right, which initially rejected Basque and Catalan claims for devolution and independence, now finds itself confined to the periphery in electoral terms. There it must compete with nationalist parties and respond to the 'regionalist consciousness' among voters. Despite these handicaps, the far Right should not be written off so easily. If the experience of Western Europe is anything to go by, neo-fascism has fed on fears centred on the linkage between immigration and unemployment and new parties are emerging that try to exploit the links. Launched in late 1993, the Movimiento Social Español (MSE) under the leadership of Ricardo Saenz Ynestrillas employs the symbols and propaganda associated with Francoism. Ynestrillas defines the MSE as a 'radical, nationalistic movement' and demands that the Catalan and Basque nationalist movements be outlawed. He included in one of his speeches to a party rally statements that demonstrate how the far Right has tried to appropriate the new vocabulary of identity and citizenship:

> We are here to fight against separatism and terrorism. We must halt the highly dangerous immigration which leads to poverty and delinquency, which limits employment opportunities and produces ghettoes in every country, endangering the national identity.[35]

In Portugal the far Right poses even less of a threat than in Spain. There are small neo-Nazi and skinhead groups like the Movimento de Accão Nacional (MAN) whose propaganda employs terminology such as 'racial purity', the repatriation of Blacks and other non-Europeans in order to ensure 'the survival of the nation, culture and identity' of the people. There have been isolated attacks on Blacks, Indians, drug addicts and heavy metal fans. In 1991 MAN was referred to the Constitutional Tribunal which imposed a ban preventing it from carrying out political activity. The question for the 1990s is whether far-Right groups find an effective way to exploit issues such as economic failure, unemployment, corruption, and democratic weariness.

CONCLUSION

The Iberian countries provide interesting insights into contemporary problems of nation and identity. In all but a handful of Spain's seventeen Autonomous Communities, an 'identity' has been artificially constructed in order to legitimise a broad state-led political project. Spain provides compelling evidence that nationalism and separatism are issues high on the political agenda and serves as an antidote to the assumption that modernisation and economic growth encourage integration and a weakening of parochial loyalties. In reality, the opposite has occurred. The increase in mobility, the erosion of class barriers and the atomisation of society have served to make nationalism and regionalism more, not less, appealing. It also underlines the failure at state level. The modern state is perceived as centralised, bureaucratic, distant, and uncaring. More worrying developments are the signs that Iberians are gradually becoming more disillusioned about Europe. They may begin to regard their immigrant populations as scapegoats for a wide range of social and economic ills. Already the link is being made with drugs, crime and the spread of the AIDS virus. One thing is certain – the themes of nationality and identity are undergoing constant redefinition and will need to be readdressed regularly in the future.

NOTES

Acknowledgement: I am indebted to Richard Gillespie for his comments on this paper.

1 S. Griffith, quote by Paul Smith in 'Of Spanish dissent', *Times Higher Education Supplement*, 16 September 1994, pp.15–16.

2 J. Junco, 'Spanish nationalism in the nineteenth century', paper delivered at the Conference on Nationalism and National Identity in Iberia, University of Southampton, 22–3 March 1995.

3 S. Payne, 'Nationalism, regionalism and micronationalism in Spain', *Journal of Contemporary History* 1991, 26: 479.

4 A de Figueiredo, *Portugal: Fifty Years of Dictatorship*, Harmondsworth, Penguin, 1975, p.187.

5 A. Brassloff, 'Spain: democracy and decentralization', in A. Brassloff and W. Brassloff (eds), *European Insights*, Oxford, Elsevier Science Publishers, 1991, p.58.

6 Payne, op. cit., p.482.

7 V. Pérez-Díaz, *The Return of Civil Society. The Emergence of Democratic Spain*, Cambridge, MA, Harvard University Press, 1993, p.197.

8 M. Hebbert, 'Spain – a centre–periphery transformation', in M. Hebbert and J. Hansen (eds), *Unfamiliar Territory*, London, Routledge, 1990, p.122.

9 Figueiredo, op. cit., p.187.

10 Pérez-Díaz, op. cit., p.198.

11 M. Siguan, *Multilingual Spain*, Amsterdam, Swets & Zeitlinger, 1993, p.281.

12 Ibid., p.282.

13 P. Heywood, *The Government and Politics of Spain*, forthcoming.

14 *European*, 21–7 October 1994.

15 R. Gillespie, 'The hour of the nationalists: Catalan and Basque parties in the Spanish general election of 6 June 1993', *Regional Politics & Policy*, 1993 3(3): 183.

16 *ABC*, 12 August 1993.

17 C. Hoffman, 'Language planning and language policies in Spain's autonomous

regions', paper presented at the Conference on Nationalism and National Identity in Iberia, University of Southampton, 22–3 March 1995.

18 Hebbert, op. cit., p.136.
19 J. Hargreaves, 'The Catalans and the Barcelona Olympic Games', paper delivered at the Conference on Nationalism and National Identity, University of Southampton, 22–3 March 1995.
20 C. de Valderrama, 'The new hosts. The case of Spain', *International Migration Review* 1993, xxvii (1) Spring: 169.
21 M. Carr, 'The Year of Spain', *Race & Class* 1993, 34 April/June: 72.
22 M. Ceu Esteves, *Portugal: Pais de Imigração*, Lisbon, Instituto de Estudos para o Desenvolvimento, 1991.
23 M. Eaton, 'Foreign residents and illegal immigrants: Os Negros em Portugal', *Ethnic and Racial Studies* 1993, 16(3) July: 550.
24 S. Ellwood, 'The Extreme Right in post-Francoist Spain', *Parliamentary Affairs* 1992, 43(3): 385.
25 *Cambio*, 16 March 1993.
26 M. Braga da Cruz, 'National identity in transition', in R. Herr (ed.), *The New Portugal: Democracy and Europe*, Berkeley, University of California Press, 1992, p.161.
27 *Expresso*, 10 June 1989.
28 Braga da Cruz, op. cit.
29 C. Brettell, 'The emigrant, the nation and the state in nineteenth and twentieth century Portugal', *Portuguese Studies Review* 1993, 2(2): 51–65.
30 Ibid., p.59.
31 A. Freeland, 'The people and the poet: Portuguese national identity and the Camões Tricentenary (1880)', paper delivered at the Conference on Nationalism and National Identity in Iberia, University of Southampton 22–3 March 1995.
32 Ibid.
33 Ellwood, op. cit., p.381.
34 Ibid.
35 *Guardian*, 14 December 1993.

SELECT BIBLIOGRAPHY

Almeida, O. (1994) 'Portugal and the concern with national identity', *Bulletin of Hispanic Studies* lxxi: 155–63.
Braga da Cruz, M. (1992) 'National identity in transition', in R. Herr (ed.), *The New Portugal: Democracy and Europe*, Berkeley, University of California Press.
Brassloff, A. (1991) 'Spain: democracy and decentralization', in A. Brassloff and W. Brassloff (eds), *European Insights*, Oxford, Elsevier Science Publishers, pp.57–68.
Brettell, C. (1993) 'The emigrant, the nation and the state in nineteenth and twentieth century Portugal', *Portuguese Studies Review* 2(2): 51–65.
Eaton, M. (1993) 'Foreign residents and illegal immigrants: Os Negros em Portugal', *Ethnic and Racial Studies* 16(3) July: 536–62.
Ellwood, S. (1992) 'The Extreme Right in post-Francoist Spain', *Parliamentary Affairs* 43(3): 373–85.
Garcia, S. (1993) *European Identity and the Search for Legitimacy*, London, Pinter.
Gillespie, R. (1993) 'The hour of the nationalists: Catalan and Basque parties in the Spanish general election of 6 June 1993', *Regional Politics & Policy* 3(3): 177–91.
Hebbert, M. (1990) 'Spain – a centre–periphery transformation', in M.Hebbert and J. Hansen (eds), *Unfamiliar Territory*, London, Routledge.

Payne, S. (1991) 'Nationalism, regionalism and micronationalism in Spain', *Journal of Contemporary History* 26: 479–91.

Pérez-Díaz, V. (1993) *The Return of Civil Society. The Emergence of Democratic Spain*, Cambridge, MA, Harvard University Press.

Siguan, M. (1993) *Multilingual Spain*, Amsterdam, Swets & Zeitlinger.

Valderrama, C. de (1993) 'The new hosts. The case of Spain', *International Migration Review* xxvii (1) Spring: 169–81.

8

ITALIAN NATIONAL IDENTITY AND THE FAILURE OF REGIONALISM

William Brierley and Luca Giacometti

In Italy's so-called first republic mass political parties dominated the political scene, giving Italians a partial sense of national identity. As the regime collapsed, old local and anti-state identities re-emerged, most strongly in the north. Between 1990 and 1994, these identities were mobilised into a political movement, the Northern Leagues led by Umberto Bossi, and it seemed for a while that they might lead the country in the formation of the second republic. The 1994 elections, however, revealed the fragility of localism in Italy: Italians chose the 'national' values expressed by the party (and even more by the personality) of the TV magnate Silvio Berlusconi. In a certain sense, this period marks the transition of Italy from a party-nation (a society which is dominated by the party-political system) to an information-nation (a society which is dominated by information and the media). This chapter seeks to explore the complexities of Italian national identity and to illuminate the recent transformation.

'MAKING THE ITALIANS': THE FAILURE OF PRE-UNIFICATION ITALY

Pre-unification models of Italy

'Italy' has been defined in a number of different ways and historical definitions of Italy influence our perception of modern Italy. Among these historical definitions, especially outside Italy, the 'Roman-Imperial' model has been dominant. According to this model, the Roman Empire is conceived as imposing itself almost without reference to pre-existing cultures. However, the modern notion of Italy was not exclusively determined by the 'Roman-Imperial model'; rather, in many ways, it came about despite it.[1] A large variety of cultures existed in Italy before Rome, and Rome absorbed and amalgamated these cultures, rather than simply inventing a new culture. The history of Italy is a history of conquerors, but also of vanquished, of the peoples who inhabited the peninsula before

Rome, and who gave it its first identifying characteristics. Pre-Roman influences have been undervalued in the definition of modern Italian identity.

Between 1200 and 1500, a second model was developed in Italy, through which painting, literature, forms of economic and political organisation and language combined to form a unique system, which could be defined as the 'merchant-commune model'. This model can be used to interpret the country as a whole not so much in the sense that the elements combine to form a national identity, but that they operate rather as a 'chorus', a collection of articulated 'objects' which form a mechanism, a global functional mechanism. Such that, for example, although the detailed politico-economic systems of Florence and Venice might have been different, they were sufficiently similar to each other and considerably different from the politico-economic organisation of France or England for a distinctively Italian model to emerge. This model did not survive long, however, and the Renaissance saw the beginning of a rapid collapse[2] as a result both of internal pressures and external intervention in internal affairs.

As the Renaissance waned, Italy lost not only its cultural unity, but also its political and economic unity, as the country, increasingly under foreign control, became fragmented into small principalities and dukedoms, lacking any unifying characteristics. In dealing with their foreign masters, the Italians became masters of rhetoric, of the art of flattery and pretence, thereby developing an 'uncivic' mentality of compromise and mediation, which functioned only to enable them to survive. The consequences of this were twofold: first, Italians placed far more emphasis on the individual, and on the social relationships absolutely necessary for day-to-day survival (the family, and the immediate local community, identified with the 'campanile' – the local church tower); and second, as solidarity and collective engagement reduced, conformism and lack of commitment to wider social objectives grew.[3] From then on, 'who the Italians are' has been a question relegated to the footnotes of the history of the nation. To the outside, it seemed that 'Italian-ness' did exist and that Italy was an identifiable entity; but in reality the conception of Italy was no longer shared or collective. The idea of Italy no longer generated those civic virtues[4] which make 'a nation of citizens', and Italy as a nation had no influence on European economic or political ideas.

Risorgimento and fascism: the defeat of the nation

The question of the 'Italian nation' became central again with the Risorgimento, which marked the beginning of the unification process and the birth of the Italian state (1861). Despite the support of democrats and proto-socialists for the unification process, Italian unification came about as the result of the efforts of Piedmontese moderates, who by force of diplomacy rather than firepower transformed the expansionist dreams of the Savoy monarchy into reality. But the post-unification social impasse between the northern bourgeoisie and the southern landowners, which led to a series of extremely moderate governments, prevented the nation from grappling with its problems, such as the very low levels of literacy and the consequent number of citizens whose only language was the local dialect; communications were very poor throughout the peninsula, and in many rural communities the Church, with its extensive network of parishes, was the only organisation larger than the family capable of transmitting values; industry had yet to develop, and agriculture was still extensive and poor. Against this background of general backwardness, a state which was present only to collect taxes or conscript young men into the army, could do nothing other than alienate popular consensus, or even revive nostalgia for a better past. So any sense of national belonging was bound to remain weak, and Piedmontese attempts to forge the nation around the myth of Rome (whose only objective was to demonstrate that Italy, whatever it might be, has rights through the 'virtues' or the 'glories' of Rome, whether republican or imperial), instead of a real collective consciousness, was bound to fail. Both the attempt to construct the nation from the top, and the sense of alienation of large masses of the people from the State, together with the lack of an authentic popular history, of heroes and victories with mythical status, taken altogether prevented the development of the social adhesive which could have made a nation of the country. 'Nationalist pomp' was used between 1861 and 1914 as a convenient scaffolding to prop up a weak nation, but it was unable to create a 'civic and democratic integration'.[5] The pre-war liberal class failed to build a popular national identity, and only the myth remained, but as industry grew and as Italy entered the list of nations with colonial ambitions, the myth was there to be exploited by nationalists before the First World War and by fascists after it.

The First World War was used by fascism in an instrumental way to create the image of Italy as a great imperial power. This did not convince the mass of the population. Nevertheless, the First World War did catalyse a sort of national consciousness, but at a mainly subcultural level. It was not that the masses, disorientated and up-rooted by the First World War, accepted the idea of Italy as designed by war propaganda, but that a real sense of solidarity, and therefore a common national identity, was forged as a result of the real trauma which the First World War created among them.

The middle classes and the rising petite bourgeoisie embraced fascism enthusiastically because they saw in it a medley of tradition and aspiration to be recognised as a great power: they really believed in the myth of the peasant empire which would defeat the decadent industrial nations, and in the 'illusion that they could overcome in one bound their economic and socio-cultural backwardness to enter the vast world of the dominators'.[6] But national-fascist ideology (as expressed by the National Fascist Party, Partito Nazionale Fascista – PNF) also included the objective of 'making the Italians', in the typical way associated with totalitarian regimes: 'by trying to subsume within itself the entire social body of the country, by aligning the social and the institutional in public life'.[7] The PNF failed in its project to 'nationalise' the Italians, because rather than attempting to construct a new national identity and instill the fascist idea, it limited itself to incorporating a variety of sectors behind the symbols of fascism. The PNF used its 'vanguards' for this purpose: party members and public employees; but also the so-called 'advanced guard of the fascist idea': school teachers, general practitioners, vets, the traditional mediators between local élites and central political power. And yet it had enjoyed a considerable amount of popular consensus: at least in terms of a facile comparison with the past, fascism guaranteed everybody (who belonged to the cadres or was in uniform) a certain social status, and it had tamed the means of communication (radio and newspapers). Thus fascism for the first time had instilled a sense of national pride in a large slice of Italians, but with the rapid collapse of the revolutionary fascist regime and its replacement by reactionary mass fascism, even this national consciousness declined. All that remained was nationalisation in a bureaucratic sense, in that Italians were controlled through their membership of state organisations. However, if the bureaucratic nationalisation of the middle classes succeeded (at least partially), that of the working class and of peripheral Italy failed miserably. The reasons for this lie in the working-class alienation from the fascist regime and the appeal that the Soviet Revolution had in the working-class imagination in the pre-fascist period, together with the persistence of deep-rooted local cultural traditions. Thus the objective of creating a national identity was reduced to that of making the masses faithful and obedient to their fascist masters. Moreover, in the long run, even the mobilisation capacity of the PNF was exhausted: 'fascist leaders and mere hangers-on subsided into a repetitive, tired routine, devoid of tension and creative impetus'.[8] To all of this, of course, must be added the Second World War, which as well as military defeat, also meant death, deportation, starvation, horror and devastation, which shattered forever the fascist illusions of grandeur.

The failure of the attempt to 'make Italians' did not lead, with the collapse of fascism, to the collapse of the idea of nation. In fact, subnational and subcultural notions persisted, which taken together gave a sense, in many ways a real sense, of 'being Italian'. In any case, there was the war emergency and, after the signing of the armistice on 8 September 1943, the moment of choice. For many Italians, that choice meant a reawakening of conscience.

Resistance as partial founding myth

The twenty-month war of liberation, long accepted as the great traumatic event that gave birth to the 'first Republic', has been recently brought into question by a number of historians in Italy. This has consequently redefined the Italians' way of seeing themselves, precisely at the time when the first Republic was coming to an end and the foundations of the second were being laid.

When the partisan war began after the signing of the armistice, Italy's army (left without orders) disintegrated, the king fled and the political class dissolved. There was a complete vacuum of power. The 'great trauma'[9] which shook the entire country, seemed to drag down with it the idea of nation. It was during those days (and the twenty months of armed struggle) that the Italians, although in limited numbers, redefined their sense of national belonging. Groups of motivated individuals took to the mountains, motivated by personal pride, feeling the need to reassert their personal identity after twenty years of fascist oppression, and therefore making a clear statement of both moral and civil responsibility. Later these individuals became groups and the partisan experience forged the political and ideological conditions for the creation or re-creation of post-war mass political parties. But there was also the majority, whose choice was to look on and wait for the storm to pass: exhausted and homesick soldiers; those who wanted only to survive (the middle classes), or to work (the peasants); those who concerned themselves with civil matters (the Church and associated bodies), or those who took to the hills to search their own consciences; those who waited for the allied victory and those who had already seen it;[10] those who simply would not get involved; or again those who had to work and confront capital (the workers). Questions may legitimately be asked about the motives which guided the partisans (and their early party-political formation), but there can be no doubt about the clear divide which separates the Italy of the conscientious minority from that of the silent majority, the so-called 'Italy of the *apoti*',[11] an example of Italian 'conformism', which is almost a virus whose typical expression was the '*uomo qualunque*' movement of the immediate post-war period.

Post-war partial attachments

What the Resistance failed to create in twenty months of political and military struggle, republican Italy has been unable to create in fifty years. Italians continued to have an exceptionally weak sense of national belonging, or rather a multiplicity of 'sub-national belongings'. Ancient divisions of the country persisted: between industrial north and agricultural south, between town and country, between the classes. And yet at the beginning, there was a strong desire for change. For many this meant 'defascistisation' and democratisation, for others the transformation of society along socialist lines. The groups included communists, socialists, the Action Party, social Christians – a heterogeneous and fragmented universe destined to ideological and electoral defeat in 1948. This period saw the failure of the defascistisation of the state, the amnesty for fascists, and the first criticisms of the Resistance. The outbreak of the Cold War froze any possible attempt at the forging of a unitary identity. And thus it was Christian Democracy (Democrazia Cristiana – DC), at the centre of all government coalitions from 1948 to 1994, which was to manage the reconstruction and modernisation of the country and bring Italy in the space of a few decades into the top league of Western industrialised nations. The DC was also able to a certain extent, through television and mass consumerism, to unify the country. But the DC managed all this by 'occupying' the state, by imposing a clientelistic system through which consensus was identified with material interests rather than ideal and/or ideological motivation. Again the idea of nation was sacrificed, especially in the south, and no collective identity developed apart from one associated with mere consumerism. In its place, what Rusconi calls 'separate allegiances' took root, in other words, allegiances to party, especially to the three great mass parties (Christian Democrats – DC; Italian Communist Party – PCI; and Italian Socialist Party – PSI).

The function of Christian Democracy, with its strongholds in the north-east and the south, was to unify the Catholic electorate politically and to delegate to the Church the education of the electorate in terms of values and identity, first against communist atheism, and second against the secularisation of society brought about by increased well-being. In terms of values, this led to personal and private morality being placed ahead of public and collective morality, and thus the relegation of the nation to a secondary status. The price which the nation paid for this 'state confessionalism' was high, and led to the Constitution paying only lip-service to liberal democracy and its more advanced social democratic principles, and the rejection of 'anti-fascism as the constituent ideology'. Even though the Resistance, as we have seen, had partly provided the values on which a democratic identity could be based, the first years of the Italian Republic emphatically rejected the transformation of the 'founding myth' (even if only partial) into a 'vehicle for a renewed national identity'.[12]

The post-war PCI, with its base in the north-west and the centre, was clearly a reformist party. It also attempted to be a national party, with solutions to all problems. With a solid base among northern industrial workers, the party needed to spread its influence throughout Italian society, and Togliatti's objective was to win over the middle classes, especially the intellectuals. After the electoral defeat of 1948, Togliatti warned that post-war Italy could not afford a confrontation between the bourgeoisie and the working class because this would lead to 'a schism in the body of the nation'; and thus the DC could not refuse to deal with the political representatives of the latter. His overtures were rejected. The PCI could do nothing during the 1950s but focus on the party itself and the education of the communist electorate. This was no easy task, given the daily dilemma of working to construct the 'socialist dream' or to 'reform capitalism', but at least the PCI, unlike the DC, immediately chose to prioritise the national-collective perspective over the narrower class perspective.

The consequences of these 'internal' and 'external' factors – respectively, the impossibility of alternative forms of government (the so-called blocked democracy) and the Cold War – led to dour confrontation, the representation of labour conflicts as if they were insurrectionary and directed by Cominform, and the permanent exclusion of political alternatives. This was achieved by Christian Democrat governments, through anti-strike laws, a public order policy which included the strengthening of the police force, the administrative censoring of the press, and the systematic exclusion of communists from public office.

The Socialist Party's (PSI) surprise success in the elections for the Constituent Assembly (1946) is explained by voters' memories of its prefascist record: the moral, civil, and social education of workers and peasants in reformist principles, together with a tradition of economic cooperation and good local government. Added to this was the energy and personality of Pietro Nenni, which helped people to forget that the party in the pre-fascist period had been strong on maximalist rhetoric, but weak on action. But this initial success could not be built upon. Its ranks still contained both revolutionaries and reformists, and the resulting ideological splits (including the loss of the social democratic Right) left the party in a very weak position at the 1948 election. Despite its electoral defeat, the PSI was again saved 'from without': the end of the DC absolute majority (1953) made the PSI pivotal in the system, and the crisis in the PCI (1956) released intellectual energy in the party's direction. Nevertheless, it was only Craxi's leadership, after 1976, which was to liberate the PSI from subordination to the communists. Craxi's leadership was, however, to have a far more devastating effect both on the people and on socialist values.

Social disintegration in the 1980s

After the crisis of the 1970s, which had been especially difficult in Italy, the economy began to expand again in the mid-1980s: production took off and a cheaper dollar led to an expansion of exports, the opening of new markets, and a reduction in the trade gap; the stock exchange boomed; large firms, including the state-owned firms, restructured, and small and medium-sized enterprises became crucial to the success of the economy, as also was the 'black' economy. To this was added the role of the media, and of private television in particular, in creating the collective euphoria surrounding the new mass consumerism of the 1980s. The development was not illusory, even if it hid the profound weaknesses of the system. An economy cannot be solid and lasting when it excludes one third of the country (the south), has huge government deficits and national debt, is constantly exposed to international influences, and is beset by organised crime which strangles the south of the country. In addition, the political class increasingly failed to represent social groups, and political parties increasingly failed to mediate social interests.

Society in the 1980s was changing. The contribution of industry to the economy was declining as the service sector grew. One consequence of this for the collective consciousness was the crisis in the so-called 'working-class centrality': an economic centrality which had been reflected in a series of values (solidarity, egalitarianism, a non-ideological democratic view of society) and clear political reference points. This was undermined in the 1980s by the urban middle classes (traditional and new), with their utilitarian values and their unstable political allegiances. Among the beneficiaries of what Turani calls 'the second economic miracle' were the members of the advanced tertiary sector: services, education, information, scientific and technological research, consultancy, which nurtured a deep feeling of trust in the private sector, which was seen as efficient and rewarding of personal initiative, and a consequent mistrust of the public sector, which was seen as inefficient and corrupt and a prey to political ambition. Milan became the symbol of these *'anni ruggenti'* ('the roaring eighties').[13]

Italians, faced with yet another major transformation, found that they had no valid political referents. They became disconnected from the political parties which had previously (at least partially) mediated their interests. The response to social pressure, which had previously been collective (both political and trade union), became fragmented and sectoral. The traditional mediators of these pressures were therefore displaced. The highest cost, at the political level, was paid by the DC, especially in its role as representative of the middle classes, as it was replaced in the north by the PSI. The 'moral vacuum' of civil society extended to the political domain and hit the parties of Craxi and Forlani hard, as the parties became ever more subordinate to sectional interests. The PSI, more than any other party, ceased completely to function as a channel for social representation and became completely artificial with neither ideological consistency nor sense of historical purpose. Lacking 'the moral tension assured by a Catholic tradition',[14] the party could not extend its roots, and the brief socialist revival (between 1983 and 1992, with the PSI vote at 11–15 per cent and Craxi as Prime Minister) was swept away by the unpredictabilities of the early 1990s. The DC and the PSI were not the only parties to pay the price: within just two elections (1992 and 1994) most of the political class of the first Republic was swept away.

The country, without entirely abandoning the values of the 1980s and the old ways of dividing up the political spoils, was however no longer prepared to put up with the excesses of *clientelismo* which the 1980s had imposed. Levels of corruption had exceeded tolerance levels and the magistracy, having sensed the new climate, took on the role of mediator of the will to change and began the job of dismantling the system. But renewal of the political system required more than just the work of the judges: a 'political' answer, from new political forces, was also necessary. Since the political class was completely discredited, and the new social forces could identify no new political class ready or able to take the place of the old one, they took on the job themselves, giving direct expression to their anti-political, productivist, utilitarian, culture and background. Political transformation, especially in the north, began to occur with the emergence of the Leagues.

THE LEAGUES

Self-determinism in Western Europe

The Leagues phenomenon, and the more general growth of ethnic and national movements, is neither new, nor conjunctural, nor uniquely Italian. The phenomenon has been developing in many countries since the 1960s.[15] In general, what unites these movements is their ideological re-evaluation of the past, and their consequent symbolic organisation of reality. A return to roots, territory, language and national customs: these elements were all used in different ways to determine the nature of the various 'ethno-national' movements as conservative, progressive, or technocratic modernisers.[16]

How did central governments respond to this phenomenon? With typical western, democratic methods: allowing partial satisfaction of negotiable claims (language policies, civil rights, some measure of admin-istrative decentralisation), while marginalising any anti-system demands (anti-capitalism, separatism). For the moment, the response seemed to work, but ethno-national problems, both long-running ones and more recent ones, continued to exist below the surface.

In considering the complex panorama of autonomist movements in Italy,[17] two distinct groups can be identified: on the one hand, the historic groups, which have existed for some time, and on the other, the new groups, and more precisely those which after 1989 constituted the Northern League. The unifying factors for the historic groups, and even for the new groups before the arrival of the Northern League, were their exclusively local dimension and their nostalgia for the past. This meant that at the national level, the handful of representatives that the voters could muster had no relevance and they attended only those parliamentary sessions where regional matters were discussed. At the local level, their participation was much more significant, and many attended regional, provincial and local assemblies. Within this category one would classify the Sardinian Action Party, the Union Valdotaine, and the South Tyrol People's Party. Further discussion of these groups is outside the scope of this chapter.

The Leagues phenomenon in Italy seemed different, influenced more by internal than external factors, and presented on the political stage as the brave, new face of politics. But this advance was accompanied by a significant metamorphosis in the movement itself. These changes in the Northern League, especially in the later stages between 1992 and 1994, were very rapid. By 1994 the League no longer behaved like the movements which represent 'small oppressed nations', but rather its interpretation of history and nation was used in an instrumental way as a means to achieving political power (at all costs). The chameleon qualities of the Northern League evoke comparisons with the ancient ill of the Italian system: *trasformismo*, whose only objective is the maintenance of the status quo and the conservation/extension of political power. The League did not sacrifice all its principles in this political game, although the right-wing alliance formed for the elections in 1994 was distinctly suspect. Rather the so-called 'Italian revolution' should be reconsidered from the point of view of 'anti-democratic conservative radicalism' as described by Melucci and Diani with reference to some 'nationalist' movements in Eastern Europe. We shall return to this later.

THE NORTHERN LEAGUE: ORIGINS AND SUCCESS

The first tremors: the Liga Veneta 1980–7

Although Bossi's League determined both the speed and shape of the so-called 'democratic revolution', in fact the first of the leagues was the Liga Veneta, led by Franco Rocchetta. Founded in 1980 as a club to promote dialect culture, it enjoyed surprising success in establishing itself in Veneto, which had previously been a solid Christian Democrat fiefdom. Its early electoral successes (1980 and 1983) attracted the attention of social and political researchers because those first few thousand votes, received almost as a gift and without any electoral battle, represented the first breach in a fortress which was previously considered impregnable. In fact, Veneto, a region of strong Catholic traditions, was a leading economic area where small landowners and small family firms predominated. Local identities (mainly anti-state) were also very strong. But the capable mediation of the Church, as guardian of universal values and identity, had managed to keep Veneto society together. The Veneto subculture had therefore become a 'white' (*bianca*) culture, indicating the extent of Catholic penetration within the subculture of the region), and had become entwined with its natural political expression: Christian Democracy. The implication was that so long as the values and identity of Church and DC coincided, political stability would be guaranteed. But ever since the 1960s, with the transition from an agricultural country to an industrial one, Italy had also become secular.[18] Thus the political crisis, whenever it broke, was bound to hit the DC, the 'political entrepreneur' which had mediated between centre and periphery in the name of Catholic universalism.[19] The secularisation of the Catholic party (*doroteizzazione*) transformed the traditional link with Veneto society (as indeed in other parts of Italy): as the religious identity weakened, the local DC changed its focus, no longer mediating between national and local values and identities, but rather merely facilitating the exchange of local interests. No alternative identity or system of values was proposed by the DC to substitute the weakening Catholic idea.

However, the political programme of the Liga in these early days was neither specific nor well developed, and having enjoyed some early success, the Liga Veneta risked losing everything during a period of stagnation (1985–7). And a second northern autonomist movement had been preparing to take the stage: the Lega Lombarda (Lombard League) of Umberto Bossi.

The early days of the Lombard League 1982–6

The Lega Autonomista Lombarda (LAL) was founded by a failed medical student, Umberto Bossi and a few close friends. The revaluation of dialect and local traditions, and of the 'local community' as the fundamental building block of society, were combined and formed part of a general attack on mass society which humiliated the individual. In Lombardy, as in Veneto before, a new *ethnie*[20] was created from scratch and was proposed as a basis for the ethno-nationalist demands of the League. This creation was totally devoid of any historical or anthropological basis. However, it did allow the whole history of the Republic (unification, fascism, and the first Republic) to be rewritten as a history of the forced suppression of regions which had the potential to become nations, and of pre-existing *ethnies*. The guilty parties were the centralisers of Piedmont (first) and Rome (later). At first, it was dialect, or rather the 'national language', the cardinal instrument in the battle for special status, which was to be the standard bearer for the oppressed 'nations'. But not for long. Bossi, unlike Rocchetta, quickly understood the limitations of the ends and the means. If the League could not change, once it had conquered the 'disadvantaged areas', it would come to the same end as the Liga Veneta, mired in the swamp of ethnic regionalism. The League had to expand, renew itself and conquer new social referents so as to move into new political arenas. It embarked therefore, as Bossi himself says, on the road to ethnic federalism (*etnofederalismo*), the unification of several ethnic nationalist movements into one political instrument. The objective: to avoid isolation in the struggle to the death with the centralist state. Lombardy became the nucleus for a very ambitious project: to create a trans-regional movement in the whole of the Po valley. This was no mere digging up of past partial paper agreements (whose purposes had been purely electoral) or of the traditional cultural links between the various autonomist movements. Rather the League set about transforming itself into a new and permanent political actor, able to take its place on the political stage and replace the old parties which were increasingly in crisis.

This represented a real break with the past, with the tradition of 'autonomy' of the autonomist movements, which (as we have seen) had never tried to look beyond their local territorial horizons to lead a movement of renewal or replacement of the entire national political class. This was an enormous challenge, thought by many at the time to be absurd. But to lead the 'federalist revolution' the League had first to become a mass party and undergo major transformation at the organisational, ideological, cultural and symbolic levels. The first requirement was a solid organisational structure (under Lombard leadership), and a revision of early values and identities. Much has already been written about the organisation of the League, and how it created a compartmentalised, pyramidal structure, in which the general secretary controlled the entire party with an iron discipline.[21] This was an authoritarian solution, and one which seemed to militate against the development of a leading cadre for the party, but it was justified as the only practical way of preventing infiltration and centrifugal tendencies. Bossi has always been obsessed with organisation: 'Organisation before votes: otherwise the movement collapses.' But among the implications of this organisation two seem quite important: the emphasis on 'anti-institutional' factors (in favour of a direct appeal to the people) and the links with 'post-democratic' representation (i.e. in which political parties are no longer the only means of organisation). In Berlusconi's government they were both to be fully displayed.

Collective identity and 'theory of the enemy'

The success of the League cannot be explained by its organisational structure alone. More important is the role played by subculture in the development of the League identity. This has positive, cohesive elements, and negative elements, whose aim is to identify the enemy. The positive elements are about peoples, territorial areas, and subnational cultures: this is the *'idea lombarda'* (the 'Lombard idea'). This collective identity is non-ideological, non-class, but purely territorial. But often more important were the negative components: the enemy, bearer of a 'negative identity', a negative concept which is often anthropomorphised. In the beginning, this enemy was simply called 'the centralist state', but it gradually became more specific, manifesting itself from time to time as: the party-political system (*partitocrazia*); welfare state and the parasitic south; immigration, crime and drugs; any individuals or groups who were in any sense different or marginal; the press, the judiciary and all the other groups who somehow or other were seen as a part of the dying system. The League was thus building up a clear 'theory of the enemy'.

This was possible because of the gradual emergence, over the past two decades, of a number of factors: the declining importance of the Left–Right divide; growing lack of confidence in the traditional political parties; the erosion of the importance and relevance of traditional subcultures and loyalties. It is on this latter factor that we shall now concentrate. The declining total vote for the DC/PCI (from 62 per cent in 1975, to 45 per cent in 1990) may also be seen as an erosion of the subcultural matrix vote. According to Mannheimer, this vote coincides with the so-called *voto di appartenenza* (allegiance vote), whereby the voter generally tends to make his/her choice regardless of actual programmes, politicians or current events. Rather, voting behaviour is determined by 'subcultural allegiances', wherein the crucial factors are family tradition, acquaintances, language, values, myths, habits, and rites. This 'allegiance' is reinforced by personal relationships and communication flows, which are maintained at subcultural level. A further element of cohesion is the identification of an enemy. Whereas for the League the enemy consists of the centralist state; previously for the DC and the Church it had been communism and atheism, and for the PCI, capital and the bosses. Under these conditions, a vote could be taken for granted. But since the 1960s things have been changing: personal geographical mobility has increased, with an integration of cultures and contexts, and the mass media has revolutionised communication, enormously increasing the range of information and cultural stimuli. This widening of the democratic base led, indirectly and quite involuntarily, to the starving of the subcultural roots of the mass parties.[22]

If one adds the progressive secularisation of Italian society and the end of the myth of communism, one can understand how the League managed to insert itself first at the subcultural level. Because, among all the forces which could have given expression to the new identities, the League offered the most 'attractive' ideas, the simplest and most immediate: the Lombard *ethnie* and the centralist state. But with one difference: that 'Lombardism', or 'Piedmontism' or 'Venetism', and so on, were from the outset used as vehicles to attack other cultures rather than to integrate with them. A subnational territorial identity (*quartiere*–city–region) in fact is neutral, a multipurpose container, which takes on form according to who is using it and how. Most often, in fact, it will coexist quite peacefully with other allegiances: religious, class, cultural, sporting. Significantly, however, in the case of the League, this identity assumed an exclusive form.

What is interesting to note here is how the process of transformation of subcultural loyalties was sought and promoted by Bossi to enable the League to move beyond the early stage of establishing itself and to attract new social referents: to take the large cities of the north Bossi needed the support of the upwardly mobile but locally attached middle classes of industry and the service sector (according to Diamanti, *efficientisti e localisti*[23]), groups which were not particularly drawn by arguments about ethnic identity or national language. Bossi, by developing the Lombard League's original ideas,[24] set out on the second phase: identifying interests to be transformed into values, and thence into identity. The territory, from being the source of historical and cultural identity, became 'a centre of identity founded on interests: a community with great traditions and productive capacity, forced into subordination to the logic of State and parties'.[25]

Birth of the Northern League

The Northern League was born on 4 December 1989 in Bergamo. This was an historic moment, as we have already noted, because it was the first time that the different autonomist movements in northern Italy had joined together into a single permanent federalist political force. Victory followed at the 1990 local elections. This success had to be consolidated. Bossi, with great foresight, organised the Pontida Assembly (20 March 1990) and the re-enactment of the medieval pact which the north Italian communes had sworn against the Holy Roman Empire. This was both a show of strength for the League and a political and personal triumph for Umberto Bossi. The regional Leagues joined together at the assembly to break forty years of Italian political stagnation. Parading in 1990 at Pontida, they indirectly recognised the authority and leadership of Bossi and the Lombard League.

The League breaks its local links

In the early 1990s, Italian public expenditure was still out of control, and less and less tolerable to the European Community. Radical reforms were necessary to bring it under control. This meant both cuts in public expenditure and tax increases. But it also meant tighter control to eliminate tax evasion among groups who had previously been left alone: small employers in craft industries, manufacturing and commerce. In other words the people who were most likely to be tax evaders were also the people most likely to jump on the League's bandwagon.

185

A new chapter was about to open in the history of the League. During this period of rapid and often dramatic change, the League underwent an important metamorphosis: from populist neo-regionalism[26] to 'invisible de-territorialisation', in other words the undeclared transformation of territorial identity into sectional interests.

Thus on the one hand the League made the symbolic proclamation of the Republic of the North, but on the other hand quite different ideas were being developed to give a much more concrete meaning to the idea of 'North', which was still lacking the legitimacy and collective memory that historical nations have, and which in Italy belong to the region and the *campanile*. To legitimise the North, it had to be given a higher symbolic content, but also a higher economic and social homogeneity: 'in the north as well as an anthropological unity, there exists an economic unity, determined by the "business culture"'.[27] Paradoxically, the link between individual and territory was reforged by moving beyond the centrality of the territory.

The entire history of the League after this point can be seen as the linking of every object, every resource, every political discourse to material interests which are continuously transformed into values. The interests produced by capitalist society (the League's natural form of social organisation) are values in themselves, and they are also values to the extent that other people want to destroy them: the state and the treasury. The adoption of economic liberalism and the unchallenged supremacy of the private sector as the locus of production and efficiency became the necessary next step.

Thus the battleground shifted again, and from the elections of 1992 on it became the apparently irreducible opposition of public versus private, collective versus individual values, conservatism versus renewal, state intervention versus free enterprise.

The League as a right-wing phenomenon

So, is the League a right-wing phenomenon? Yes, even if it is not a traditional Right, but an 'integral federalist' Right. The League is clearly against economic levelling and egalitarianism, justifying its stance by saying that these imply a strong interventionist state, and it is precisely the grip of the state on this area of civil society which the League wishes to loosen. So the League is in favour of a reduction in the cost of labour by allowing increases only in areas where the cost of living was actually greater.[28] Other proposals include: wide-scale privatisation, reform of the health service (including abolition of the subsidised prescriptions) and of the pension system, priority to residents in the competition for jobs in the public sector and in the allocation of housing. But at the same time, the

League declares that family, maternity and unemployment allowances should be maintained. The appellation 'right-wing' does not frighten the League, in so far as society's perception of the gap between Right and Left was already slight. Being labelled conservative gave them rather more cause for concern.

But other labels were used as well: fascist, anti-democratic, racist. These were serious accusations levelled by all and sundry: the old guard, the bishops and the majority of the Catholic world, both the old and the new Left, lay and democratic intellectuals, television commentators, the press both in Italy and abroad.

Italian commentators replied: this is not a neo-fascist (even less a neo-Nazi) movement. 'The League does not show the aggressive nationalism of fascism ... it does not have the will to power, nor does it wish to impose Lombardism on anyone.'[29] Some did see analogies with Mussolini, and the economic factors which were at the root of his rise. But fascism promised more. In comparison the League 'seems a more modest movement .... The doctrine of the League can be summed up as wanting to break up Italy because they don't like southerners' and because they don't want to pay taxes.'[30] For Massimo Salvadori too, comparisons with Le Pen or the Republikaner were off target. These analyses seem correct, at least from a formal point of view. The League cannot be compared to the extreme, violent Right. People were convinced that the real enemy of the League was the inefficient state, even if it was sometimes called by another name (immigration, marginalised categories, inefficient public services). The aggressiveness of the League was therefore entirely instrumental, it served simply to break the ring of indifference and/or hostility around it, to force the discussion of its issues, and then to move on to other subjects, raising the stakes all the while. However, just because the League declares that it has long since abandoned its dangerous ethnic themes, this does not mean that it may now be considered blameless.

The League as a racist phenomenon

Giorgio Bocca charges Italian society with a barely concealed intolerance which becomes racism when in contact with the other. Thus the League cannot be accused of racism, since without the phenomenon of migration, and the consequent social reaction, it would not be able to make racist statements or programmes. This is a very weak argument which ignores the role of the League in stoking the latent racism of northern society. This can be demonstrated by an analysis of the problem of immigration by non-Union nationals.

Italy, despite the alarming data published by the media and other sources, has not in fact been the target of mass immigration: the figure is tiny compared to other European countries. However, reaction to the phenomenon has been disproportionate, creating an invasion syndrome among Italians, and a fear of being under siege.[31] But this didn't happen by itself: 'political entrepreneurs' have taken facts and fear and manufactured action. Those most responsible for this have been the League and the MSI (Movimento Sociale Italiano), who have become 'organisers of intolerance'.[32]

As regards the League, it is difficult to accept without reservation its image as an authentically democratic movement and its 'post-ethnic' conversion. But even if we do accept this hypothesis, its federalism still maintains both its 'economic exclusivism' (purified of racism) and its 'ideological exclusivism' (or racism *tout court*, which is denied). We have already described the former. For the League anyone who cannot or will not adopt their views of a productive economic society, and who therefore constitutes a drain on resources, cannot be integrated and must be excluded. This includes not only dependants on the welfare system, but anyone who is 'different' (homosexuals, gypsies, the handicapped, the homeless, etc.).

But it is also true that the 'exclusivism' of the League is cultural and socio-biological and that it has become more and more ideological: the Lombard League party conference of 1989 demonstrates this clearly, as does the constitution of the SAL (Sindacato Autonomista Lombarda) and the pro-Le Pen statements of the mayor of Monza in 1993.[33] The proposal for special schools for handicapped children is not motivated by economic reasons, but cultural ones ('they upset the normal children'). Bossi has already described homosexuals as 'old women, weaklings, unstable'. Miglio just sees homosexuals as 'sick'.[34]

Thus even if one were to accept the economicist (and non-racist) vision of human relations, it would still be difficult to think of League supporters as purified of the 'cultural racism', even less as guardians of a collectivist message. At the subcultural level, a 'culture' based solely on the logic of exclusion has built up among League supporters (particularly in Lombardy and Veneto). The emphasis on its own identity goes hand in hand with the devaluing and denigration of the other's identity. The reason for this can be found in the 'irresistible need for an enemy'; and that enemy needs sometimes to be more visible and concrete than the centralist state. The enemy thus evoked may be used as an agent for intermittent mobilisation, but it may also be the source of a more deeply rooted ethnic intolerance. Thus 'racist outbursts' (acute) become 'racist situations' (chronic).

Triumph

Before the 1992 election, the League registered a major victory at the local level: in Brescia, a DC stronghold, the League won 24.4 per cent of the vote and became the second party. This was the prelude to triumph. The date 5 April 1992 marks the end of the regime: with 55 deputies and 25 senators, and 8.7 per cent of the votes, the Northern League became the fourth largest political party in Italy. No party in post-war Italy had achieved so much (after only ten years in existence).

Although not officially announced, the 'death' of the first Republic was there for all to see. The DC were forced to give up the reins of power and the formula whereby the DC, the PSI and their allies were considered irreplaceable no longer applied. Once the threat of communism (both Soviet and PCI) had been removed, an alternative was possible without risk to democracy. The Italian electorate no longer needed to 'hold its nose' and it could no longer ignore the stench of corruption which had pervaded the old party system. The magistrates' investigations could now proceed unhindered and they put an entire political class on trial without fear of repercussions or accusations of a 'judges' coup'. The League, although it was still lacking votes in sufficient quantity, according to preliminary analyses had appeared to begin replacing the DC. An analysis of the results region by region seemed to confirm this: everybody lost a little, but the DC was almost wiped out. The transformation of the League into a 'national federalist force' continued.

The strongly anti-national sentiments which had characterised much of even the most recent phase were no longer repeated: initiatives like the 1990 creation of the Republic of the North (at Pontida) were considered 'broadsides' from an 'infantile' period. There was no more talk of breaking up the fiscal unity of the state, or boycotting the economy or state finance, but rather of privatisation and budget cuts. At the institutional level, the League supported the first-past-the-post electoral system and the direct election of the prime minister, and thus was working for the 'reinforcement and revitalisation of the central government, which is the last thing one would expect from a movement once considered secessionist'.[35] The League became a 'responsible' political force, the coordinator of the various leagues, and no longer called for the dismantling of the state. The years of protest were over and Bossi did not force the pace of the crisis. He understood that it was only a matter of time and that the system was no longer able to reform itself.

BERLUSCONI AND THE ADVENT OF THE RIGHT

Forza Italia: a media tycoon at the head of a virtual party

But when the crunch came (the general election of March 1994), it was not the Northern League that took the prize, but the media tycoon Silvio Berlusconi, and his new party, Forza Italia. For the first time, Italy had a major industrialist at the head of the government:

Berlusconi controls half the TV audience, a third of the market for magazines, and a quarter of the book market; he owns the largest share of advertising; he has the Italian cinema industry in his hands, from production to distribution; he has a bridgehead in newspapers, and even in the theatre. He is the biggest employer of intellectual labour in the history of the country.[36]

Not to mention building, finance, supermarkets, and football. Italy had voted into power a Right which was at the same time both clear and anomalous: 'a right composed ... of three components which were in different ways unelectable'.[37] For the first time, a Western democracy had changed into a 'soft autocracy, a tyranny of good sense',[38] in which the nature of politics, its structures and protagonists, had changed radically. Conservative populism, which had come about as a result of the enormous power of information systems, had taken politics out of its traditional sanctuaries and was experimenting with the first post-democratic form of government.

Forza Italia, the company party (*partito-azienda*) was born officially in mid-January 1994. Its existence depended entirely on the president of Fininvest and the employees of Publitalia, the publicity company which conducted a lightning campaign to recycle centrist policies by placing its employees in strategic and politically vital nerve centres.[39] Forza Italia, even more than the Lega, was born and began to function without any of the basic democratic rules or structures (party statutes, elections, conferences) thus ensuring that the infiltration of undesirable elements was impossible.[40] Berlusconi's launch of his product on the political market was nothing other than a marketing operation. The selection of policies, candidates, methods, messages, tones were all subordinated to the conquest of power. And the entire power of Fininvest was employed to support this project, especially television: spot advertising, biased news broadcasting, mixing entertainment and propaganda, and most effective of all, the domestically conducted opinion surveys.[41]

Then there was Berlusconi himself: good-looking, good-natured, vain, eclectic, fascinated by power. He made even more use than Bossi of the idea of an 'enemy', but for him it was communism, disguised as the welfare state, which was poised to destroy the natural values of society: the free market, the family, the state itself. Only he, the self-proclaimed 'man of destiny', could confound their wicked ambitions, and at the same time guarantee to maintain the values on which Italian society had been based in the 1980s. Berlusconi, then, was the guarantor of this society, and its post-modern, videocratic regime: a regime which created and sustained its own televisual, non-party-political subculture, creating and transmitting through the TV screen the images and values of the 1990s.

Videocracy and identity[42]

This was a new regime, then, for a society in which communication has a vital function. As never before, communications media allow the individual to experience a plurality of worlds, cultures and ways of life. Everything is an 'object of communication' (though not necessarily of understanding), and everyone sooner or later gets a chance to express themselves, but without the need to identify with any universals, because dialogue has been abolished and there is no time or need to go into anything in detail. Individuals live in an ahistoric present in which the principal (if not only) identity is one which is insinuated with Berlusconi's commercial TV 'culture' (to which Italians have been exposed for fifteen years): the free market, consumerism, unconstrained individualism.

There is no doubt that one feature of Berlusconi's world is the loss of collective national memory. The loss has been particularly observed among the so-called 'Five Generation' ('*Generazione Cinque*') – those 18–25-year-olds who have grown up in front of Canale 5 TV screens, and who have had the 'dubious pleasure of spending their youth and adolescent years during the fabulous 80s when all the world was marketing-orientated'.[43] But the ideology of spot advertising has become as diffuse as the products of the 1980s: the world is represented as epic and positive, rewarding determination and victory. But the philosophy of Berlusconi, entrepreneur, goes further and is less noble: 'sport as metaphor of war, expansion as surrogate for the defeat of the enemy, suffering as a mask for violence'.[44] The Berlusconi generation has grown up anaesthetised by TV commercials and the fantasy world of television, living only in the present. And from this world they have absorbed the optimistic spirit and the winning mentality of their leader. But they have also become very individualistic and emotional ('I do what I want') and effectively neutral ('I don't give a damn'), and tending towards the violent since they have no respect for rules and prioritise personal over collective interests.[45]

The radical Right: Alleanza Nazionale

The two new political formations, the Lega Nord and Berlusconi's Forza Italia formed a coalition with the third rising political formation of the Right in Italy, Alleanza Nazionale (AN). This, third, partner in the coalition of the so-called Polo delle Libertà, was, unlike its political allies, not a new party but a 'modernised' version of the neo-fascist Movimento Soziale Italiano (MSI). The AN has emphasised the renaming of the party as part of a process of radical reform and renewal within the organisation and represented itself as an essentially post-fascist party that has broken away from its neo-fascist past.

Indeed, it could be argued that the founding of AN has represented a victory for the 'moderate' wing of the MSI which has been advocating the integration of the MSI into mainstream politics. The Movimento Soziale Italiano – whose name has been deliberately reminiscent of the Repubblica Soziale Italiana or the Salò Republic, established by Benito Mussolini in the north of Italy in 1943 as the Italian fascist regime collapsed in Rome – had been a marginal political formation in Italian politics since its birth in 1946 and until the early 1990s had averaged a mere 4–5 per cent in general elections.[46] Since its establishment, the MSI had defined itself as an essentially anti-systemic party; initially it did not accept the constitutional framework of the Italian Republic and pursued a strategy of tension and confrontation, although it progressively moved from its fundamental opposition to opposition to specific aspects of the political system (such as *partitocrazia*, or the weakness of the executive power in Italian politics).

The relaunching of the party in the 1990s under the new name Alleanza Nazionale, its participation in the Polo delle Libertà and its subsequent electoral victory has thus been the product of a long process of de-radicalisation of the party's politics and of gradual integration of the MSI into the Italian political system and has its roots in the post-war political arrangements as well as in the changes brought about by the end of the Cold War.

The polarisation of the post-war Italian political system between the Centre (DC) and the Centre Left has lead to a growing tendency of the political parties to contend for the political middle ground[47] in order to have a chance to attract the votes of the electorate and to be able to participate in coalition governments. This political reality prompted a review of the political options and strategy of the MSI and gave rise to an internal struggle for the party's future which was often translated to an ambiguity as to the party's repertoire of political action and long-term objectives. Unofficially, the MSI had been engaged in a dialogue with the DC between the late 1940s and 1969, its leader, Giorgio Almirante, had formulated a strategy of *inserimento* (gradual integration to the political system) and in the early 1980s the party appeared to have become more acceptable to the political establishment: in 1982 the leader of the Partito Radicale (Radical Party), Mario Pannella, attended the MSI conference; in 1984 official representatives of the DC, and the Partito Liberale Italiano (Liberal Party) also attended. More important, in 1983, the Socialist leader Bettino Craxi consulted the MSI while he was forming his government making thus a gesture of political significance to the MSI. However, the integration of the party into the Italian political system was given a further impetus after the eventual succession – after a bitter internal struggle – of MSI's founding leader, Giorgio Almirante, by the current leader of AN, Gianfranco Fini. Fini and most of Alleanza Nazionale's spokespersons have been repeatedly stressing the break of the party with its fascist and neo-fascist past by claiming that the AN is a post-fascist political formation committed to the democratic system although advocating a stronger government able to respond to the economic and political challenges Italy faces today.

Although AN is, admittedly, different from the MSI, in the sense that it represents the victory of the latter's moderate wing over its hardline elements, it, nevertheless, retains a substantial part of the MSI political tradition. It is characteristic that alongside the party's contention that it provides the answer to the problems of 'post-industrial' Italy, prominent members of the party have been engaged in the Europe-wide debate on 'historical revisionism' and have attempted to 'rehabilitate' the interwar Italian fascist regime, or key personalities associated with it. In addition, traditional links of the MSI with specific social groups have been strengthened and mobilised by AN. It is characteristic that the Alleanza Nazionale – and the Berlusconi government – has supported the demands of Italians who had been expelled or had fled from Istria and the Dalmatian coast after the establishment of post-war Yugoslavia for the return of their properties at a time when the successor states of former Yugoslavia concerned are most vulnerable. This strategy echoes the calls of some MSI and AN members for the reincorporation of the 'lost territories' to Italy.[48]

Although it is too early to see how AN is going to evolve after its integration into mainstream politics, it is evident that the element of continuity between itself and its fascist predecessors is by no means negligible. It is this continuity that has been central in shaping the party's and – to a lesser extent – the Berlusconi government's nationalist discourse.

The victory of the Right

On 27 March 1994 Italian society, more localised and individualist than ever, rewarded the parties of the Right, those which had best interpreted its needs and (more to the point) its dreams. With 366 seats (out of 630) in the lower chamber and 155 (out of 315) in the Senate, the Right was forced to work without an absolute majority in the Senate. And Umberto Bossi had no alternative but to hitch his war chariot to Berlusconi's bandwagon, but in the name of the free market, rather than federalism, which had been the real issue of the election. Bossi began to speak of the liberalisation of the labour market, and the free market became synonymous with dismantling the welfare state and privatising social services (health, communication systems, transport, education, social security) along American or Thatcherite lines.[49] This was the only way the Right could see of saving the Italians from their predicament.

CONCLUSION

Bossi's League having been a principal agent of renewal, had arrived at the winning post of the second Republic, but at a cost which was so high as to snatch final victory from it. Even as late as December 1993, the League had still been growing in strength: it was the largest party in the north even if it had failed to capture some of the major cities. But these partial victories had strange psychological effects on League members: on the one hand, it seemed that the defeats in the major cities (Turin, Genoa, Venice, Trieste) had been willed by the 'Centre', by Bossi himself, who was thought to have imposed weak candidates 'to reinforce his centrality and his hegemonic capacity on the movement as a whole'; on the other, they seemed to indicate that the League was no longer 'on the right side of history', which feeling had been engendered by the previous succession of electoral victories. This together with the feeling that they were 'alone against everyone' could only lead to frustration and disillusion. The League, like the PDS, had also had to embark on a policy of alliances. This was far from easy for the League, because of its 'genetically' hostile attitudes to other parties. The League had to hold itself together while at the same time preparing its base for alliances with very unusual bed-fellows: Berlusconi and Fini. In the end, it failed. The middle classes are the 'glue' holding the League together (Mondi's term was 'jelly'). They are essentially pragmatic: they have no values to defend, only interests. In order to provide 'a back-bone for the jelly of its voters', the League had no alternative but to link up with 'the business model guaranteed of success by the structures of Fininvest'.[50] Berlusconi was able to superimpose his interest-values on the League's middle classes, but he explicitly denied the League's other major demands, such as collective action and the idea of politics as the extension of the life of the common people, affirming at the same time the idea of 'politics as theatre', nothing more than artificiality and manipulation. When put to the test, territorial identity as a basis for politics melted away before a national identity provided by the much more concrete consumerism and the fantasy dream-world of television.

NOTES

1 R. Romano, *Paese Italia*, Rome, Donzelli, 1994.
2 Ibid., pp.3–19.
3 Marino Livolsi, *L'Italia che cambia*, Florence, La Nuova Italia, 1993, pp.5–25.
4 G. E. Rusconi, *Se cessiamo di essere una nazione*, Bologna, Il Mulino, 1993, p.13.
5 Ibid., p.13.
6 Livolsi, op. cit., p.19.
7 G. De Luna, 'La Lega e il progetto di "fare gli italiani"', in G. De Luna (ed.), *Figli di un benessere minore*, Florence, La Nuova Italia, 1994, p.3.
8 Ibid, p.3.
9 S. Folli, 'Italia delle bombe. Nata l'8 settembre', interview with Renzo De Felice, in *Corriere della Sera*, 10 August 1993. See also V. Foa, *Il cavallo e la torre*, Turin, Einaudi, 1991, p.137; G. De Luna, 'Dalla spontaneità all'organizzazione', in De Luna (ed.), *Figli di un benessere minore*, op. cit., p.4; P. Scoppola, 'Un'incerta cittadinanza italiana', *Il Mulino* 1/91: 52.

10 The partisans, on the other hand, felt the need to reassert an autonomous freedom for Italy in order to build a real democracy. G. De Luna, 'Tutti a casa. Quasi tutti', *Il Manifesto*, 8 September 1993.

11 Lanaro defines this as a person who is 'attracted neither by the gentle attraction of utopia nor by the manly fascination of decisiveness, but rather by the ideal of absence of disputes, of a harmony among all the legitimate interests, of a unanimous agreement around the ruling class'. S. Lanaro, *Storia dell'Italia repubblicana*, Venice, Marsilio, 1992, p.256.

12 Ibid., p.58.

13 'Chiude la "Milano da bere"'; 'Il Cavalier Guido: "Una città che non c'è più", *Corriere della Sera*, 6 February 1994.

14 G. De Luna, 'Dalla spontaneità all'organizzazione', in De Luna (ed.) *Figli di un benessere minore*, op. cit., p.39.

15 A. Melucci and M. Diani, *Nazioni senza Stato. I movimenti etno-nazionali in Occidente*, Turin, Loesher Feltrinelli, 1992.

16 F. Alberoni, *Movimento e istituzioni*, Bologna, Il Mulino, 1977.

17 For more information on the autonomist movements in Italy see S. Salvi, *Le lingue tagliate. Storia delle minoranze linguistiche in Italia*, Milan, Rizzoli, 1975.

18 For example, in thirty years (1960–90) the attendance at Mass has collapsed from 80 per cent to 29 per cent. S. Magister, 'Tutti casa e poco Chiesa', *L'Espresso*, 11 October 1992.

19 I. Diamanti, *La Lega. Geografia, storia e sociologia di un nuovo soggetto politico*, Rome, Donzelli, 1993, p.46.

20 In common speech the word *'ethnie'* has become highly evocative. Transposing the term, 'without any solution of continuity', from the original ethno-anthropological meaning to the 'more general' cultural identity, now every-thing is *'ethnie'*. So '"ethnic" is equal to "someone different". . . . More precisely ethnicity has become a feature of elected difference . . . a polemical strategic resource either to get something or to deny something to someone else.' With the risk of hiding the 'race' behind the softer and decent *'ethnie'*. G.E. Rusconi, *Se cessiamo di essere una nazione*, op. cit., pp.151–3. The Leagues of Piedmont and Veneto, for example, give the following definition of *'ethnie'*: 'the cultural-social-biological-evolutionary moment', I. Diamanti, *La Lega*, op. cit., pp.59–60.

21 D. Vimercati, *I Lombardi alla nuova crociata*, Milan, Mursia, 1990, pp.32–5.

22 'When different channels send differing messages, the attitudes and beliefs which form the normative core of a subculture are inevitably weakened', R. Mannheimer, 'La crisi del consenso per i partiti tradizionali', in R. Mannheimer (ed.), *La Lega Lombarda*, Milan, Feltrinelli, 1991, p.18.

23 I. Diamanti, 'Una tipologia dei simpatizzanti della Lega', in R. Mannheimer (ed.), *La Lega Lombarda*, op. cit., pp.180–1.

24 But even in its early days (1983) the Lombard League gave a 'post-ethnic' definition of Lombards: all those 'who have been residing in the region for at least 5 years'. The Lombard identity is therefore 'the result of a condition and of shared values', more than a matter of ethno-racial homogeneity, I. Diamanti, 'Una tipologia', op. cit., pp.58–60.

25 Ibid., p.57.

26 R. Biorcio, 'La Lega come attore politico: dal federalismo al populismo regionalista', in R. Mannheimer (ed.), *La Lega Lombarda*, op. cit., pp.34–82.

27 Il federalismo per la libertà dei popoli. Una scelta nel senso della storia', *Lombardia Autonomista*, 19 June 1991.

28 M. Rosi, 'Gabbie salariali per un'economia europea', *Lega Nord*, 25 June 1993.

29 G. Bocca, *La disunità d'Italia*, Milan, Garzanti, 1990.

30 P. Ottone, 'Vediamo se Bossi è un altro Mussolini', *L'Espresso*, 1 November 1992.

31 See V. Cotesta, *La cittadella assediata. Immigrazione e conflitti etnici in Italia*, Rome, Editori Riuniti, 1992, pp.x–xi.

32 L. Balbo and L. Manconi, *I razzismi reali*, Milan, Feltrinelli, 1992; F. Torriero, 'Imparate da me . . .', interview with Jean-Marie Le Pen, *L'Italia settimanale*, 28 July 1993; R. Biorcio, 'La Lega come attore politico: dal federalismo al populismo regionalista', op. cit., pp.58–67.

33 'Only the legal immigrants are allowed to stay by us, provided that they are not Muslim. We cannot accept that the Koran will destroy our culture', C. Valentini, 'Amministrare stanca', *L'Espresso*, 12 December 1993

34 I. Sales, *Leghisti e sudisti*, Rome, Bari, Laterza, 1993; *Atti del primo congresso nazionale della Lega Lombarda*, Segrate, December 1989; C. Valentini, 'Amministrare stanca', *L'Espresso*, 12 December 1993; V. Moioli, 'Il razzismo delle leghe', *Critica Marxista*, 1992.

35 G. Sacco, 'Les Ligues Régionales', *Politique Etrangère*, 1/93.

36 L.Ballio, 'E ora prendiamo i voti', *L'Espresso*, 21 November 1993

37 A company (Forza Italia), a potentially separatist movement (Lega Nord) and a tendentially fascist party (Alleanza Nazionale). C. Rinaldi, 'L'Etat c'est lui', *L'Espresso*, 13 May 1994.

38 Ibid.

39 G. Quaranta, 'La loro Weltanschauung', *L'Espresso*, 3 June 1994.

40 P. Criscuoli, 'Forza Publitalia', *L'Espresso*, 29 April 1994; G. Bocca, 'Contro i comunisti alla ricerca di alleati', *La Repubblica*, 27 May 1994.

41 C. Gallucci, 'Se non c'è Silvio che notizia è', *L'Espresso*, 25 February 1994; C.C. Gallucci, 'E Ambra dà la linea', *L'Espresso*, 4 February 1994.

42 For more information see G. Perelli, 'L'Italia stravidea, parola di Dan Rather', *L'Espresso*, 11 March 1994; Ennio Caretto, 'USA: la videocrazia fa i presidenti. Ma è imparziale', *Corriere della Sera*, 26 January 1994; M. Lichtner, 'Il razzismo nella cultura post-moderna', *Critica Marxista*, 1992, p.93; G. Vattimo, *La società trasparente*, Milan, Garzanti, 1989, p.15; 'The third revolution has replaced the written word with the screen. The screen is everything that we forget at once, everything that dazzles and fascinates without leaving a trace. The screen carries oblivion, it is industrialized oblivion. In this sense Italy is leader of oblivion: it is the end of politics, the end of democracy [. . . meant as] the synthesis of reflection and temporal detachment.' Berlusconi aims 'to turn the world back five centuries, to the time of the "condottieri". Democratic power, the power of the Republic, of the nation, becomes personalized once again. Thanks to TV a new feudalism is spreading all over Europe', P. Virilio, 'La politica non c'è più resta la tv', *L'Espresso*, 6 May 1994.

43 G. Romagnoli, '"Generazione Cinque" vuole vincere', *La Stampa*, 28 March 1994.

44 E. Pirella, 'Spot: ripetere e competere', *L'Espresso*, 21 January 1994.

45 C. Gatto Trocchi, 'Malcostume senza gaudio', *La Repubblica*, 28 February 1994.

46 Roberto Chiarini 'MSI a historical profile of Neofascism in Europe' in L. Cheles, R. Ferguson and M. Vaughan (eds), *Neo-fascism in Europe*, London, Longman 1991.

47 Ibid.

48 James Gow, 'The first test case for integration', *War Report*, 1994, no. 30, pp.25–6.

49 C. Valentini, 'Attenti che qui vi rifanno il Quarantotto', interview with Paul Ginsborg, *L'Espresso*, 4 March 1994; M. Pirani, 'Il sogno liberista', *La Repubblica*, 20 May 1994.

50 G. De Luna, 'Dalla spontaneità all'organizzazione', op. cit., pp.67–9.

SELECT BIBLIOGRAPHY

Allum, P. (1994) 'Chronicle of a death foretold: First Italian Republic', University of Reading Occasional Paper.

Calabrese, O. (ed.) (1994) *Modern Italy: Images and History of a Natural Identity,* vol. 5, *1860–1980 Visions of the Country,* Milan, Electa.

De Luna, G. (1994) 'La Lega e il progetto di "fare gli italiani"', in G. De Luna (ed.), *Figli di benessere minore,* Florence, La Nuova Italia.

Ginsborg, P. (1994) *Contemporary History of Italy,* London, Penguin.

Hellman, S. and Pasquino, G. (1994) *Italian Politics: A Review,* London, Pinter.

Lanarco, S. (1992) *Storia dell'Italia repubblicana,* Venice, Marsilio.

McCarthy, H. (1994) *Italy and its Regions: A Resource Book of Regional Geography, History and Culture,* Carlton, Victoria, CIS Educational.

Melucci, A. and Diani, M. (1992) *Nazioni senza stato. I movimento etno-nazionali in Occidente,* Milan Loesher Feltrinelli.

Procacci, G. (1991) *History of the Italian People,* London, Penguin.

Romano, R. (1994) *Paese Italia,* Rome, Donzelli.

Rusconi, G.E. (1993) *Se cessiamo di essere una nazione,* Bologna, Il Mulino.

Part IV

THE NATION-STATE AFTER COMMUNISM

9

THE FAILURE OF NATIONALISM IN POST-COMMUNIST POLAND 1989–95

An historical perspective

Frances Millard

The resurgence of nationalism in post-communist Eastern Europe and its manifestation in ethnic conflict, tension and civil war received considerable public and academic attention after 1990, not least because of the visibility of the Yugoslav tragedy. Many observers explained this re-emergence of nationalism using a 'deep freeze' analogy. In brief, this view argued that communism suppressed nationalist tensions, which simmered under an ice cap of political control. The thaw enabled the ancient historic enmities to gush once again to the surface.

Yet nationalism did not flourish in all the former socialist states, including some states where it was a thriving political project in the pre-communist period. Poland is a case in point, with its pre-communist history of vigorous ethnic antagonisms, yet little sign of support for nationalist parties after 1989. The notion of the suppression of nationalism by the communist regime also needs qualification. The Polish communists were not immune to patriotic and nationalist aspirations. Furthermore, from time to time elements within the Polish Communist Party attempted to mobilise nationalism in its xenophobic form as a mechanism of intra-party struggle. This chapter seeks to document and elucidate these points by examining the nature of Polish nationalism in the pre-communist and communist periods and its lack of appeal in Polish democratic politics after 1989. It will also offer reasons for the disjuncture. They may be summarised as follows. First, the boundaries of the Polish state changed dramatically as a consequence of the Second World War, giving rise to a largely homogeneous nation-state without immediate threats to its security or integrity. A strong sense of nationhood was firmly rooted in the myths of a glorious history of resistance to oppression and rich political and cultural traditions. Second, after 1989 there was no external enemy to provide a focus for nationalist mobilisation. Third, the population proved un-responsive to the issues identified by nationalist elements, while nation-alist parties remained bitterly divided. Nationalism also failed because of the dominance of liberal secularism in the first post-communist govern-ments. At the same time there was a clear alternative focus of opposition in the successor parties, the former-communist Socjaldemokracj Rzecz-pospolitej Polskiej (SDRP – Social Democracy of the Kingdom of Poland), which successfully transformed itself into a respectable social democratic party, and the PSL, which succeeded in capturing the discontented peasant electorate. We should note here that nationalism is conceived as a political project, with a focus on the nation as the prime object of political allegiance.[1] This means that citizens may be deeply imbued with national sentiment without being nationalist. It also means that nationalism may be contingent, attracting in times of threat adherents whose 'normal' prime loyalty is to the individual, the family, the community or some other collectivity. The argument here is not that nationalism has been perman-ently eradicated as a major feature of the Polish landscape, but that in the first years of post-communism it was of minor importance. Nor is the discussion intended to obscure the suffering caused to individuals and groups by manifestations of bigotry and xenophobia. The thesis is that nationalism at the level of the Polish state was largely irrelevant.

NATIONALISM IN THE INTER-WAR PERIOD

After more than a century of foreign domination, the Polish state re-emerged in 1919 from the peace settlement following the First World War; this was based, at least rhetorically, on the international acknowledgement of the right to self-determination. By this time Polish national con-sciousness was highly developed. By the end of the nineteenth century nationalism, once the preserve of the gentry, had emerged as a strong mobilising ideology for the masses, and an educated intellectual élite was ready and anxious to take power. However, the boundaries of the Polish state did not conform to the principle of 'one people, one state'; Poles comprised some two-thirds of the population of Poland, with a rich ethnic admixture in all its border areas. Jews, Ukrainians, Belorussians, and Germans were the major minority nationalities. According to census data from 1921 (universally judged to understate minority numbers), 14.3 per cent of the population were Ukrainian, 3.9 per cent Belorussian, 10.5 per cent Jewish, and 3.9 per cent German.

Ethnic tension was a prime characteristic of inter-war politics from its outset, as two conceptions of the state vied for political primacy. The first was the federalist concept associated with Marshall Józef Piłsudski, seeking a multi-ethnic state dominated by Poland but with autonomy for the eastern minorities. The concept of the nationalist leader Roman

Dmowski was that of an ethnically Polish, unitary state. However, the feasibility of Piłsudski's approach was undermined by his failure to re-establish Poland's historic boundaries of 1772. The eastern boundary, effectively determined as a result of the Polish–Russian War of 1920 and the Polish seizure of Lithuanian territory, meant the inclusion of numerous non-Poles into the reborn state; but they were not sufficiently numerous for a viable partnership. The new Polish constitution was unitary, and the state, despite its multi-ethnic composition, was depicted as a Polish state. In the eastern border areas class and ethnic tensions reinforced one another, as the Poles constituted the landowning class, while except for the Jews, most non-Poles were peasants. In this area ethnic nationalism served the interests of the dominant class.

Polish policies towards the eastern minorities in the inter-war period had the effect of stimulating national consciousness among peoples whose prime loyalties had not hitherto been 'national' but rather regional or religious. In the 1920s policies were either themselves chauvinist or thwarted by 'the chauvinism and incapacity of local officials.'[2] Piłsudski's 1926 coup failed to resolve these problems.[3] Indeed, the notorious 'pacifications' of Ukrainians by Polish cavalry took place under his auspices. As Ukrainian parties increasingly resorted to terrorism, official reprisals intensified in a spiral of violence, including the razing of villages suspected of aiding rebel Ukrainian nationalists and also the settlement of Polish military colonists. The national aspirations of the Belorussians were also suppressed after the mid-1920s, and outlets for enhancing cultural identity, including Belorussian schools, were closed. Internment at the notorious Bereza Kartuska camp was the penalty for minority nationalist dissidence, and large numbers sought refuge in emigration. Neither did the situation of the Slav minorities improve after Piłsudski's death in 1935. After a brief period of 'normalisation', his successors in the Camp of National Unity (Obóz Zjednoczenia Narodowego – OZN) competed with Dmowski's nationalist opposition in demanding the wholesale polonisation of social, economic and political life, and they came to adopt a number of openly fascist themes.[4] The Belorussians remained quiescent and their ethnic consciousness relatively undeveloped, but the Ukrainians responded to 'the increased dynamism of German foreign policy, which led the majority of Ukrainians to look to Hitler for the realization of their national objectives'.[5] The Poles responded with efforts at forcible assimilation.

Although the German minority was relatively small, it was highly significant. In Poznania, Pomerania and Upper Silesia many large landowners and industrialists were German. In other parts of Poland they were largely peasants. Unlike the eastern minorities the Germans had seen their status fundamentally altered from that of ruling nationality in the former Prussian partition to that of a minority separated from their co-nationals and humiliated by military defeat. The Germans were well organised and resistant to polonisation. After the Polish–German non-aggression pact of 1934 the Polish government furthered German cultural and economic rights and generally treated the Germans with circumspection, despite the growing attraction of Nazism for the local German population. It was not until mid-1939 that the Poles moved against the potential (and in many cases actual) fifth column, prompting many Germans to leave for the Reich.

The Jewish minority was the most visibly distinctive, since the majority of Jews retained their singular style of dress and their devout religious observances. The 3-million-strong Jewish population was concentrated in cities, where it played a key role in trade, commerce, and the free professions.[6] Jewish influence on Polish culture was considerable, and the Jewish villager also played a role in rural life.[7] After the Great Depression the position of the Jews deteriorated markedly, and economic ruin faced many. Historians of varied persuasions noted the phenomenon of Jewish pauperisation in the 1930s,[8] accompanied by the growth of both popular and official virulent anti-Semitism.[9] For many years official policy stressed Jewish emigration as the 'solution' to the 'Jewish question' (a view shared by the major political parties and by sections of the Jewish community itself). By the mid-1930s anti-Semitism infused the content of government policy, mainly economic policy; this included such measures as prohibiting Jews from certain professions and imposing heavy taxes on 'Jewish' occupations. Many government spokesmen and deputies from the government camp (OZN) articulated much harsher sentiments, including advocating the deprivation of the civic and political rights of the Jewish population. Intelligentsia, bourgeoisie and artisans alike felt increasingly threatened by Jewish economic competition. The government did not oppose the Nationalist Party's promotion of a boycott of Jewish shops and reacted half-heartedly when the campaign deteriorated into violence, with pogroms in a number of towns. Nor did it prevent the harassment of Jewish students or anti-Jewish manifestations among the free professions.

Negative attitudes to national minorities were not merely aspects of government policy; they were deeply embedded in popular attitudes and culture. Ukrainians and Belorussians were stereotyped as inferior types of Slav, and stories and anecdotes circulated about their backwardness and primitivism. This was assisted by the major role played by the *kresy* (borderlands) intelligentsia, itself a product of the gentry and retaining its perceptions as the dominant class. The increasing violence of Ukrainian nationalists provoked deep animosity in the eastern regions. Popular anti-Semitism in particular had deep roots, both economic and religious;[10] but it intensified from the latter part of the nineteenth century after an influx of Russian Jews escaping new repressive legislation and mass pogroms in central Russia. In 1883 Jan Jeleński founded the journal *Rola* on an explicitly anti-Jewish platform. 'The Protocols of the Elders of Zion' had a profound impact in the early years of the new century, and the Catholic Church played a role with its continuing stress on Jews as responsible for the murder of Christ. The National Democratic Party (later the National Party) incorporated anti-Jewish elements into its programme of 1903.[11] The issue smouldered in the first years of Poland's regained independence and acquired a new virulence in the desperate economic circumstances of the Great Depression.[12] The National Party, itself deeply imbued with anti-Semitism, generated a number of small splinter groups such as the Falanga of Bolesław Piasecki[13] which were overtly fascist and pro-German. The 1936 Peasant Party programme was also 'more anti-Semitic'.[14] Foreigners found anti-Semitism visible and pervasive.[15] This was 'naive' anti-Semitism, the emotive response to those who are perceived as alien, as distinct from the instrumental anti-Semitism of many politicians.[16] Because of their economic position the Jews could stand both as a symbol of modernity and the dislocations of industrial development. Yet they could also be portrayed as an obstacle to modernity on several, contradictory counts.[17] They were viewed as a barrier to the development of a Polish middle class. They were also viewed as themselves an obstacle to modernism: alien, obscurantist, deeply tied to tradition, unassimilable.

The inter-war period, then, was one in which the nationalist project dominated. Nation-building now went hand in hand with state-building, the task of reintegrating Poles into a common political unit after a century of division. Internal economic and political dislocations were coupled with extreme external vulnerability.

NATIONALISM AFTER 1939

War and the communist assumption of power

The invasion of Poland by her neighbours and its wartime occupation by Nazi Germany brought a renewal of the romantic, heroic strand of Polish nationalism characteristic of the first part of the nineteenth century.[18] Occupation brought a considerable measure of reconciliation as nationalists, liberals, socialists, agrarians, and conservatives united in defence of the nation. The Polish resistance movement was the largest in Europe. It was both a military organisation devoted to sabotage and intelligence-gathering and a movement to protect and preserve the nation by means of a parallel, underground Polish state, which developed its own institutions, press, and education system.[19] Its main element was the Armia Krajowa (Home Army), loyal to the London government-in-exile. A smaller, communist resistance movement, the AL or Armia Ludowa, operated separately. However, elements of intolerant ethnic nationalism did not vanish. In 1944 the National Armed Forces (Narodowe Siły

Zbrojne – NSZ) detached itself from the AK and began to cooperate with the Gestapo against Jews and communists, whom the NSZ linked together and viewed as a greater threat to Poland than even the Germans.[20]

The war had a searing effect. To the massive physical loss of some 6 million citizens, mass dislocation, psychological degradation, and exhaustion were added a sense of national betrayal by the Western Allies, who finally gave Stalin virtual *carte blanche* in Poland's erstwhile eastern territories.[21] The Soviet Union retook and then retained the territories earlier incorporated into the Belorussian and Ukrainian Soviet republics under the terms of the Nazi–Soviet Pact of 1939. Lithuania, including territory regarded by many as 'Polish', had also been forcibly incorporated into the USSR. In return, Poland acquired German lands, known as 'the recovered territories'. Many Poles opted to leave the former eastern territories for the western region, while the border minorities, especially Ukrainians, also moved to the USSR. Later, in 1947, as a result of continuing nationalist resistance, clusters of Ukrainians remaining in south-eastern Poland were forcibly deported to the western territories in the infamous Action Vistula (*Akcja Wisła*).[22] Flight and expulsion also removed some 3 million Germans from Poland altogether, leaving a small German population whose existence was officially denied. The Jews had of course been subject to mass murder by the Nazis, and of those remaining, large numbers emigrated to Israel.[23]

This new Poland was, then, largely homogeneous, in regard to both ethnicity and religion. Some 97 per cent of its population was now Polish and most Poles were Roman Catholic. The multi-ethnic inter-war state was now genuinely a nation-state, its civic bonds strengthened by the shared experience of Nazi occupation. However, the potential basis for Polish irredentism remained. The eastern borderlands (*kresy*) had enormous symbolic significance for Polish culture. The capital of Lithuania, Vilnius (Wilno, Vilna), and the major city of the western Ukraine, Lviv (Lwów, Lemberg), had been Polish cities. Nor could deeply embedded anti-minority cultural attitudes be erased overnight. However, in the new circumstances anti-communism provided the main motor of nationalist sentiment.

With Soviet aid the Polish communists rapidly established their power. After 1945 groups of disparate nationalist anti-communist partisans in isolated areas continued to fight against communist forces. Some were linked to the Home Army (AK), some to the ultra-right NSZ, others to the Peasant Party (and still others to Ukrainian nationalists). By late 1948 this armed resistance had been defeated. The Communist Party (the Polska Zjednoczona Partia Robotnicza – PZPR, or Polish United Workers' Party) was firmly in control and the Soviet variant of socialist internationalism rapidly became the sole permitted ideology. In these circumstances it proved impossible openly to articulate a concept of the Polish nation different from the official version, which presented the USSR as the saviour and guarantor of Poland's national and state sovereignty against a resurgent threat from (West) German imperialism. There was ample anti-German popular sentiment to feed the constant reminders of Nazi atrocities, while the censor prohibited all mention of the experiences of the Polish population in areas now under Soviet rule, including the notorious Katyń massacre of Polish officers by the NKVD (Soviet secret police) in 1943. History was rewritten, for example denying the central role of the Home Army in the wartime resistance. The German community became largely invisible. National symbols were altered, with the Polish eagle deprived of its crown and cross. After the Soviet split with Yugoslavia in 1948 repression intensified further. Those communists, like the erstwhile leader Władysław Gomułka, who advocated a specifically 'Polish' road to socialism, were dismissed and arrested for the sin of 'nationalist deviation'.

Even in the immediate post-war period, however, the strong vein of anti-Semitism manifested itself once again. The exodus of Jews from Poland had begun immediately at the end of the war. Many of those remaining were resettled in the western territories, in an attempt to render them 'invisible'. According to Checinski, 'Anti-Semitism was widely used as a weapon against the government, which not only included Jews, but which also seemed excessively tolerant towards them.'[24] Anti-Jewish violence affected several Polish towns, culminating in the notorious (and still not fully explained)[25] Kielce pogrom of 1946, which stimulated a further exodus. By the time anti-Semitism took on an official hue, on directives issued from the Soviet Union, where Stalin was inaugurating a new campaign against 'Zionists and hostile elements', Polish Jewry was but a tiny remnant. A new onslaught was prevented by Stalin's death in 1953. By then the majority of the small element which remained, estimated at some 60,000, consisted of assimilated 'Poles of Jewish origin'.

Popular protest and national sentiment

From 1956 onwards one can identify two distinct strands of nationalism in Polish politics. The first was the (failed) attempt by the communists to generate legitimacy through the manipulation of popular anti-Semitism to provide a scapegoat for Poland's ills. The second was the strand, detectable within the Party but widespread in society at large, of resistance to Soviet dominance. In the aftermath of Stalin's death a power struggle broke out among the communist leadership, soon giving rise to a general crisis of the Party. One element favoured moves to a less repressive system, while the other remained associated with Stalinist policies and methods. Gomułka was quietly freed and rapidly became the leader of the more 'liberal' wing of Polish communism, as well as a symbol of repressed

Polish nationalism for communists and non-communists alike; his defiant refusal to repent of his 'nationalist sins' was widely known. The death of the Party leader Bierut in March 1956 provided a convenient scapegoat for Polish Stalinism. His successor Edward Ochab set a steady de-Stalinising course. The Stalinist, 'Natolin', faction of the PZPR once again used anti-Semitism as a political weapon and found an echo both in the Party *apparat* and in society at large, where traditional stereotypes of an insidious Jewish cobweb of political influence and economic gain resurfaced, but now in the context of 'Judeo-communism', the *żydokomuna*.[26]

Ochab himself stepped aside in Gomułka's favour later that year. In June, however, liberalisation appeared threatened by workers' discontent. Although economic grievances were the major cause of the Poznań riots, national aspirations also surfaced; among the protesters' slogans were calls for a withdrawal of Soviet troops. Initially the protests were suppressed by force and officially blamed on anti-socialist provocateurs. This view quickly yielded to the recognition that the workers had legitimate grievances. Increasingly the Party looked to Gomułka, who demanded *inter alia* the departure of the Polish-born but russified Minister of Defence, Konstanty Rokossovsky, along with numerous Soviet 'advisors'. An attempted coup by the Natolin wing was successfully thwarted, and the way was paved for the now dominant reformers to reinstate Gomułka as party leader. Khrushchev's arrival with a high-powered Soviet delegation and the mobilisation of Soviet military units increased the level of tension, but Gomułka reassured the Soviets of his unswerving loyalty to the socialist camp. On 21 October Gomułka became leader and reaffirmed the legitimacy of a Polish 'national road to socialism'.

The exhilarating sense of national unity under a popular, reformist leader gave the communists a brief period of genuine legitimacy. Certainly there were enduring consequences, including a *modus vivendi* with the Church and political accceptance of the spontaneous decollectivisation of the peasantry. Also, until the rise of Solidarity the Polish communists ran domestic affairs without Soviet interference, although they remained subordinate in foreign policy matters. It is true that rapid popular disillusion set in with Gomułka's failure to implement serious reforms. During the 1960s he became increasingly unpopular in the country at large, which lost the outlet for its national and patriotic emotions. However, 1956 may be regarded as a major watershed in Polish post-war history, setting the relationship between Party and society on a new course.[27] The expression of national aspirations became legitimate, albeit curtailed within the Soviet orbit. Humanitarian values were articulated strongly; indeed, much intellectual discourse became infused with liberalism, while xenophobic attitudes were vehemently condemned. Undoubtedly 1956 had set the Polish variant of communism on a path of fundamental change, although its future development was far from linear.

Indeed, gradually Gomułka's incipient failures gave rise to a new faction within the PZPR, claiming to represent the national interest by once again mobilising traditional sentiments against threats to 'Polishness'. In March 1968 new protests erupted, this time among students and intellectuals. They centred on issues of censorship but also reflected a broad desire for wider political reform. Demonstrations provided the opportunity for the 'Partisan' wing of the PZPR, led by Interior Minister Mieczysław Moczar, to launch a bid for power. This right-wing variant of Polish communist nationalism began to orchestrate a new anti-Semitic campaign, thinly disguised as an attack on the 'Zionism' allegedly pervading the universities. Gomułka rode the storm, but his position was further weakened. Although the anti-Semitic campaign was clearly orchestrated from above, there were signs that Moczar had struck a chord among part of the population, as well as rank and file communists. Large numbers of Poles of Jewish origin were expelled from Poland, including reformers from within the PZPR itself.[28] Gomułka's loss of touch was amply confirmed by major political blunders two years later, leading to his replacement by Edward Gierek. Gierek sought to base his rule on expectations of material progress rather than appeals to sentiment. The right-wing nationalist strand within the PZPR sank into temporary abeyance.

Polish society, however, continued its turbulent battles with the party-state with two further developments in the 1970s. December 1970 saw another outbreak of workers' protest in the Baltic region. The political impact of dozens dead and thousands wounded not only ensured Gomułka's removal but reinvigorated powerful collective memories of communist repression. After a brief period of prosperity, the economy began to decline. The gap between Party and society again loomed wide, fuelled by resentment at the privileges of the ruling élite. In 1976 a new attempt to increase prices led to another outburst of working-class discontent, cut short by a hasty political retreat. However, nationalist feelings of resistance to the communist system intensified in Polish society.

This year was important because of this new test of working-class strength against the authorities. It also saw successful resistance to a proposed constitutional amendment deeply wounding to national sensibilities. The draft promised to strengthen the 'indissoluble ties of friendship' with the USSR. Protests from intellectuals and from the Episcopate, criticising this formulation as limiting Poland's sovereignty and inviting interference in her internal affairs, led to revision of the offending text. The protest helped stimulate the development of political opposition. Later that year the Workers' Defence Committee (Komitet Obrony Robotników – KOR) emerged to assist striking workers. KOR provided the first linkage between disaffected workers and the intelligentsia.[29]

By the end of the 1970s the Party appeared bankrupt. The economy was in dire straits. There were drastic shortages, endless queues and a deterioration in social services. A Party-sponsored group of experts produced reports analysing the bankruptcy of the polity, the moral exhaustion of society and the wide gulf between the two.[30] Yet dissent was spreading and providing the basis of an active alternative culture, notably but not exclusively among the intelligentsia. Discussion groups and illegal publications proliferated, filling the gaps in history, politics and literature left by the censor. The Flying University, whose name echoed national resistance to tsarism and the underground Polish state of the Second World War, challenged the Party's monopoly of scholarship and education. The Confederation for Independent Poland (Konfederacja Polski Niepodległej – KPN), the first modern underground political party, preached an intensely anti-communist and anti-Soviet message. Furthermore, there emerged a renewed sense of spiritual community, intensified by the election of the Polish Pope John Paul II in October 1978, and culminating in the first papal visit in June 1979. The regime itself seesawed between repression and uneasy toleration.

The birth of Solidarity came a year later in August 1980 as a result of a new wave of industrial unrest. The culmination of the 'hot summer' was the negotiation of the Gdańsk Agreement. The workers achieved far-reaching, fundamental concessions, in particular the right to establish an autonomous trade union movement free of Party control and buttressed by the right to strike. This was an unprecedented departure from communist practice.

Solidarity rapidly developed not only as a trade union but as a mass social movement some 9 million strong.[31] It aimed for change within the framework of the existing system of communist political domination and alliance with the USSR; this reflected the notion of a 'self-limiting revolution'. Yet it also represented a unified national challenge of society against the polity, in which some one-third of rank and file party members also took part. National and religious symbolism was pervasive.[32] The PZPR was unable to cope with an independent mass movement commanding the disciplined support of its members. The vestiges of authority drained from the Party, which remained divided over strategy and tactics (Stanisław Kania replaced Gierek in September 1980 and General Wojciech Jaruzelski succeeded Kania in October 1981). The Party leadership was unable to contemplate the radical changes needed to cope with the deteriorating economy; they also faced unremitting Soviet pressure to 'deal with' Solidarity.

As the stalemate appeared to generate a paralysis of both sides, Solidarity itself became increasingly divided, its more radical elements becoming bolder in their anti-communist rhetoric. Initially Solidarity was nationalist *faute de mieux* by virtue of its unified challenge to communist authority and its recognition as the legitimate representative of the national community. Its main concerns stressed workers' rights, including principles of self-management and social justice.[33] By autumn, 1981, however, a more specific political agenda was being articulated, including calls for free elections. The ability of Solidarity's leader Lech Wałęsa to control the escalation of demands was also being called into question.

The introduction of martial law in December 1981 was primarily a result of the Communist Party's impotence in the face of this social challenge. The military under Jaruzelski moved into the political vacuum, not to displace the Party but to make possible its ultimate restoration. Senior Party leaders feared increasing civil strife at home and the imminence of Soviet intervention. They justified martial law in terms of *raison d'état*, as the lesser evil and the last chance to preserve some elements of the reform programme.

Jaruzelski remained indelibly associated with what was widely seen as an act of national betrayal. Although he moved relatively quickly to a renewed strategy of controlled participation, including amnesties and some institutional innovations, the rhetoric of democratisation and re-newal had been heard too often before, and the population remained passive. Nor was he uniformly supported by the Party, which remained divided. Alternative focuses of national loyalties remained in Solidarity and the Church. Solidarity clung to a tenuous underground existence but the mythologised memory of 1980–1 remained strong in society at large. The continuation of a vast network of underground publishing was also important; it meant not only that alternative sources of current news were available, but that elements of the Polish intelligentsia remained exposed to West European currents of thought. When the turning point came in 1988, however, it was not Solidarity but a new generation of young workers whose strikes finally convinced the exhausted regime that dia-logue was the sole remaining option.

The communists did not lack national aspirations, but they were ideologically and politically disposed to accept a nation-state with limited sovereignty under a Soviet guarantor. The pre-war variants of Polish nationalist thought were suppressed, but elements within the Communist Party were not averse to stressing the threat posed by a resurgent (West) Germany or to mobilising traditional cultural stereotypes of the Jews for their own political ends. They largely failed, not least because they had inherited a homogeneous nation-state, from which they had created a modern society with an educated population and a now vastly different social structure.

NATIONALISM AFTER COMMUNISM

The round-table negotiations of 1989 between the party-state and Solid-arity paved the way for Solidarity's victory in partially free elections in June 1989 and for the first non-communist-led government in the contemporary era. The fall of communist regimes elsewhere in Eastern Europe, followed by the disintegration of the Soviet Union, made it possible to embark on a process of system transformation, aimed at creating a democratic political system based on a capitalist economy. Poland appeared to have considerable advantages in comparison with other post-communist states. The state was ethnically homogeneous, with ethnic identity buttressed by widespread allegiance to Roman Catholicism and shared memories of successful resistance to repression. There was a sense of national pride and a body of sustaining myth. Poland faced no crisis of identity, and no significant conflicts over the concept of citizenship.[34] Ethnic minorities constituted no more than 2–3 per cent of the population; they could now express their own aspirations, but they were too small to threaten the integrity of the state. Gone, too, was the forced link with the USSR, which had dominated security policy and external economic relations. Poland's geopolitical position was transformed.

Attempts to revive the nationalist parties of the inter-war period failed. They remained tiny groupings of nostalgic old people with no prescriptions for the modern world, and none achieved electoral representation. It was the liberal wing of Solidarity, firmly committed to a 'return to Europe', which succeeded the communists in power. It viewed accession to the European Community as a means of enhancing Poland's status, security and economic position. Entering the EC/EU would constitute a recognition of Poland's historic links with Western civilisation. Nor did the communist successor party, Social Democracy of the Polish Republic (SDRP) take the nationalist route, as in Russia, Romania or Serbia. The reformist wing of the Communist Party had triumphed, and the SDRP defined itself in the mould of European social democracy, committed to a mixed economy and the welfare state. Those who dominated the political scene after 1989 were patriots, but they were not nationalists.

Yet if nationalism failed, it was not absent. Numerous new right-wing parties attempted to mobilise the population with different combinations of typically nationalist themes: the nation, sometimes the Catholic nation, as the supreme focus of political allegiance; its strong ethnic base and its organic unity; a hierarchical, patriarchal view of society; and a marked xenophobia. This contrasted with the non-nationalist, pragmatic, rational, patriotic approach, which perceived the nation as a civic association of common laws and shared history and culture. Certainly adherents of both approaches claimed to act in the service of the Polish national community, affirmed the significance of national identity and endorsed the restoration of national symbols. Indeed, the two approaches could become blurred, since most contemporary political discourse was permeated with the rhetoric of the national interest. Still, the differences loomed large and conflicts between these different emphases provided much of the stuff of Polish politics, especially between 1991 and 1993.

Increasingly, however, a gap developed between the priorities of the politicians and those of the population. Between the elections of 1991 and 1993 there was a marked shift in popular mood. Its beneficiaries were not the nationalist Right but the social democratic Left. It was not simply a lack of popular appeal but also the divisions among the right-wing groupings which rendered them relatively impotent. Their differences of emphasis regarding many key political issues, coupled with bitter personal animosities, contributed to marginalising them in many areas. The Right paid a high price for these divisions in the September 1993 election, when it was virtually excluded from the new parliament.

Yet the political situation was far from stable after 1989. Between 1989 and 1993 Poland had a presidential election, from which Lech Wałęsa emerged victorious in December 1990; and two further parliamentary elections, in October 1991 and September 1993. This period saw five post-communist prime ministers. Of these, Mazowiecki, Bielecki and Suchocka belonged firmly to the liberal camp, while Pawlak, who failed to form a government in June 1992 but who became prime minister in October 1993, was the leader of the Polish Peasant Party (PSL), successor to the Communist Party's peasant satellite after 1945. Only Jan Olszewski laid claim to firm nationalist credentials, which took the form of anti-communist clericalism.

Nationalism, parties and issues

In the 1991 election numerous small, self-consciously nationalist parties failed to gain representation. Most had attempted to revive pre-war political formations; they were anti-Semitic and some preached a neo-fascist message. By 1993 they were politically irrelevant. Yet within the highly fragmented Polish parliament of 1991–3 different nationalist strands could certainly be identified in right-wing parties. These divisions, personal as much as programmatic, constituted a major reason for the defeat of the Right in 1993.

The best-known parties with strong nationalist tendencies were the Christian National Union (Zjednoczenie Chrześcijańsko-Narodowe – ZChN) and the KPN (Confederation for Independent Poland). Both of these parties were also tinged with anti-Semitism, though it formed no part of their official programmes. For the ZChN the concept of national identity was closely linked to Catholicism; it often came close to suggesting that only a Catholic could be a 'true Pole' (reviving the old concept of *Polak-Katolik*). It vigorously opposed the separation of Church and state and served as the mouthpiece of the Church in parliament. It was hostile to abortion and divorce, favourable to state use of religious symbols, sympathetic to censorship (especially of 'pornography') and saw women as properly belonging in the home, where they could realise their natural, caring functions.[35] It also supported attempts to rehabilitate the NSZ. However, the ZChN owed its relative electoral success in 1991 primarily to its support from the Church, rather than to its nationalist appeal as such. Many of its attitudes were shared by the Centrum, Solidarity (the trade union) and the peasant parties of Solidarity provenance, though they lacked the overt clericalism of the ZChN.

By 1992 the Porozumienie Centrum (PC – Centre Accord), conceived as a Christian Democratic grouping formed to support Wałęsa's presidential candidacy, focused mainly on the alleged significance of a continuing communist threat, which it now condemned the president for ignoring. In June 1992 after his government's fall Olszewski left the Centrum and formed the Ruch dla Rzeczpospolitej (RdR – Movement for the Republic), but the latter was generally indistinguishable from the former. Within Solidarity (the trade union) an increasing militant nationalist–populist radicalism began to gain the upper hand. Several extra-parliamentary populist groups also attempted to mobilise nationalist sentiments.

Decommunisation first emerged as an issue in the 1990 presidential election, when it served as one of Wałęsa's campaign slogans. He emphasised the ability of the former communist élites to take advantage of new freedoms for private enterprise to transform their political assets into economic ones. The Mazowiecki government (1989–90) introduced regulations to prevent private firms' exploiting state assets, but it opposed retrospective legislation and it was bitterly attacked for complicity in *nomenklatura* exploitation of public assets. The second dimension of decommunisation concerned the removal of communist personnel and so-called collaborators of the old regime. Government opponents also attacked the slow progress in disbanding the communist media empire and the retention of many ex-communist officials in government ministries. The absence of trials for criminal acts committed for political reasons appeared further evidence of attempts to forestall a reckoning with the past and to protect 'communist friends'. Mazowiecki resigned after coming third in the presidential election to Wałęsa and to the expatriate Stan Tymiński, both of whom promised a painless economic transformation.

During the parliamentary election campaign of October 1991 the Centrum, the ZChN and the KPN stressed decommunisation as essential to cleanse the nation, polluted by its experience of communism. Decommunisation was the major platform holding together the parties of the Olszewski coalition government from January to June 1992 (the Centrum, the ZChN, and the small Solidarity Peasant Party, the PL). The crusading Olszewski and his colleagues labelled their opponents communist sympathisers and themselves became known as 'Olszewiks' or 'White Bolsheviks'. Olszewski's view that even the president was soft on the old ex-communist officer corps generated growing animosity between president and premier. Such issues finally brought the defeat of Olszewski's government over the 'lustration affair'.

Proponents of lustration (a religious term meaning purification) favoured a vetting system blacklisting those who had 'collaborated' with the former regime. They argued that Poland could be neither sovereign nor secure so long as Soviet agents and informers occupied important positions within the state. Furthermore, they argued that former 'collaborators' could prove a security risk, susceptible to blackmail if their past were hidden. Lustration would also demonstrate that collaboration was not just distasteful but morally repugnant.

The issue came to a head in June 1992, when Olszewski lost a vote of confidence after his government issued a list of politicians allegedly guilty of collaboration with the communists. The list, including the president himself, the speaker of the Sejm (Parliament), and KPN leader Leszek Moczulski, was immediately compromised; but the issue rumbled on, including numerous attacks on Wałęsa from those claiming better to represent the national interest. 'Whose Poland is it to be?', asked Olszewski metaphorically, 'ours' or the communists?[36] Pro-lustration elements were also vocal within the Solidarity trade union. Wałęsa received an icy reception at its congress shortly after Olszewski's fall. Solidarity condemned the president's support for the defeat of Olszewski and his nomination of peasant leader Waldemar Pawlak as the new prime minister (Pawlak could not form a government). Spokespersons for the Centrum, the ZChN, and the Solidarity peasant movement depicted Pawlak's nomination as a *de facto* return to communism, despite an earlier readiness to welcome him into their governing coalition.

Lustration, however, split the ranks of the decommunisers. Leaders of the Confederation for Independent Poland (KPN) and Christian National Union (ZChN) were both on the highly dubious 'lustration list', though the ZChN had participated in Olszewski's coalition. The ZChN preferred to remain in government and joined the new seven-party Suchocka coalition, whose members opposed lustration or accorded it low priority, while Olszewski and Jarosław Kaczyński of the PC intensified their personal attacks on Wałęsa, his alleged role as 'Agent Bolek', and members of his entourage.[37] However, lustration was not a major issue for the population, which was more preoccupied with the hardships of daily life. The combined weight of Olszewski's RdR and Kaczyński's Centrum in the 1993 election was some 7 per cent, and neither entered parliament.

The clerical nationalists (ZChN) achieved many of their aims between 1989 and 1993. On issues such as abortion, religious education in schools and the privileged restitution of Church property they had the support of Christian elements in various parties, from the RdR and the Centrum to the Catholic wing of the liberal Democratic Union. However, the prestige of the Church declined, and it attracted much criticism for excessive

215

political interference.[38] It remained politically neutral in the 1993 election, and the ZChN failed to cross the electoral threshold.

Economic deprivation is often associated with the rise of nationalist sentiments, especially in regard to minority groups. Certainly unemployment, insecurity, a deterioration in state social provision, and visibly widening income differentials all played their part in increased working-class and peasant hostility to the new political élites. Manifestations of populist demagoguery were plentiful, usually with nationalist overtones. Indeed, most observers (mistakenly) predicted wide electoral gains in 1993 for the KPN, which had devoted particular attention to organising among the working class.[39] Much of the Polish Right embraced interventionist policies to mitigate the social impact of economic transformation. This was so for the Centrum, the ZChN, the KPN, and Olszewski's RdR. Unlike the Left, their inspiration was paternalist rather than egalitarian. The KPN in particular was often described as embodying populist nationalism, and its cavalier economic policies favoured an unlimited budget deficit and massive social expenditure. The extra-parliamentary peasant organisation, Self-Defence, preached an anti-Western, anti-Semitic message. Trade unions, including Solidarity, also began to express growing xenophobia. Immigrants came under criticism for competing with the local labour force, exporting currency and non-payment of taxes.[40] Skinhead violence made an appearance.

The key to the failure of the nationalist Right to benefit from society's frustration and insecurity lay in the availability of strong parties traditionally associated with the economic interventionism and egalitarianism of the old regime. The successor parties, the SDRP and the PSL, were well organised and had retained significant elements of their former constituencies.[41] Their leaders were impressive in articulating their programme of 'capitalism with a human face' and a strong welfare state. The SDRP won 20.4 per cent of the vote in 1993, yielding 171 seats, while the PSL won 15.4 per cent and 132 seats. Those who could not bring themselves to vote for the SDRP had an attractive social democratic alternative in the Labour Union (Unia Pracy – UP), whose origins lay in the self-management wing of Solidarity. The UP won 7.3 per cent of the vote and 41 seats.

Towards the middle of 1995 the political temperature soared again as the parties prepared for the second presidential election at the end of the year. Strikes and extra-parliamentary protest increased, with renewed bursts of anti-communist and xenophobic rhetoric. However, the leading candidates, including the SDRP leader Aleksander Kwaśniewski, remained committed to the democratic process, the rule of law and tolerance of minority interests. The Right found it impossible to agree on a single candidate and by August 1995 the position seemed similar to that on the eve of the 1993 election, with the 'Left' overcoming a fragmented fractious 'Right'.

Poland's minorities

Traditionally in Poland the insecurities of economic dislocation had been linked with a rise in anti-minority sentiment, especially anti-Semitism. It would be surprising if no tensions remained, not least because all modern societies display manifestations of intolerance. Indeed, the post-communist years saw numerous instances of harassment or violence against Ukrainians, Gypsies, Germans, and Jews. Ukrainians along the eastern border were involved in local disputes over the return of their churches. The most vicious anti-Romany manifestations took place in Mława in summer 1991.[42]

The discovery of a German minority ready to take advantage of new opportunities for political and cultural expression came as a shock to many,[43] and in some cases stimulated renewed fears of German expansionism. When in July 1991 Brandenburg Prime Minister Manfred Stolpe proposed a comprehensive programme of bilateral cooperation for the Polish–German border zone, elements of the Polish press portrayed it as a new weapon of German imperialism. In Silesia demands of the German minority for autonomy stirred fears of a potential fifth column. A spiral of mutual misunderstanding accompanied the proliferation of anti-immigrant attacks by German neo-fascists, which in turn stimulated Polish nationalism in German areas, while elements of the German community in Poland proved themselves highly insensitive to Polish historical sensibilities by erecting statues to honour German wartime dead. New German asylum regulations increased Polish fears of a mass influx of refugees expelled from Germany. The KPN was particularly adept at anti-German insinuations and veiled allegations. Clearly Polish–German relations could constitute a future regional issue of some significance, but up to 1995 tensions were not serious and the Germans enjoyed parliamentary representation in the first post-communist parliaments.

The phenomenon of 'anti-Semitism without Jews'[44] attracted greatest attention after 1989. Although only some 12,000 Jews remained in Poland,[45] most of them polonised, anti-Semitic invective was noticeable in the 1990 presidential election[46] and in party broadcasts in the 1991 (but not 1993) parliamentary elections. However, anti-Semitism was no longer a respectable or accepted part of élite political discourse, mainly because of the Holocaust and the influence of West European liberalism.[47] Most parties remained careful to avoid imputations of intolerance, though their supporters could not always be relied upon to exercise restraint. Similarly, the public displayed no wide attraction to anti-Semitic rhetoric.[48]

Certainly anti-Semitic slogans and graffiti remained common, and cases of physical violence against Jews or alleged Jews occurred, along with desecration of tombs and memorials. There remained more than fifty extreme nationalist groupings,[49] whose rhetoric often sounded as though it were taken directly from the 1930s. Virulent anti-Semitic literature was easily accessible. Many older people in particular retained the negative associations of the term 'Jew' and its stereotypical association with evil or exploitation.[50] Groups of young skinheads attacked 'Jews' and 'foreigners', and some gained a spurious ideological veneer through association with certain small extremist parties. The way in which these notions became embedded in language was also illustrated by the way in which 'Jew' could be used merely as a term of abuse, regardless of the religious or cultural persuasion of its object.[51] Yet anti-Semitism remained a marginal phenomenon, a vestige of the inter-war political culture. Profound changes in social structure, resulting in a secular, educated population, had largely removed the conditions to which mass anti-Semitism had been a response.

The return to Europe

The 'return to Europe' remained a constant theme of Polish politics after 1989. The coalitions formed after the 1993 election, first under Pawlak and from March 1995 under the Social Democrat Józef Oleksy, maintained the earlier thrust of Polish foreign policy. Indeed, a remarkable measure of consensus remained, not least because of the growing sense of physical security derived from the perceived absence of external threat. Joining the European Union and NATO were given high priority and enjoyed broad popular support. The SDRP–PSL coalition recognised the need to include Russia in the new security architecture of Europe and accepted that American concerns with Russian fears of isolation were not groundless. The coalition responded positively to President Clinton's 'partnership for peace' initiative, though the foreign minister pressed unsuccessfully for a specific timetable for the gradual extension of NATO's membership and the enunciation of specific criteria to be met by new members;[52] and President Wałęsa himself did not hide his disappointment at the second-rate status implied by the 'partnership'. Generally, problems with the EU/NATO strategy lay rather with the prospective partners, who preached a warm welcome but in practice laid an obstacle course for the East Europeans to negotiate.

As with other areas, some circles did express a degree of ambivalence. Peasant politicians responded to concerns that the EU discriminated against Polish agricultural products. Social Democrats had some anxieties about joining a capitalist club. The Catholic Church and its spokespersons favoured Europe as the potential site of a new Polish 'civilising mission'. At the same time they opposed insidious Western influences, threatening the Poles' moral fibre: the scourges were materialism generally and sexual mores, notably abortion (perceived not only as the murder of the unborn but as a 'genocidal threat to the Polish nation'), contraception, pornography, and homosexuality in particular. The underlying unity of approach however stressed that Poland's national identity had always been European, not only for geographical but for historical, social and cultural reasons.

CONCLUSION

Ethnic nationalism, so strong in inter-war Poland and rooted in the multiplicity of national minorities, class conflict and geopolitical insecurity, was only partially suppressed under the communist regime. After 1945 nationalism was used as an instrument of intra-party struggle, albeit rather unsuccessfully, given the now considerable homogeneity of the Polish state. Attempts to convince the population that the Soviet Union was the appropriate guarantor of national sovereignty also succeeded only partially. In the immediate post-communist state, nationalism also failed, although it continued to have residual effects on the political system. Numerous right-wing parties attempted to base their appeal on modern nationalist themes, but they failed to mobilise the population whether in support of decommunisation, a clerically oriented state based on the identification of the nation with the Catholic Church, or an economically interventionist, xenophobic populism. They retained a constituency, but their fragmentation and inability to cooperate was to spell (at least temporary) political demise in the 1993 elections. Economic discontent and social frustration increased support for secular, reformist and pro-European left-wing parties rather than for the parties of the Right.

NOTES

1 A.D. Smith, *Theories of Nationalism*, London, Duckworth, 1971.
2 A. Polonsky, *Politics in Independent Poland 1921–1939*, Oxford, Oxford University Press, 1972, p.139.
3 For an assessment of Piłsudski see J. Rothschild, *Piłsudski's Coup d'Etat*, New York, Columbia University Press, 1966, pp.359–71; cf. N. Davies, *God's Playground. A History of Poland*, Oxford, Clarendon Press, 1981, vol. II, pp.53–6.
4 Edward Wynot, *Polish Politics in Transition*, Athens, GA, University of Georgia Press, 1974, pp.104ff. and chapter 9.
5 Polonsky, op. cit., p.460.
6 See Ezra Mendelsohn, *The Jews of East Central Europe between the World Wars*, Bloomington, Indiana University Press, 1983, pp.23–32.
7 Aleksander Hertz, *Zydzi w kulturze polskiej*, Warsaw, Biblioteka Więzi, 1988.
8 Polonsky, op. cit., p.44; Wynot, op. cit., p.16; Andrzej Albert (pseudonym of Wojciech Roszkowski), *Najnowsza Historia Polski 1918–1980*, London, Polonia (2nd edn), 1989, pp.246–7; Mendelsohn, op. cit., p.74.
9 See Mendelsohn, op. cit., pp.68–81.
10 See, for example, Hillel Levine, *Economic Origins of Anti-Semitism. Poland and Its Jews in the Early Modern Period*, New Haven, CT, Yale University Press, 1991.

11 *Program stronnictwa demokratyczno-narodowego w zaborze rosyjskim*, Cracow, Przegląd Wszechpolski, 1903, p.22, paragraph 12.
12 For a somewhat different interpretation see Davies, op. cit., pp.262–3.
13 Lucjan Blit, *The Eastern Pretender. Bolesław Piasecki, His Life and Times*, London, Hutchinson, 1965, provides a partial biography.
14 Polonsky, op. cit., p.416.
15 See Wynot, op. cit., p.17.
16 K. Dunin-Horkawicz, 'Jak nie być antysemitą w Polsce? Antysemityzm w dyskursie publicznym', *Studia Socjologiczne* 1991, nos 3–4: 126. The inter-war collection of *Pamiętniki bezrobotnych* (Memoirs of the Unemployed) contains numerous unself-conscious references to Jews (Warsaw, Państwowe Wydawnictwo Ekonomiczne, 1967 reprint).
17 See Michel Wieviorka, 'Analyse sociologique et historique de l'antiSemitisme en Pologne', *Cahiers Internationale de Sociologie* 1992, XCIII: 237–44.
18 See Peter Brock, 'Polish Nationalism', in Peter Sugar (ed.), *Nationalism in Eastern Europe*, Seattle, University of Washington Press, 1969, pp.311–28.
19 Stefan Korboński, *The Polish Underground State*, New York, Hippocrene, 1978.
20 K. Kersten, *The Establishment of Communist Rule in Poland, 1943–1948*, Berkeley and Oxford, University of California Press, 1991, pp.126–7. Documents relating to NSZ–Gestapo collaboration were published in *Polityka* 46, 14 November 1992.
21 On Western negotiations with Stalin see Jan Karski, *The Great Powers and Poland 1939–1945. From Versailles to Yalta*, London and New York, University Press of America, 1985, pp.581–5.
22 Z. Anthony Kruszewski, *The Oder–Neisse Boundary and Poland's Modernization. The Socioeconomic and Political Impact*, London, Praeger, 1972, pp.59–60.
23 Ibid., pp.15–19, on the German expulsions. However, estimates of the size of the minority populations vary; and official statistics were not published; see R.F. Leslie (ed.) *The History of Poland since 1863*, Cambridge, Cambridge University Press, 1980, p.444.
24 Michael Checinski, *Poland. Communism, Nationalism, Anti-Semitism*, New York, Karz-Cohl Publishing, 1982, p.17.
25 But the fullest discussion is in ibid., pp.21–34.
26 Paweł Machewicz, *Polski Rok 1956*, Warsaw, Oficyna Wydawnicza 'Mówią wieki', 1993, pp.216–31. Machewicz provides evidence to question Checinski's earlier judgement that Natolin attempts to stimulate anti-Semitism found no response; see Checinski, op. cit., pp.107–8.
27 This is also Kersten's view; see K. Kersten, 'Rok 1956 – punkt wrotny', *Krytyka* 1993, 40: 136–42.
28 Checinski, op. cit., pp.156–73; see also Josef Banas, *The Scapegoats*, London, Weidenfeld & Nicolson, 1979, for some documents and first-hand accounts.
29 On KOR see Jan Józef Lipski, *KOR: A History of the Workers' Defense Committee in Poland 1976–1981*, Berkeley, University of California Press, 1985.
30 The English version is *Poland. The State of the Republic*, London, Pluto Press, 1981.
31 The literature on Solidarity is vast. Among the most readable works are still those of Neal Ascherson, *The Polish August: The Self-Limiting Revolution*, London, Penguin, 1981; and Tim Garton Ash, *The Polish Revolution: Solidarity 1980–82*, London, Jonathan Cape, 1983.
32 See Barbara Törnquist Plewa, *The Wheel of Polish Fortune*, Lund, Sweden, University of Lund, 1992, especially pp.175–253, for a discussion of Solidarity's use of Polish Romantic national myths.
33 For a different view see Peter Stachura, 'Polish nationalism in the post-communist era', in José Amodia (ed.), *The Resurgence of Nationalist Movements*

in Europe, Bradford, Department of Modern Languages, University of Bradford (Bradford Occasional Papers No. 12), c. 1992, pp.96–7.

34 Cf. Claus Offe, 'Capitalism by democratic design? democratic theory facing the triple transition in East Central Europe' 1991, *Social Research* 58 (4) Winter: 868–9.

35 The link between gender and ethnicity in right-wing political formations is explored in K. Verdery, 'From parent-state to family patriarchs: gender and nation in contemporary Eastern Europe', *East European Politics and Societies* 1994, 8 (2) Spring: 225–55.

36 Jan Olszewski, *Olszewski. Przerwana Premiera*, Warsaw, Tygodnik Solidarność, 1992.

37 J. Kurski and P. Semki, *Lewy czerwcowy*, Warsaw, Editions Spotkania, 1993.

38 Jerzy Wiatr, *Wybory parlamentarne 19 września 1993: Przyczyny i następstwa*, Warsaw, Agencja Scholar, 1993, pp.77–87; see also the interview material in J. Hayden, *Poles Apart. Solidarity and the New Poland*, London, Frank Cass, 1994.

39 Janina Paradowska, 'Kroki po skoku', *Polityka* 24, 12 June 1993.

40 CBOS poll of October 1992, cited in M. Henzler, 'Rzeczpospolita przechodnia', *Polityka* 7, 13 February 1993.

41 For more detail see Frances Millard, 'The Polish parliamentary elections of September 1993', *Communist and Post-Communist Studies* 1994, 27 (3): 295–314.

42 'Tabor z Mławy', *Wprost* 30, 28 July 1991.

43 W. Kalicki, 'Niemcy za Pazuchą', *Gazeta Wyborcza*, 21 September 1991.

44 The term derives from Paul Lendvai, *L'anti-Semitisme sans juifs*, Paris, Fayard, 1971.

45 Z. Lentowicz, 'Przykłady hańby', *Rzeczpospolita* 94, 22 April 1991.

46 K. Gebert, 'Antisemitism in the 1990 Polish presidential election', *Social Research* 1991, 58 (4): 723–55.

47 Dunin-Horkawicz, op. cit.; see also Antony Polonsky (ed.), *'My Brother's Keeper?' Recent Polish Debates on the Holocaust*, London, Routledge, 1990.

48 See the reports of extensive public opinion surveys in *Rzeczpospolita* 158, 9 July 1991.

49 Mariusz Janicki, 'Jedna trzecia Rzeczpospolitej', *Polityka* 17, 23 April 1994.

50 See the opinion polls reported in *Rzeczpospolita* 158, 9 July 1991. Lentowicz reported that as late as 1978 80 per cent of survey respondents in the countryside still associated the Jews with ritual murder; Lentowicz, op. cit.

51 Dunin-Horkawicz, op. cit., p.133.

52 See Olechowski's proposals in *Rzeczpospolita* 293, 16 December 1993.

SELECT BIBLIOGRAPHY

Brock, P. (1969) 'Polish nationalism', in P. Sugar (ed.), *Nationalism in Eastern Europe*, Seattle, University of Washington Press, pp.311–28.

Checinski, M. (1982) *Poland, Communism, Nationalism, Anti-Semitism*, New York, Karz Kohl.

Davies, N. (1981) *God's Playground. A History of Poland*, vol. 2, Oxford, Clarendon Press.

Kersten, K. (1991) *The Establishment of Communist Rule in Poland, 1943–1948*, Oxford, University of California Press.

Korboński, S. (1978) *The Polish Underground State*, New York, Hippocrene.

Millard, F. (1994) *The Anatomy of the New Poland. Post-Communist Politics in Its First Phase*, Aldershot, Edward Elgar.

Polonsky, A. (1972) *Politics in Independent Poland 1921–1939*, Oxford, Oxford University Press.

Prazmowska, A.J. (1995) 'The new right in Poland: nationalism, anti-Semitism and parliamentarism', in L. Cheles, R. Ferguson and M. Vaughan (eds), *The Far Right in Western and Eastern Europe*, London, Longman, pp.198–214.

Tittenbrun, J. (1993) *The Collapse of 'Real Socialism' in Poland*, London, Janus Publishing.

10

FROM SOVIET TO RUSSIAN IDENTITY

The origins of contemporary Russian nationalism and national identity

Paul Flenley

In 1986 the new Soviet Communist Party programme adopted under Mikhail Gorbachev declared that 'the nationalities question, as inherited from the past, has been successfully resolved in the Soviet Union'.[1] Five years later the Soviet Union had disintegrated under the weight of demands for sovereignty from the national minorities and indeed the Russians themselves and the ideology of Marxism–Leninism had seemingly been replaced by strident nationalism. The main aim of this chapter is to examine the relationship between Russian and Soviet identity in the Soviet period and analyse the way in which the concept of Russia emerged out of the collapse of the Soviet Union. It will be argued that the Soviet system at one and the same time exploited, controlled and attempted to supersede Russian nationalist sentiment. Eventually as the Soviet system began to weaken under Gorbachev it was Russian nationalism which emerged both from within and outside the Party/state to deal the final blow. In the politics of these final years of the USSR and in the subsequent period conservative communists and ardent nationalists could often find common ground. The chapter will seek to illustrate the basis of this strange alliance. Finally it will be seen that while the emergence of Russia may have played a crucial card in bringing the end of the Soviet Union the question of Russia's existence as a modern nation-state remains unresolved.

MAJOR THEMES IN RUSSIAN IDENTITY

Some of the major problems of Russian identity derive from the lack of obvious physical boundaries to the nation and the fact that from the mid-sixteenth century onwards Russia had been a multi-ethnic entity. The definition of where or what the nation is, therefore, has and continues to be a problem. When overt Russian nationalism began to emerge in the early nineteenth century, however, there was one element that was agreed on – the fate and development of Russia was inextricably tied to the existence of a strong central authority whether it be defined as state or autocrat. For Nicholas Karamzin (1766–1826) author of a twelve-volume, *History of the Russian State*, autocracy was to be defended as 'the Palladium of Russia'. History had taught that undivided autocratic power was better than the foreign models of constitutional limitations to authority with which the then Tsar Alexander I was toying.[2] Indeed even in 1564 Ivan IV (the Terrible) justified autocracy to the rebellious boyar Kurbsky on the grounds that not only was it long associated with the emergence of Russia and its survival against external enemies but that its preservation under him would prevent Russia from falling apart through conflict within[3]. For Nikolai Danilevsky, the theorist of Pan-Slavism in the nineteenth century 'the goal that justified all the cruelties of Russian history was the creation of a powerful state organism whose expansion would be subject only to the natural laws of evolution.'[4]

Identification of national integrity with the state was reinforced by the memory of those periods when the collapse of central authority seemed to be directly associated with the disintegration of Russia. The accession of a weak tsar in 1584 was seen to have led to the 'Time of Troubles' when between 1598 and 1613 Muscovy (seen by Russian historians as the precursor of Russia) was convulsed in boyaral strife, foreign intervention and peasant revolt. The installation of the Romanov dynasty with full autocratic powers marked the beginning of the reconstruction of the nation. When that autocracy itself was overthrown in 1917 even many opponents of the Bolsheviks applauded the historic role the Bolshevik dictatorship played in preventing the total collapse of Russia. In N.A. Berdyaev's view Lenin 'stopped the chaotic disintegration of Russia, stopped it in a despotic, tyrannical way. In this are features of similarity with Peter (the Great).'[5] Subsequently the Soviet state under Stalin despite its repressiveness was seen as engaging in a 're-gathering of the lands' lost to Russia after 1917. Above all, the period 1941–5 was seen as the point when the survival and integrity of Russia was most identified with the strength of the Soviet state.[6] Not surprisingly the Second World War became a key element in sub-sequent attempts to legitimise the Soviet state. Even some of the most ardent critics of Stalin conceded his positive role in this period.[7]

A political culture which identified the well-being of the nation with the assertion of central power and strong leaders persisted into the con-temporary period. While Gorbachev's policy of glasnost was widely supported, surveys undertaken in the late 1980s showed that the idea of democratisation tended to be supported only in the abstract.[8] The ex-perience of the multi-candidate elections of 1989 and 1990 and the presidential election of 1991 made people supportive of the idea of competitive elections and of the opportunity to remove leaders. However other surveys showing negative attitudes to minorities and sizeable percentages supporting state restrictions on freedoms of the press reveal the vulnerability of support for a civic and political culture which would make democracy stable in practice.[9] A majority still looked to a few people to run everything. Even in the summer of 1991 some 70 per cent of those surveyed agreed that 'Russia's salvation would be a person able to lead the people and bring order to the country.'[10] In 1992 between 24 per cent and 43 per cent supported the idea of dictatorship or authoritarian rule.[11] Not surprisingly politicians in the post-Soviet period have exploited this sentiment. In his battles with the Russian Parliament in 1992–3 Yeltsin frequently played the 'it's-either-me-or-chaos' card. On 9 December 1993 speaking on television in favour of his new constitution which would strengthen presidential power he declared 'Civil war has not simply knocked at the door, it has already entered our house.' As a solution he advocated 'A president elected by the whole population by all the peoples, all the citizens of all regions or as they used to say in Rus [old Russia] – of the lands – called upon to personify the whole of Russia, to be the main guarantor of its unity and to bear the main responsibility for the country. But for this he should have the necessary powers.'[12] While Yeltsin did not demand absolute powers others were emerging on the scene who claimed that that was exactly what Russia needed. In the context of rising crime, loss of territory and economic and social despair Vladimir Zhirinovsky polled unexpectedly well in the December 1993 elections on the basis of a progamme which included the view that dictatorship could restore Russia. 'I will immediately declare a dictatorship – the country cannot afford democracy for now. I will stabilise the situation in just two months,' he announced.[13]

While the theme of strong central authority and identification of the Russian nation with the Russian state was common in Russian tradition this should not be confused with support for despotism. For Karamzin autocracy meant undivided but not unlimited power.[14] Freedom was not seen as incompatible with the idea of autocracy. It was only with the writings of such conservatives as Leontiev at the end of the nineteenth century and the activities of such anti-Semitic groups as 'The Black Hundreds' in 1905 that the Russian nationalist tradition becomes identified with repression. Indeed the Slavophiles of the nineteenth century saw freedom as essential to their philosophy. For them autocray was to be valued precisely because it guaranteed the people a unique form of freedom superior to the so-called freedoms of the West. This involved the freedom to live according to unwritten laws of faith and tradition in a community of Orthodox Christian believers. The legalistic, alienated individualism of Western 'freedom' would be avoided.[15]

From the early nineteenth century onwards, then, a strong theme in Russian thought tended to assert Russian identity in terms of difference to Western Europe. The Russian road entailed a mixture of communalism, moral truth, authority and an interpretation of freedom which was somehow lost in the West. The campaigns of Slavophiles in the nineteenth century and so-called neo-Slavophiles in the post-Soviet period have been concerned to preserve the uniqueness of Russia against the threat of westernisation and so-called 'modernisation'. It is this latter point that provides a basis for cooperation between nationalist and communist politicians in the post-Soviet era – what Yeltsin termed, the 'Red–Brown alliance'. For overt 'nationalists', despite the horrors of the Soviet period, communism sustained certain fundamental ideals which are now threatened by the post-Soviet rush to embrace the free market and Western models of government. Seeing Stalin's collective farms as a continuation of the old peasant commune may appear grotesque. Nevertheless, the view that the Bolsheviks and contemporary communists believed in the community as an organic whole rather than a collection of individual market consumers enabled an effective alliance of Right and Left to flourish. In the organisation of blocs for the December 1993 elections the Socialist Party of the Working People found it could ally with Cossacks and monarchists on the basis of favouring the preservation of the communal ownership of land.[16] I. Konstantinov, co-president of the Front for National Salvation talked of the need for a new social structure based on *sobornost* (the old Slavophile concept of community) and identitifed this as basically the same principle as the *kollektivizm* of the communists. It was not therefore surprising to find the former Soviet dissident Alexander Solzhenitsyn being applauded by both nationalist and communist deputies when he addressed the State Duma on 28 October 1994 and condemned Yeltsin's free-market economic reforms.[17] For some observers the above phenomenon is part of a re-run of the nineteenth-century debate between Slavophiles and Westernisers over the future road which Russia should take. There are those, as above, who stress 'the distinctiveness of Russian development and the specific mission of the Russian people' and those who 'emphasize the unifying features of the world civilization' who prefer to see Russia as just another normal country.[18]

TSARIST AND SOVIET NATIONALITY POLICY

The degree of continuity between Russia and the Soviet Union has been a major source of debate among historians.[19] The parallels particularly between Stalinism in the late 1930s and the politics of old Muscovy are certainly compelling, while the peculiar structure of a highly militarised Soviet state with its service-dependent social structure could be said to have been laid out by the end of the fifteenth century.[20] Yet when the Bolshevik Revolution occurred the break with the past seemed greater than in any previous revolution. The Bolsheviks advocated a clear break with the traditions of the Russian empire. To begin with they professed an internationalism which claimed that the solidarity of the proletariat would overcome traditional loyalty to individual states. Even when this failed to materialise in the form of successful European revolutions Bolshevik policy internally seemed geared towards constructing a new type of person or 'New Soviet Man'. In nationality policy in particular the Bolsheviks advocated a new relationship between the peoples of the former tsarist empire which would not be based on Great Russian chauvinism.

The tsars had not pursued a wholly consistent policy towards ruling a multi-ethnic state. Nevertheless they generally adhered to the principle of maintaining Russia as a single unit and ultimately defining all citizens of Russia as those subject to the rule of the autocrat. Major exceptions to this policy included Poland and Finland which at times had been governed as constitutional monarchies. The Ukraine, Livonia and Estonia had also enjoyed periods of extensive autonomy and many of the nomadic peoples of the empire were granted some self-rule.[21] Overlaying this policy was the periodic pressure on the various minority peoples, especially Jews and Moslems, to convert to Orthodoxy and especially in the late nineteenth century the pushing of Russian culture and language in overt campaigns of russification. By 1917 the resentment of many national minorities was sufficient to ensure that the fall of the autocracy was accompanied by the growth of national movements with a range of demands from greater autonomy to outright independence in the case of Poland and Finland. The success of the Bolsheviks in retrieving the situation and rebuilding a large multi-ethnic unit, which more or less restored the former boundaries of the old tsarist empire, is still a feat in need of further detailed research by historians. A vital part of that success was Bolshevik nationality policy itself and the idea that the Soviet Union was not just a cover for renewed Russian imperialism. In the field of nationalism, as in other areas of policy in 1917, the Bolsheviks geared their programme in order to benefit from the tide of the popular revolution.[22] Lenin compromised his traditional predilection for centralism and championed the right of self-determination for national minorities. This factor was undoubtedly a major reason for the Red Army's success in the subsequent Civil War.[23] The White armies on the opposing side were never able to mobilise the resentment of the national minorities. Their leaders espoused the cause of the restoration of 'Russia, One and Indivisible'. Even the Russian liberals of the Kadet Party continued to support the idea of maintaining the unity of the state as a Russian state.[24]

After the Civil War the Bolsheviks translated the concept of self-determination into a formula based on the 'national–territorial' principle rather than the 'national–cultural' principle favoured by the Austrian Marxist, Otto Bauer. The Soviet territorial solution in part derived from Stalin's concept of the nation which he put into practice as Commissar of Nationalities. For him a nation was an 'historically constituted, stable

227

community of people formed on the basis of a common language, territory, economic life and psychological make-up, manifested in a common culture'.[25] In practice this meant that certain ethnic groups in the Soviet Union were accorded territorial units and degrees of formal autonomy depending on their size and qualifications as a 'nation'. In the 1924 constitution of the USSR certain sizeable ethnic groups were granted the status of a titular republic with full rights of secession, in theory, and their own political structures, ministries, etc. Such republics had to have an external boundary and contain a majority of the eponymous nationality. At the other end of the scale smaller ethnic groups were granted auton-omous areas with the right to organise cultural institutions. Many groups received no territorial recognition, especially if they were very small or were dispersed throughout the Union.

The problem with this approach emerged almost immediately in the 1920s and reappeared in the Gorbachev era. The boundaries of the national territories did not always accord with the actual distribution of ethnic groups. Especially in areas such as the Caucasus and Central Asia the mixing of ethnic groups was such that it was inevitable that large numbers of people found themselves living outside the area identified with their ethnic group. For the Communist Party leadership this was seen as a temporary problem. Separate ethnic and national identity would gradu-ally cease to be important as socialism developed. Even in the initial period of its history the fact that 'the proletariat and peasantry' (i.e. the Commun-ist Party) was to be in power within each of the territories would lessen the likelihood of ethnic conflict. Moreover, that power would ensure that national autonomy would not convert into demands for secession. As Stalin declared on the creation of a Tatar-Bashkir Autonomous Soviet Republic in May 1918: 'Autonomy is a form. The whole question is what class control is contained in that form. The Soviet Government is for autonomy, but only for an autonomy where power rests in the hands of workers and peasants.'[26] The Soviets developed a federal system but underlying it was an increasingly centralised state held together ultimately by the Communist Party. It was only when the latter began to collapse under Gorbachev that some of the consequences of following the 'national–territorial' solution to the national question began to manifest themselves. For example, in 1988 Armenians living in the Nagorno-Karabakh enclave within Azerbaidzhan took advantage of the demo-cratisation encouraged by Gorbachev and voted to leave the Azerbaidzhan Republic and unite with Armenia. The subsequent conflict developed into a major ethnic war in the Caucasus.

Although the Soviet system in practice relied on coercive powers and central institutions such as the Communist Party to overcome nationalist unrest and ethnic conflict there was always the residual belief that the ultimate solution would lie in the sphere of changes in peoples' consciousness as socialism developed. Under Khrushchev it was argued that a fusion (*sliyanie*) of the different nations of the Soviet Union was occurring and some officials even suggested that perhaps the rationale for the existence of individual republics had gone. Khrushchev himself saw the administrative divisions between the republics to be so much a formality as to transfer the Russian-populated Crimea as a 'gift' from the Russian to the Ukrainian Republic in 1954 to celebrate the tercentenary of the union between the Ukraine and Russia.[27] In the post-Soviet period such a 'formal' act had very real political consequences when Russians in the Crimea resented being administered by an independent Ukraine.

Brezhnev tended to talk in terms of a 'drawing together' ('*sblizhenie*') of the ethnic groups. However, in 1971 he announced that a new supranational identity had developed: 'the Soviet people' which was 'a new historical community'.[28] Whereas the tsarist empire had ultimately used identity with the Russian state and tsar as a way of holding a multi-ethnic state together the Soviets claimed to have developed a new national concept, 'the Soviet People' with which all ethnic groups, Russian and non-Russian, could equally identify. In politicians' speeches and in the ideology generally the Soviet leadership promoted such ideas as 'Soviet patriotism' and love for the 'Soviet homeland'. Indeed the State Emergency Committee (GKChP) which temporarily seized power on 18 August 1991 did so to overcome the deep crisis which 'threatens the life and safety of the citizens of the Soviet Union, the sovereignty, territorial integrity, freedom and independence of our Fatherland [*Otechestvo*]'.[29] In its 'Address to the Soviet People' it talked of 'our multinational people' living 'full of pride in their Motherland [*Rodina*]' and called for their support as a realisation of 'their debt to the Motherland [*Rodina*]'.[30]

SOVIET IN FORM, RUSSIAN IN CONTENT?

For many, especially among the national minorities, this Soviet identity was simply a mask for Great Russian nationalism. Ivan Dzyuba, a history teacher from the Ukraine, interpreted sovietisation as a cover for the russification of the national minorities.[31] Although the Russian republic (RSFSR) was only one of the republics of the Soviet Union there was always a certain overlap between Russian and Soviet identity. Even at the end of the USSR many considered the interests of Russia and the Soviet Union to be identical. Not long before the failed August coup an appeal was published in *Sovetskaya Rossiya* signed by a range of political figures and nationalists including two members of the subsequent coup leadership. It talked of the need for a patriotic movement to prevent the breakup of the 'motherland' and halt the disintegration of the Union. The fact that they apealed to 'Dear Russians! Citizens of the USSR! Fellow Country-men!' suggests that the fate of Russia and the Union were seen as inseparable.[32]

The origins of this overlap in identity lie right at the birth of the Soviet state. Despite the internationalist emphasis given to the Russian Revolu-tion by its leaders its significance as a national revolution must not be forgotten. In 1924 Kritsman, the former Left Communist,[33] commented that the Revolution was 'national in form but international in essence'. In the context of an increasingly global economy dominated by international finance capital the Revolution was the 'national ... Russian expression of the world revolutionary crisis, of the crisis of world capitalism'. He goes on to say: 'It is national above all in the sense that it ... embraced the entire Russian population.'[34] In this sense the Russian Revolution can be seen as the first twentieth-century movement for national liberation. The identification of the early Soviet state with a Russia 'liberated from foreign capital' was reinforced during the Civil War when Bolshevik propaganda was able to portray the Whites as unpatriotic because they were backed by foreign interventionists. In addition during most of the Civil War the Bolsheviks controlled only the old Muscovite heartland of Russia. In this period therefore Soviet Russia 'was now a land overwhelmingly domin-ated by Great Russians'.[35] Not surprisingly the Bolsheviks were able to benefit from the nationalism of their predominantly Great Russian Red Army and urban workforce.[36]

The view that the Bolsheviks were the heirs to Russia's destiny con-vinced many of their political opponents to work for the new state. This was particularly so for the technical intelligentsia and many former tsarist officers.[37] The introduction of the New Economic Policy in 1921 further persuaded many members of the intelligentsia and 'bourgeois specialists' to reconcile themselves with the regime. Symbolic of this were the 'smenavekhovtsy' who argued for loyal Russians to support Soviet rule. In 1924 Boris Pilnyak felt able to write 'I am with the Communists – that is insofar as the Communists are with Russia, I am with them.'[38]

Bolshevik ideology in the 1920s also seemed to be bending to a more nationalist theme. The October Revolution had been seen as the precursor to socialist revolutions in more advanced European countries where the proletariat was in a stronger position. They would then be able to assist the development of socialism in Russia. The failure of that international revolution had left the Russian proletariat isolated. It was now faced with the prospect of beginning the construction of socialism on its own. The theory of 'Socialism in One Country' which grew out of this had the advantage of being able to draw on much deeper nationalist strains in Russian thought. After the fall of Constantinople to the Moslem Turks in the fifteenth century the Muscovite princes had begun to project them-selves as the leading defenders of Orthodox Christianity. Moscow began to be referred to as the 'Third Rome' and Russia as the 'New Israel'. As the monk Philotheus wrote to Vassili III – 'Two Romes have fallen, and the third stands and a fourth there shall not be.'[39] From then on the concept of a special mission for Russia periodically appeared to be confirmed by history, whether it be defending Christianity or later rescuing Europe from Napoleon in the early nineteenth century or from fascism in the twentieth. The Russian philosopher N.A. Berdyaev observed that 'in Russia, in the Russian people there is an exceptional nationalism going beyond its borders and a fierce, exceptional, Jewish messianism but also a truly Christian, sacrificial messianism'.[40] He saw this messianic consciousness running 'through Russian history down to the communist period'.[41] For the Soviet regime the fact that it was to be the Russian proletariat which was the first chosen by history to construct socialism was an important boost to the ideology that underpinned the regime. Stalin's programmes of forced collectivisation and rapid industrialisation were conducted in an atmosphere of national mission. Critics, fainthearts or oppositionists such as Trotsky and the Left Opposition could be undermined as having no faith in the Russian people or even worse, as 'enemies of the people'.

Closer identification between the concepts of Russia and the Soviet Union affected relations with the national minorities as well. Originally Lenin and the Bolsheviks had been sensitive to the charge that their Revolution had only attained power by winning the support of the Russian and russified working class in the non-Russian areas. Lenin had specifically championed the idea of a federal system of union republics, the USSR, in order to reduce the possibilities of a continuation of the Great Russian nationalism which had been a feature of tsarist rule. In 1923 the Party also formalised the policy of 'korenizatsiya' ('indigenisation') to win over the national minorities. Apart form declaring the equality of non-Russian languages and cultures vis-à-vis Russian the policy involved the deliberate promotion of non-Russians into leading positions in the Party and state, especially in the national republics.[42] In the Ukraine for example Mykola Skrypnik pushed a policy of the maximum Ukrainianisation of the Party and government of the Ukrainian Republic. In the early 1930s, however, a more overt Russian centralist policy was pursued. 'Korenizatsiya' appeared to be encouraging a national assertiveness which would undermine the control of central authorities. Communists who had championed the rights of smaller nationalities and those such as Skrypnik arguing for genuine federalism were condemned as 'bourgeois nationalists'.[43] Many of these more 'nationalist' communists perished in the purges. It became the custom from now on to appoint Russians to key positions in the republics, especially as second secretary of the relevant republican Communist Party.[44] The role of the Russian language was reassessed. The end of the old ruling classes meant that Russian was no longer oppressive but was to be seen as a tool for introducing non-Russians to highly developed Russian culture.[45]

In the mid-1930s a reassessment of pre-1917 Russian history began. On 5 March 1934 the Politburo highlighted the need for new history textbooks. One such textbook written for the third and fourth grades of secondary schools in 1937 fulfilled the new criteria – a fusion of 'the idea of exalting the old state and the idea of the inevitability and beneficial effect of the victory of socialism in Russia'.[46] The overtly Marxist interpretations of history developed by such historians as M.N. Pokrovsky were replaced by those which stressed the continuity of Russian and Soviet history and applauded key developments and rulers in the tsarist period. In parallel with this there was a revival of interest in Russian traditions. Having been under attack during the cultural revolution of the early 1930s, folklorism now reappeared in popular culture. A Theatre of Folk Art was established in Moscow in 1938 and by the late 1930s one and a half million balalaikas and domras were being produced by Soviet factories each year.[47]

In the run-up to the war and during the war itself the Russian past was used as a way of mobilising the population. Eisenstein's 1938 film *Alexander Nevksy* reminded the population of an earlier threat from the West. In both this case and that of the film *Ivan the Terrible*, released in 1945, the parallels with Stalin's national leadership role were barely disguised. Stalin himself cultivated the image by adopting the uniform of Marshal which recalled the military dress of pre-1917 days. In 1941 he appealed to soldiers 'Let the manly images of our great ancestors – Alexander Nevsky, Dimitry Donskoi, Kuzma Minin, Dimitry Pozhorsky, Alexander Suvorov and Mikhail Kutuzov – inspire you in this war.'[48] To boost the effect the Russian Orthodox Church was rehabilitated.

The decisive role played by the Red Army in the defeat of Hitler in Europe led to a period of self-confident Russian assertiveness paralleled only by the boost to Russian nationalism which followed the defeat of Napoleon over a century before. This was reinforced by the isolationism of the Cold War which allowed campaigns of 'anti-cosmopolitanism' to hit anyone including Jews, with links, real or not, with the West. Russians were credited with inventions and achievements normally associated with non-Russians[49] and within the Soviet Union Russians were singled out as the nationality which contributed most to victory, while some others were tainted with the suspicion of collaboration. For most historians this Russian nationalism of the post-war period was deliberately orchestrated by Stalin as a way of restoring his authority.[50] How far ordinary Russians actually identified with this is not yet clear.

While it is possible to portray Stalin as a Great Russian nationalist and identify continuities with the Russian tradition it is important to remember, as Robert Tucker has pointed out, that Stalin was still a revolutionary.[51] The 1930s and 1940s were by no means a period of restoration after the Revolution of 1917. The traditional Russian countryside and urban life were changed beyond recognition. Indeed it was Stalin's Great Turn at the end of the 1920s which prevented Lenin's revolution from running into the sand.[52] For Tucker, Stalinism's continuity with the Russian past lay in the political culture, the methods used and in its similarity to earlier revolutionary periods in Russian history when state-building and revolution from above were the main features of radical change.[53]

In the post-Stalin period the overt use of Russian tradition was toned down. Indeed on the official level nationalism and chauvinism were decried. The 1961 CPSU progamme called for a fight against 'manifestations and survivals of nationalism and chauvinism of all types, against all trends of national narrow-mindedness and exclusiveness, idealisation of the past'.[54] For Russians this manifested itself in Khrushchev's reversal of the comparatively liberal policies applied to the Orthodox Church by Stalin. Although Khrushchev was often remembered fondly by many intellectuals for the 'Thaw' and the beginnings of de-Stalinisation, for many ordinary Russians the closure and in some cases destruction of some 10,000 churches between 1959 and 1964 was a major cause of his unpopularity.[55]

While the Soviet leadership was to use Russian nationalism and was not averse to allowing the concepts of Russia and Soviet Union to merge in ordinary Russians' consciousness this did not mean that Soviet identity was in fact the same as Russian identity. In the absence of terror and systematic coercion of the national minorities russification was not a viable nationality policy. Even in the early 1930s the Soviet leadership had begun to promote the idea of a hierarchy of identities with the concept of 'Soviet people' being an identity that could embrace all nationalities. On passports people had to register their ethnic identity as their nationality and 'Soviet' as their citizenship.[56] From the late 1950s onwards attempts were made to construct specifically Soviet rituals[57] and invoke a collective 'Soviet memory'. Rituals surrounding the Second World War were particularly important in this. While previous Soviet history had been socially divisive with policies pursued in a context of civil war against one class or another the war was seen as the first time that the Soviet state and Soviet peoples had come together as one.

In the 1970s Brezhnev sought to give greater meaning to this Soviet identity and inculcate a greater sense of the Soviet people sharing one overarching identity rather than consisting of wholly separate peoples. This new historical identity called the 'Soviet people' was not seen as a new ethnic identity. To be 'Soviet' was to be a citizen of the Soviet Union and to share certain officially approved values. These included loyalty to the Soviet state and Soviet 'patriotism'. They also included such values as love of work, collectivism, discipline and internationalism. The vehicles for promoting such an identity were the schools and youth programmes.[58] As Ligachev declared in 1988, 'In the school classroom itself, at Pioneer gatherings, and later, in training workshops and student auditoriums, the younger generation learns to feel involvement with the traditions and values of the Soviet homeland, the spiritual make-up and culture of the peoples, the activities and preoccupations of the country and its prestige in the modern world.'[59]

It is difficult to ascertain whether this identity was little more than a charade. A five-republic study conducted in the late Brezhnev years predictably claimed to show that the idea of a hierarchy of identities was working. Most respondents listed both the USSR and their individual republic as their homeland.[60] Equally unsurprising are results of surveys which show little support for the maintenance of the Soviet Union in the national republics in the late 1980s. In 1989 one poll showed only 10.6 per cent of Armenians and 10.2 per cent of Baltic peoples believing that the maintenance of the Soviet Union was a high priority.[61] What is more interesting is to trace the degree to which Russians identified with the Soviet Union. In interviews of the Russian population in Moscow in autumn 1987 70 per cent still saw the entire Soviet Union as their motherland. Only 14 per cent identified the RSFSR (the Russian Republic) alone.[62]

The fact that 'Sovietism' was felt more strongly among Russians could be interpreted as evidence that Soviet identity was indeed nothing more than a mask for Russian identity. It is true that many rituals developed to underpin Soviet identity appeared to draw heavily on Russian folklore and culture. However, most were torn from any traditional organic meaning. They tended to be a mishmash of contrived images and symbols, which had as little fundamental ethnic meaning for Russians as any other national grouping.[63] Indeed one of the main arguments put forward by Russian nationalists when they became more open under Gorbachev was that Russians perhaps more than any other nationality had been deprived of their specific national identity within the Soviet Union. As the writer Vladimir Soloukhin exclaimed in 1989, 'Everything Russian had to be suppressed. Why did they (the Soviets) destroy ninety-two percent of our churches? Because they had to neutralise the national feelings of Russians. Why were all the towns and villages renamed? In order to weaken the national feelings of Russians.'[64] By 1991, however, Russians themselves were beginning to disentangle their identity from that of the Soviet Union and assert a more specifically Russian identity. In the March 1991 referendum on the preservation of the Soviet Union only 53.5 per cent of voters in the RSFSR voted for the Union.[65] By 1991 many ordinary Russians were beginning to think that their interests were not inextricably entwined with the maintenance of the Soviet Union.

THE ORIGINS OF OVERT RUSSIAN NATIONALISM
WITHIN THE USSR

As in the case of nationalisms elsewhere the original vehicle for the development of Russian nationalism in the post-Stalin period was the intelligentsia. The late 1950s and early 1960s was a period in which the policies of de-Stalinisation had created hope of the possibility of socialism with a human face. However, paradoxically it was also one in which many intellectuals saw signs that the system was beyond redemption. Khrushchev's denunciations of Stalin at the Twentieth and Twenty-Second Party Congresses permanently undermined the credibility of the Party. Moreover, Khrushchev's fluctuating and often repressive policies in the arts and religion convinced many that the system was still essentially the same. This was confirmed by the attempted 're-Stalinisation' under the Brezhnev–Kosygin leadership from 1964 onwards. As a result a more politicised dissident 'movement' began to emerge, part of which turned to Russian tradition for its critique of the Soviet system and for inspiration as to future development.

Like all emerging nationalisms the initial interest was in the re-discovery of Russia's past and a desire to preserve it. In 1965 the All-Russian Society for the Preservation of Historical Monuments was formed and numbered 3 million members within a year.[66] Moscow intellectuals began to decorate their homes with icons and other symbols of Russian Orthodoxy.[67] From 1967 this interest began to form into a neo-Slavophilism which was pursued particularly in the pages of the journal *Molodaya Gvardiya*. Articles criticised the pro-Western fascination of much of the intelligentsia and called for greater heed to be paid to the true sources of Russian culture, especially the people (*narod*).[68] The fact that this journal was one of the official organs of the Komsomol (the Young Communist League) was interpreted by some as indicating that sections of the leadership itself were temporarily using Russian nationalist sentiment to combat the influence of the liberal intelligentsia as exercised through such journals as Tvardovskii's *Novyi Mir*.[69] It has even be seen as an attempt to stimulate popular anti-Westernism in order to head off any potential sympathy with the fate of Czechoslovakia in 1968.[70] This seems unlikely however. There certainly was a revival of popular interest in Russia's past in the 1960s.[71] However, subsequent ethno-sociological studies have shown that only a fraction of the population was even aware of the arguments between *Molodaya Gvardiya* and *Novyi Mir*, i.e. mainly the humanitarian intelligentsia.[72] As yet the traditional gulf which existed between the Russian intelligentsia and the mass of the population militated against the percolation of nationalist ideas downwards. It was only when popular economic and social discontent with the Soviet system escalated in the late Gorbachev period that such intellectual nationalism could be transformed into a mass phenomenon.

While perhaps dallying with Russian nationalism the regime was not prepared to tolerate any threat it might have posed. In 1964 the All-Russian Social Christian Union for the Liberation of the People (VSKhSON) argued for the overthrow of the Soviet government. In rejecting both the Communist Party and Western alternatives they called for 'a theocratic, social, representative and popular entity' echoing earlier Slavophile ideas.[73] The group was arrested in 1967. At the end of 1970 overt Russian nationalism began to be generally discouraged by the regime. The editorship of *Molodaya Gvardiya* was condemned and changed. From now on until glasnost, explicit Russian nationalism would only penetrate the official press on the occasion of the celebration of specific literary or historical events such as the 1980 celebrations of the Russian victory over the Mongols at Kulikovo in 1380.[74] The discussion and development of the political ideas of Russian nationalism were now largely confined to the ranks of dissidents such as Solzhenitsyn and such samizdat publications as the collection of essays *From under the Rubble*, produced in 1974, and the journal *Veche*.[75]

Culturally, however, neo-Slavophile themes were echoed in official literature in the works of the so-called 'village prose' writers ('*derevenshchiki*'). Stories by V. Rasputin, V. Shushkin, V. Belov, F. Abramov and others concentrated on life in the countryside and in doing so seemed to emphasise some apparently authentic moral Russian values supposedly found among the people there.[76] Their concern for the protection of the countryside against the ravages of industrialisation linked up with the beginnings of an ecological 'movement' in the 1970s. Such writers as V. Rasputin joined scientists and others in concern at the damage done by pollution to areas of natural interest, in particular Lake Baikal in Siberia.

The 'neo-Slavophilism' which emerged in the 1960s and 1970s while not acquiring a mass status was at the time predicted by several observers as an important trend for the future – 'Neo-Slavophilism is a system of ideas which may well supplant a moribund Marxism–Leninism in the Soviet Union.'[77] While united in their hostility to Western democracy as an alternative to Soviet communism, some neo-Slavophiles actually envisaged the possibility of a future accommodation with the Soviet system. Shimanov, a 'centrist' neo-Slavophile saw the potential of the political structure which the communists had established but argued it would have to be reformed in a Christian direction. 'If we encourage the imminent transformation of the Communist Party into the "Orthodox Party of the Soviet Union" we shall really achieve the "Ideal State",' he wrote in 1975[78] – a foretaste perhaps of the common ground which neo-Slavophiles and communists would find in the post-Soviet era when challenging rapid marketisation and westernisation and their effects.

THE BEGINNINGS OF POPULAR RUSSIAN NATIONALISM

Perestroika under Gorbachev had a number of fundamental consequences. First it undermined those forces for centralisation which had kept
the regional centrifugal forces of the Soviet Union in check. The All-Union
Communist Party lost its authority and its capacity to impose central
discipline behind the façade of a federal state. The agencies of central
planning were also weakened. Adequate replacements did not emerge
either in the form of alternative nation-wide political organisations or in
the form of an effective national market system. Second, the promotion of
democratisation within the system forced local élites to look to the
demands of their constituents rather than simply obey Party discipline
from Moscow. In republics where nationalism was growing this often
meant championing nationalist demands if local élites wished to survive.
Third, revelations of the crimes of the past and of the inadequacies of the
present eventually killed off any remaining claim to superiority for the
ideology of Marxism–Leninism and destroyed the Communist Party's
moral claim to monopoly rule. All this not only undermined the cohesion
of the Soviet Union but also made the idea of a Soviet identity meaningless
for most people. In the confusion of collapse most citizens turned to the
nearest most obvious identity – that of their ethnic group. Paradoxically
it was the Soviet system itself which had made this the most likely choice.
While Stalinism in its destruction of civil society had dispersed most group
identities, it had sustained ethnicity as an official source of identity. The
federal structure of the Soviet system enshrined ethnicity as an organising
principle. In some areas in the 1920s, particularly Central Asia, ethnically
defined units such as Uzbekistan were established for the first time as a
deliberate policy of promoting a secular ethnic identity, for example, Uzbek,
in order to combat more dangerous religious allegiances such as Islam. At
the time the 'rights' given to ethnic groups and national republics might
have appeared relatively formal and confined to cultural expression.
Moreover open assertion of nationalism was periodically repressed.
However, when the Soviet Union began to collapse the ethnic forms and
structures began to be filled from below with real meaning and content.[79]
The prior existence of forms of ethnic identity meant that there was a
ready-made identity or 'we' to which the 'I' could turn when Soviet
identity began to disappear.[80]

For Russians the turn to a more ethnically based identity was to be just
as important as for other nationalities. However, for them, it was and
remained more problematic. First, more than any other nationality within
the Soviet Union their identity was linked to the Soviet idea. Second, while
they had 'their' Russian Federation within the USSR they did not have the
national institutions which other nationalities 'enjoyed'. There was no

Russian Academy of Sciences while there were Estonian and Georgian Academies. Russia had to be asserted and created as a separate state within the Soviet Union while for other republics it seemed to be largely a matter of secession from the Union. Third, the assertion of Russian as an ethnic identity was sometimes to let loose certain sentiments which the Soviet system had in the main sought to check, that is, hostility to non-Russian minorities and Jews.

Russian nationalism as a mass phenomenon developed largely as a reaction to the national movements in the national republics, especially the Baltic states. It was fired by a number of emotions. First, Russians resented the anti-Russian sentiments which appeared to motivate the other national movements. There was a feeling that Russians were being unjustly blamed for the mistakes of the Soviet system and that, if anything, Russians had suffered more than others.[81] In reply to the demands of the Baltic secessionists at the Congress of Peoples' Deputies in June 1989 the novelist V. Rasputin articulated those sentiments, 'Believe me when I say that we are tired of being scapegoats, of enduring the slurs and the treachery. . . . The blame for your misfortunes lies not with Russia but with that common burden of the administrative-industrial machine, which turned out to be more terrible to all of us than the Mongolian yoke, and which has humiliated and plundered Russia as well, to the point of near suffocation.'[82] A second sentiment was the feeling that Russians should no longer feel embarrassed about asserting their separate Russian identity. Despite the continuities with Russian identity the Soviet system had generally discouraged Great Russian nationalism and portrayed it in a negative light while the national identity of others had been seen as generally positive.[83] Because Russia lacked its own political institutions separate from the central Soviet state, no one seemed to be articulating the interests of Russia and Russians in the arguments between Gorbachev and the national republics.

As in the early nineteenth century the reasssertion of Russian identity under Gorbachev was accompanied by an interest in history. Glasnost provided the opportunity for journalists and historians to begin filling in the 'blank spots' in recent Soviet history. This was facilitated by official action in releasing previously closed archival material particularly on the 1920s and 1930s.[84] There was also renewed interest in pre-1917 Russian history exemplified on a popular level by the historical novels of such writers as V. Pikul' and the revival of interest in Cossack organisations and traditions. In the realm of ideas there was an effort by many intellectuals to familiarise themselves with the mainstream of pre-1917 Russian thought which had been blotted out by Marxism–Leninism. Again this was partly officially encouraged by such ventures as the publication from 1989 onwards of a series entitled *Iz istorii otechestvennoi filosofski mysli* (From the History of National Philosophical Thought) as a supplement to the mainstream philosophy journal *Voprosy Filosofii*. Under these auspices works by such figures as Berdyaev, Florenskii, Frank, Losev, Tkachev and Kropotkin were made available.[85] The publication of volumes of works by such figures as Chaadaev (1987), Khomiakov (1987) and Vladimir Soloviev (1988) associated with nineteenth-century debates about Russia's destiny fed into the resurgence of that debate between modern versions of the Slavophiles and pro-Westerners.

In view of the above it is perhaps no coincidence that two organisations most associated with the beginnings of more open political activity in the Russian Republic stressed the idea of historical memory – Memorial and Pamyat' (Memory) – albeit from widely different political perspectives. At the founding conference of Memorial Iurii Afanas'ev declared, 'The most important task of Memorial is to restore to this country its past. But the past is alive in the present. Therefore Memorial is a political movement, in so far as today has not yet settled accounts with yesterday.'[86] The immediate aim of the organisation was to expose the illegal repressions of the past and erect a memorial to the victims of Stalinism. Its effect, however, was to mobilise up to 20,000 members including scholars and artists and as such it became an important stimulant to further political development.[87]

The national movements in the Baltic states had similarly been stimulated by anger at the crimes of the Stalinist past, especially after exposure of the circumstances of the incorporation of the Baltic states into the USSR under the Molotov–Ribbentrop Pact of 1939. There the mood had been channelled into the formation of Popular Fronts from April 1988. This example was taken up in the RSFSR with the attempts to form a Russian Popular Front. At first such fronts appeared in major cities such as Moscow and Leningrad to combat the attempts by the old Party/state machine to manipulate the elections to the 19th Party Conference in 1988. As such, they were organisations in support of Gorbachev's perestroika. Eventually on 21–2 October 1989 a founding congress in Yaroslavl with representatives from forty-one areas established a Popular Front for the Russian Republic (RSFSR) as a whole. Although this Russian national-level organisation was never as successful as those in the Baltic states, its programme outlines some of the principles of the 'liberal' side of the debate over the future of the Russian nation. As was common to Russian nationalists of both liberal and conservative variety the programme called for the establishment of the political, territorial and cultural sovereignty of the republic (i.e. the RSFSR) and the restoration to the Russian Federation of full statehood.[88] Its specifically 'liberal' nationalist agenda was confirmed in such proposals as the need for all nationalities within the RSFSR to be given equal rights and in its support for the mixed economy and the extension of democratic freedoms.

On the other side of the developing debate about the future of Russia were groups of conservative Russian nationalists, who emphasised the ethnic dimension of Russia and the Russians, and conservative communists opposed to perestroika. The sentiments of these two tendencies often overlapped, for example, the barely disguised anti-Semitism of articles in *Molodaya Gvardiya*, the Komsomol journal. They were united by seeing the boundaries of the Soviet Union as their rightful 'homeland' and by their opposition to market reform. However, they shared the liberal agenda of greater recognition for Russia and Russians within the USSR. The most famous of the conservative Russian nationalist groups, Pamyat' (Memory), came to prominence after a speech delivered by one of its leading activists Dmitrii Vasilev to a meeting on 8 December 1985 in which he asserted the authenticity of the anti-Semitic forgery 'The Protocols of the Elders of Zion'.[89] From 1987 Pamyat' split into some ten major groupings in all. They paraded a strong belief in a Judaeo-Masonic plot, a veneration for Stalin and an identification with what they considered to be 'healthy' forces within the Communist Party. By 1988 the majority of Pamyat' groups had abandoned any support for the communist system and were calling for the restoration of the monarchy and Russia's spiritual revival. They nevertheless still tied Russia's destiny to the maintenance of the USSR.[90]

A whole range of other Russian 'patriotic' groups developed alongside Pamyat' including 'The Russian Party of Russia' (1989), 'Patriot' (1988), 'National Patriotic Union "Loyalty"' (1987),[91] 'The Union of Spritual Rebirth' and 'The Society of Russian Artists'.[92] The titles of nationalist newspapers on sale both then and now reflect the obsession with images of Russia's past – *Tsar' Kolokol*, *Tretii Rym* (The Third Rome). Although many of these groups were small and fragmented certain common themes emerged which have become perennial features of Russian conservative nationalist organisations: the need for Russian spiritual and cultural rebirth and a belief in a Jewish conspiracy as the cause of Russia's ills. Such groups also shared a belief that the area of the Soviet Union was rightfully Russian and that Russians should fight off Westernism and Russophobia. The latter views gave them much common ground with conservative communists. They differed, however, in their tendency to take their models of the desirable political system for Russia from a romanticised view of the past. Many argued for such 'solutions' as return of the tsar and the calling of a traditional medieval '*zemskii sobor*'[93] to deal with Russia's ills.

The need to maintain the integrity of the Soviet Union was brought home by the organisation of so-called 'Interfronts' and 'Soviets of Labour Collectives' among the Russian populations of the Baltic republics. These developed in response to perceived threats to the civil rights of the substantial Russian minorities in those republics posed by such moves as the Estonian Supreme Soviet's attempts to remove the rights of recently arrived Russian migrants to vote in local elections. For many Russian nationalists therefore the maintenance of the USSR was not simply part of some imperialist agenda but a consequence of the more practical real-isation that its collapse would leave 25 million Russians outside the territory of the Russian Republic and transform them into foreigners overnight.

NATIONALISM WITHIN THE PARTY/STATE AND THE END OF THE USSR

While the above groups were vocal on the streets their real significance depended on the extent to which they could link up with sympathetic groupings within the Party/state. The real battle over Russian identity and the most effective uses of Russian nationalism were to be found within the Soviet Communist Party and state apparatus itself. Here the problems associated with Gorbachev's reforms were to force two increasingly distinct nationalist reactions as both liberal and conservative critics of perestroika used Russian nationalism to mobilise opinion behind them.

The conservative–nationalist tendency which began to emerge within the Party was responding to the apparent destabilising effects of Gorba-chev's perestroika. Not only were crime and social dislocation growing but the reforms were threatening the future of the Soviet Union itself. In their view it was time for Russia and Russians to assert themselves within the Union, both to defend their interests against Gorbachev and the secessionists and in particular to defend the Union. On the other side of the argument were the enthusiasts for reform who felt that perestroika was not going far enough. They eventually became convinced that it was the central Party/state bureaucracy which was the main obstacle. For them, asserting the sovereignty of Russia and indeed of the other republics was a way of challenging and eventually undercutting the power of this central bureaucracy. The Union was increasingly seen as a burden on any progressive democratic developments for Russians themselves. For these liberal nationalists Russian nationalism was to be used to push reform even further than Gorbachev intended.

The first most successful 'conservative' grouping within the Party/state, the United Front of Working People (OFT), emerged out of political clubs in Leningrad which had supported candidates of 'Communist Orien-tation' in the elections to the new Congress of Peoples' Deputies in March 1989. Its coordinating council included five USSR Peoples' Deputies, a CPSU *obkom* instructor, a Komsomol *obkom* secretary, First Secretary of the Petrograd *raikom* as well as several Communist Party workers, military personnel, managers, members of the intelligentsia and ordinary workers. Its political programme could be taken as an early statement of the conservative–nationalist agenda within the Party. They claimed to stand for the defence of the interests of the working class against all those groups who were profiting from Gorbachev's reforms, maintenance of the social guarantees of Soviet society in housing, education, etc., opposition to market reform and the maintenance of strong central government. They also advocated maintaining the Union of fifteen republics intact while giving the Russian Republic its own national institutions.[94] By the end of 1989 the OFT had joined with other groups outside the Party/state such as Otechestvo (Union for the Spiritual Revival of the Fatherland) and other 'social-patriotic movements' to organise a bloc with which to fight the republican and local elections within the RSFSR in 1990. Published in the sympathetic newspaper *Sovetskaya Rossiya* their 'Towards a National Agreement' could be seen as the first programme of a 'Red–Brown alliance' between conservative communists and non-Party nationalists. In addition to the concerns reflected in the OFT's programme the document presaged the agenda which communists and nationalists would come to share in the post-Soviet period. They asserted Russia's right to defend Russians in the non-Russian republics and the need for a strong army and powerful law-enforcement agencies to combat crime and defend Russia. They condemned 'amoralism and individualism, pornography and violence' and they called for the Russian Orthodox Church to participate in the development of the spiritual life of the Russian people. Finally, in a pseudo-Slavophile gesture they claimed that, 'We have had enough of experiments with the Russian soil and peasant – its power and protector.'[95]

Subsequently the OFT became one of the main initiators in founding the Russian Communist Party in Moscow in June 1990. The original Russian Communist Party had disappeared in the 1920s under the umbrella of the All-Union Communist Party (CPSU). Apart from being seen as a significant step towards giving Russia its own national organisations the new Party was conceived as a way of undercutting the power of the reformers within the CPSU since in theory all RSFSR members of the latter could now belong to the Russian Party as well. In practice by December 1990 the new Party had become a major focus of organisation for conservative elements within the CPSU.[96] The First Secretary of the new Party, Polozkov, was hailed by Pamyat' as 'the Saviour of Russia'.[97]

In October 1990 Polozkov called for a 'union of patriotic and democratic forces in the name of saving the fatherland'. Such an open basis for a 'Red–Brown alliance' was established in the major cities in early 1991 in the form of Committees of National Salvation.[98] The context for these was the increasing confidence of conservatives in 1991 and the apparent success of their pressure on Gorbachev to backtrack on perestroika. The Soyuz group of conservative deputies in the USSR Congress of Peoples' Deputies reflected the sentiments of many when at the Second Congress in April 1991 they called openly for an immediate state of emergency.[99] The attempted coup of August 1991 marked the culmination of the conservative communists' efforts to defend the Soviet homeland. The proposed new Union Treaty to be signed between Gorbachev and the leaders of the republics in August 1991 would have drastically shifted power from the centre. For conservative communists this would have marked the end of the Soviet Union. The State Emergency Committee which briefly assumed power on 18 August 1991 made a nationalist 'Appeal to the Soviet People' calling for the support of all 'true patriots'. Evoking historical memories of the major Russian national crisis at the beginning of the seventeenth century they saw themselves as putting an end to 'the current time of troubles'.[100]

While the Emergency Committee could be seen as the culmination of the conservative–nationalist campaign within the Party/state, it also dramatically exposed the weakness of conservative–nationalism in general before 1991. By 1991 Russian national consciousness had at last been mobilised on a mass popular scale but it did not translate into support for the view that the maintenance of the status quo of the Soviet Union was in Russia's best interests. Groups such as Pamyat' and conservative elements in the Party failed to achieve any significant success in terms of electoral support. It is true that there was some sympathy with the coup, especially in the countryside.[101] However, as yet, Boris Yeltsin's 'liberal' interpretation of nationalism had won more popular appeal at the ballot box and even though the population did not exactly turn out *en masse* to defend the 'White House' in August 1991 they were even less moved by the old Soviet patriotic rhetoric of the Emergency Committee.

The 'liberal' interpretations of nationalism within the Party/state shared with the conservative–nationalists a sense that Russians and Russia had unjustly lost out within the Soviet Union and that they lacked effective representation. Perestroika did not seem to be rectifying this situation but for the liberals within the Party this was because reform was not radical enough. Boris Yeltsin in particular began to effect a populist Russian nationalism in criticism of the Party and its bureaucracy. In a speech in Karangada on 18 August 1990 he declared that 'we cannot go on living in such conditions. Seventy billion roubles are being taken from Russia. Where to?'[102] As Moscow Party chief Yeltsin championed popular discontent against the Party élite and its privileges and was sacked for it. Subsequently he showed the extent to which he had touched a popular chord by being elected to the RSFSR Parliament from Sverdlovsk at a time when more conservative Party officials were losing such elections. Elected to be chair of the RSFSR Parliament in May 1990 Yeltsin used his position to spearhead the strategy of asserting the rights of Russia in order to push reform forward.

'Liberal' nationalists had originally come together in the 'Democratic Platform' within the CPSU. However, by the beginning of 1990 they had largely despaired of the central Soviet apparatus's capacity to deliver meaningful reform. From May 1990 onwards the Democrats began to leave the Party to join democrats outside it and form new political parties such as the Democratic Party of Russia (Travkin's party) or the Republican Party of Russia. Many, including Yeltsin, left at the 28th Party Congress in July 1990. In July 1991 the Movement for Democratic Reform attempted to unite the liberal viewpoint into a broad coalition calling for a parliamentary republic, constitutionalism, a free economy, and promising that people would retrieve their history and traditions and that the army would have 'the proud feeling of defending the Motherland'.[103] The popular strength of the liberal nationalist view was confirmed by the direct election of Yeltsin to be Russian President on 12 June 1991 with 57 per cent of the vote.

By now the strategy had already been developed of using Russia and Russian nationalism to circumvent the obstructive central Party/state altogether. At the Congress of Peoples' Deputies of the RSFSR on 12 June 1990 delegates had voted that the laws and constitution of the RSFSR should take precedence over those of the USSR within the Russian Republic. At the time this was largely a gesture given that the institutions running Russia were in central Soviet hands. However, the Russian Parliament headed by Yeltsin increasingly constructed direct horizontal relations with the national republics rather than going centrally via Gorbachev. A coalition of republics was being constructed against the centre and the conservatives.

The real coup of 1991 was that of the 'liberal' Russian nationalists. While the Emergency Committee claimed to have assumed power, Yeltsin as President of Russia declared on 20 August that all Soviet institutions within the territory of the USSR now came under control of the Russian (RSFSR) government. After the collapse of the conservatives' coup Yeltsin's actions were confirmed by a series of decrees. On 24 August all-union ministries were placed under RSFSR control. With its centre officially russified the Soviet Union as a country was finally killed off by the agreement between the leaders of the Russian, Belorussian and Ukrainian republics to establish a new entity, the Commonwealth of Independent States on 8 December 1991. As the founding signatories of the Union Treaty of 1922 which had established the USSR they now declared that the latter was ceasing its existence.[104] Soon most of the other former republics of the USSR joined the new arrangement as independent states.

THE PROBLEMS OF RUSSIAN NATIONAL IDENTITY IN THE POST-SOVIET ERA

The relationship between Russian and Soviet identity had been highly contradictory. At one and the same time the Soviet system used and repressed Russian national sentiment. For Russians in particular the concepts of identity with the Soviet Union and identity with Russia tended to merge. Separate Russian nationalism on a mass scale developed comparatively late in the day. Yet when it was mobilised politically it was to be the instrument which ultimately sealed the fate of the Soviet Union.

The assertion of Russia and Russian identity was not, however, accompanied by the emergence of Russia as just another nation-state nor did it solve the problem of Russian national identity. The Soviet and tsarist heritage still exercise enormous influence on people's consciousness. For many observers the main problem for Russians is the transition from an imperial consciousness.[105] Roman Szporluk even characterised the conflict between conservative and liberal nationalists outlined earlier as one between 'empire-savers' and 'nation-builders'.[106] However this is to oversimplify the problem. Russia's continued 'imperialism' stems from three practical problems. First, the collapse of the Soviet Union left some 25 million Russians as minorities in the new independent states of the former Soviet Union. No Russian politician sensitive to public opinion could afford to ignore their fate. Their potential dissatisfaction presents a continual source of material for exploitation by more extreme Russian nationalists. Second, Russia itself is still a federation containing a large number of non-Russian ethnic groups and twenty-one ethnically based republics. Some of the latter, Chechnya, for example, have even refused to recognise the legitimacy of rule from Moscow. Third, both economically and strategically it has been difficult for Russians to recognise that the rather arbitrary Soviet administrative divisions between the Russian Republic and others now have the status of international borders. The use of the concept 'the near-abroad' is one which shows that Russians will take some time, if at all, to accept the idea that Ukraine is a foreign country in the same way that France is. For all these reasons, just as in the case of the tsarist empire and the Soviet Union, modern Russia cannot behave simply as though it is the nation-state of the Russians. Whether that makes it imperialist is another question.

Other major problems associated with the emergence of the new Russian 'nation' concern its institutions, both political and economic. Those which it inherited were ones developed for the Soviet Union. In the post-Soviet period the project has been to construct alternatives. Many of the crises of the post-Soviet period are linked to the problems involved with this. For example, the old Soviet constitution had not effectively defined the division of powers between president and parliament leading to conflict between the two in the period after 1991. The Communist Party had provided a way of linking administration in the centre with the localities. With its reduction to just another political party Russia lacked effective integrating mechanisms. Even by 1995 it still proved difficult to build a multi-party system. Parties tended to cohere around personalities rather than concrete programmes and involved shifting alliances between individuals. New parties lacked nationwide organisations with mass memberships. The moves to replace the centrally planned, state-controlled economy with the free market confronted both structural and social obstacles. In particular, the end of the relative security provided by the Soviet system and the impoverishment of many, particularly the old and those in state employment, resulted in a backlash against the 'liberals' which manifested itself most starkly in the successes of both Zhirinovsky and the Communist Party in the December 1993 elections.

While the liberal interpretations of Russia's future were in the ascendant at the time of the collapse of the USSR, experience since tended to change the balance of forces in favour of conservative–nationalists. It was against this background that the Russian leadership decided to reassert Moscow's control over the rebellious Chechen Republic within the Russian Federation. The human costs of the use of force and its consequent unpopularity caused a disarray which cut across the former liberal versus conservative-nationalist/communist divide. Some 'liberals' joined the extreme nationalist Zhirinovsky in supporting the action while the majority of both liberals and conservatives in the Russian Parliament saw it as a mistake. For many people, Chechnya showed the limitations of attempting to maintain the integrity of Russia by force. However, the question of how to provide effective government of Russia as an enormous multi-ethnic unit still remained. In addition, while Chechnya may have finally brought home the negative consequences of pursuing any 'imperial' identity the questions of what Russia is and where it and its interests properly lie still remain contested.

NOTES

1 *Programma kommunisticheskoi partii sovetskogo soyuza: novaya redaktsiya. Prinyata XXVII s'ezdom KPSS*, Moscow, Politizdat, 1987, p.43.
2 R. Pipes (ed. and transl.), *Karamzin's Memoir on Ancient and Modern Russia*, New York, Atheneum, 1966, p.139.
3 J.L.I. Fennell (ed. and transl.), *The Correspondence between Prince A.M. Kurbsky and Tsar Ivan IV of Russia*, Cambridge, Cambridge University Press, 1955, pp.13–15, 105.
4 A. Walicki, *A History of Russian Thought from the Enlightenment to Marxism*, Oxford, Clarendon Press, 1980, p.292.
5 G.A. Bordyugov and V.A. Kozlov, 'Voennyi kommunizm: Oshibka ili Proba Pochvy', in V.A. Kozlov (ed.), *Istoriya Otechestva: Lyudi, idei, resheniya*, Moscow, Politizdat, 1991, p.54.
6 In order to bring home the idea that this was a war of national survival, the Second World War was referred to as the 'Great Patriotic War'. (The 1812 war against Napoleon had been known as the 'Patriotic War'.)
7 A. Mertsalov, 'Mif o velikom stratege', in G.B. Nikanorova and A.Ya. Razumov (eds), *Stranitsy istorii*, Leningrad, Lenizdat, 1989, pp.167–72.

8   S. White, 'Post-Communist politics: towards democratic pluralism', *Journal of Communist Studies* 1993, 9(1): 27.

9   M. Wyman, 'Russian political culture: evidence from public opinion surveys', *Journal of Communist Studies* 1994, 10(1): 25–54.

10   White, op. cit., p.27.

11   Wyman, op. cit., p.45.

12   *Krasnaya zvezda*, 11 December 1993, p.1.

13   *Time International*, 27 December 1993, p.17.

14   W.J. Leatherbarrow and D.C. Offord (eds and transls), *A Documentary History of Russian Thought*, Ann Arbor, MI, Ardis, 1987, p.15.

15   Walicki, op. cit., p.97.

16   *Guardian*, 2 November 1993.

17   *Guardian*, 29 October 1994.

18   V. Zaslavsky, 'The evolution of separatism in Soviet society under Gorbachev', in G.W. Lapidus and V. Zaslavsky (eds), *From Union to Commonwealth*, Cambridge, Cambridge University Press, 1992, p.80.

19   See C.E. Black, *Understanding Soviet Politics: The Perspective of Russian History*, Boulder, CO, Westview Press, 1986.

20   See R. Hellie, 'The structure of modern history: towards a dynamic model', *Russian History* 1977, 4: 1–22 and E.L. Keenan, 'Muscovite Political Folkways', *Russian Review* 1986, no. XLV: 115–81.

21   R. Pipes, *The Formation of the Soviet Union: Communism and Nationalism 1917–1923*, Cambridge, MA, Harvard University Press, 1964, pp.3–6.

22   H. Carrere d'Encausse, *Decline of an Empire*, New York, Newsweek Books, 1979, pp.13–14.

23   E. Mawdsley, *The Russian Civil War*, London, Allen & Unwin, 1987, p.281.

24   J.D. Smele, 'What Kolchak wants: military versus polity in White Siberia, 1918–1920', *Revolutionary Russia* 1991, 4(1): 91, 93.

25   J.V. Stalin, 'Marxism and the National Question', (1913) in B. Franklin (ed.), *The Essential Stalin: Major Theoretical Writings 1905–52*, London, Croom Helm, 1973, p.60.

26   Quoted in M. Fainsod, *How Russia is Ruled*, Cambridge, MA, Harvard University Press, 1953, p.303.

27   R. Medvedev, *Khrushchev*, Oxford, Basil Blackwell, 1982, p.113.

28   L.I. Brezhnev, *Otchetnyi doklad Tsentral'nogo komiteta KPSS XXIV s'ezdu Kommunisticheskoi Partii Sovetskogo Soyuza*, Moscow, Gospolitizdat, 1971, p.135.

29   G. Yanaev, V. Pavlov, O. Baklanov, 'Zayavlenie sovetskogo rukovodstva', *Pravda*, 20 August 1991.

30   Gosudarstvennyi komitet po chrezvychainomu polozheniyu v CCCP, 'Obrashchenie k sovetskomy narodu', *Pravda*, 20 August 1991.

31   See I. Dzyuba, *Internationalism or Russification: A Study in the Soviet Nationalities Problem*, London, Weidenfeld & Nicolson, 1968.

32   'Slovo k narodu', *Sovetskaya Rossiya*, 23 July 1991.

33   The Left Communists were a group within the Communist Party who advocated a more radical, internationalist policy after the October 1917 Revolution.

34   L. Kritsman, 'Geroicheskii Period Russkoi Revoliutsii', Introduction and chap. 1 (translation), *Revolutionary Russia* 1989, 2(2): 1–12.

35   Mawdsley, op. cit., p.76.

36   E. Acton, *Rethinking the Russian Revolution*, London, Edward Arnold, 1990, p.146.

37   K. Bailes, *Technology and Society under Lenin and Stalin*, Princeton, NJ, Princeton University Press, 1978, pp.23–4.

38 S. Carter, *Russian Nationalism: Yesterday, Today, Tomorrow*, London, Pinter Publishers, 1990, p.47.

39 G. Vernadsky *et al.* (eds), *A Source Book for Russian History from Early Times to 1917*, vol. 1, New Haven, CT and London, Yale University Press, 1972, p.156.

40 N.A. Berdyev, *Sud'ba Rossii*, Moscow, 1918, reprinted Moscow, Izdatel'stvo MGU, 1990, pp.107–8 (my translation).

41 N.A. Berdyaev, *The Russian Idea*, London, Bles, 1947, p.8.

42 G. Liber, 'Korenizatsia: restructuring Soviet nationality policy in the 1920s', *Ethnic and Racial Studies* 1991, 14(1): 15–23.

43 J. Borys, *The Sovietization of the Ukraine*, Edmonton, Canadian Institute of Ukrainian Studies, 1980, pp.330–5.

44 A. De Jonge, *Stalin and the Shaping of the Soviet Union*, New York, 1986, pp.81–2.

45 Liber, op. cit., p.21.

46 A.N. Artizov, 'To suit the views of the leader: the 1936 competition for the (best) textbook on the history of the USSR', *Russian Social Science Review* 1993, 34(3): 89.

47 R. Stites, *Russian Popular Culture*, Cambridge, Cambridge University Press, 1992, pp.78–9.

48 I. Deutscher, *Stalin: A Political Biography*, 2nd edn, Harmondsworth, Penguin, 1972, p.458.

49 Stites, op. cit., p.116.

50 See R. Pethybridge, *A History of Post-War Russia*, London, Allen and Unwin, 1960, p.49, and R. Conquest, *Stalin: Breaker of Nations*, London, Weidenfeld & Nicolson, 1991, ch.14.

51 R. Tucker, 'Stalinism as revolution from above' in R. Tucker (ed.), *Stalinism: Essays in Historical Interpretation*, New York, Norton, 1977, p.108.

52 E.H. Carr, *Studies in Revolution*, London, Frank Cass, 1962, p.214.

53 Tucker, op. cit., pp.90–8.

54 *Programma kommunisticheskoi partii sovetskogo soyuza. Prinyata XII s'ezdom KPSS*, Moscow, Gospolitizdat, 1962, p.116.

55 J. Dunlop, *The New Russian Revolutionaries*, Belmont, MA, Nordland Publishing, 1976, p.203.

56 D.V. Dragunskii, 'Navyazannaya etnichnost', *Politicheskie Issledovaniya (POLIS)* 1993, no.5: 23.

57 N. Sadomskaya, 'New Soviet rituals and national integration in the USSR', in H.R. Huttenbach (ed.), *Soviet Nationality Policies*, London, Mansell, 1990, pp.94–120.

58 See K.A. Collias, 'Making Soviet citizens: patriotic and internationalist education in the formation of a Soviet state identity', in H.R. Huttenbach (ed.), *Soviet Nationality Policies*, London, Mansell, 1990, pp.73–93 and G. Simon, *Nationalism and Policy Towards the Nationalities in the Soviet Union*, Boulder, CO, and Oxford, Westview Press, 1991, pp.307–14.

59 *Pravda*, 18 February 1988, quoted in Collias, op. cit., p.90.

60 Collias, op. cit., p.87.

61 J. Dunlop, 'Russia: confronting a loss of empire', in I. Bremmer and R. Taras (eds), *Nations and Politics in the Soviet Successor States*, Cambridge, Cambridge University Press, 1993, p.62.

62 L.M. Drobizheva, 'The role of the intelligentsia in developing national consciousness among the peoples of the USSR under perestroika', *Ethnic and Racial Studies* 1991, 14(1): 97.

63 Sadomskaya, op. cit., p.116

64 H. Smith, *The New Russians*, New York, Random House, 1990, p.390.

65 A. Sheehy, 'USSR – The All-Union and RSFSR Referendum of March 17: results', *RFE/RL Research Report*, 26 March 1991.
66 J. Dunlop, *The New Russian Revolutionaries*, op. cit., p.204.
67 A. Yanov, *The Russian New Right*, Berkeley, CA, Institute of International Studies, 1978, p.12.
68 J. Dunlop, *The Faces of Contemporary Russian Nationalism*, Princeton, NJ, Princeton University Press, 1983, pp.218–27.
69 V. Zaslavsky, 'The evolution of separatism in Soviet society under Gorbachev', in G.W. Lapidus and V. Zaslavsky (eds), *From Union to Commonwealth*, Cambridge, Cambridge University Press, 1992, p.80.
70 Yanov, op. cit., p.17.
71 J.V. Haney, 'The revival of interest in Russia's past in the Soviet Union', *Slavic Review* 1973, 32(1): 3.
72 Drobizheva, op. cit., p.91.
73 J. Dunlop, *The New Russian Revolutionaries*, op. cit., p.288.
74 Drobizheva, op. cit., p.88.
75 Yanov, op. cit., chs IV, V; P. Walters, 'A new creed for Russians? The ideas of the Neo-Slavophils', *Religion in Communist Lands* 1976, 4(3): 20–31.
76 See G. Hosking, *Beyond Socialist Realism: Soviet Fiction since Ivan Denisovich*, London, Elek, 1980.
77 Walters, op. cit., p.20.
78 Ibid., pp.24–5.
79 Dragunskii, op. cit., pp.26–8.
80 G.Ch. Guseinov and D.V. Dragunskii, 'A new look at old wisdom', *Social Research* 1990, 57(2): 389–433.
81 V. Aksiuchits, 'Westernizers and nativists today', *Russian Social Science Review* 1993, 34(3): 23.
82 Smith, op. cit., p.386.
83 Aksiuchits, op. cit., p.25.
84 See R.W. Davies, *Soviet History in the Gorbachev Revolution*, London, Macmillan, 1989.
85 R. Aizlewood, 'The return of the Russian idea in publications, 1988–1991', *Slavonic and East European Review* 1993, 71(3): 490–9.
86 G. Hosking, 'The beginnings of independent political activity', in G.A. Hosking, J. Aves and P.J.S. Duncan (eds), *The Road to Post-Communism*, London and New York, Pinter Publishers, 1992, p.18.
87 Ibid., p.17.
88 P.J.S. Duncan, 'The rebirth of politics in Russia', in G.A. Hosking, J. Aves and P.J.S. Duncan (eds), *The Road to Post-Communism* op. cit., p.78.
89 J. Wishnevsky, 'Pamiat takes to the streets', in Vojtech Mastny (ed.), *Soviet-East European Survey, 1986–1987*, Boulder, CO, and London, Westview Press, 1988, pp.208–9.
90 M.Hughes, 'The rise and fall of Pamyat', *Religion, State and Society* 1992, 20(2): 213–29.
91 V. Pribylovsky, 'A survey of radical right-wing groups in Russia', *RFE/RL Research Report* 22 April 1994, 3(16): 28–37.
92 Drobizheva, op. cit., p.93.
93 '*Zemskii sobor*' can be roughly translated as 'Assembly of the land'. It was an assembly of nobles and officials periodically called together by the tsar to give approval to policies. The first one was called in 1549 by Ivan IV (the Terrible). In 1613 a *zemskii sobor* elected Mikhail Romanov to be tsar after the period of civil war and foreign invasion known as the 'Time of Troubles'.

94 R.W. Orttung, 'The Russian Right and the dilemmas of Party organisation',
    Soviet Studies 1992, 44(3): 451–4.
95 Carter, op. cit., pp.153–8.
96 Orttung, op. cit., pp.456–69.
97 M. Hughes, 'The never ending story: Russian nationalism, national Commun-
    ism and opposition to reform in the USSR and Russia', *Journal of Communist
    Studies* 1993, 9(2): 50.
98 Ibid., p.52.
99 M. Buckley, 'Political groups and crisis', *Journal of Communist Studies* 1993, 9(1):
    174.
100 *Pravda*, 20 August 1991.
101 Buckley, op. cit., p.175.
102 L. Drobizheva, 'Perestroika and the ethnic consciousness of Russians', in G.W.
     Lapidus and V. Zaslavsky (eds), *From Union to Commonwealth*, op. cit., p.107.
103 Buckley, op. cit., p.178.
104 See related documents in C.F. Furtado and A. Chandler, *Perestroika in the Soviet
     Republics: Documents on the National Question*, Oxford, Westview Press, 1992,
     pp.352–8.
105 See V.B. Pastukhov, 'Novye russkie: Poyavlenie ideologii', *Politicheskie Issle-
     dovaniya (POLIS)* 1993, no.3.
106 R. Szporluk, 'Dilemmas of Russian nationalism', *Problems of Communism*, July/
     August: 1989, 15–35.

SELECT BIBLIOGRAPHY

Bremmer, I. and Taras R. (eds) (1993) *Nations and Politics in the Soviet Successor
    States*, Cambridge, Cambridge University Press.
Carrere d'Encausse, H. (1979) *Decline of an Empire*, New York, Newsweek Books.
Carter, S. (1990) *Russian Nationalism: Yesterday, Today, Tomorrow*, Pinter Publishers.
Dunlop, J. (1983) *The Faces of Contemporary Russian Nationalism*, Princeton, NJ,
    Princeton University Press.
—— (1993) *The Rise of Russia and the Fall of the Soviet Empire*, Princeton, NJ,
    Princeton University Press.
Dzyuba, I. (1968) *Internationalism or Russification: A Study in the Soviet Nationalities
    Problem*, London, Weidenfeld & Nicolson.
Hosking, G.A., Aves, J. and Duncan, P.J.S. (eds) (1992) *The Road to Post-Communism*,
    London and New York, Pinter Publishers.
Hughes, M. (1993) 'The never ending story: Russian nationalism, national Com-
    munism and opposition to reform in the USSR and Russia', *Journal of Communist
    Studies* 9(2): 41–61.
Huttenbach, H.R. (ed.) (1990) *Soviet Nationality Policies*, London, Mansell.
Lapidus, G.W. and Zaslavsky, V. (eds) (1992) *From Union to Commonwealth*,
    Cambridge, Cambridge University Press.
Pipes, R. (1964) *The Formation of the Soviet Union: Communism and Nationalism
    1917–1923*, Cambridge, MA, Harvard University Press.
Smith, H. (1990) *The New Russians*, New York, Random House.
Szporluk, R. (1989) 'Dilemmas of Russian nationalism', *Problems of Communism*
    July/August: 5–35.
Walicki, A. (1980) *A History of Russian Thought from the Enlightenment to Marxism*,
    Oxford, Clarendon Press.

11

CULTURE, POLITICS AND IDENTITY IN FORMER YUGOSLAVIA

Spyros A. Sofos

Yugoslavia, as a political and social project, was, from its inception, precarious. Former Yugoslavia is an area where battles over not only territory but also history and culture have been frequent and intense since the inception of the notion of South Slav unity at the end of the last century. A variety of political projects has inspired the political imagination of the élites and the peoples of the area throughout the past two centuries, ranging from monocultural nation-state, to multicultural territorial-state-building experiments. In the post-war period, the failure of the Yugoslav Federation to provide and sustain a collective political imaginary which would not suppress the multicultural character of Yugoslav society, and to address issues of socio-economic justice and development, provided a fertile ground for the re-emergence and strengthening of mono-ethnic nationalist movements and discourses; not for the first time, nationalist movements in all republics and provinces of former Yugoslavia have attempted, apparently successfully, to construct nationalist histories and cultures,[1] testifying to the long and continuous existence of their respective nations in the territory of former Yugoslavia, and hence, their rightful sovereignty over contested territories and identities.

This is not unusual, as ethnicity and nation, as well as their cultural and historical markers, are the product of social *imagination*.[2] They all involve, and depend upon, selective – sometimes consciously and purposefully organised – remembering, as well as forgetting, and their function is to offer a meaningful interpretation of the *social* to those who share them, to restore a measure of certainty in a world of ambiguous, fluid and multiple identities, and to conceal the precarious character of the cultural and political identities they support. However, it should be made clear that *imagination* is not merely a 'mental' or 'intellectual exercise'; it is *material*, lived, tangible. War, genocide, ethnic cleansing, displacement, are just some of the most well-known facets of this process of *imagination* in former Yugoslavia; the visions of multiculturalism, plural democracy and 'civil society', often aspired to by the little publicised anti-nationalist opposition movements in the successor republics, are also products of *imagining* –

albeit alternative to the dominant nationalist imagination of the post-communist period. Bearing in mind these brief remarks, in the following pages I will attempt to examine the processes of *reification, naturalisation* and *closure* of national identities, histories and cultures and to shed some light on the discontinuities and internal contradictions in nationalist discourses in former Yugoslavia.

A BRIEF HISTORY

Former Yugoslavia has often been referred to as a country situated on 'civilisation faultlines'.[3] The demarcation line between Eastern Orthodox and Western Christianity roughly split its territory in the middle, almost coinciding with another, slightly earlier, demarcation line, separating the Eastern (later Byzantine) and Western Roman empires. More recently, it has been argued that an additional faultline divides former Yugoslavia: the dividing line between the 'civilised' West and the 'barbaric' Balkans.[4] However, borders in former Yugoslavia have been extremely fluid and permeable; populations, religious and political ideas, merchants and commodities, armies were in constant motion defying state, adminis-trative and so-called 'cultural' or 'civilisational' boundaries.

The first Slavic groups – ancestors of today's South Slavs – arrived in the Balkans during the fifth and sixth centuries. The newcomers' settle-ment in the Balkan peninsula led to the displacement of some of the previous inhabitants of the area, as the indigenous rural populations sought refuge to the mountainous areas of contemporary Montenegro and Albania and the Byzantine Empire managed to hold on only to its Dalmatian ports. Although it is quite difficult, and possibly misleading, to draw clear distinctions between the Slavic groups of the period – especially along ethnic lines – the political formations of the medieval period have often been considered to be the outcome of ethnic differentiation in the area and used as historical precedents for the legitimation of the alleged inevitability of separate statehood for the different ethnic groups of former Yugoslavia, or for the delegitimation of rival claims.[5] In the tenth century, a union of the – mainly Catholic – lands of Dalmatia, Slavonia and Croatia under King Tomislav, often considered the first Croatian kingdom, was established. It, however, quickly declined and soon became a satellite of the Magyar kingdom. Towards the end of the tenth century, the southern part of the territory of former Yugoslavia, including the area that today comprises the territory of the former Yugoslav republic of Macedonia was incorporated, together with the territory of modern-day Bulgaria as well as other parts of the Balkans, in the 'Bulgarian' or, according to some historians, Macedonian–Slavic empire of King Samuil.[6] Two centuries later, Stefan Dusan established a new empire, extending from eastern Bosnia and the northern borders of Serbia to Central Greece and assumed the title 'Tzar of Romans and Serbs'. Soon after his death and the subsequent disintegration of his empire, another kingdom comprising the territories of Dalmatia, Bosnia and Montenegro was established under King Tvrtko, providing a haven for the local Bogomil Christians who had been persecuted by both the Catholic and Eastern Orthodox religious authorities as heretics.

The Ottoman advance in the Balkans accelerated the disintegration of the last remnants of the medieval South Slav political formations. The defeat of the Serb and Albanian armies under Prince Lazar, in the 1389 battle of Kosovo, initiated a massive northwards, and later – after the Christian insurrections of 1690 and 1737 – westwards, migration of Orthodox Slavs (to the territories of contemporary Vojvodina, Slavonia and the Croatian Krajina). A part of the Slavic population of Bosnia eventually converted to Islam, while Albanians and Vlachs migrated to the depopulated plains of Southern Serbia and Kosovo. Eventually Dalmatia fell under Venetian rule, while much of the territory of contemporary Croatia was incorporated in the Habsburg empire after the Magyars' defeat by the Ottomans in 1526. In order to protect themselves from the Ottoman threat, the Habsburgs created a *cordon sanitaire*, the Military Frontier (*Vojna Krajina*), extending from the Adriatic coast to the south-eastern extremes of the Hungarian plains, and situated between their empire and the Ottoman lands. To guard part of this military zone, they recruited the Slav–Orthodox settlers who, having fled the Ottoman advance, established their new communities in the area. Finally, during the late medieval period, Spanish Jews fleeing persecution in Spain settled in major cities of the more tolerant Ottoman Balkans and established vibrant communities like those of Monastir (Bitola) and Sarajevo.

The division of the Ottoman subjects on the basis of the religious or ecclesiastical community (*millet*) they belonged to, and not their ethnic or linguistic group,[7] did not facilitate processes of ethnic/linguistic differentiation of the population of the Balkans, especially as several communities were already or eventually were to become bi- and multilingual.[8] Often, linguistic and religious markers would complicate the situation as Bulgarian, Slav-Macedonian or Serbo-Croat-speakers would be under the ecclesiastical authority of either the mainly Greek Orthodox Patriarchate of Constantinople, or the Bulgarian Orthodox Exarchate. Thus, the often contradictory character of linguistic and religious affiliations, rendered language and religion insufficient, and often unreliable markers of ethnic or national identity.[9]

National consciousness was the product of nineteenth-century ethnic cultural movements, byproducts themselves of the European Romantic movement. These sought to demarcate national cultures and languages out of the linguistic and cultural continuum of the Balkans, and to prepare and sustain the national uprisings of the emergent Balkan peoples. They all encompassed the formation of national educational institutions, the establishment of print presses in major cities of the Balkans, the establishment and standardisation of national literary languages and the codification of national folklores. Among the South Slavs, it was the Serbs who first developed such a cultural movement, and who attempted to standardise the Serbian language. This project, inspired by Romantic/ Herderian definitions of nationhood as cultural community based on language, provided a powerful motor for the construction of national consciousness among Orthodox speakers of Serbo-Croat.[10] The formation of an independent Serbian Principality in the 1830s, combined with this intellectual project, boosted Serbian nationalism whose objectives, summarised in Ilija Garašanin's *Načetanije* (Outline) of 1844, were the unification of all Serbs under a Greater Serbia with the cooperation and submission of all other South Slavs of whom Serbia was thought to be the 'natural protector'.[11]

However, alongside the Serbian nationalist movement and its politically less significant Croatian counterpart emerged Yugoslavism (*Jugoslovenstvo*), the doctrine of South Slav unity. To this process contributed the slow disintegration of the Habsburg and Ottoman empires throughout the nineteenth century, combined with the 'proximity', or commonality of the Serb and Croat languages[12] which gave rise to the doctrine of 'national oneness' ('*narodno jedinstvo*') according to which the South Slavs were essentially one people, the distinct Serbian, Croatian and Slovenian identities being merely the outcome of 'tribal' divisions. It was this conjuncture that gave rise to Yugoslavism as an alternative to imperial dependency, although it was the First World War, and the ensuing disintegration of the Habsburg Empire, that brought Yugoslavism to the foreground, mainly as a result of political necessity. Slovenes and Croats, weary of the emergence of Italy as a regional power, already possessing Istria and parts of the Dalmatian coast and of the danger of Hungarian expansion, saw in the union with the Kingdom of Serbia a possible way out of the instability and insecurity which followed the collapse of the Habsburg empire. It was South Slav intellectuals of the period, mainly from the Habsburg territories, who saw in Yugoslavism an appealing formula offering possibilities for some form of autonomy for Croatia and Slovenia within a South Slav state with Serbia as its core, and became the vanguard of a 'Yugoslavian' movement.[13]

The Kingdom of the Serbs, Croats and Slovenes, established in December 1918 under the Serbian Karadzeordjevic dynasty was – or, at least, was intended to be – the political expression of this Yugoslavian project. It was however characterised by considerable ethnic, religious and cultural diversity. If one tried to draw a simplified geopolitical sketch of the country one could not avoid recognising this: Yugoslavia contained numerous national and denominational groups. This ethnic and cultural mosaic was further complicated by the distinct history of some of its regions: Slovenes endured over five centuries of Habsburg rule. Croats claimed a period of statehood in the Middle Ages and then spent seven centuries under the Hungarian crown. Dalmatia has had its own tradition of city-states, and a significant post-medieval literary culture. Montenegro had been an independent state under a Montenegrin dynasty. Finally, after the disintegration of Stefan Dušan's empire, Serbs came under the rule of the Ottoman empire until the establishment of an independent Serbian kingdom in the nineteenth century.

The new state enjoyed a short period of grace as, very soon, Slovene and Croat intellectuals and politicians perceived it as inspired by a rigid Yugoslavism, or by a Serbian vision of Yugoslavia – as the shell of a Greater Serbia encompassing primarily all 'Serbian peoples' of the Balkans, and secondarily other South Slavs.[14] This realisation soon gave rise to tensions and widespread dissatisfaction among the ethnic groups of the kingdom. A Croatian movement for the dissolution of the union and the proclamation of a Croatian republic, a more muted Slovene centrifugal movement, and rising Bulgarian and Macedonian-Slav nationalisms in the south threatened the stability and future of the kingdom.

In 1929, King Aleksandar proclaimed a dictatorship and attempted to stabilise and unify the kingdom by pursuing one-nation, Yugoslavist, policies premised on the principle of national unity (*narodno jedinstvo*). Although this doctrine cannot be equated with Yugoslavism in general, nevertheless it represented a not insignificant, mono-ethnic variant of Yugoslav identity which inspired the dominant élites of the state. However, his *coup d'état* and authoritarian rule, instead of achieving unity and cohesion, increased the divisions within the Kingdom of Yugoslavia – as it was then renamed. King Aleksandar was killed in 1934 by an assassin paid by the Ustaše ('Insurgents'), a Croatian nationalist secret organisation. The impending Second World War convinced his caretaker successor, Prince Regent Paul, to negotiate with Croat nationalists in order to reduce the nationalist tensions within the kingdom. Thus, the 1939 *Sporazum* (Agreement), signed by the Yugoslav Prime Minister, Dragoljub Cvetković, and the Croatian Peasant Party leader, Vladko Maček, offered home rule to a 'Greater Croatia', encompassing parts of Bosnia and Herzegovina as well as Dalmatia, Slavonia and the Krajina and effectively recognised the existence of a Croatian nation. This short-lived arrangement – it eventually collapsed with the occupation and dismemberment of Yugoslavia by the Axis powers – appeased only a small part of the Croatian nationalist opposition as it fell short of independence. It did, however, undermine the legitimacy of the state among Serbs and the other nationalities of Yugoslavia as it was widely perceived that the *Sporazum* offered only one nationality a distinct status denied to the rest.

The occupation of Yugoslavia by the Axis powers (Germany, Italy,

Hungary and Bulgaria) temporarily disrupted this, precarious, cohabitation of the South Slav nations. Whereas the bulk of Yugoslavia was put under the direct control of the Axis powers, a Greater Croatia was established under the Ustaše leader Ante Pavelić, a friend of the Italian fascist leader Benito Mussolini. This strategy was highly successful: the establishment of a Greater Croatia under a fascist Ustaše poised to 'cleanse' the state's territory from Serbs, Jews, gypsies as well as Croat dissidents, and which proclaimed Muslims to be 'Croats of the blood' and a target for conversion, alienated and divided the population of occupied Yugoslavia.

The dismemberment of Yugoslavia, and the persecution of the Serbian populations outside the rump Serbian territory under Nazi occupation, constituted a blow to inter-war Yugoslavism, as it turned the mutual mistrust between Serbs and Croats into open animosity and unleashed ultra-nationalist feelings. The animosity was reflected in the atrocities perpetrated by the Croatian Ustaše and the Serbian-royalist and, on occasion, collaborationist Četniki (Chetniks) and the war between these two political forces. In this highly divisive atmosphere emerged the partisans, a new liberation movement, advocating a new post-war socialist order, based on an 'open' version of Yugoslavism that would respect and promote the distinct national cultures, including those of the smaller national and ethnic communities which had been totally disregarded in the inter-war political arrangements; federalism, combined with the promise of an egalitarian society allowed the communists (CPY – Communist Party of Yugoslavia), under the leadership of Josip Broz Tito, to attract support across ethnic and – to an extent – political boundaries, and to achieve hegemony over the movement.

THE POST-WAR PERIOD: OPPORTUNITIES AND OBSTACLES

These factors, combined with a series of military and political successes in the resistance and internal campaigns in 1943, helped the partisans achieve hegemony over Yugoslav society and, after the end of the war, allowed their leadership to establish a socialist state under the name People's Federal Republic of Yugoslavia. Even before the end of the war, the CPY leadership had realised that if post-war Yugoslavia was to survive it needed to deal with *the politics of ethnicity* which had been unleashed in the inter-war period and exacerbated during the occupation, and to invent a *collective imaginary* – a new version of Yugoslavism, sustained by a *social contract* which would not only achieve the economic development of a destroyed, under-developed and differentially developed country but also sustain economic and social progress and a vision for the future. These areas – the national issue, the identity of post-war Yugoslavia and the task of economic development – became the main battlefields on which the political struggle for hegemony over Yugoslavia and its destiny would be fought throughout the post-war period.

The regime's solution to the national issue was the formation of a federation of six republics and two autonomous units, coupled with an active promotion of Yugoslavism. The new state was premised on the principle of federalism within the context of a supranational Yugoslav socialist order. According to the CPY, the uniting force behind the Federal Republic was 'Yugoslavism', or rather the fusion between Yugoslavism and socialism, combined with respect for the cultures of the different ethnic groups that comprised Yugoslavia. The majority of the republics established by the first post-war constitution – Macedonia, Montenegro, Bosnia-Herzegovina, Slovenia, Croatia and Serbia – were considered to be 'homelands' of a particular national group (*narod*) which lived within Yugoslavia, while the provinces were federal units in which nationalities (*narodnosti*), which had a 'homeland' in another state, were concentrated. However, due to the complexity of the ethnic map of the country, and the political objectives of the post-war political class, the geographical distribution of ethnic groups did not neatly conform to republic divisions – the boundaries of the latter were primarily administrative. Thus, Serbs lived also in the republic of Croatia, three South Slavic communities – Serbs, Croats and Muslims – were living in Bosnia. Albanians constituted the ethnic majority in Kosovo and Western Macedonia and a minority in Montenegro. Serbia's Sandžak region had a Slav-Muslim majority with cultural affinities to the Muslims of Bosnia, Vojvodina had a significant Hungarian community, while Roma (Gypsies) and Vlachs were dispersed all over the country. In reality, the communists' solution to the 'national problem' of Yugoslavia was not the outcome of the appreciation of its complexity, but the result of a series of tactical concessions and calculations during the process of the mobilisation and consolidation of the partisan alliance during the occupation, and of the new state in the aftermath of the war. One of their main preoccupations was to balance or, whenever possible, to suppress ethnic/national antagonism, aspirations and grievances. They thus granted some degree of autonomy within Serbia to the predominantly Albanian Kosovo ('Kosovo i Metohija')[15] and Vojvodina which contained a large Hungarian minority, and opted for the formation of the republics of Macedonia and Bosnia-Herzegovina. This formula, in theory, reduced the possibility of Serbian dominance over the federal institutions, prevented the potential tensions the dismemberment of Bosnia by Serbs and Croats would entail, and rendered visible and offered a say to the smaller national and ethnic groups of the country (Slovenes, Muslims, Macedonians, Albanians and Hungarians). Thus, the recognition of the multi-ethnic and multicultural composition of Yugoslavia was more due to reasons of political expediency than to sensitivity regarding ethnic and national identity. This instrumental attitude towards the national question in Yugoslavia was best reflected in the arbitrary republic and region border demarcation and the, also arbitrary, decision of the CPY leadership to recognise 'nation' or 'nationality' status to some of the cultural/ethnic groups of the Federation, while denying this to the rest. Thus, the Slav-Muslims of Yugoslavia were recognised as a nation only in 1974 – this recognition however did not affect the status of the Serbian region of Sandžak in which Slav-Muslims were the majority, while Vlachs and Roma were at best statistical categories.

Although the first post-war constitution – inspired by its Soviet counter-part – defined the six republics as sovereign, in fact, the principles of federalism and republic sovereignty were largely decorative as political power resided with the CPY. However, the republics were endowed with their own republican administrative – and later, political – and cultural institutions and were allowed to promote the distinct identities of the nations they were supposed to be 'homelands' of, within the limits, however, of the official policy of *bratstvo i jedinstvo* (brotherhood and unity). In this sense, post-war Yugoslavism was developed not as ant-agonistic, but rather as complementary to the other identities of former Yugoslavia, as a form of civic-socialist identity. It should, of course, be pointed out that during the first two decades of post-war Yugoslavia, the regime attempted to stress similarities and to suppress divisive factors among the South Slav ethnic groups. Efforts to reinforce Yugoslav unity were officially sponsored: the federal authorities encouraged and sup-ported the 1954 Novi Sad declaration of Croat, Montenegrin and Serb linguists, regarding the 'oneness' of the Serbian, Croatian and Monte-negrin language; official versions of 'Marxist' Yugoslav history were promoted and the formation of a Yugoslav 'cultural space' was en-couraged, especially in the sphere of high culture.

The second significant challenge for the communists was the re-construction and development of a destroyed economy and the elimi-nation of the substantial economic disparities among the regions of Yugoslavia. On the eve of the war, Yugoslavia was an under-developed country, characterised by low industrialisation and rural overpopulation. What is more, the war, the occupation and the subsequent civil war had a devastating effect on the economy of the country: the transport and production infrastructure was almost entirely destroyed, the financial system had disintegrated and just under a quarter of the population was left homeless.[16] The regime's initial response to the economic problems was the adoption of a Soviet-type development programme: a five-year plan whose primary goal was to develop heavy industry and strategic investments at the expense of agriculture and other primary-sector economic activities. The deterioration of the relationship between Yugo-slavia and its main ally, the USSR, the Tito–Stalin rift of 1948, and the subsequent need of the regime to survive in an international system of bipolar competition, however, necessitated a rethink of the ideological and political identity and, therefore, of the developmental strategy of Yugoslavia. The five-year plan was abandoned and Soviet-style state capitalism rejected in favour of the principle of 'direct social self-management'. Despite this not insignificant change in the principles underlying its social and economic philosophy, the League of Communists of Yugoslavia (LCY – as the CPY was renamed) remained influenced by the developmental philosophy of the Soviets outlined above. Thus, the LCY policies between 1948 and 1961 yielded high growth rates, 'largely achieved by the very high rate of investment expenditures'[17] but undermined the traditional economies of the less developed republics. The effects of this fragile development were initially cushioned by the generous Western aid and – as time passed – loans. Thus, Yugoslavs experienced a period of continuous increase of their standard of living throughout the 1950s and early 1960s which was largely manifested in a rise in personal consumption.

In the early 1960s, however, the crisis started having visible effects: an inflexible economy geared towards the continuing development of heavy industry, an increasingly unequal differential development between the republics,[18] an increasing balance-of-trade deficit and high inflation clearly marked the end of the post-war economic boom and threatened to undermine the post-war social contract. This atmosphere of economic malaise prompted a debate over the future of the economy and, more generally, the future of Yugoslavia. The definition of the objectives of Yugoslavia's economic strategy became in fact the object of a struggle between the competing political and economic élites – the party reformers, market economy advocates and allied technocrats on the one hand, opposing the old political and bureaucratic élites, faithful to socialist orthodoxy, (re)centralisation and a considerable degree of central planning, on the other.

MOVES TOWARDS CONFEDERALISATION

The debate culminated in Yugoslavia's decision to pursue a 'third way to socialism' – the liberalisation and, later, decentralisation of the economy – an objective eventually called *market socialism*. The reformers, who had won the argument, found in the articulation of economic demands with the awakening national grievances a convenient vehicle for the advancement of their programmes. It was in this conjuncture that economic nationalism – the legitimation of devolution of economic, and eventually political, power to the republics in the name of national well-being – became a significant factor in Yugoslav politics. Thus, Tito's decision to remove his conservative vice-president Aleksandar Ranković in 1966, to purge his supporters and to restrict secret police activities, marked the regime's recognition of the power of the articulation of economic and national issues and indicated a strategic shift 'in the management of ethnic diversity and conflicts'.[19] In this 'pluralist socialist' phase,[20] Yugoslavism became discredited as a reactionary notion associated with the forces which sought to undermine 'market socialism',[21] as a centralistic and anti-reformist force, whereas nationalism and reform became inextricably linked.

By the late 1960s, a mixture of discontent with the economic situation and awakening nationalism gave rise to a chain of political protest. The Albanian movement in Kosovo and Western Macedonia which culminated in the 1968 'Kosovo riots', the mobilisation of Serb liberals in the 'Belgrade Summer' of 1968, the assertion of Croatian identity and separatist feeling by the emerging technocratic élites and the *maspok* (mass movement) which led to the 'Croatian Spring' of 1971, the campaign of Bosnian Muslims to redesignate Bosnia a 'Muslim Republic' in the late 1970s and the Albanian–Macedonian dispute over the 'national status' of Muslims in the Republic of Macedonia were some of the reasons which triggered the process towards the confederalisation of Yugoslavia. Despite Tito's purge of the nationalist and liberal opposition, the 1974 constitution sanctioned many of the demands of the former, changing radically the centre/republic balance of power within the federation: it endowed republics with extensive economic and political powers – including a degree of foreign policy competence[22] – and virtual sovereignty; it rendered the autonomous provinces almost equal in status to the republics and, finally, left limited authority and jurisdiction to the federal authorities. Even federal officials, due to a complex system of rotation of office among representatives of each republic and the introduction of ethnic/republican quotas, were effectively primarily, or even exclusively, loyal to their republic. The only counterbalances to the power of the republics were the personal authority and charisma of the federal president, Tito, and the Yugoslav People's Army (JNA).[23]

In fact, the 1974 constitution, instead of enabling the expression of the social diversity of Yugoslavia and its republics (including, but not limited to, ethnic and religious diversity), *reified* republican and, by extension, ethnic and national identities and rendered them the primary form of differentiation within Yugoslavia, by legally sanctioning and 'naturalising' them, at the expense of other social and political identities which remained suppressed, or at least excluded from the universe of political debate. The post-1974 period saw also the progressive 'confederalisation' of the LCY in a way shadowing the confederalisation of the country. This development, apart from generally reinforcing the significance of ethnic and national identity referred to above, also allowed and institutionalised the fragmentation of the political, administrative and economic élites along republican lines and facilitated and reinforced the political segmentation of Yugoslav society by creating republican/ethnic constituencies. These changes, however, did not satisfy the nationalists: in Serbia, confederalisation was perceived as a step towards the fragmentation of the Serbian nation – Kosovo and Vojvodina had been granted autonomy, while the position of Serbs living in other republics was uncertain; grievances regarding the differential development of the country's regions were incorporated in nationalist discourses – a prominent element in the Croatian and Slovenian universe of public debate was the 'burden imposed to their economies by their subsidising the black-hole economies of the South', whereas a dominant theme in Serbian and other 'Southern' republic politics was 'their economic subordination to the North' – despite the continuing inability of Yugoslavia to address successfully the issue and to tackle the unfair distribution of resources and advantages among Yugoslavia's regions.[24]

In addition, after Tito's death in 1980 one of the remaining federal institutions, the presidency, was also 'nationalised' as it was subjected to a system of rotation, based upon the principle of republic representation at the level of federal presidency. This eventually led to a collective leadership, stifled by inter-republic conflict, unable to respond to the new circumstances.

These political developments gathered pace as the political dynamics unleashed by the constitutional and party changes were complemented by the dramatic deterioration of the economic and social conditions during the late 1970s and throughout the 1980s. The international oil crisis and the world recession of the 1970s, combined with a poorly coordinated investment strategy based on excessive borrowing from foreign creditors, and directed towards capital-intensive projects into Macedonia and Kosovo failed to address the unemployment problem and to reduce the widespread feeling of regional economic disparity. By the end of the decade, the country was almost entirely dependent on foreign loans, aid and investment,[25] while by 1983 the repayments of the country's international debt, which had been mainly used to sustain consumer spending, had drained Yugoslavia's foreign exchange reserves.[26] Unemployment, falling living standards, high inflation, a restrictive monetary policy, combined with economic mismanagement and the failure of the principles of self-management had seriously undermined the foundations of the 'social contract' and triggered waves of discontent and created an atmosphere of widespread disappointment. Confidence on the part of the population that these problems could be resolved using existing political formulas and social practices dwindled.[27] In addition, the increasing social dislocation in the south of the country gave rise to internal migration, mainly of Kosovo and Macedonian Albanians, to the northern, more prosperous republics. In addition, partly for the same reasons and partly due to the political situation in Kosovo, local Serb and Montenegrin migration to Serbia and other republics intensified.[28] These developments increased the tensions within the republics and migration provided a unifying issue in public debate and a valuable mobilisation resource: in Slovenia internal migrants (mainly Albanians, but also Serbs) were seen as a threat to Slovenian culture and language,[29] while in Serbia and Montenegro, the migration of fellow Serbs and Montenegrins out of Kosovo, considered to be the outcome of the 'Albanisation' of the province, constituted the raw material for the unleashing of a profound 'moral panic'.[30]

Meanwhile, the segmentation of Yugoslavia was advancing. As political, economic and cultural powers resided with the republics and provinces, commercial, cultural institutions and the mass media became primarily or entirely 'republican' as far as their control and framework of reference was concerned. Virtually each republic and province, despite the multicultural and multi-ethnic composition of Yugoslavia's constituent units, progressively provided a framework for the promotion of the national identity and attainment of sovereignty of a specific ethnic group, facilitating in this way the fragmentation of the already precarious Yugoslav public sphere.[31] Yugoslavia's artificial and arbitrary internal, administrative, borders were 'upgraded' to national or 'civilisational' faultlines;[32] the Federation was disintegrating as a result of the 'ethnicisation' or 'nationalisation' of its republics and autonomous provinces and the pursuit of essentially mono-ethnic policies. These developments affected the strategies, and later the composition, of republic élites in a variety of ways.

More precisely, and at the risk of over-simplification, in Serbia, where the post-1974 federal order was perceived to be undermining the unity and rights of the Serbian nation, Serbian communists realised that nationalism was an important political force and source of legitimation. The Serbian communist leadership resorted to a mixture of pro-Yugoslavist and Serbian nationalist rhetoric and campaigned for the restoration of centralism and, of course, the restoration of Serbian control over the autonomous provinces of Kosovo and Vojvodina. On the other hand, the leaderships of the provincial parties were ardent supporters of decentralisation, Slovenian communists pushed for political liberalisation and decentralisation, while the Croatian party's aversion towards liberalisation of the political system was coupled with support for decentralisation – economic nationalism and the economic prospects of such a development were the primary reasons for this. The Macedonian LCY and the Montenegrin and Bosnian parties advocated the preservation of the Federation, although their tactical positions and the degree of their commitment varied. Despite, however, the diversity of positions, a bipolar division was slowly taking shape as Slovenia and Croatia supported the provincial party leaderships against Serbian demands of recentralisation. This confrontational atmosphere could not but lead to a deep rift between the republic élites and, more generally, the republics, as Serbian communists temporarily intimidated the provincial leaderships and managed to secure the reluctant cooperation of their Macedonian and Croatian counterparts.[33]

THE 1980s: DISARTICULATION OF THE OFFICIAL DISCOURSE AND THE EMERGENCE OF POPULIST NATIONALISMS

A combination of international and internal developments in the mid and late 1980s affected these precarious relations of power between republic élites and enabled dissent towards the more powerful 'centralist bloc' to emerge. Yugoslavia's distinct international position as a leading member of the non-aligned movement – a not insignificant marker of Yugoslav identity – was swept away by the sea-change that the end of the Cold War brought about. The protest waves which brought down the East–Central European state socialist regimes, combined with European Community demands for political reform in exchange for financial assistance increased the pressures for the legalisation of opposition parties and democratic elections. As the last vestiges of Yugoslavism withered, the official discourse and system started to break down.

In this conjuncture, Ivan Stambolić, former leader of the Serb communists and President of the Republic of Serbia, lost control of the nationalists which he had tolerated, and even manipulated for tactical reasons, in the Serbian campaign for recentralisation, while sections of the state bureaucracy and the party, having realised the potential of nationalism, supported a policy of change in the party and the state apparatus which would allow the fusion of the nationalist movements of Serbia and Montenegro[34] and the old institutional actors of the Republic (mainly the Serbian LC). This realignment of the party and republic élite eventually led to a party takeover in September 1987. In this process, Slobodan Milošević', a relatively young dynamic leader emerged and occupied the foreground of Serbian and Yugoslav politics. Milošević, a protegé and friend of Stambolić, put himself in the centre of the emerging nationalist movement after his 1987 visit to Kosovo Polje, where he pledged to protect the members of the Serbian and Montenegrin minority of the province from 'persecution by the Albanian majority'. By adopting a nationalist rhetoric, allying himself with the Serbian Orthodox Church, reinforcing the moral panic regarding the 'Albanisation' of Kosovo and mobilising aspects of folk and popular culture,[35] a variety of elements of popular concern such as the ever-widening Serbian perception that Yugoslavia was undermining 'Serbian rights', the emotional ties of Serbs with Kosovo,[36] and the widespread popular dismay with the inflexible administrative-bureaucratic system, he bid for the party leadership.

In late 1988, one year after capturing power, Milošević launched the 'anti-bureaucratic revolution', a campaign intended to 'cleanse' the party and state apparatus of 'inefficient bureaucrats'. In the name of the antibureaucratic revolution and of the restoration of Serbian rights and 'pride', Milošević used the 'moral panic' which had emerged in Serbia and Montenegro over the sensitive issue of the alleged 'Albanisation' of Kosovo[37] to justify the need for constitutional reform. He thus initiated a purge of civil servants, industry managers, journalists and university staff who might pose obstacles to his reforms or were likely to be disloyal, introduced a new Serbian constitution, and effectively abolished the autonomous status of Kosovo and Vojvodina. In Kosovo, Albanians were forced out of positions in the civil service, universities, schools, state enterprises and other organisations and institutions in a process of 'Serbianisation' of the province. As the emigration of Serbs and Montenegrins from Kosovo had been elevated to the status of national disaster, Milošević pledged to formulate an (illegal) federal government-funded programme to assist Serb communities in Kosovo and to encourage the resettlement of Serbian emigrés. Having gained the support of the radicalised Kosovo Slavs, he tacitly encouraged the emergence of 'street democracy' (*ulična demokracija*) in Serbian and Montenegrin politics: since the mid-1980s, but especially after Milošević's ascendance to power, mass rallies have progressively become part of the political life of Serbia and Montenegro. More representative of this type of popular mobilisation were the Kosovo solidarity demonstrations and the anti-bureaucratic rallies of 1987, the 1988 march of 100,000 Milošević supporters to Novi Sad, the capital of Vojvodina, to 'convince' the LC officials to resign in favour of Milošević supporters, the 1988 mass pro-Milošević demonstrations in Serbia, the 1989 Montenegrin rallies which led to the resignation of the anti-Milošević government, and the 'Meetings of Truth' organised all over Yugoslavia to 'enlighten' fellow Yugoslavs regarding the positions of Serbia and its leadership. These constituted 'extra-institutional' rituals through which the regime claimed legitimacy, the identity and unity of the nationalist-populist movement were forged,[38] and which established a 'plebiscitary' form of legitimation, parallel to that associated to the representative institutions of the socialist and post-socialist period and reinforced the 'charismatic' authority of Milošević.[39] Partly as a result of 'street democracy', Milošević achieved the establishment of a pro-Serbian government in Montenegro and the assumption of control in the provinces of Kosovo and Vojvodina; this constituted a coup at the federal level: Serbia controlled four out of the eight votes of the federal presidency and the League of Communists.

It was by then obvious that the Serbian leadership had set Serbia on a collision course with the other republics. The reaction of the Slovene and Croat communists was rather muted, although Milošević's constitutional coups had undermined their already wavering commitment to the Federation. In 1989, the Slovene and Croat communists, opting for political reform at the republic level, endorsed multi-party elections, while in January 1990 the Slovene representatives walked out of the fourteenth LCY congress, after the latter had refused to consider their proposals for full confederalisation of the party.

However, before the collapse of the congress, and despite the pre-dominance of conservative delegates, the LCY, bowing to the inevitable, adopted multi-party democracy. As a result, the political opportunity structure of the Federation was radically transformed, paving the way for the recomposition of the political élites of the republics, as non-communist political organisations, already operating in the republics, re-emerged as legal political parties.[40] The republic Leagues of Communists intensified the ideological and organisational changes that would enable them to function in the post-communist political system; these involved the *de facto* break-up of the LCY and the transformation of the former into 'national' political parties.

By 1990 Yugoslavia was only officially alive: the federal authorities had become effectively caretakers of a transitory political structure, while the republics were being transformed into nation-states. Slovene and Croat communists – the Party of Democratic Renewal, and the Party of Social Reform as they had been renamed – paid the price of their reluctance to confront Milošević's constitutional coups by losing in the first multi-party elections in their republics to more uncompromising nationalists un-tarnished by participation in the federal government. In the same year, the Serbian Socialist Party (SPS, formed by the Serbian Communist Party and the Socialist Alliance) won 40 per cent of the votes and 77.6 per cent of the parliamentary seats, while its leader, Slobodan Milošević, got two-thirds of the votes in the second round of the presidential election. What is more, his Montenegrin allies, the LC of Montenegro won an impressive 66.4 per cent of the legislature seats, and its leader, Momir Bulatović, became president of the republic. In Macedonia, despite a majority electoral system during the elections of 1989, a hung parliament led to the formation of a coalition government of former communists, Macedonian and Al-banian nationalists, and the election of the reform communist Kiro Gligorov as president. In Bosnia-Herzegovina, the legalisation of multi-party competition led to the formation of ethnic parties – Muslim (Party of Democratic Action – SDA) and the more secular Muslim Bosniak Organisation – MBO), Serbian (Serbian Democratic Party – SDS), and Croat (the Bosnian branch of the Zagreb-based party of Franjo Tudjman, Croatian Democratic Community – HDZ) which defeated the communists and federalists in the 1990 elections; the three ethnic parties formed a short-lived coalition government, before the outbreak of the war in March 1992.

SLOVENIA

In Slovenia, the mainly Centre Right coalition DEMOS won the 1990 elections on a pro-independence ticket, while reform communist Milan Kučan was elected president. All parties shared an essentially secessionist and moderate nationalist discourse and objectives often disguised by their '"return" to Europe' rhetoric. At the level of popular discourse nationalism was more clearly discernible, and often mixed with 'cultural fundamentalist' arguments emphasising the clearly distinct cultures of Serbs, or other southern Yugoslavs and Slovenes. Characteristic of this 'cultural fundamentalism' has been the contradictory character of the position displayed by the Slovenian authorities as well as the majority of Slovenes regarding the issue of Kosovo: whereas Slovenia had consistently been the most ardent supporter of the demands of the Albanian majority population of Kosovo for autonomy and republic status, and often clashed with Serbia in apparent solidarity with the Albanians, the panic regarding the influx of migrants from other Yugoslav republics and provinces often took, in addition to its anti-Serbian or anti-southern bias, an explicitly anti-Albanian dimension. This ambiguous attitude of the Slovene public and policy-makers indicated that the republic's pro-Albanian stance constituted part of a broader anti-Yugoslav or anti-Serbian orientation during the late 1980s and early 1990s.

During 1990, Slovenia remained only formally a constituent part of Yugoslavia, as it rapidly prepared for independence.[41] In June 1990 the Slovenian legislature proclaimed the republic's sovereignty, in October the JNA occupied the Slovenian Territorial Defence Force headquarters and in July 1991, after the proclamation of Slovenian independence, a ten-day military confrontation, in which the JNA unsuccessfully tried to resume control of the republic's international borders and bombed the airports of Brnik and Maribor, led to the withdrawal of the Yugoslav army from the republic.

After the initial euphoria, it became clear that the post-independence period would be more difficult than expected. Slovenia's 'return to Europe' has proved to be more elusive than anticipated as the European Union has refused to discuss the possibility of Slovenian membership before the beginning of the next millennium, contrary to popular expectations. Slovenia has to face minor border disputes with Croatia and, after the victory of the Berlusconi coalition in Italy, unofficial demands for compensation or even return of the emigré Italian-Istrian community and implicit claims that the Slovenian borders may have to be renegotiated. In addition, unemployment has risen to more than 130,000, partly as a result of the disengagement of the Slovenian economy from its traditional markets of former Yugoslavia and partly due to the inability of its industrial infrastructure to withstand the shock of integration to the international markets. In this climate of insecurity, xenophobia and nationalism have developed: the peace movements and citizens' initiatives which had flourished in Slovenia before independence have almost disappeared, while nationalist right-wing political organisations like the Social Democratic Party of Slovenia, which has been demanding 'Slovenia for the Slovenes', are growing rapidly and gaining supporters and sympathisers.[42]

CROATIA

In Croatia, the demise of the communists paved the road to power of Franjo Tudjman's nationalist Croatian Democratic Community (HDZ), and led to his election as president of the republic. Tudjman's programme included calls for a confederal Yugoslavia and an independent Croatia, demands for the annexation of part of the territory of Bosnia-Herzegovina and the 'Croatisation' of the civil service and other institutions of the republic in which Serbs had been over-represented.[43] Tudjman, a former partisan, communist official and army major general, persecuted and imprisoned for nationalist activity in the 1960s and 1970s, has also been an historian who had consistently attempted to rehabilitate aspects of the Ustaše-led Independent State of Croatia during the Second World War, by arguing that despite its fascist leadership it nevertheless constituted the legitimate expression of the Croats' wish to live in a sovereign state of their own. In addition, his engagement in the historical debate on the running of concentration camps and the scale of mass killing by the Ustaše during that period alarmed Croatian Serbs.[44] The inept management of inter-community relations by the HDZ authorities exacerbated the situation: the government tolerated the creation and arming of the Croatian Party of Right (HOS), a paramilitary Ustaše-inspired organisation loyal to the Croat nationalist warlord Dobroslav Paraga; did not react towards the vandalism of Serbian properties in Zadar in the spring of 1991;[45] introduced policies of 'Croatisation' of the civil service forms and implemented them so rigidly that Serbs perceived them as purges; and pronounced the Croatian variant of Serbo-Croat as the only language of administration, and removed the cyrillic script from public buildings, documents or road signs.[46] These policies alienated the Croatian Serbs and enabled the Belgrade-based nationalists and their local allies to mobilise historically conditioned fears of the re-emergence of a fascist Croatia. In July 1990, Croatian Serb leaders proclaimed their autonomy, called for their integration within Yugoslavia and requested permission to conduct a referendum to determine their status within Croatia or Yugoslavia. The Croatian justice ministry banned it while Tudjman accused the Serbs of destabilising Croatia. The process of ethnic polarisation and confrontation escalated as the Serbian referendum went ahead followed by a declaration of sovereignty of Croatian Serbs, sporadic violence, the setting of barricades in predominantly Serbian districts and a plea for protection to the JNA. In 1991 as Croatia proclaimed its independence, Serbian irregulars – local and Chetniks from Serbia – attacked targets in Slavonia and the Croatian Krajina, while the Croats retaliated in Slavonia; in October the JNA imposed a naval blockade of Dalmatia, joined forces with the Serb irregulars of Eastern Slavonia in a protracted and bitter fight which eventually culminated in the capture of the area by the Serbian forces and the total destruction of the Slavonian town of Vukovar, and a few days later the airforce launched attacks on Zagreb. The war in Croatia was eventually temporarily 'frozen' when the combatants agreed to UN peacekeeping troops' deployment in the disputed areas. This, however, was not a long-term solution, as Croatia's military offensives of May and August 1995 against the Serbs of Western Slavonia and the Croatian and Bosnian Krajina respectively led to the elimination of the self-styled Serbian republic of the Krajina and the relief of the Bosnian Krajina 'Bihać enclave' which had been under siege by Croatian and Bosnian Serb forces for over three years.

The nationalist and irredentist orientation of the HDZ and Franjo Tudjman, combined with the war against the Croatian Serbs and the JNA, and the determination of the Krajina and Slavonian Serbs to secede are some of the factors which have led to the exacerbation of an already virulent nationalist discourse. Like its Serbian counterpart, Croatian nationalism has also drawn on nationalist mythologies and 'demonisations' of the 'national enemy': in the Croatian nationalist imaginary, Knin, the capital of the self-styled Serbian republic of the Krajina, and the city where medieval Croat royalty was crowned, has an aura somewhat similar to the one that Kosovo has in Serbian nationalism,[47] while the Serbs are represented as mortal enemies of the Croatian nation, and as belonging to a non-European civilisation.[48]

Since independence, Croatian nationalism has been a central feature of social and political life in Croatian society. Indeed, as the 'restoration of Croatia's national rights' seems to have been the main theme in Croatian political debate and has acquired absolute priority over pressing economic and social problems and the imperative of democratisation, the opposition had to subscribe to the hegemonic nationalist ideology to avoid being accused of not being committed to the survival of Croatia. The fact that virtually all Croatian opposition parties participated in the nationalist euphoria and triumphalism promoted by the ruling HDZ after the recapture of the Krajina in August 1995 constitutes a clear indication of a lack of a public sphere characterised by plurality of opinions and identities. The fusion of nationalism with the ideology of conservative circles within the Catholic Church has also led to the emergence of a powerful *nationalist social majority* movement which, in the name of the nation, has been systematically pursuing the establishment of a 'morally healthy' society in which the national interest would prevail over sectional and individual interests and rights.[49] By relying primarily on this social and political constituency, the ruling political élite has managed to maintain its control over the state, the economy and the mass media and to suppress demands for democratisation.[50]

In addition, Croatian nationalism seems to have undermined any possibility of a multi-ethnic and multi-confessional Croatia as it has legitimised the principle if not the practice of ethnic cleansing. Indeed, it appears that the Croatian government has tacitly opted for an ethnically cleansed Croatia. This is indicated by the fact that Croatian military strategy during Croatia's successful attempt to recapture the Krajina region was clearly designed to prompt and facilitate the massive exodus of its Serbian population and by the reaction of the Croatian government to the mass fleeing of Serbian refugees from the region over the next few days: despite the repeated assurances that the government did not wish to see Croatia cleansed of its Serbian citizens, the ensemble of the political leadership of the country merely shed crocodile tears as the exodus unfolded and a number of Croatian citizens attacked the bleak convoys of refugees.

Finally, it seems that the period of the predominance of nationalism over Croatian cultural and political life will be protracted as the restoration of Croatia's sovereignty over its internationally recognised territory is, at the time of writing, by no means complete (the region of Eastern Slavonia, which is rich in natural resources, is still under rebel Serb and ultimately Yugoslav control). In addition, it seems that, after a period of successful military operations within both Croatia and Bosnia, Croatia has become a regional power and, through a series of political and military pacts with Bosnia-Herzegovina, including the US-brokered option of a confederation agreement between the two states, is rapidly becoming a senior partner in its relationship with the Bosnian government. In this new situation, Croatian nationalist claims over part of Bosnia-Herzegovina appear more feasible than ever and have been regaining legitimacy. Even if a Croat–Bosnian military confrontation has at present been averted through the acceptance, in March 1994, of the still inactive 'confederation' between the Bosnian Muslim–Croat Federation and Croatia proper, the formation of some sort of a Greater Croatia in which the latter would dominate politically and militarily over the western part of former Yugoslavia is almost certain.

BOSNIA-HERZEGOVINA

The situation in Bosnia-Herzegovina was much more complicated as, according to the 1991 census, the population of the republic was 43.7 per cent Muslims, 31.4 per cent Serbs, 17.3 per cent Croats and 5.5 per cent

'Yugoslavs'.[51] The formation of ethnic parties, the Muslim Party of Democratic Action (SDA), under the leadership of Aliji Izetbegović, and its more secular offshoot Muslim Bosniak Organisation (MBO), the Serbian Democratic Party (SDS), and the Croatian Democratic Community (HDZ), indicated that the war in Croatia, and the claims of Croat and Serb nationalists over its territory would not leave the republic unaffected. Despite the multicultural character of Bosnian urban centres and of some of the rural areas, each party was committed to the creation of an 'ethnicised' Bosnia-Herzegovina in which sovereignty would not lay with its citizens but with the 'constituent nations' of the republic – a solution somewhat reminiscent of former Yugoslavia's response to the national issue. In the 1990 legislature elections, the republic's electorate opted for the national parties, leading to the formation of a coalition between the three larger nationalist parties – the SDA gained 34 per cent of the seats; the SDS followed with 30 per cent; and the HDZ won 18 per cent. Initially, the leaderships of the three national parties succeded in maintaining a *modus vivendi* by sharing government and administration offices among them. In addition, crucial ministries and organisations, like the Ministry of the Interior, allocated to the SDA, or RTV Sarajevo, the republic's radio-television service, maintained a degree of impartiality. Despite this façade of a democratic Bosnia-Herzegovina, however, the reality was grim: in a climate of tension and suspicion among the three ethnic parties, the operation of the legislature and other representative institutions was merely decorative. Most of the decisions were taken at extra-institutional sittings after 'subterranean' dealings among the three coalition partners, while, due to the frequent inability to reach a decision, the presidency and its Crisis Command (*Krizni stab*) had acquired exceptional powers.[52]

Throughout 1991, as it was becoming evident that Yugoslavia was rapidly disintegrating, and the debate over the prospect of sovereignty of Bosnia unfolded, Serbian nationalist irregulars loyal to the Serbian politician and warlord Vojslav Šešelj were crossing the Bosnian–Serbian border and engaging in terrorist activities in rural areas, the SDS was setting up shadow governmental institutions and seizing JNA armour in preparation for the possibility of confrontation. Similarly, HOS, a Croatian ultra-nationalist party, and its paramilitary forces, who demanded that all Bosnia be annexed to Croatia,[53] was also preparing for war.

At the same time disagreements over the future of Bosnia were becoming unbridgeable as Alija Izetbegović and his SDA increasingly rejected an arrangement that would leave Bosnia within a rump Yugoslavia, and Radovan Karadžić and his SDS increasingly felt marginalised by their coalition government partners. The Bosnian-Serbian position was that Bosnia's constituent nations should have the right to self-determination and self-government and, as a first step towards that direction, Bosnian

Serbs – followed by the Bosnian-Croat HDZ in February 1992 – demanded the partition of ministries and government organisations along ethnic lines and the acceptance of the principle of unanimity among the three partners in the decision-making process, a solution that effectively amounted to the creation of three separate administrations for each major ethnic group. In October 1991, when the republic legislature proclaimed Bosnia a sovereign state, the seventy-three Serbian delegates walked out denouncing the decision. In February 1992, when the Bosnian government, encouraged by the decision of the European Community to recognise Slovenia and Croatia,[54] declared independence, the Serbian leadership set an alternative Serbian administration at Pale, a winter-sports resort near Sarajevo. In the spring of 1992, following an unsuccessful Bosnian-Serbian attempt to erect barricades in Sarajevo and to undermine the Bosnian government, the siege of Sarajevo began and fighting between local Serbs and paramilitary groups of warlords from Serbia proper like Željko Raznjatović (Arkan) and Vojslav Šešelj on the one hand and Muslims (regular as well as irregular) on the other, erupted in several areas of Bosnia. In the next few months, and after the assumption of the leadership of the HDZ by the leaders of the Herzegovinian, ultra-nationalist faction of the party, the war escalated as the Croats also joined the fight to carve Herzegovina (or Herceg-Bosna as the self-styled statelet became known) and areas of central Bosnia out of the war-torn republic.

Following this implicit agreement between Serbs and Croats on the principle of partition along ethnic lines, the EC effectively endorsed the notion of a divided Bosnia in a document circulated in the Lisbon meeting (February 1992) and its numerous subsequent proposals to the three parties. The radical wing of the SDS, however, thought that what these documents offered in terms of territorial rewards, especially as there was no clear agreement on the boundaries of the proposed ethnic regions, was much less than what could actually be gained *de facto* on the ground and assumed an intransigent position. War escalated and the imperative of creating ethnically homogeneous territory led to large-scale expulsion of undesired populations from areas occupied by the different national forces.

The protracted war and inconclusive negotiation over the years have led to the belief among the dominant élites of the three sides that the solution to the Bosnian question will be solved on the battlefield rather than in conference rooms. Alliances (like the recently agreed Bosnian Croat/ Muslim federation and the envisaged confederation between the new entity and Croatia) and ceasefires have therefore been more opportunistic than lasting and reliable, whereas the will to preserve a multicultural and multi-confessional society seems to be increasingly weakening. Recent developments, like the successful military cooperation between Croatia and the Bosnian Federation in central Bosnia and the Bihać enclave, have reinforced the resolve to continue the war until an enforced solution is found. What is more, in addition to the clashing Serbian and Croatian nationalisms, a third, Muslim nationalism has emerged and is competing for ascendancy.[55] This was expressed by members of the SDA and part of the Muslim clergy of Bosnia. It should be stressed at this point that Bosnian Islamic identity has historically been moderate and opposed to clericalism and strict religious observance. Indeed, it could be argued that it has been more a cultural identity in the broad sense of the term than a religious one. However, in 1990 the secular wing of the party was forced to abandon it and form the Muslim Bosniak Organisation, leaving the SDA under the control of Alija Izetbegović, whose agenda included the promotion of an Islamic Muslim identity as a central component of the identity of the Muslim nation. Izetbegović, possibly realising the political and economic advantages of association with the Muslim countries of the region and worldwide, promoted links with Turkey, Iran and Saudi Arabia and in 1994 made a high-profile pilgrimage to Mecca. However, in contrast to what could be called the 'fundamentalist' wing of his party which envisage a future Islamic – as opposed to civic – Bosnian identity, he has adopted a more pragmatic line, recognising the need for a coalition among the three ethnic communities of the republic and for a multicultural[56] Bosnia. It should, however, be emphasised that the protracted war in Bosnia has reinforced the 'fundamentalist' wing of the Muslim political élite, which has increasingly been attacking the secular forces within Bosnian society and the multicultural ethos which members of the political and cultural élites remain committed to. Characteristic examples of this tendency are the increasingly vociferous Islamic clergy under the Muslim religious leader Mustafa Cerić which has been denouncing mixed marriages and the secular character of Muslim culture, and the frequent attacks against the Sarajevo daily *Oslobodenje* for its commitment to a multi-ethnic and multicultural Bosnia, by a new publication, *Ljljan*. *Ljljan* has also criticised mixed marriages and has urged the Bosnian government to encourage the adoption of Islamic traditions and Islamic holidays as the new state's public holidays. Although there are indications that this extremist variant of Muslim nationalism is not hegemonic among Bosnian Muslims, the polarisation brought about by the brutal conflict in the republic has created fertile ground for its development.

More generally, the war among the three major ethnic groups in Bosnia and the associated practice of 'ethnic cleansing' have undermined the possibility of restoration of a multicultural and multi-confessional society, at least in the foreseeable future. Deep hatred and suspicion have destroyed the memory of tolerance and peaceful coexistence, and have broken the fabric of pre-war Bosnian society.

MACEDONIA

The southernmost part of former Yugoslavia, Macedonia, had different challenges to face once the dissolution of the federation became evident. A landlocked territory surrounded by hostile or suspicious neighbours, the former Yugoslav Republic of Macedonia was hesitant to abandon the federation until it became clear that the rump Yugoslavia, after the secession of the northern republics, would consist essentially of Serbia and its ally Montenegro. The first political voices for Macedonian independence were manifested in the calls of the Internal Macedonian Revolutionary Organisation–Democratic Party (VMRO–DPMNE), a new Macedonian nationalist party, for Macedonian independence, while the first clear signs of popular dissatisfaction with the republic's membership of Yugoslavia were the May 1991 demonstrations against the participation of Macedonian conscripts in the JNA operations against the republics of Slovenia and Croatia. Although these demonstrations raised, at least indirectly, the issue of sovereignty and independence of Macedonia, they were not entirely or primarily inspired by nationalist feelings; a widespread desire to avoid involvement in the conflict was the central factor in these mobilisations. However, the legitimation of the demand for independence achieved through the citizens' anti-war initiatives reintroduced into public debate the issue of Macedonian national identity. Due to a number of reasons, including the relatively recent attainment of national identity of Macedonians, the uncertain position of the republic among its neighbours and its unclear international status, the issue of Macedonian nationhood has been controversial as national identity constituted a significant battlefield in the political life of the emerging state. At the time of writing, the debate continues with no signs of consensus in the near future, as the emerging nationalist parties, the diaspora radical nationalists, the Macedonian-Albanian and other minority political and cultural organisations as well as the more moderate centrist and left-wing political forces formulate their particular definitions of Macedonian identity and visions of the future of the Macedonian state. For the nationalists, the Macedonian state was seen primarily as the state of ethnic Macedonians,[57] while for a not insignificant number of activists among them – especially in the diaspora – its establishment was perceived as a mere step towards the fulfilment of their vision of a Greater Macedonia encompassing regions of Greece and Bulgaria.[58] More moderate political forces would, in contrast, promote a civic concept of Macedonian nationhood, encompassing all the citizens of the former Yugoslav republic, and the emerging nation-state, irrespective of ethnic and cultural background,[59] while Albanian minority political organisations were oscillating between this, civic and ethnic versions of nationhood by arguing that the Macedonian state should be a state of all its citizens and claiming that the Slav-

Macedonian and Albanian communities should be recognised as the constituent nations of an independent Macedonia.[60]

Realising the change caused by the irrevocable disintegration of Yugoslavia, sensing the growing popular apprehension regarding their republic's membership of a Serbian version of Yugoslavia, and becoming increasingly aware of the new political mood in the republic, in July 1991, the Macedonian government carried out a referendum on the future of the republic in which approximately 74 per cent of the electorate voted for independence. In November 1991, the republic's legislature adopted a new constitution and in December the republic, following Slovenia, Croatia and Bosnia-Herzegovina, applied for European Community recognition. The Community, however, declined to recognise the Republic of Macedonia as a sovereign state, mainly due to the objections of its southern neighbour, Greece, which maintains that the use of the name 'Macedonia', and of symbols derived from Greek antiquity (like the 'Vergina sun', an ornament found in the ancient Macedonian royal graves in Vergina, Northern Greece, and which is claimed to be the basis of the flag of the new state) constitute a 'usurpation of Greek history'. This, combined with a number of clauses in the November 1991 constitution which affirmed the interest of the Macedonian state in the welfare and protection of ethnic Macedonians living in neighbouring states, was interpreted by Greece as expressing expansionist aspirations and paving the way towards territorial demands over the Greek region of Macedonia (called by Slav-Macedonians Aegean Macedonia).[61]

Other neighbouring states also refused or offered conditional recognition: Albania refused to recognise the new state until it deemed that a 'satisfactory' arrangement regarding the substantial minority of Macedonian Albanians had been made; Serbia kept an ambiguous stance as it did not denounce any territorial claims made by Serbian politicians like Vuk Drašković Vojslav Šešelj who have reaffirmed the pre-Second World War Serbian position that Macedonia is merely Southern Serbia, and declined to recognise the new state; Bulgaria, maintaining a tradition of Bulgarian claims that the Slavophone Macedonians are essentially Bulgarians, recognised the new state but declared that this did not imply the existence of a Macedonian nation.

This prolonged period of uncertainty has definitely affected the political life of the new state. The inability of Macedonia to achieve economic integration in the world economy due to a Greek economic blocade in the south (Macedonia's only access to sea had traditionally been the Greek port of Thessaloniki) and the UN embargo against its major commercial markets in the former Yugoslavia have tested the economy of the country. Unemployment has risen to 30 per cent[62] and the government has attempted to keep social peace through a strategy of fragile development, premised on bolstering consumer power at a time when the GDP of the republic is declining.[63] One of the casualties of political and economic uncertainty has been the initial spirit of inter-ethnic cooperation within Macedonia. The increasing politicisation of the Macedonian Orthodox Church, the also increasing militancy of the Macedonian-Albanian leadership, the questionable legitimacy of the Alliance for Macedonia government after the withdrawal of the two strongest opposition parties, the VMRO–DPMNU and the Democratic Party from the second round of the 1994 elections have created an explosive political mix.

In this climate, the Macedonian president and government, recognising the sensitive nature of identity politics, have occasionaly resorted to the use of the nationalist card in order to increase their legitimacy and hold on to power. Devices included the adoption of an ambiguous national symbol, a star resembling to the 'Vergina sun'. The Macedonian president also attempted to create a nationalist history by claiming (in a session of the United Nations General Assembly) that St Kiril and St Methodius, the creators of the Slavonic alphabet (cyrillic) who were born in Thessaloniki, had been ethnic Macedonians, despite the fact that in the ninth century the concept of nation did not exist and Macedonia was a term referring to a geographical area.[64] His unfounded references, in March 1993, to imminent Greek invasion and annexation of part of Macedonia[65] have been other characteristic examples of the flirting of moderate forces with the power of nationalism.

As far as inter-ethnic relations are concerned, the violent police intervention in the Tetovo area to close down the illegal Albanian University and the subsequent incidents and death of one Albanian have strained relations between the Slav and Albanian Macedonian communities. It is doubtful if the notion of a state premised on the ideal of citizenship, as opposed to ethnicity, would survive the current internal and international strains. The hope is that normalisation of Macedonia's relationship with its neighbours and an improvement in the economic situation might come in time to salvage a pluricultural society which is at the moment at the brink of disintegration and to give new impetus to the building of a multicultural society.

CONCLUSION

The dissolution of Yugoslavia seems to have partly been due to the 'internal' dynamics of the federal political system. The subordination of social conflict to the notion of nationhood and the logic of nationalism seems to have survived the transition from the state-socialist to the post-communist era. What is more, the disintegration of Yugoslavia seems to have been linked with the emergence of populist discourses in the political spheres of the former Yugoslav republics: national identities have been asserted through the positing of oppositional, or antagonistic relationships between the nation and its 'other', and the complexity of the 'political' has been reduced to bipolar antagonisms. However, the inter-ethnic conflict in former Yugoslavia is also linked to a number of external factors: the international economic climate of the late 1980s led to the collapse of the social contract upon which the Federation was established, international and EC pressure for liberalisation of the economy as a condition for loans and aid, German encouragement to the northern republics to secede, the antagonism between the EC, the US and Russia over the acquisition of spheres of influence in the region and the eventual EC and US endorsement of the division of Bosnia-Herzegovina along ethnic lines are some of the key factors which sustained the conflict. At present there is no indication of a waning of the populist nationalisms that have torn former Yugoslavia apart – one might say that the fierce and violent confrontation between communities which had coexisted in close proximity or even in interaction over the centuries may have totally undermined any possibility of a future of mutual understanding and cooperation. In addition, the issues of integration of Macedonia to the world community and of the status of the Albanian communities in this country and in the neighbouring Serbian province of Kosovo are still urgent and unresolved; long-term uncertainty in Macedonia and continuation of the Serbian suppression of the Albanian nationalist movement would almost certainly culminate in further conflict.

NOTES

1 This, of course, is not an exclusively Yugoslav phenomenon. For an examination of the politicisation of history and tradition in recent years see F. Füredi, *Mythical Past, Elusive Future: History and Society in an Anxious Age*, London, Pluto, 1992.

2 This has been demonstrated in B. Anderson, *Imagined Communities: Reflections on the Origin and Spread of Nationalism*, London, Verso, 1983; E.J. Hobsbawm, *Nations and Nationalism*, Cambridge, Cambridge University Press, 1990 p.46; E. Gellner, *Nations and Nationalism*, Cambridge, Cambridge University Press, pp.48–9.

3 This view has recently become very popular. For example the highly acclaimed Channel 4 'Bloody Bosnia Season', despite its undoubted merits, on several occasions reproduced this perception of the 'legitimate' or 'unavoidable' disintegration of Yugoslavia because of the underlying civilisation faultlines, resorting very often to distortion of geopolitical and historical information. It is characteristic, for example, that the Drina River (the natural boundary between contemporary Serbia and Bosnia) was represented as the boundary between West and East, and Bosnia often as an integral part of the West, sustaining in this way an 'orientalist' symbolic geography.

4 M. Bacić-Hayden and R.M. Hayden, 'Orientalist variations on the theme "Balkans": symbolic geography in recent Yugoslav cultural politics', *Slavic Review* 1992, 51: 1–15.

5 However, the territories of these political entities and the religion of their leaders are by no means sufficient to substantiate such claims. On some of the

problems that such attempts entail see B. Denitch, *Ethnic Nationalism: The Tragic Death of Yugoslavia*, Minneapolis, University of Minnesota Press, 1994, pp.113–14.

6 See on this D. Dakin, *The Greek Struggle in Macedonia, 1897–1913*, Thessaloniki, Institute for Balkan Studies, p.7, or J.B. Allcock, 'The contradictions of Macedonian nationality', *Journal of Area Studies* 1994, no. 4: 143.

7 It has to be pointed out however that the Ottoman *millets* of the nineteenth century, and the ecclesiastical and educational authority accorded to them by the Ottoman Porte, were utilised by the nationalist movements of the Balkans as instruments of nation-building. Thus, the persistent efforts of the Patriarchate of Constantinople, the Exarchate and the Serbian representative in the Patriarchate of Constantinople to be allocated Archbishoprics and dioceses in Macedonia, Serbia and Thrace, were linked with the Greek, Bulgarian and Serbian nation-building projects of the period.

8 Until the late nineteenth century one could encounter Greek-speaking Bulgarians and Vlachs, or Bulgarian and Macedonian-speaking Vlachs. These bilingual populations were eventually absorbed by the dominant linguistic communities in the areas they were settled; thus, the majority of the Vlachs of northern Greece became primarily Greek-speakers, while the Vlachs of the Monastir (Bitola) area became Macedonian-speakers. See, for example, Dakin, op. cit., pp.16–23.

9 Indeed, this ambiguity persisted well after the establishment of national states in the Balkans, especially in the Ottoman province of Macedonia, and was partly responsible for the intense and long struggle among the emerging Bulgarian, Greek, and Serbian national states for 'converting' the populations of the province to their nationalist ideologies.

10 It should be pointed out that the decision of the 'founder' of the Serbian literary language, Vuk Karadžić, to premise it on the dialects used by Orthodox or Serb inhabitants of Herzegovina, instead of eastern Serbian dialects, was highly significant, as it produced a literary language very similar to that spoken by Croats. Thus, although the establishment of the Serbian literary language was instrumental in the Serbian nation-building process, it also allowed proponents of Yugoslavism to support their political project on the grounds that South Slavs shared a common Serbo-Croat language. See also Allcock, op. cit.

11 Quoted in N. Scott and D. Jones (eds), *Bloody Bosnia; A European Tragedy*, London, *Guardian* and Channel 4 Television, p.17.

12 In fact, and despite attempts to 'purify' the Croat variant, or earlier claims that *Bosanski*, the dialect used by Bosnians, should be recognised as a distinct language, the majority of the inhabitants of Serbia, Montenegro, Croatia, and Bosnia-Herzegovina speak the same language, allowing, of course, for some regional variations. The majority of Orthodox populations (although, until recently, not the Šerbs of the Krajina) use the cyrillic script, whereas, the Catholic and Muslim speakers of the language use a modified Latin script. Hawkesworth compares the differences between British and American English to those between the Serbian and Croatian variants in order to describe the relationship between the latter two. For more details on the language see C. Hawkesworth, *Colloquial Serbo-Croat*, London, Routledge, 1993, pp.xvii–xx. Slovenian also belongs to the South Slavic linguistic family and although it is generally intelligible to speakers of Serbo-Croat, it is distinct in terms of grammar and syntax.

13 See R. Okey 'The historical background to the Yugoslav crisis', *Journal of Area Studies* 1994, no. 4: 126.

14 For a more detailed discussion of the politics of the national issue in that period, see L.J. Cohen, *Broken Bonds: The Disintegration of Yugoslavia*, Boulder, CO, Westview Press, 1993, pp.13–17.

15 The name of the province has been the object of contestation between Serbs and Montenegrins on the one hand, and the Albanians on the other. It was called Kosovo i Metohija until 1968, when the clearly Serbian part of the name of the province Metohija was dropped. But even then, the demand of the majority Albanian Kosovars for the official adoption of the Albanian 'Kosova' was not met. I have followed customary English usage and used the Serbian term Kosovo instead of using the more appropriate form, whether Kosovo or Kosova.

16 D. Pleština, 'From "Democratic Centralism" to decentralised democracy? Trials and tribulations of Yugoslavia's development', in J. B. Allcock *et al.* (eds), *Yugoslavia in Transition: Choices and Constraints*, Providence, RI, Berg, p.128.

17 Ibid., p.132.

18 Pleština points out that in 1960s dependency of less developed republics had increased: difference in GDP between Slovenia and Kosovo from 1:3 (1950) was 1:5 (1960), see ibid., pp.133–4.

19 L.J. Cohen, op. cit., p.29.

20 Ibid.

21 The reforms of 1964 indeed met strong resistance by federal institutions and Belgrade-based financial and commercial organisations, which increased the pressure for decentralisation.

22 I. Duchacek, *The Territorial Dimension of Politics, Within, Among and Across Nations*, Boulder, CO, Westview Press, 1986, p.123.

23 The JNA continued to be a pro-Federation force until its 1991 intervention in the conflict between the Croatian government and the Krajina Serbs. It proved extremely resistant to the tendencies towards confederalisation – indeed the fate of the JNA was linked to the preservation of the Federation in a way similar to the Red Army. In Yugoslavia the Army's link to the federal order was institutionalised as its agreement was needed when major policy decisions were to be made at the federal level. A Serb-dominated army in terms of its officer-corps composition although not necessarily pro-Serb, it was pro-Yugoslav, mainly because its corporate interests were best served by the preservation of the Federation. For a more extensive discussion of these issues see A. Bebler, 'Political pluralism and the Yugoslav professional military', in J. Seroka and V. Pavlović (eds), *The Tragedy of Yugoslavia: The Failure of Democratic Transformation*, Armonk, NY, M.E. Sharpe, pp.111–39.

24 See C. Martin and L. D'Andrea Tyson, 'Can Titoism survive Tito? Economic problems and policy choices confronting Tito's successors', in P. Ramet (ed.), *Yugoslavia in the 1980s*, Boulder, CO, Westview Press, 1985; also Pleština, op. cit., pp.148–51.

25 F. Gozzano, 'La Jugoslavia fra Pressioni Esterne e "Contraddizioni Dialettiche" Interne', *Affari Esteri* 1979, 11: p.324.

26 Pleština, p.151.

27 A September 1982 poll found that only 44 per cent of workers felt positive about the system, while in 1983, a mere 38 per cent of poll respondents in Belgrade expressed confidence in the Party (as contrasted with 64 per cent in 1974), in P. Ramet, 'Apocalypse culture and social change in Yugoslavia', in P. Ramet (ed.), *Yugoslavia in the 1980s*, Boulder, CO, Westview Press, 1985, p.6.

28 S. Ramet, *Nationalism and Federalism in Yugoslavia, 1962–1991*, Bloomington, Indiana University Press, 2nd edn, 1992, pp.198–9.

29 *East Europe Report*, no. 81989, 15 October 1982

30 For more on 'moral panic' see S. Cohen, *Folk Devils and Moral Panics: The Creation of the Mods and Rockers*, Basingstoke, Macmillan, 1974, pp.1–2. On the reaction of Serbian, Montenegrin and Macedonian reactions to the perceived 'Albanisation' of Kosovo and western Macedonia, see S. Ramet, op. cit., pp.196–201.

31 This process had already been under way since the early 1970s. By 1987 intra-republic communications and commercial transactions had reached 76 per cent of total activity, compared to 69 per cent in 1970 (C. Ocić, 'O federalizmu i regionalizmu: promene u medjuzavisnosti Jugoslovenkih Republika i pokra-jina 1970–1987', Naucni skup: *Kriza u Jugoslaviji i uporista reformi*, Belgrade, Institut za evropske studije Konzorcijum instituta, p.10). In addition, the educational system increasingly became fragmented and by the mid-1980s it could be argued that there were effectively eight distinct federal unit curricula for primary education.

32 Bacić-Hayden and Hayden, op. cit., pp.3–6.

33 For a detailed analysis of inter-republic rivalries in the 1980s, see S. Ramet, op. cit., pp.215–24.

34 The term 'nationalist movement' does not imply homogeneity of the con-siderably diverse cultural and political networks and institutions (groups of dissidents, intellectuals, Slav migrants from Kosovo, the Serbian Orthodox Church, ultranationalist parties and paramilitary groups, or Vuk Drašković's opposition Serbian Renaissance Movement), and the widespread popular feelings of bitterness for what was widely perceived to be the 'betrayal' of Serbia by Yugoslavia (which consisted among other things, of the granting of autonomy to Kosovo and Vojvodina, and hostile acts by fellow Yugoslavs like the Slovenian support of provincial 'separatisms'). In fact, it was not until the arrival of Slobodan Milošević at the centre of the political scene that the majority of these disparate elements was mobilised and articulated within the context of the Serbian nationalist-populist movement, although nationalist forces (the Serbian Renaissance Movement) are also predominant in the opposition. As far as the relationship between the Serbian and Montenegrin nationalist movements is concerned, in both republics there have been advocates of the unity of the two peoples, as they share language, religion and – to an extent – folk memories and tradition. It would seem that the moral panic regarding 'the loss of Kosovo' reinforced unifying tendencies as Serbs and Montenegrins were represented as being subjected to the same hardships by the same enemy.

35 The regime encouraged revived Serbian-Orthodox rituals such as the mass baptisms of Serbs and Montenegrins in Kosovo Polje, or the 'procession' of the alleged remains of Prince Lazar through a series of sacred sites and monasteries en route to Kosovo Polje where they were reinterred. The return of the defeated prince to the place where the Serbs had been defeated by the Turks and he lost his life gave the impression of a complete circle, a 'new beginning'. Both rituals constituted a symbolic confirmation of the will of the Serb nation to restore and reclaim its dignity. Other instances of mobilisation of popular culture were the revival of a Četniki subculture, as uniforms, insignia, flags and other aspects of the dress code of the Četniki became popular among the youth of the fringe of the nationalist movement (the Radical Party of Vojslav Šešelj, and the ultranationalist circle of Belgrade politician and warlord Željko Raznjatović (Arkan)). Finally, the revival of Serbian folk, or the emergence of the popular *turbofolk* (neo-folk), music was also linked to the nationalist movement.

36 Serbs consider Kosovo to have been the centre of the medieval Serbian empire which was eventually destroyed by the Ottoman conquest of the Balkans. The nineteenth-century Serbian nation-building project was premised on the promotion of collective memory associated with the sanctity of Kosovo, and the importance of the Serbian defeat there. A collective memory of the battle survived in local oral tradition, folk songs, while the Serbian Orthodox Church invested the defeat of Prince Lazar with a mystical dimension. Such is the power of the history and mythology of Kosovo that the head of the Association of Serb Writers, Matija Becković, stated that Kosovo would be Serbian even if not a single Serb lived there, while in 1986, members of the Serbian Academy of Sciences, in their *Memorandum*, presented the situation in Kosovo as equivalent to a national defeat. However, in modern-day Kosovo the Albanian population outnumbers the Serbs and Montenegrins nine to one.

37 In fact, there was a series of moral panics regarding the 'Albanisation' of Kosovo. The first climaxed in 1987, when Milošević while visiting Kosovo met local Serbs and Montenegrins who accused the Albanian majority of intimidation and violence against persons and property. These allegations became a permanent or recurrent theme of news reports from the province and triggered reaction from political, religious and cultural leaders as well as from the public. In the same year, cases and rumours of rape of Serbian women by Albanians were quickly taken up and exploited by the media. Rape acquired a dimension of ethnic antagonism as it was argued that these rapes were premeditated attacks against the Kosovo Serbs and the Serbian nation. Rape victims were often represented as 'Serbian mothers' (their prescribed role as reproducers of the nation) and public interest was directed not towards the individual cases of rape but towards the 'rape of the nation by Albanians'. See A. Milić, 'Women and nationalism in the former Yugoslavia', in N. Funk and M. Mueller (eds), *Gender, Politics and Post-Communism*, New York, Routledge, 1993, pp.115–6, R. Salecl, 'National identity and socialist moral majority', in E. Carter, J. Donald and J. Squires (eds), *Space and Place; Theories of Identity and Location*, London, Lawrence and Wishart, 1993.

38 It is characteristic that in one of the 1988 demonstrations, the poet Milovan Vitezović addressing the crowds revealed this aspect of 'street democracy': 'Honourable people, this will be recorded in our history as the year when "the people" was born' (my translation), quoted in N. Popov, *Srpski Populizam*, Belgrade, 1993, p.73.

39 'Plebiscitary' legitimation was derived by the 'spontaneous' physical presence of the 'people' in these rallies and the rapport between the 'leader' and the people: these rallies were often represented as mass 'meetings', and the relationship between the audience and the leader/enunciator as a dialogue. Thus, Milošević would respond to slogans chanted by his audience, or would 'interpret' them, appearing to 'express' the 'popular will'.

40 By October 1990, there were 150 legal parties. For the post-communist political sphere see V. Goati, 'The challenge of post-Communism', in Seroka and Pavlović (eds), op. cit., pp.3–22.

41 L. Cohen, *Broken Bonds*, op. cit., p.119.

42 G. Suhadolnik, 'The dark side of the Alps', *Balkan War Report* 1995, no. 30: 41–2.

43 Ibid, pp.94–102.

44 J. Feffer, *Shock Waves; Eastern Europe after the Revolutions*, Montreal, Black Rose Books, pp.264–6.

45 Denitch, op. cit., p.41.

46 M. Glenny, *The Fall of Yugoslavia; The Third Balkan War*, London, Penguin, 1992, pp.11–14.

47 Ibid.
48 J. Feffer, op. cit., p.265.
49 A. Arić, 'The HDZ's "Contract with Croatia"', *Balkan War Report* 1995, no. 32: 33; R. Tsagarousianou, '"God, patria and home": reproductive politics and nationalist redefinitions of women in East-Central Europe', *Social Identities* 1995, 1(2); A. Milić, 'Women and nationalism in the former Yugoslavia', in N. Funk and M. Mueller (eds), *Gender, Politics and Post-Communism*, op. cit., pp.115–16; R. Salecl, *The Spoils of Freedom; Psychoanalysis and Feminism after the Fall of Socialism*, London, Routledge, 1994, pp.20–37; R. Ivecović, 'The new democracy; with women or without them?', in S.P. Ramet and L.S. Adamovich (eds), *Beyond Yugoslavia: Politics, Economics, and Culture in a Shattered Community*, Boulder, CO, Westview Press, 1995, pp.399–402.
50 A. Arić, op. cit., p.33; M. Thompson, *Forging War; The Media in Serbia, Croatia and Bosnia Hercegovina*, London, Article 19, pp.130–46; B.K. Tristo, 'The President's Press', *Balkan War Report* 1995, no. 32: 32.
51 L. Cohen, *Broken Bonds*, op. cit., p.139.
52 Paul Shoup, 'The Bosnian Crisis in 1992', in S.P. Ramet and L.S. Adamovich (eds), *Beyond Yugoslavia*, op. cit., p.159.
53 S. Ramet, p.259.
54 For the role of the EC in the development of the crisis see P. Shoup, op. cit., pp.164–70.
55 This of course does not mean that Muslim nationalism is the product of the inter-ethnic conflict. The politicisation of Muslim consciousness can be traced back to the debates of the late 1960s over the status of the Yugoslav Muslims. For a discussion of the Muslim question, see S. P. Ramet, *Nationalism and Federalism*, op. cit., pp.177–86.
56 The term 'Islamic' here refers to Islam and the cultures developed within the framework of Islam. It should not be confused with the term 'fundamentalist' which I use to refer to radical, exclusionist and extremist uses of Islam. Among Bosnian Serbs as well as part of Western public opinion, Islam and fundamentalism were indistinguishable. However, such an assumption constitutes over-simplification of the role of Islam in Bosnian Muslim identity.
57 This has been the view of the Internal Macedonian Revolutionary Organisation – Democratic Party for Macedonian National Unity (VMRO–DPMNU) which emerged as the largest party in the first elections of 1991.
58 Representative of this is the 'International Macedonian Congress' which has recently launched its Internet home page *Virtual Macedonia*.
59 The main moderate force is the Alliance for Macedonia, a three-party coalition force which has so far kept the nationalist VMRO out of the post- independence governments.
60 See D. Perry, 'Civil society or civil strife?', *War Report* 1995, no. 35: 27–30.
61 On Greek reactions to the independence of the former Yugoslav Republic of Macedonia, see S. Sofos and R. Tsagarousianou, 'The politics of identity: nationalism in contemporary Greece', in J. Amodia (ed.), *The Resurgence of Nationalist Movements in Europe*, Bradford, University of Bradford, *Bradford Occasional Papers* no. 12, 1993; also, for an excellent overview of the context in which the dispute has developed, see M. Mazower, 'Classic errors in the Balkans', *Guardian*, 12 April 1994.
62 V. Milčin, 'Sofia, Skopje and the "Macedonian Question"', *War Report* 1995, no. 35: 26.
63 See D. Perry, 'Civil society or civil strife?', *War Report* 1995, no. 35: 29.
64 I. Dimitrova, 'The names devouring the people', *War Report* 1995, no. 35: 37–8.

65 S. P. Ramet, 'The Macedonian enigma', in Ramet and Adamovich, *Beyond Yugoslavia*, op. cit., p.229.

SELECT BIBLIOGRAPHY

Allcock, J.B *et al.* (eds) (1992) *Yugoslavia in Transition: Choices and Constraints*, Providence, RI, Berg.

Banac, I. (1984) *The National Question in Yugoslavia: Origins, History, Politics*, Ithaca, NY, Cornell University Press.

Cohen, L.J. (1993) *Broken Bonds: The Disintegration of Yugoslavia*, Boulder, CO, Westview Press.

Glenny, M. (1992) *The Fall of Yugoslavia: The Third Balkan War*, London, Penguin.

Jelavić, B. (1983) *History of the Balkans* (2 vols), Cambridge, Cambridge University Press.

Magaš, B. (1993) *The Destruction of Yugoslavia: Tracking the Break-up 1980–92*, London, Verso.

Poulton, H. (1994) *Who are the Macedonians?*, London, Hurst.

Ramet, S. (1992) *Nationalism and Federalism in Yugoslavia; 1962–1991* (2nd edn), Bloomington, Indiana University Press.

Ramet, S., and Adamovich, L.S. (eds) (1995) *Beyond Yugoslavia: Politics, Economics, and Culture in a Shattered Community*, Boulder, CO, Westview Press.

Thompson, M. (1992) *A Paper House: The Ending of Yugoslavia*, London, Vintage.

van den Heuvel, M., and Siccama, J. (eds) (1992) *The Disintegration of Yugoslavia*, Amsterdam and Atlanta, GA, Rodopi.

Part V

CONCLUSION

12

CONCLUSION

Brian Jenkins and Spyros A. Sofos

Nationalism is one of those terms which convey so much and at the same time so little. Indeed, although today *nation* is a globally recognisable notion, an irreducible component of identity, it remains a term incapable of meaningfully conveying the diversity of national experiences in the variety of social-historical contexts in which national identity and nationalism become salient. Etienne Balibar recognises this multiplicity and diversity of the processes of construction of national identities and nationalisms, and its significance, as he argues that these 'do not work everywhere the same way: in a sense, they must work everywhere in a *different* way, this is part of the national "identity"'.

On the other hand, the resurgence of nationalism in contemporary Europe, the speed with which questions of national identity, otherness and citizenship have colonised the spaces of public debate and the designing boards of policy-makers all over Europe indicate the existence of underlying key elements in the quest for identity in contemporary European societies.

Our general aim has been to achieve a comparative understanding of this multifaceted phenomenon, and to identify the diversity of social-historical contexts in which it finds fertile ground and the variety of raw material upon which nationalist projects draw. At a more concrete level, we sought to explore the state of nationalism in some of the major European societies in the current global, regional and national context; to examine the relationship of contemporary nationalist projects with the processes of socio-economic and cultural globalisation and the demise of the bi-polar international system after the end of the Cold War.

In our preliminary debates and during the process of writing and editing this book, the diversity of narratives of the nation, of the historical forms nationalism in Europe has taken, and the different collective experiences upon which the latter grew became evident. In terms of the relationship between nation-state and nationalism, the forms nationalism took in established nation-states like Britain and France have been clearly distinct from those in the so-called 'late developers' (Germany, Italy) and in the very latest additions to the European club of nation-states (Poland, former Yugoslav Republics and, in a sense, Russia). What is more, the diversity of societal responses to the demise of the bi-polar system was reflected in the variety of identity formation strategies in different European societies. German unification prompted a re-examination of the issue of national identity, premised on a reappraisal of the relationship between Germans and non-German residents of the country, between Western and Eastern Germans, and between Germans and their fellow Europeans within the European Union and the new Europe. The redundancy of the traditional bi-polar political system in Italy was accompanied by the emergence of an uncompromising regionalism or even nationalism, premised on an obsessive rejection of the possibility of coexistence between northerners and southerners. The disintegration of the USSR initiated a process of re-formulation of Russian identity premised on contradictory perceptions of the Russian nation as the inheritor of the Soviet legacy and as its victim. The collapse of Yugoslavia in which *ethnic identity* had been a privileged form of identification set in motion a lengthy process of ethnic hatred and brutal ethnic conflict in which the notion of *alterity* became synonymous to that of *antagonism*.

On the other hand, as is clearly indicated in this book, similar themes appear to be shared by most European nationalisms. The urgency with which issues of migration and citizenship have occupied a prominent position in the public debate all over Europe, the quest for, or pinpointing of, an 'other' to be blamed, excluded or eliminated, the longing for and susceptibility to narratives of national homogeneity, or the systematic re-reading (and rewriting) of history, from Iberia to Poland and the former Soviet Union and from Britain to the Balkans, are indicative of this common ground upon which contemporary European nationalisms have grown.

Throughout the book, we have not attempted to formulate or impose any general theory of nationalism as it is clear that this would have obscured the astonishing diversity of nationalist projects in contemporary Europe. However, we have attempted to address a series of common challenges faced by European societies in the run-up to the new millennium which we deemed relevant to the resurgence of nationalism, in order to mark the tension between the simultaneous claims of nationalism to universality and difference, to openness and closure. To return to the European setting which has been central in this book, our ambition has been to emphasise the internally contradictory nature of contemporary European nationalisms: their visions of an enhanced citizenship and democracy coexisting with the longing to exclude and disenfranchise, their narratives of liberation coexisting with processes of cultural closure and political authoritarianism.

INDEX

APO 136–7
Abercrombie, P 97
Absolutism 101, 102–3
Action Française 41
Action Vistula 206
Ad Hoc Group on Immigration 58, 60, 61
Adenauer, Konrad 134, 135
Albania 252, 253, 274
Albanians 257, 262, 265, 276; emigration
  to north 261; in Macedonia 273–4, 275;
  protests in Kosovo 260; purge of 264
Aleksandar, King of Yugoslavia 255
Alexander Nevksy 232
Algeria 109
Algerians 34–5; citizenship rights in
  France 70
All-union Communist Party (CPSU)
  228, 237, 242, 243–4, 246
Alleanza Nazionale 191–3
Almirante, Giorgio 192
Alter, P 130–1
Ancien Régime 14, 105
Anderson, Benedict 12, 117
anomie 112, 116, 117, 118, 119, 120
Anthias, Floya 36–7
anti-communism 108–9, 111, 135, 206,
  209–11
anti-imperialism 25
Anti-Racist Commission 61–2
Anti-Semitic League 41
anti-semitism 39–42; in France 40–2,
  106; in Germany 128; images of 43; in
  Poland 204–5, 207–9, 211, 213, 217–18;
  post communism 42–3; in Russia 240;
  scientific 39
Ardanza, Jose Antonio 160
Armenians 228, 234
Armia Krajowa 205, 206, 207
Armia Ludowa 205
Arzalluz, Xavier 160
assimilation 22, 67, 71; of Algerians 70,
  75; in Britain 69
asylum 59, 60, 61, 144; curbs in
  Portugal 165; Dublin Convention 1990

61; policies 62–4; seekers 44, 47, 48, 55,
  60, 73
Asylum and Immigration Appeals Act
  1993 63
Austria 126, 127, 128; annexation of 129,
  133
autonomy 3, 26; in Italy 180–9; in Soviet
  Union 227–9; Spanish regional 159;
  under Tsars 227; in Yugoslavia 257–63
Azerbaidzhan 228

Bahr, Egon 137, 138
Bahring, A 148
Bakhtin, Mikhail 35, 36
Baldwin, Stanley 94–6
Balibar, Etienne 285
Balkan peoples 253–4
Balladur, Edouard 115, 119
Baltic states 239
Basic Law 131, 133, 143
Basque Nationalist Party (PNV) 160–1
Basques 3, 158, 159, 168;
  nationalism of 160–1; Statute 1937 157,
  161
Baudrillard, Jean 117
Bauer, Otto 227
Belorussians in Poland 202, 203, 204, 206
Berdyaev, N.A. 224, 231
Berlusconi, Silvio 172, 183, 189–91, 193–4
bi-polar system 286
Bihać enclave 268, 272
Bismarck, Otto von 13, 127
Bocca, Giorgio 187
Bogomil Christians 253
Bolsheviks 227, 229–31
Bosnia 252, 253, 255, 260, 262, 269
Bosnia-Herzegovina 257, 262, 267, 274;
  ethnic parties in 265, 269–72; Muslim
  nationalism in 272
Bossi, Umberto 181, 182–5, 189, 193, 194
Boulanger Affair 120
Boulangist movement 106
bourgeoisie 12, 16, 102–3
Brandt, Willy 138

Brennan, Timothy 19
Bretell, C 166
British Nationality Act 1981 63
Britishness 2–3, 84, 85–6; on film 90–5, 96
Brubaker, R 72
Bulatović, Momir 265
Bulgaria 252, 253, 255, 274
Burke, Peter 16

CPSU *see* All-union Communist Party
Calder, Angus 88
Camoes, Luis de 166–7
Camp of National Unity (OZN, Poland) 203, 204, 214
capitalism 16, 20, 40, 42
Carriers Liability Act 1987 63
Catalans 3, 159, 162, 168; monolinguism in 161; Statute 1932 157
Catholicism 106, 111, 112, 126, 127, 157–8, 160, 174, 181–2, 202–15 passim
Cerić, Mustafa 272
Četniki 256, 268
Chechnya 245, 246
Chirac, Jacques 115
Christian Democracy (DC, Italy) 177–8, 179–80, 182; decline of 184, 188–9
Christian Democratic Union (CDU, Germany) 63, 72, 131, 134, 139, 140, 146, 147
Christian National Union (ZChN, Poland) 213–4, 215, 216
Christian Social Union (CSU, Germany) 47, 131, 147
cinema 90–5
citizenship 9, 285, 286; assimiliationist model 66–7, 75, 76; exclusionist model 66, 67–8, 71–2, 75, 76; and immigration 73; models 20–2, 66–8, 76, multi-cultural model 67, 68; and national identity 74–7; and nationalism 13, 14, 15, 20, 28, 29; and nationality 65–72, 104; policy 2, 64–77; rights 64– 7, 70–1
class 1, 12, 16–18, 24, 36, 106, 107, 117; in France 50–1; and nationalism 16–18, 24
classical body 35–6, 37
Cold War 1, 9, 26, 27, 44, 108, 111, 114, 129, 134, 232; political effects 139–40, 177, 178, 263
Colley, Linda 87
Colls, R 87
colonialism 38, 51
Committee of the Regions 160–1
Common Agricultural Policy 165
Commonwealth of Independent States 244
communism 27, 88, 107, 114, 135, 190, 226
Communist Party of Poland (PZPR) 201, 206, 210; Natolin faction of 208; right-wing faction in 209
Communist Party of Russia *see* All-union Communist Party
Communist Party of Yugoslavia 256,

257, 258, 264–5 (later League of Communists of Yugoslavia)
Confederation for Independent Poland (KPN) 210, 213, 215, 216, 217
constitutional patriotism 139, 145–6
constitutionalism 13
consumerism 117, 179, 191, 194
Corfu Summit 1994 61
Council for the Preservation of Rural England 97
Craxi, Bettino 178, 179, 192
Crimea 229
Croatia 148, 252, 253, 254, 257, 264–5, 271, 273, 274; Croatian Spring 1971 260; declaration of independence 1991 268; nationalism 255, 256, 267–9; nationalist mythology 268; Serbs in 267–9
Croatian Democratic Community (HDZ) 265, 267, 268, 270–1
Croatian Party of Right (HOS) 267, 270
Cronin, AJ 91
Cruz, Braga de 166
cultural determinism 21
cultural fundamentalism 23, 28
cultural separatism 45–51

Dalmatia 252, 253, 254, 255, 268
Danilevsky, Nikolai 224
de Gaulle, Charles 109–10
decolonisation 46, 108
Democratic Party of Russia 244
Demos 266
Denmark 60, 61, 127
Deutscher Flottenverein 128
Deutscher Wehrverein 128
Deutschlandpolitik 137–9, 140
dialect 182
Diamanti, I 185
Diani, M 181
differentiation 2, 45
Dmowski, Roman 202–3
documentary movement 91
Dodd, P 87
Dreyfus Affair 41, 107
Dublin Convention 1990 61
Dzyuba, Ivan 229
Drumont, Edward 40–1

ETA 158, 160
Ellwood, S 164
English Journey 89
English nationalism 85–7
Englishness 83, 85–6, 94–5; images of 86, 89–98
Enlightenment 10, 12, 103
Essay on the Inequality of Races 37
Estonia 227, 240–1
ethnic cleansing 23, 269, 272
ethnic federalism 183, 259–63
ethnic identity 237, 240, 286 *see also* individual countries and minorities
ethnic nationhood 3, 11, 14, 15

ethnicity 4, 11, 14, 15, 21, 75–6, 112, 118, 261–3; and citizenship 66; and minorities 202–5, 212, 217–18, 224–45, 269–72; and nationalism 4, 9, 15, 66–7, 142
Eurodac 63
European Commission 57, 58–60
European Council 60
European Court of Justice 59
European Economic Area 57
European Free Trade Association 55, 57
European Union 9, 10, 54, 114–15; citizenship rights 65; immigration policies 58–9; regionalism in 165; social policies 59
exclusivity 19, 20, 21, 28; of Lombard League 184, 188; 'others' 33–4, 106, 285, 286 see also citizenship, imagery, nationalism

Falklands Conflict 83, 88
fascism 22, 88, 107, 120–1; Italian 174–5, 187
Fatima cult 158
Fini, Gianfranco 192–3
Fininvest 190, 194
Finland 227
folklore 232, 234, 254
Ford, Caroline 112
Foreigners Law 1985 63, 168
Fortress Europe 28, 44, 56, 57
Fortress Iberia 164–5
Forza Italia 4, 189–91
France 2, 3, 9, 10, 12, 14, 17; anti-immigration 44–5; anti-semitism 40–2; asylum policy 62; Catholicism in 106, 111, 112, 127; centralised administration 101 – 3, 111; citizenship rights 66–7, 70–1; class 50–1; forces for nationalism 105–8; Front National 3, 44, 45, 48–51, 62, 70, 76, 115, 116–21; illegal immigrants 165; immigration 46, 48–51, 117, 118, 120, 163; immigration controls 62; multiculturalism 70; and nation 102–5, 111–16, 118–19; nationalism of Right and Left 105–8; nationhood 101–5; pluralism 112, 120; post-communism 114–16; post-war nationalism 108–13; racism in 46, 75–6
Frankfurter Allgemeine Zeitung 148
French Nationality Code 71, 104
French Revolution 13, 14
Frente Nacional 167
Frey, Gerhard 47
From under the Rubble 236
Front for National Salvation (Russia) 226
Front National (France) 3, 44, 45, 48–51, 62, 70, 76, 106, 113, 115, 116–21
Fuerza Nueva 167

Galicians 3, 157, 159

Garasanin, Ilija 254
Gargantua and Pantagruel 35–6
Gdansk Agreement 210
Gemeinschaft 15
gender 36, 104, 112; stereotypes of 51
general will 13, 14, 16
German Confederation 126–7
German Democratic Republic 129–39, 132–3, 135, 146–7; and FRG 137–9, 142–4
German People's Union (DVU) 47–8, 132, 144
Germanness 136, 141
Germans in Poland 202, 203–4, 206, 207, 217
Germany 2, 3, 9, 15, 26–7, 48; anti-communism 135; asylum 55, 62–3, 145; borders of 133–4, 137; Catholicism in 126, 127; citizenship rights in 64–5, 66, 71–2; 75, 76, 145; commemoration 141–2; constitution 133; constitutional patriotism in 139, 145–6; and European Union 130, 147–8; extremist parties 131–2, 144–5; historical consciousness 136–7, 140–2, 146–7; immigration 44–5, 46–8, 55, 163; immigration controls 62–3, 71; imperialism of 128, 129; militarism in 128, 130; national identity 126–9, 131, 140, 143–5; national identity and history 125, 136–7; National Socialism 128, 130, 131, 136–7 141; national symbols 127, 131, 132–3, 141; nationalism 125–9, 130–3, 138–9, 140–1, 143–5, 146–7; racism in 38, 46, 75, 128–9, 144–5; relations with GDR 129–30, 137–9, 142–4; reunification 71, 75, 130, 133–4, 135, 137, 138–9, 142–4, 148; and western integration 134–6, 140
Gesellschaft 15
Gierek, Edward 208, 210
glasnost 238
Gligorov, Kiro 265
globalisation 1, 9, 10, 28–9, 73; economic 27; effects on France 111, 113–20
Gobineau, Arthur, Comte de 37–8
Gomulka, Wladyslaw 207–9
Gonzalez, Felipe 161–2, 168
Gorbachev, Michail 142, 223, 224; and perestroika 237, 241, 242
Grass, Gunter 142–3
Great Britain 2–3, 10, 83–4; asylum seekers in 55, 63; conservatism 94, 95–6; economy 84, 90; fragmentation of 85–7; immigration controls 63; inter-war society 88–98; multiculturalism in 68–70, 76; national identity 85–6, 89, 90, 96, 98; racism in 76; sovereignty 84
Greece 274, 275
grotesque body 35–6, 37, 41
Gulf War 83
Gypsies 129, 188, 217, 256 see also Roma

Habermas, Jürgen 139
Habsburg Empire 15, 253, 254
Hainsworth, P 116
Hallstein Doctrine 1955 135
heimat 135, 139, 141–2
Heimat (TV series) 140
Henderson, Robert 83
Herri Batasuna 160
Herzegovina 255, 271
Heuss, Theodor 132
history and identity 136–7, 140–2, 146
Hobsbawm, Eric 9, 17–18, 21, 24–5, 26,
    87, 114, 121
Hockenos, Paul 42
The Holocaust and the Liberal Imagination
    51
Holtby, Winifred 91
homosexuality 33, 50, 129, 188, 219
Honecker, Erich 139
Howkins, Alun 97
Hungarians 254, 257
Hungary 43, 142,

Ignazi, P 120
imagery 40, 86; of otherness 34–7, 38,
    40–2, 43, 45, 50–1, 106, 285, 286
Imagined Communities 12
'imagining' 14–16, 166, 251–2
immigrants 3, , 44, 54; illegal 44, 55, 64,
    84, 73; imagery of 46–9 *see also*
    individual countries
immigration 27–8, 54–7; to Australia 67;
    and citizenship 73; controls 54–61, 74–5;
    amd European Commission 57, 58–60;
    inter-governmental responses 60–2, 63,
    64; New Commonwealth 84; primary
    54; and racism 44–51; threshold of
    tolerance theory 118
Immigration Act 1971 68
imperialism 128, 129, 245
Inglehart, Ronald 119–20
International Labour Organisation 55
International Monetary Fund 43
Islam 49, 50
Islamic fundamentalism 56, 272
Italian Communist Party (PCI) 177–8,
    184, 189
Italian Socialist Party (PSI) 177, 178,
    179–80
Italy 3, 9, 15, 54–5, 176, 177, 179–80;
    autonomist movements in 180–9;
    Berlusconi's victory 189–94; fascism in
    174–5, 187; historical definitions of
    172–6; immigration to 187–8; leagues in
    180–9; racism in 187–8; role of church
    174, 181–2; role of judges 180, 189; role
    of media in 172, 179, 184, 189–91, 194;
    socialism in 177, 179; state identity
    177–8
Ivan the Terrible 232
Izetbegović, Alija 270, 272
Jaruzelski, General Wojciech 210, 211

Jelenski, Jan 204–5
Jewish France 40–1
Jewish Invasion 42
Jews 253; immigration of 40, 84;
    stereotypes of 39–40, 43; in Poland 202,
    204, 207, 208, 209, 211, 213, 217–18; in
    Russia 227; in Yugoslavia 253
Johnson, Paul 84, 85
jus sanguinis 67, 71, 75
jus soli 67, 70, 71, 72, 76

Kaase, M 136
Kaczynski, Jaroslaw 215
Karadzić, Radovan 270
Karamzin, Nicholas 224, 225
Katyn massacre 207
Khrushchev, N 235
Kielce pogrom 1946 207
Kohl, Helmut 63, 72, 138–9, 140, 142,
    146
Kosovo 253, 257, 268, 276;
    Albanisation of 262, 263–4;
    autonomy of 261; riots in 260, 261,
    263; serbianisation 264
Krajina 253, 255, 268–9
Kritsman, L 230
Krockow, Ch von 126
Kučan, Milan 266
Kulturnation 15, 16, 126
Kushner, Tony 51
Kwasniewski, Aleksander 216

Labour Union (UP, Poland) 216
Lafontaine, Oscar 143
Lamers, K 147
language 11, 14, 15, 161, 182, 253, 254;
    Portuguese 166; of racism 40, 45, 47–8,
    49–51; Russian 231–2
Law of Asylum and Refuge 1992 64
Le Pen, Jean-Marie 45–6, 49–51, 76
League of Communists of Yugoslavia
    259, 262, 265
Lenin, I 227, 231
liberal democracy 13, 14, 102
liberal nationalism 243–4
La Libre Parole 41
Liga Veneta 181–2
Light, Alison 86, 89, 94, 95, 98
The Lion and the Unicorn 90
Lithuania 203, 206
Livonia 227
Lombard League 182–5

Maastricht Treaty 9, 57, 58, 60, 147;
    French campaign against 115
McCrone, D 85
Macedonia 252, 255, 265, 273–5, 276;
    Albanians in 273–4; Muslims in 260;
    nationalism in 273–4; part of
    Yugoslavia 257
Maghreb 45, 55, 56, 63, 70, 75, 76, 163
Major, John 86, 87

Mannheimer, R 184
market economy 1, 4
Marquand, David 84–5
Marxism 12, 16, 17, 24, 167
Marxism-Leninism 223, 236, 238
Mass Observation 91
Maurras, Charles 41, 42
Melucci, A 181
Memorial 239
micronationalism 9–10, 157
migration 2, 44–5, 54, 262–3, 264–5, 286;
    between Yugoslav republics 261–2; and
    elections 265; post colonial 1; post
    communist 1; to France 46, 48; to UK 55
militarism 128, 130
Milośević, Slobodan 263–4
minorités agissantes 22, 25, 26, 102, 103, 104
Minute 50
miscegenation 37–8, 46
Mitterrand, François 114, 147
Moczar, Niecyslaw 209
Moczulski, Leszek 215
modernity 40, 41
Molodaya Gvardiya 235, 236, 240
Montenegro 252, 253, 255, 257, 262, 263,
    264, 265, 273
Mooers, Colin 102
Morgan, KO 85
Movimento de Accão Nacional 168
Movimento Sociale Italiano (MSI) 4,
    188, 191–3
Movimiento Social Español 168
multiculturalism 46, 49, 68–71, 76, 156;
    fear of 68, 75; in France 70; in the UK
    68–70, 76
Municipal Council for Immigrant
    Communities and Ethnic Minorities 165
Muslim Bosniak Organisation (MBO)
    270, 272
Muslims 45, 46, 257, 258, 260, 265, 269,
    271; in Bosnia-Herzegovina 272; in
    Britain 69; in France 70; in Macedonia
    260; nationalism 272; in Russia 227
Myth of the Blitz 88

Nato 130, 134, 135, 218
Nairn, Tom 10–11, 19, 24
nation-state 1, 9, 10–13, 113; citizenship
    model 21; decline 114–16, 118–120;
    exclusionist model 21–2; monocultural
    251; multicultural 251; and nationalism
    285–6; particularist 15; pre-requisites
    for 14; universalist 15
National Armed Forces (NSZ, Poland)
    205–6
national consciousness 22–6, 203;
    German 130–1; Polish 202; Yugoslav
    253–5
National Democratic Party (NPD,
    Germany) 132
National Democratic Party
    (Poland) 205

National Fascist Party (PNF, Italy) 175
National Front (UK) 63
national identity 33–4, 86, 286; and
    citizenship 74–5; exclusionist 33–4; and
    immigration 73; language in 160, 161;
    threats to 73–4
National Patriotic Front (Hungary) 43
nationalism 2, 11–13, 17, 285–6;
    ambiguity of 13–14, 19, 28; as anti-
    communism 206; and anti-fascism 24–5;
    bourgeois 17, 18, 20–1, 27, 28; and
    citizenship 13, 14, 15; citizenship model
    15–16, 20, 28, 29; and class 16–18, 24;
    and communism 201; ethnic model 15;
    exclusionist model 19, 20, 21, 28, 106,
    113–14; and modernity 19; national
    symbolism 20, 22–3; political model 19;
    post communism 201; pre-requisites for
    11–12; state led 104–5, 112–13; and state
    legitimacy 23–7; suppression 201 see
    also individual countries and
    nationalities
nationalist movements 19–22, 42–3, 158,
    180–9, 251
nationality 1, 3, 5, 9; and citizenship
    65–72; malleability of 1, 2, 13, 23, 29;
    models of 10–13; socio-economic
    factors in 12
nationhood 11–13, 254; models of 3, 14
Nazi-Soviet Pact 1939 206
Nazism 33, 128–9, 130, 131, 136, 137,
    204; commemoration of 141–2, 146
Nenni, Pietro 178
neo-fascism 132, 144, 168, 191, 192
neo-Nazis 26, 44, 62, 75, 145, 168
neo-Slavophilism 235, 236
newsreels 92–5, 96
Nolte, E 141
Nordic Union 57
North Africans 45–6, 48–50;
    immigration to Spain 156; stereotypes
    of 51
Northern League 4, 9, 180–1, 185–9, 191,
    193–4
Novyi Mir 235

Ochab, Edward 208
Oleksy, Josef 218
Olszewski, Jan 213, 214–5, 216
Orwell, George 89, 90
Otechestvo 242
Ottoman Empire 15, 253, 254, 255

Pamyat' 42–3, 239, 242, 243; anti-
    semitism in 240
Paraga, Dobroslav 267
Paris Commune 105, 108
particularism 3, 10, 15
Party of Democratic Action (SDA) 265,
    270, 272
Party of Democratic Socialism (PDS,
    Germany) 143, 144

Pasqua, Charles 62
Patriotic Grunwald Association (Poland) 43
Pavelić, Ante 256
Payne, Stanley 156, 157
Peasant Party (Poland) 205, 206
perestroika 237; opposition to 240, 241, 242
Perez, Lucrecia 164
Perez-Díaz, V 158, 159
Petit, Henri-Robert 42
Piasecki, Boleslaw 205
Pilsudski, Marshall Jozef 202–3
Pinar, Blas 167
pluralism 67, 68, 112, 120
Pokrovsky, MN 232
Poland 4, 4, 43, 71, 201, 218, 227; anti-semitism in 203–4, 207, 208, 209, 211, 213, 217–8; civic unrest 209–11; communism in 206–7, 208–9; decommunisation 214–5; ethnic tensions in 202–5, 212, 219; and European Union 218; lustration affair 214; Nato 218; post-communism 212–13; role of Catholicism 202, 205, 206, 208–15 passim
Polish nationalism 201–5, 207–11, 213, 216–19
Polish Peasant Party (PSL) 213, 216
political legitimacy 13 see also state legitimacy
Politics and Poetics of Transgression 34
Polo delle Liberta 191
Pope John Paul II 210
popular sovereignty 13, 14
populism 4, 190
populist nationalism 237–41, 243–4, 263, 276
Porozumienie Centrum (PC, Poland) 214, 215
Portugal 3, 54–5, 155–7, 158–9; asylum law 165; Catholicism in 158; emigrant 166; extremist parties 168; immigration 64, 162–5, 169; language 166; national identity 165–7; racial tension 164–5; state legitimacy 158
post-colonialism 116, 121; in France 117–18
post-industrialism 116, 117, 118, 121
post-materialism 120, 121
post-modernism 29, 113, 116–21
post-socialism 116, 121
Poujadist Movement 106, 108
Poznan riots 208
Priestley, JB 89–90, 91, 96
Pronay, Nicholas 92
Protocols of the Elders of Zion 39, 43, 205, 240
Prussia 15, 126, 127, 134
Publitalia 190
Pujol, Jordi 161

Quebecois 25

Rabelais and his world 35–6
Race Relations Act 1976 68
Racialized Boundaries 36–7
racism 28, 34–5, 37, 38, 75, 76; anti-immigrant 44–5, 47; attacks 48, 144; in Europe 73–7; in Italy 174–5, 187–8; language of 45, 47–8, 49–51; post-communism 42–52, 75–6; scientific 37–8, 49; stereotypes of 38
Ramsden, J 95
Ranger, Terence 87
Rasputin, V 236, 238
Re-Admission Agreements 57
red-brown alliance 226, 242
regionalism 155, 159–62, 168, 169
religion 1, 11; in nationalism 14, 15 see also Catholicism
Republican Party (REP, Germany) 44, 45, 47
Republican Party of Russia 244
resistance movements 176–7, 205–6
Richards, J 91
Risorgimento 13, 173
Rocchetta, Franco 181, 182
Rokossovsky, Konstanty 208
Rola 204–5
Roma 43–4, 48; in Poland 217; in Yugoslavia 257, 258 see also gypsies
Romania 43, 47
Ross, George 111, 112
Rostock, racist attacks in 48, 144
Ruch dua Rzeczpospolitej (RDR, Poland) 214, 215, 216
Rushdie, Salman 57, 69
Russia 224–5, 231–3, 238–40; democratisation 237; ethnic minorities 227–9; modernisation 226; in Soviet Union 226–36, 239, 242, 243, 244; Tsarist 226–7, 229
Russian nationalism 223–4, 230–1, 245; authoritarism in 224–5; continuity of 226; distinctive nature 225–6; identification with the state 224–6, 237–8, 241–4; national minorities 229–45; nationality policy 226–9; popular nationalism 237–41, 243–4; post Stalin 235–6; resurgence of 238–41; and Soviet identity 229–35, 244–5

Salazar, A 156, 157, 158
Salisbury Review 84, 84
Salvadori, Massimo 187
Sarajevo 253, 271
Sardinian Action Party 181
Schauble, Wolfgang 146, 147
Schengen Accord 1985 57, 60, 62, 63
Schengen Convention 1990 60, 64
Schengen Information System 60–1
Schonhuber, Franz 47
Self Defence (Poland) 216
self-determination 13–14, 180, 202, 227
separatism 9–10, 25–6, 27, 45–51, 169

Serbia 252, 253, 257, 273, 274; diversity of 254–5; grievances 261; internal migration 261–2; nationalism in 254, 263–5
Serbian Democratic Party (SDS) 265, 270–1
Serbian Socialist Party 265
Serbs, in Bosnia-Herzegovina 269–72; in Croatia 267–9
Šešelj, Vojslav 270, 271, 274
Silverman, Max 46, 117
Single European Act 1987 9, 54, 55
single market 55
Skrypnik, Mykola 231
Slav immigrants 33, 46, 203
Slavonia 252, 253, 255, 268, 269
Slavophiles 225, 226, 239
Slovenes 254, 255, 262, 264–5
Slovenia 148, 274; identity 254, 262, 266, 271, 273; independence 266–7; in Yugoslavia 257
Smith, Antony 33
Smith, Malcolm 95
Soares, Mario 159, 165
Social Democracy of the Kingdom of Poland (SDRP) 202, 212, 216
Social-Democratic Party (SDP, Germany) 63, 72, 137, 147
Social Democrats 134, 135, 137
socialism 17–18, 135, 228–9; in Italy 177–9; market 259–60; Soviet 230
Socialist Party of the Working People (Russia) 226
Socialist Reich Party 131
Socialist Unity Party (SED, Germany) 137, 143
Solidarity 4, 210–12, 214, 215
Soloukhin, Vladimir 234
Solzhenitsyn, Alexander 226, 236
Sonderweg 128, 130, 147
Sontag, Susan 40
South Slavs 252–8 passim
South Tyrol People's Party 181
sovereignty 1, 3, 5, 73, 84; and European integration 166; and immigration control 58; popular 12–13, 14; of Yugoslav federal states 260
Soviet identity 229, 233–4, 237, 244–5
Spain 3, 10, 54–5, 155–7; asylum policies 63–4; Catholicism in 157–8, 160; centre nationalism 157–8; constitution 1978 159; extremist parties 167–8; immigration 162–4, 168; immigration controls 63–4; Law on Foreigners 168; national symbols 155; racial tensions 164, 167, 169; role of monarchy 162; regional autonomy 159–62; separatism 168–9; state legitimacy 156, 158, 168
Sporazum 255
Stalin, Josef 227–8, 232–3
Stallybrass, Peter 34, 35, 36, 37
Stambolić, Ivan 263

State Emergency Committee (GKChP, Russia) 229, 243
state legitimacy 1, 3, 5, 12–13, 20, 23–7, 73, 108, 156, 158, 168
state patriotism 13–14, 21, 23
state socialism 4, 9
Stead, P 91
Sternberger, Dolf 139
Stevenson, J 97
Stolpe, Manfred 217
Suarez, Adolfo 159
Suez crisis 1956 88
supranational action 58–60, 60–2, 63, 64, 74–5, 114, 134, 155
Sweden 67
Szporluk, Roman 245

Taguieff, P-A 119, 120, 121
Tallack, Sir Stephen 91
Tito, Josip Broz 256, 259, 260, 261
Tong, Raymond 85
Tonnies, Ferdinand 15
Touraine, A 113–14, 116
Treaty of Versailles 128
Treitschke, Heinrich von 38–9
Trevi group 58, 60
Tucker, Robert 232–3
Tudjman, Franjo 265, 267–8
Turkish immigrants 46, 47–8, 72, 75
Two-Plus-Four Treaty 1990 130, 135
Tyminski, Stan 214

USSR Congress of People's Deputies 242, 244
Ukraine 5, 227, 229, 231, 244
Ukrainians in Poland 202, 206, 217; nationalist activities 203, 204
Unia Pracy (UP, Poland) 216
Union Valdotaine 181
United Front of Working People (OFT, Russia) 241–2
United States of America 135–6
Ustaše 255, 256, 267
Uzbekistan 237

Veche 236
Vichy government 42
Visegrad group 56
Vlachs 253, 257, 258
Vojvodina 253, 257, 261, 262, 264
Volksgeist 126
volksgemeinschaft 47
Volksnation 126
Voprosy Filosofii 239
Vukovar 268

Walesa, Lech 211, 213, 214, 215, 218
Wallace, W 73
Warsaw Pact 130
Weber, Eugen 103
Weimar Republic 128, 131
Weissbrod, L 145

Weizsacker, Richard von 141
West European Union 135
White, Allon 34, 35, 36, 37
Williams, GA 85
Wisden Cricket Monthly 83
Wistrich, Robert 39
Workers Defence Committee (KOR, Poland) 209
Yeltsin, Boris 225, 226, 243; election as Russian President 244
Ynestrillas, Ricardo Saenz 168
Yugoslav People's Army (JNA) 260, 267, 270, 273

Yugoslavia 1, 4, 9, 47; confederalisation of 259–63; dissolution of 275–6; economic developments in 258–9, 261, 276; ethnic groups 257–8; ethnicisation of 261–3; history 252–9; market socialism 259–60; multi-party elections in 265; national consciousness 253–4; populist nationalism 263, 276 *see also* the ethnic nationalities
Yugoslavism 254–6, 257, 258, 260, 263
Yuval-Davis, Nira 36–7

Zhirinovsky, Vladimir 225, 246